a–z of reflective practice

Professional Keywords series

Every field of practice has its own methods, terminology, conceptual debates and landmark publications. The *Professional Keywords* series expertly structures this material into easy-reference A to Z format. Focusing on the ideas and themes that shape the field, and informed by the latest research, these books are designed both to guide the student reader and to refresh practitioners' thinking and understanding.

Available now

Mark Doel and Timothy B. Kelly: *A–Z of Groups & Groupwork*
David Garnett: *A–Z of Housing*
Jon Glasby and Helen Dickinson: *A–Z of Interagency Working*
Richard Hugman: *A–Z of Professional Ethics*
Glenn Laverack: *A–Z of Health Promotion*
Glenn Laverack: *A–Z of Public Health*
Jeffrey Longhofer: *A–Z of Psychodynamic Practice*
Neil McKeganey: *A–Z of Addiction and Substance Misuse*
Steve Nolan and Margaret Holloway: *A–Z of Spirituality*
Marian Roberts: *A–Z of Mediation*
Fiona Timmins: *A–Z of Reflective Practice*
David Wilkins, David Shemmings and Yvonne Shemmings:
  A–Z of Attachment

a–z of
reflective practice

Fiona Timmins

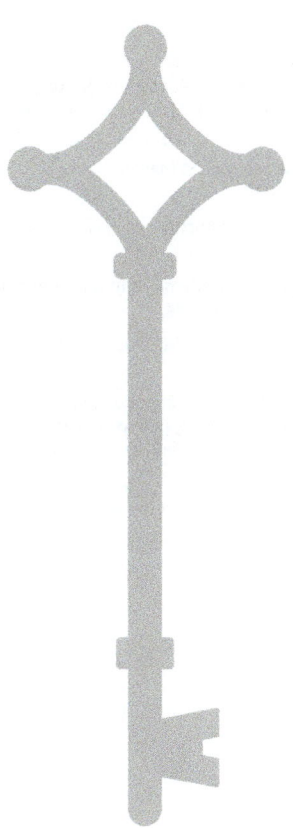

 macmillan education palgrave

First published 2015 by
PALGRAVE

Palgrave in the UK is an imprint of Macmillan Publishers Limited, registered in England, company number 785998, of 4 Crinan Street, London, N1 9XW.

Palgrave Macmillan in the US is a division of St Martin's Press LLC, 175 Fifth Avenue, New York, NY 10010.

Palgrave is a global imprint of the above companies and is represented throughout the world.

Palgrave® and Macmillan® are registered trademarks in the United States, the United Kingdom, Europe and other countries.

ISBN 978-1-137-00504-5   ISBN 978-1-137-00505-2 (eBook)
DOI 10.1007/978-1-137-00505-2

This book is printed on paper suitable for recycling and made from fully managed and sustained forest sources. Logging, pulping and manufacturing processes are expected to conform to the environmental regulations of the country of origin.

A catalogue record for this book is available from the British Library.

A catalog record for this book is available from the Library of Congress.

*For Melanie Jasper (1954–2014), a bright shining light
who led the way*

contents

how to use this book

Reflective practice has been recognized as a strategy for personal and professional development within health and social care for more than 20 years. There is a plethora of texts, from basic introductions to advanced theoretical level, which aim to enable understanding and utility of reflective practice for the practitioner. This book provides a jargon-busting user guide to the key concepts and techniques of reflective practice, and can be used as a handbook and to guide the reader to other sources of information. It aims to be a one-stop resource book for both the beginner and the experienced practitioner, and an aide-memoire for the aspiring reflective practitioner.

The book is intended as a useful resource to quickly look up topics of interest in the field of reflective practice. It is intended as an interdisciplinary text with application in health-related academic and practice disciplines where the practice of reflection is encouraged. Examples of these are physiotherapy, nursing, occupational therapy, medicine, psychology, radiography, pastoral care, clergy and dentistry. The practice of reflection is of growing importance and also has some useful application in practical disciplines such as teaching, law and engineering. For this reason practical applications and examples are deliberately broad and not necessarily applied to one discipline or the other. Situations where reflection can be used across disciplines are often those that concern people and relationships, such as creating trust; building relationships; confronting challenging behaviour; maintaining a focus in a conversation; breaking bad news; responding to difficult emotions such as guilt, anger or sadness; ending a piece of work; learning from mistakes; and evaluating practice. These factors and how they apply in your particular learning or work setting need to be borne in mind when reading the entries.

In keeping with the A–Z style of the series, there is an alphabetical structure. As such, topics are not presented sequentially but rather intended to be read as self-contained entries. Each entry provides a brief overview of the topic in question and for further in-depth reading around the area you are guided to the list of key texts provided. There is a four-fold referencing system insofar as you may be guided to your areas of interest by scanning the alphabetical entries either manually or by looking at the contents page. There are also 'see also' lists and italicized cross-references embedded in narrative and index. Readers new to the topic might like to begin by exploring basic concepts such as reflection and reflective practice first and exploring the 'see also' lists of these. It is useful for those seeking a more in-depth knowledge of the topic to explore the area through further reading and bibliography for a fuller grasp of the field.

acknowledgements

The author and publisher would like to thank McGraw-Hill for their permission to reproduce Figure 1 'The Johari Window' from J.Luft *Group Processes: An Introduction to Group Dynamics* (1984) and Pearson for their permission to reproduce Figure 2 'Learning Cycle' from D A.Kolb *Experiential Learning: Experience as the Source of Learning and Development* (1984).

acknowledgements

introduction

Reflective practice is increasingly being recognized as a useful strategy for personal and professional development within the healthcare fields for more than 20 years. Indeed almost every modern professional espouses the notion of reflection on practice (Hargreaves and Page 2013). There is a plethora of texts, from basic to conceptual levels, which aim to enable understanding and utility of reflective practice for the practitioner. The proposed text will provide a jargon-busting user guide to the key concepts and techniques of reflective practice, and can be used as a handbook and to guide the reader to other sources of information. Hence it will be a one-stop source book for both the beginner and the experienced practitioner, but will attempt to provide an overview that enables any reader to start a journey to becoming a reflective practitioner.

Many qualified practitioners need to provide evidence of continued professional development (CPD) for professional registration, and often require reflective reviews as evidence. Similarly, students may have assessments driven by reflective processes, reviews or writing. Work-based learning is becoming an increasingly popular mechanism of CPD for practitioners without removing them from the workplace. This book supports all of these approaches.

Reflective practice is a valued and embedded method of obtaining CPD in a number of disciplines. This book will be a useful resource which will provide a quick guide to students and practitioners across disciplines. In particular, reflection is embedded in nursing, social work and counselling. In addition this book will be of value to all students and practitioners who use reflection as a process of professional development (e.g. psychology students and psychologists, psychotherapists and occupational therapists). All disciplines with a practice focus will find this book to be of value.

Reflective practice is at the heart of professional education across a range of disciplines. It is established as a key aspect of adult learning and is used as part of the process and the assessment for students undertaking applied training. Reflective practice is now a core topic in professional social work education and other disciplines including nursing, becoming a 'pedagogical signature' (Shulman 2005:52) concept within these courses. This means that reflective practice has become a dominant paradigm in education across many disciplines and is inextricably linked with teaching and practice in these areas. However, despite the centrality of reflective practice, many students struggle to understand what is meant by the term and also how to apply such concepts to their assessed practice. A book such as this promises an applied and welcome practical guide in an everyday context. This is also an area that many students find difficult to both understand and evidence. This book will help to distil some of the core concepts of reflective practice, making it easier to comprehend, and will hopefully be a useful adjunct to your reading library. This book will also appeal to the qualified workforce.

Much of the work of the modern university has its basis in science and scientific discovery to inform and improve our knowledge and to pass this inspiration on to students who form the future workforce. Regardless of the academic discipline, there is an emphasis on basing both teaching and practice on the best available scientific evidence. At the same time, all disciplines, including those in health-care, are encouraged to practise using an evidence base. There is continuous questioning and exploration of this evidence base, using scientific methods of research, largely due to humans' enlightenment in the 1700s. Prior to this, traditions, practice, folklore and religion were largely responsible for determining knowledge and practice in various fields. As such, the modern notion of science and scientific methods informs both our education and practice across many disciplines including health-care. Given the exponential nature of man's understanding of human science, medicine and technology, particularly in recent decades, it is essential that firm understanding of the evidence that informs practice forms part of disciplinary development and practice. At the same time the growth of scientific evidence means that there are also options available, and increasingly health-care practitioners, for example, are encouraged not just to be informed by evidence, but to critically evaluate that evidence to determine its potential contribution to clients' well-being and health-care in general.

However, at the same time, alternative approaches to this singular approach to using a scientific knowledge base have become increasingly popular in the health-care disciplines over the past 30 years. In recognition that many disciplines operate in the real world of practice, where human relationships and situations are complex, and where practitioners can develop a practice wisdom that is informed by, but not necessarily a direct result of, scientific endeavour (Ruch 2009b), writers such as Dewey (1933) and Schön (1983) opened the possibly of alternatives to scientific knowledge and espoused the benefits of reflective practice as a form of knowledge production. Put simply, John Dewey saw reflection as a further dimension of thought, and as such in need of education: 'while we cannot learn or be taught to think, we do have to learn to think well, especially acquire the general habit of reflection' (Dewey 1933). Dewey, an educationalist, was particularly concerned about the context in which the practice (of education, for example) takes place, suggesting that practitioners need to be mindful and responsive to this (Dewey 1933). The education and training of professionals who interact with society, in his view, needed to focus less on the technical skills required and more on creating reflective thinkers who are responsive to each society's needs (Dewey 1938). Dewey viewed experience as an important tool for learning, but one which needed guidance in order to yield rich learning (Dewey 1938).

While Dewey (1933, 1938) focused much of his attention on teaching, his novel approach to learning influenced much of the development of reflection as a tool for professional development in the health-care professions in recent decades. From a historical perspective Dewey first began to articulate the need to think reflectively in order to solve problems (Høyrup and Eltjaer 2006). However, it wasn't until the 1980s that reflection began to emerge as a popular mechanism for professional development (Høyrup and Elkjaer 2006). Schön (1983), in particular, concerned with professionals' development of skills and knowledge, outlines reflection in and on action. Schön's conceptualization of reflection has been influential in suggesting less reliance on traditional and scientific forms of enquiry and encouraging practitioners to learn from reflecting both within practice and on their practice (Rolfe et al 2011). Opposed to the dominance of positivism, Schön (1983) proposes reflection as an alternative method of practice theory generation.

Schön's seminal work subsequently underpinned many structured models of reflection that developed for practitioners (Rolfe et al 2011). These two scholars (Dewey 1933, Schön 1983) along with Freire (1970), who espoused critical enquiry of local, cultural and political contexts, served to form a cohesive bedrock upon which modern approaches to reflective practice within the disciplines have been built (Lyons 2010). The contributions of these three theorists to reflective practice are outlined by Lyons (2010) below.

Theorist	Characterization	Implications for practice
1. Dewey 1933	Reflective enquiry as thinking	Learning is understood as learning to think
2. Schön 1983	Reflective enquiry as a way of knowing	Reflection requires knowing in and on action
3. Freire 1970	Reflective enquiry as critical consciousness, interrogation of the contexts of learning	Uncovering critical contexts: political, social and cultural, through investigation

Identification of major contributors to the concept of reflective practice (Lyons 2010:19).

Although not without its critics, reflective practice has increasing worth within the professional disciplines (Lyons 2010). Increasingly, professions are realizing the importance of simply thinking, in a structured way, about their practice (Lyons 2010). While there are few texts that address reflection for all the disciplines as a whole, Nona Lyons, who has taught and lectured on this topic for more than 20 years, provides key chapters on reflective practice within disciplines such as nursing education, medicine, law and occupational therapy that are a useful resource for those disciplines. It is important to remember that, while useful, this A to Z will form a preliminary reading text only and needs to be substantiated by further reading if an in-depth knowledge and understanding is required.

While not all thinking results in meaningful learning (Lyons 2010, Dewey 1933), thoughtful, insightful reflection can assist us to develop new understandings and address complex situations. Reflection is gaining increasing importance among disciplines, including more fact-based traditional disciplines, such as law (Lyons 2010) and engineering (Babapour and Rahe 2013), particularly in light of emerging societal crises (The Mid Staffordshire NHS Foundation Trust 2013, Laming 2003) that show that in spite of the wealth of information and science available contemporarily the 'failure to *think*' and respond accordingly and effectively in situations are important contributory factors in catastrophic failures in modern times (Lyons 2010:5). Shulman (2005:52) points to three responsibilities of the modern professions: to think, to perform and to act with integrity. All three require reflective practice (Lyons 2010). As this approach is personalized – aimed at developing a personal and local wisdom – generalizing from it is difficult. However, modern approaches to disciplines such as social work place increasing emphasis on the importance of developing practice knowledge and initiating personal and social change through reflection (Fook 2012). As such there is little scientific and empirical evidence that this approach actually works (Lyons 2010). However, the literature is replete with discussions on, encouragement of and approaches to reflective practice and there is a firm belief in health and social care disciplines such as nursing (Rolfe et al 2011), physiotherapy, social work and medicine in its benefits. Moreover, reflection and reflective practice are espoused by the regulatory bodies of many of the aforementioned disciplines. It is for this reason that you are approaching this topic and within this book you will find many entries of interest in this regard.

The book's focus is on the underpinning principles of reflection and reflective practice and providing simple, easy-to-read definitions of these while at the same time pointing to useful resources for further reading. The book's intended audience is primarily students and professionals within health and social care, but it will also have relevance to other professionals that interact with the public and espouse reflective practices. It would also suit professionally qualified staff needing to refresh their knowledge. The book draws on generic approaches to reflection and reflective practice that have developed within the health and social care literature over the past 20 years. It is beyond the scope of this book to explore any one of the disciplines and their approaches in any great detail; however, important overarching principles that most disciplines draw upon will be developed. The book specifically draws upon the discipline of nursing in health-care, which, compared with other disciplines (such as social work, occupational therapy, physiotherapy) has both a longer history of usage and greater scope of writing, research and application than other disciplines (Nelson 2012). In addition, as reflective practice needs to occur within the scholarly discipline of writing and education, the book takes a novel approach to some concepts with the introduction of ideas that are non-standard in approach. Depending on your rationale for reading this book, you might like to select entries according to your current needs. For example, if you are a practising social worker who is required to complete a reflective diary then 'diary' would be your first selection. If you are a nursing student who has a reflective essay to write, then perhaps 'writing' or 'assessment' might be sought out first.

a

analysis

SEE ALSO awareness; critical reflection; criticality; group reflections; models; reflection; reflective practice; work-based learning

Analysis is a key component of reflection and *reflective practice* (Jasper 2013). In the context of reflective practice, analysis refers to the action of re-examining a situation, usually retrospectively, and breaking down the experience into its constituent parts in order to examine it carefully, and to the process of becoming more self-aware. Analysis aims to explain and understand something more fully (Jasper 2013) and helps to make sense of the experience (Gardner 2014). Professionals often come across situations that are intriguing or puzzling to them and therefore difficult to make sense of. As such, giving these situations careful attention through analysis is helpful to uncover truths and meanings.

Models of *reflection* generally provide clear guidelines for assisting you to analyse situations and events. Many of the models and frameworks for reflection prompt you to analyse the incident, the situation, your experience and your feelings. This is to provide you with a better understanding of what has gone on, new perspectives on this and new knowledge and ways of working. In *critical reflection* this analysis also includes an exploration of the contribution of the environment to the situation. The analysis that you are prompted to do during reflection involves breaking the experience down in some way, so that it may be understood clearly and from a new perspective. However, in addition to being a conceptual thinking exercise, very often reflection will guide you towards an examination of the underpinning knowledge, theory and research in the field (Brookfield 1995). By examining policy, procedures, guidelines, textbooks, research and other sources, you get to learn more about what should or could have been done in the situation and what could be done the next time to improve matters. This analysis does not merely occur as an intellectual (thinking) or paper (writing) exercise; rather it is an active process. Analysis may also apply to your gradual 'getting to know yourself' and growing *awareness* as you grow in *criticality* through reflection and reflective practice. You may undertake an analysis of your personal strengths and weaknesses or of opportunities and barriers in order to facilitate a growing self-awareness.

implications for reflective practice

In the busy world of professional practice there is often little time to look back over events in order to examine the experience. In keeping with the growing awareness of adults' capacity for independent learning and the benefits of *work-based learning*, reflective practice is becoming increasingly popular among professionals. Many professionals, in some cases guided and/or instructed by their regulatory authority, are actively engaging in reflection and reflective practice. Analysis is intrinsic to the models of reflection that guide reflection and reflective practice. While the level and type of analysis will vary according to the model used, the basic premise is that you will be encouraged to look back over experiences and reframe those experiences in a new way. This analysis can provide new understandings and awareness and ultimately contribute to new knowledge and ways of practice as the reflective cycle is completed.

For some professions this level of analysis and the use of reflective practice are very familiar, for others it is new. Pastoral care workers, counsellors and social/health-care workers, for example, are often presented with human suffering and traumatic or life-changing events. The use of reflection and reflective practice as a result has both grown and been embraced in these professional spheres. Analysing situations that were stressful, traumatic, sad or complex can have real benefits for such professionals, and reflecting in a group can be particularly useful and is growing in popularity. While analysis of work-based problems and cases is typical in professions such as law, science and engineering, the retrospective analysis of situations often required by reflective practice is less common. Again, reflection and reflective practice are gaining popularity in these fields, particularly for the education of new and graduating practitioners. There has also been a huge growth and development of reflection within the teaching professions (Brookfield 1995).

The main benefit of analysis across all of the professional disciplines is to trigger work-based learning. It is increasingly being recognized that work-based learning has incredible value in the modern, complex work environments, and there is rich learning to be gained by revisiting situations, analysing them and reflecting upon them (Boud 2006, Boud et al 2006). Our own interpretations and memories of events are often unreliable or of limited perspective (Brookfield 1995); analysis of events opens up the possibility for re-interpretation in a way that improves practice.

As a teacher, for example, you may have determined that your novel teaching idea was a failure as the students' reaction was initially poor, and you may decide to abandon it. However, this analysis relies only on your personal (and emotional) interpretations. A more thorough analysis, using a model of reflection, may prompt you to seek more student feedback (by survey for example), which reveals that the majority enjoyed the innovation. You might explore the research in the field and find that resistance is commonplace and come up with ideas to combat this. Through critical reflection you might find a contextual factor that affected the class environment that day. The point being demonstrated here is that a reliance on oneself to objectively interpret an event, using the thinking process, is potentially unreliable. The analysis prompted by reflection asks you to go beyond simple reflection to a more thorough and searching reflection on, and analysis of, practice. Through these means, which can be enhanced greatly by working in groups, you can become adept at analysing situations in order to develop better practices and learn from experiences.

KEY TEXTS

- Gardner, F. (2014) *Being Critically Reflective* (Basingstoke: Palgrave Macmillan).
- Jasper, M. (2013) *Beginning Reflective Practice*. 2nd edn (Hampshire: Cengage Learning).

andragogy

SEE ALSO **lifelong learning; portfolios; reflection; reflective practice; wisdom; work-based learning**

Within the concept of *reflective practice*, 'andragogy' is a rarely heard term. However, it is important to understand that the move towards reflective practice and *work-based learning* has been underpinned in educational terms by theories that propose greater learner independence and responsibility. 'Andragogy' is a term used to describe an approach to adult learning developed by Malcolm Knowles (1989). Notably in this theoretical approach, how children learn is differentiated from adult learning. It is claimed that while children require structured directive approaches in the educational setting, adults require much less structure and can learn independently. Andragogy proposes that adults control and predict when best learning will take place and that this need not always occur in the classroom. As such, adults are capable of taking responsibility for their learning; therefore their learning can be independent and self-directed. The notion that learning needs to take place in a classroom (virtual or otherwise) becomes redundant. Consistent with the notion of *lifelong learning*, adults may continue to strive to educate themselves beyond the formal learning setting. This can occur in many ways. For example, through active reading, perhaps in libraries, and through work-based learning. *Reflection* and reflective practice are important mechanisms by which informal learning like this can be harnessed and developed into meaningful learning for adults (Pearce 2003).

Knowles (1989) identified four key components of adult learning: self-concept, past experience, readiness to learn and the self-diagnosis of learning needs. Self-concept refers to adult learners having the ability to take responsibility (Knowles 1989). Adults are deemed capable of taking this responsibility. Past experience has a significant impact on adult learning, as adults will learn in different ways and at different speeds according to their past experiences. In fact they may resist some learning as a result of this, or excel at others. Being ready to learn is also of fundamental importance in this theory. Self-diagnosis of learning needs involves self-assessment of learning needs, formulation of objectives, design of learning experiences and evaluation (Knowles 1989).

Adults may or may not be ready to learn at the time of teaching (say, for example, in the classroom) but rather will learn in their own time. Teaching methods may also prove ineffective if the person is not ready to learn (Knowles 1989). Several factors may influence this readiness. The motivation of adult learners is generated from internal rather than external sources (Knowles 1989) and this intrinsic motivation affects the readiness to learn. A professional who strives for excellence in practice may explore their practice carefully to see where improvements may need to be made. This demonstrates an internal motivation, as the need for high-quality practice is driven for the most part by personal standards rather than external forces. It is partly due to this belief in human internal motivation that professions and organizations are prompted to foster reflective practice, often with little or no guidance as to how it might be done and what it might entail. Increasingly this view is being seen as naïve, as although adults are capable of self-direction and are motivated, it is becoming obvious from the limited empirical evidence that exists in the field that support and guidance for independence in reflective practice are required.

Although whether self-direction ability is universal to all is a subject of debate (McCauley and McClelland 2004), the self-direction movement has paved the way for many self-directed learning initiatives. At the same time, national and international policies have advocated that the major responsibility for learning lies with individuals (rather than the state), which is encapsulated in the notion of the lifelong learner (Field 2012).

Continued learning and development among adults is thought to improve well-being and satisfaction (Field 2011) although these benefits are largely associated with overall changes to literacy and education, which can have major effects on lifestyle and well-being (Field 2011). Specific courses of study have also been found to improve disposition; however, it is unclear whether reflective practice yields any benefits in this regard. At the same time, making generalizations about the overall benefits of adult learning is difficult due to methodological issues with the data collected (Field 2011). However, ongoing professional development initiatives do appear to increase personal confidence and belief in oneself (Timmins and Nicholl 2005).

Reflection and reflective practice build upon this premise of self-direction, as learning is not teacher-directed, but rather initiated and developed by the learner or practitioner. There is recognition that the technical mastery required of a profession is only part of the requirements of a modern practitioner (Dewey 1933). Instead, today's complex environments require a practitioner who can think on their feet and who is propelled towards learning for its own sake, based on their experiences in practice.

However, for some there are some doubts about the ability of adults to be their own critic. Miller et al (2012) term this 'the illusion of the self-regulatory professional', drawing our attention to research which indicates that the ability to self-assess is generally quite poor.

implications for reflective practice
While there may be a tendency to expect all fundamental principles that apply to your discipline to be taught directly to you, an understanding of andragogy, and how adults learn, informs us that we can do a lot of this learning by ourselves. This notion gains increasing importance when we work in complex environments such as health and social care, law or industry. Our preparatory education may not always equip us with everything we need to know. This is especially true with regard to human relationships, where many challenges arise. It is only through experience that meaningful learning takes place. Knowing that you as an adult learner are capable of independent learning, and beginning to value learning from practice, unlocks the potential for rich learning in the practice setting. Students will be quite familiar with this, and may receive instruction on how to go about this. However, this is also of great relevance to qualified practitioners who may have finished their courses of study. Their learning is ongoing, not in school, but rather in practice. Acknowledging themselves as lifelong adult learners is important. Reflection and reflective practice are mechanisms to capture this important practice *wisdom* and turn it into meaningful learning.

This is especially important in disciplines that, for part of their ongoing registration with their regulatory body, are required to submit evidence of learning in practice. Recognizing that as an adult learner you can direct and guide your own learning, rather than relying on others to do this for you, is an important step here. So too is the recognition that in addition to courses, reading and further studies, the ability to reflect on practice and document this in some way can provide good evidence of your adult learning in practice.

KEY TEXTS

- Field, J. (2011) 'Researching the Benefits of Learning: The Persuasive Power of Longitudinal Studies', *London Review of Education*, 9 (3): pp. 283–292.
- Field, J. (2012) 'Transitions in Lifelong Learning: Public Issues, Private Troubles, Liminal Identities' *Studies for the Learning Society*, 2–3. ISSN 1736-7107, available at: http://dspace.stir.ac.uk/bitstream/1893/7380/1/SLS%20fulltext.pdf, accessed January 20, 2015.

assessment

SEE ALSO analysis; andragogy; awareness; barriers; competence; consequences; diary; ethical issues; experiential learning; journals; learning logs; models; portfolios; reflection; reflective practice; reflective processes; supervision; writing

Assessment is an important consideration for anyone embarking on *reflective practice*. It is 'a complex moral and ethical act' (Bolton 2010:145). There is much debate and discussion within the literature on the benefits or otherwise of assessing *reflection* and reflective practice (Bolton 2010), with an emerging view that assessing these concepts may affect creativity, honesty and engagement with the process. At the same time, providing an assessment of reflection or reflective practice attaches a certain importance to these activities (Bolton 2010).

One of the first questions that you need to ask is whether or not your reflective practice will be assessed; assessment is more likely if you are a student engaging in primary studies or ongoing continuous professional development. You may also be an assessor. If you are neither student nor assessor, then assessment of reflection is of less relevance to you. However, an understanding of the principles of assessment and the notion of peer assessment might still be useful to you as you might like to have some of your reflective *writing* informally assessed by another, perhaps asking them to offer comments on it to form part of your work-based *portfolio*.

Assessment within university and other courses refers to the measurement of student achievement of learning outcomes. The approaches to assessment vary and include measurements such as examinations, practical assessments and essays/assignments. Reflection and reflective practice are most commonly assessed using either practical assessment or essay/assignment, although elements of reflection may also appear on examinations, either oral or written. Reflection may also form a component of a portfolio and may be assessed under its auspices. In addition to formal assessment by your teacher, informal assessment by either yourself (self-assessment) or your peers (peer assessment) is becoming increasingly popular, although there is little evidence of the benefits of either of these, in the context of reflection and reflective practice, over more traditional forms of assessment (Xie et al 2008).

An immediate concern for the student regarding this is that reflection is often seen as a personal activity and as such sharing with others could lead to discomfort (Timmins and Dunne 2009). Understanding the assessment requirements from the outset will help to prevent this discomfort. Generally when reflection forms part of an assessment that involves writing, it becomes more public and one needs to be mindful of the potential *consequences* of this writing.

'*Competence*' is a term increasingly used to describe the knowledge, skills and behaviour required of students taking practical courses, especially those in health and social care. Explicit competence requirements for professions, such as those required for nursing students, have become increasingly common (NMC 2010b) and are usually linked to the official professional regulation of that profession. Reflective practice is often a required competence.

Reflection may be used in part, or indeed in full, to support the assessment of learning outcomes in health-care at both undergraduate and post-graduate levels (Schutz 2013). The approach to the use of reflection in this way varies considerably. Summative assessment of reflection focuses on learning outcomes and looking for evidence that these have been achieved. This aims to measure students' skills or knowledge, and a grade or mark is awarded. Where reflection is used as part of the learning process, but where no final mark/grade is awarded, this is known as formative assessment.

Assessment of reflection is likely to require some knowledge and explanation of *models* of reflection and it is likely to have a clinical focus or focus on clinical skills. For summative written work, you might be asked to consider an experience and reflect on this.

There are inherent challenges with both approaches. There are also acknowledged challenges to the use of assessment, such as:

- Lack of consistent understanding and interpretation of meanings of reflection
- Lack of consistent approaches to the process of reflection and which models to use
- Potential dishonesty in reflective writing
- Lack of reliable marking criteria for reflection (Schutz 2013)

Assessment of the reflection may relate to the specific programme requirements for the module or the experience, or competency requirements. However, students can sometimes lack motivation with this, or find it difficult to get started, and where there is no summative assessment the work may not be completed (Timmins and Dunne 2009). Furthermore, where reflections are summatively assessed, there can be difficulty assigning a grade to what are very unique and individual pieces of work (Timmins and Duffy 2011).

implications for reflective practice
Although there are mixed views about assessment of reflection and reflective practice, ascribing value to reflection by including it as a course assessment during either formal or informal learning is important. This can motivate professionals to attend to the required *reflective processes* and help prevent *barriers* to reflection. In your own circumstances you need to be clear whether or not your reflective work will be assessed, or form part of an assessment, so that you are sure about your own personal learning goals and what needs to be done to achieve these. At the same time, knowing whether or not your models of reflection, *journals, diaries* or *learning logs* are going to be either public material or viewed by an assessor is important as it might influence what you choose to write. While you need to be mindful of *ethical issues* with reflection and reflective writing, there is also a need to keep private those thoughts and feelings that may be part of your self-development and ongoing self-awareness.

KEY TEXT
- Schutz, S. (2013) 'Assessing and Evaluating Reflection' in Bullman and S. Schutz (eds), *Reflective Practice in Nursing* (Oxford: Wiley Blackwell): pp. 201–224.

autobiography

SEE ALSO analysis; awareness; barriers; critical friend; critical incident; critical reflection; criticality; diary; facilitator; journals; learning logs; mentor; models; narratives; procrastination; reflection; reflective practice; reflective processes; reflexivity; supervision; writing

Autobiography is an approach to reflective writing that is self-confessional and self-revealing (Howatson-Jones 2010). As people progress through life, they develop a story, and autobiography helps to record this by *writing* the story down. In popular culture autobiography generally refers to the writing out and publication of the story of one's life. This is later sold for profit. In the university and practice setting, autobiography is used as a means of learning about oneself and the impact that this can have on practice. Autobiography is also used as a research method, for example, in professions such as teaching (Hartog 2004, Whitehead 2004). Autobiography in this way has an important contribution to knowledge because it:

> tells a recognisable [professional] story, portrays character development in the face of serious issues within a complex setting, gives place to the dynamic struggle of living life whole, and offers new perspectives. (Roberts 2003:300)

However, pure autobiographical writing for the purposes of professional practice runs the risk of being superficial and merely an extended and descriptive curriculum vitae or listing of events or happenings (Bleakley 2000). As such, in professional settings the confessional style of autobiographical *narratives* might have limitations (Bleakley 2000). Although personal and reflective, they may be purely introspective and lack the *analysis* or *reflection* that is required to develop practice knowledge. For autobiography to contribute authentically to *reflective practice*, it needs to be 'interesting ... [it] need[s] to have aesthetic depth, as well as ethical focus' (Bleakley 2000:23).

Nonetheless, autobiography may be used as a tool for reflection (Howatson-Jones 2010). As we progress through life, we develop a life story. Through exploration of these stories we can come to know more about ourselves, our motivations, our desires and our drives. This can support or enhance our increasing self-awareness.

Autobiographical reflection is a 'way of making sense of what is happening, within the context of a person's life' (Howatson-Jones 2010:37). Using a *model* of reflection to structure this autobiography is suggested (Howatson-Jones 2010), although free writing is also possible. Applying this structure to autobiography addresses some of Bleakley's (2000) concerns about the limitations of autobiography. Personal autobiography can also be developed through narrative, perhaps by story writing or keeping a *diary*.

Reflection on these entries can then assist in examining one's actions and reactions in life. Restrictions on this approach are that when used alone it is quite limiting in terms of objective learning, and thus it may be useful to have a *facilitator, mentor* or supervisor to share the autobiography with. However, as an autobiography is inherently personal this might not suit the situation, and clear guidance within the local professional setting is required. Autobiographical writing may also bring up painful memories and it is important to seek professional help in such circumstances.

implications for reflective practice
Reflection and reflective practice often require writing in order to facilitate the revelation of important circumstances and/or feelings and reactions to this. Writing, for some, can be challenging and it can be difficult to know where to start. Autobiography is an approach to reflective writing that permits a story to unfold in a relatively free way, which may prompt reflective writing. Autobiography may be used when using a *journal* or diary perhaps to keep an ongoing record of your thoughts, feelings, actions and emotions related to a particular period of your professional life or a particular situation. The personal revelations entailed would serve as an aide-memoire for reflection using a model of reflection and permit you some accuracy in your remembrances and reflections rather than relying solely on memory. This could be useful if you are required to submit regular reflections or *learning logs* as a component of a preparatory or post-graduate education programme or training course. The autobiography also serves as a useful guide to choosing *critical incidents* for your reflections. While you may find it difficult to isolate one situation that was puzzling or disturbing by re-reading your autobiography of that period, you might identify patterns and trends that point to another area that needs reflection. You might

notice over a period of practice, for example, that attitudes to certain groups or individuals are negative and you might choose to reflect on this.

The autobiography may also be retrospective, looking back over your professional life or childhood in order to develop self-awareness or inform your practice. In teaching, for example, autobiography is used to explore personal ideas about teaching and teaching philosophies, many of which have their basis in personal experience rather than teacher training (Brookfield 1995).

KEY TEXT
- Howatson-Jones, L. (2010) *Reflective Practice in Nursing* (Exeter: Learning Matters).

awareness

SEE ALSO **analysis; barriers; critical friend; critical reflection; criticality; facilitator; mentor; models; reflection; reflective practice; reflective processes; reflexivity; supervision**

Reflection, *critical reflection* and *reflective practice*, all foster self-awareness. Through the use of *models* of reflection you are encouraged to get to know yourself better and to understand your motivations and actions. You are also encouraged to think not only about your own part in situations but also about the reactions and actions of others and the environments within which events take place. As such, developing an increased awareness is a key goal of reflection and reflective practice, which encourages *reflexivity*. Developing self-awareness is of utmost importance as the premise of reflective practice is that you can develop and improve personal practices. This can be done effectively only by coming to know oneself and the reasons for actions/reactions in certain circumstances. Reflective practice requires action, and knowing yourself better will facilitate you to act. Often *barriers* exist to reflection and reflective practice, and knowing yourself well will help you to circumvent these rather than be distracted by them.

The emphasis on exploration and coming to know the self is a relatively modern phenomenon. The notion of 'self' as a distinct entity (that is, separate from God and community) and the increased need for self-awareness developed mostly since the Enlightenment (after the 1700s) (Tarnas 1991). Developing awareness in the context of reflection and reflective practice means not only increasing your own personal self-awareness but also increasing an awareness of what's going on around you. This contextual awareness, the increased ability to understand situations and their ability to contribute to the success or otherwise of your actions in practice, is a crucial step in the *reflective processes*, reflective practice and critical reflection. As such, awareness requires developing an increased understanding of:

> Individuals (including oneself) in relation to socio-political and ideological context within which meanings are socially constructed. (Brechin 2000:35)

Developing a growing awareness of self, together with an increased understanding of context, spurs personal and professional growth and enables you to more aptly solve problems that occur in practice (Brechin 2000). Getting to know yourself, your values and your practice requires maturity in terms of openness to feedback. Increasing awareness goes hand in hand with reflection and reflective practice as the skills of self-awareness develop during the reflective processes, as you are uncovering and learning more about the opportunities and challenges faced in your life and how these might be best addressed. You are also becoming increasingly aware of your strengths and weaknesses (Timmins and Duffy 2011). Skills of self-awareness develop naturally alongside the reflective processes and by using reflection, critical reflection and models of reflection. As you grow in awareness and explore practice using critical reflection, you develop reflexivity.

Reflection often requires working with a *mentor* or *critical friend* and this enhances your self-awareness as this mentor or friend is likely to either challenge you or reflect back your own thoughts and actions to you, thus increasing your awareness. By sharing your personal thoughts and reflections you will grow in your awareness; however, this process requires an openness to constructive criticism (Timmins and Duffy 2011).

You may also uncover and learn more about yourself by attempting a personal strengths and weaknesses *analysis* (Jasper 2013). Questions for consideration in this exercise include the following:

- What things are you good at?
- What features about yourself are you satisfied with?

- How would you describe your relationships with others?
- What are your most proud achievements so far? (Jasper 2013).

When you are considering your weaknesses you might like to consider the following cues:

- What would you most like to change about yourself?
- In what activities have you been less than successful?
- What goals would you like to have achieved by now but did not?
- What disappointments have you had and how do these affect you?

The Johari window (Figure 1) is a frequently used exercise that can help you to develop self-awareness. It asks you to explore yourself in various aspects. The first is the self that is known to others. Part of this self (known to others) we are aware of (open/free area) and some of it we are 'blind' to. We can be completely unaware of aspects of ourselves in terms of desires, motivations, ambitions and assumptions. Exploring this element of ourselves is useful as it is often a new and surprising discovery which strengthens self-awareness. Working with a mentor, *facilitator* or supervisor is particularly useful in this regard as they can assist you with exploring yourself by using the Johari exercise, but also by providing feedback on your reflections which might provide some insight into those hidden parts of the self.

At the same time, the Johari window suggests that there is a part of the self that is not known to others (but it is known to you). This hidden area is a natural part of the human condition as there is always a private part to the self which may be unknown to at least some others. In many professions it is also important to separate the personal/private and professional persona, and as such during reflection and reflective practice you are often acting out, and developing, the aspects known to others (the open/free area). However, at the same time private or hidden aspects of your persona can influence your actions as a professional. By analysing yourself using the Johari window, you can examine ways in which your hidden self may affect your interactions and practices. What may come as a greater challenge is the unknown area, that part of our personality that we know least about. Not only is this hidden, but not much

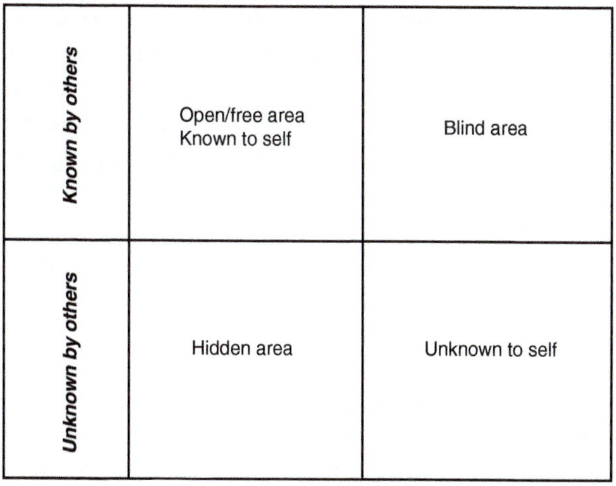

	Open/free area Known to self	Blind area
Known by others		
Unknown by others	Hidden area	Unknown to self

FIGURE I   *The Johari window*

Source: Luft (1984)

is known about it by others or indeed ourselves. In fact, it could be questioned how you might begin to explore such an area. However, it is this very area that requires careful attention during reflection, critical reflection and reflective practice as by exploring your actions, feelings and reactions you may come to know aspects of yourself, or hidden assumptions that you had not previously been aware of.

Here too there is a hidden part that we are unaware of. Again, through working with others and through regular self-reflection we can come to know what lies in this area.

implications for reflective practice

Reflection, critical reflection and reflective practice all entail the ongoing development of self-awareness. Many adults and professionals always strive to come to know themselves better by questioning their thoughts and actions. However, by developing *criticality*, reflexivity and timely reflective practice you become accustomed to self-analysis. Ultimately, and to an extent unbeknownst to yourself, you will develop a growing awareness of yourself and the multiplicity of factors, both internal and personal and also external and contextual, that influence your practice. Through the use of models of reflection you will become accustomed to seeing matters through different lenses as Brookfield (1995) described. By using models of reflection and reflective practice, you are encouraged to get to know yourself better and to understand your motivations and actions. Using SWOB and Johari window analysis in conjunction with reflective processes will strengthen your growing awareness and also provide for a more in-depth awareness of your personal contribution to a situation.

This is particularly useful in challenging professional situations where the fall-back position is often to cast blame on another person. Only by fearlessly and honestly getting to know ourselves can we aim to develop the awareness that is required for genuine reflective practice. Being able to clearly see your own personal contribution to situations through developing awareness is crucial to reflective practice (Laing and Humphries 2013). Having a mentor, facilitator or supervisor is a very useful adjunct to this type of personal development. These people can challenge you but also affirm and support your growing awareness. As true awareness may uncover some deep-rooted assumptions, beliefs or memories that you were unaware of yourself, you need to be mindful of the boundaries in those professional relationships, and seek counselling and/or professional help if painful memories emerge that you either would like to explore in more detail with a professional or are finding difficult to deal with as a result.

KEY TEXT
- Jasper, M. (2013) *Beginning Reflective Practice*. 2nd edn (Hampshire: Cengage Learning).

b

barriers

SEE ALSO analysis; andragogy; assessment; awareness; critical incident; critical reflection; criticality; diary; ERA cycle; experiential learning; journals; learning logs; mentor; models; narratives; reflection; reflective practice; reflective processes; supervision; writing.

There are several barriers to *reflection* and *reflective practice*. While barriers exist that can impede the development of reflection and reflective practice, it is important to see and interpret these as challenges that if understood and negotiated correctly will not necessarily impede reflective practice. These are matters that must be understood and integrated into your approaches in order to make your reflective activity a success. Firstly the idea of personal reflection may be daunting for some. There is also the tendency to put it off and procrastinate especially if there is no particular obvious reward (for completion) or punishment (if not completed). For some, it can also be a source of concern about potential consequences.

Another barrier that applies particularly to busy practitioners is a lack of confidence in the benefits of reflection. Although it does appear to increase personal self-awareness (Timmins and Dunne 2009) there has been little overall exploration of the benefits (if any) of the approach. As it forms part of an *experiential learning* cycle, reflection has not been subjected to rigorous scientific enquiry.

It is important in these contexts that there are clear guidelines to support reflection and reflective practice with clear pathways for disclosure if necessary. It is important to create a climate of trust and safety where reflections can be made and learning enhanced (Bleakley 2000). The organizational climate too can cause a great barrier to reflection and reflective practice and it is difficult to say with confidence that an organization can become reflective or support reflective practice if a culture of reflection is not fostered (Gardner 2014), supported by clear guidelines.

Reflection and reflective practice are also time-consuming activities (Manning et al 2008). Mechanisms for recording reflection take time to complete, and professionals, even when motivated, can falter with these commitments (Duffy 2008, Xie et al 2008). Addressing this issue for professionals may require factoring time into the workplace hours so that reflection is not only completed but valued. Group reflections in particular require this level of organizational commitment to ensure success (Manning et al 2008). Group reflection also needs strong leadership and careful guidance and planning in order to succeed.

Sometimes reflection and using *models* of reflection can become very formulaic, that is, it is followed in a step-by-step fashion with simplistic answers given, almost in a yes/no fashion. This type of reflection can be superficial and yields limited learning. There is also a possibility that one model or another may not suit you (Hargreaves and Page 2013) or your practice. The best thing to do in these situations is to choose one that suits best, or indeed practise free reflection, either thinking through or *writing* out your experiences without a formalized structure (Hargreaves and Page 2013). You might also wish to move on from using a model for the following reasons:

- It is no longer challenging
- There are items that you need to address or include that are not considered within the model
- You are spending a lot of time analysing the model rather than reflecting on your practice (Hargreaves and Page 2013)

However, having others, including facilitators, *mentors* or supervisors, read reflections can be a barrier for some and make them reluctant to share honest reflections (Levett-Jones 2007). This is particularly pertinent when the expression of feelings which are innately personal is required during reflection. While this might inhibit expression, explanation of the purposes of reflection and the putting of boundaries on the reading, for example reading selected work only, might help this. It is also important, however, if the reflections are to be shared in a group, or with a facilitator, that the professional concerned is aware of this public nature and the reasoning behind it so that they can alter their expression accordingly.

Keeping some thoughts and reflections personal and private, in a *diary* for example, might be useful for exploring personal feelings on situations, and less detail can be shared with colleagues, depending on the circumstances.

Apathy can also occur. This means that people lose interest and motivation towards reflection. Reasons for this include lack of direction: leaving people to their own devices with perhaps too many assumptions about and too much reliance on adult independent learning. This is sometimes prompted by a general lack of knowledge in the area and limited understanding of reflection (Timmins et al 2013). Without specific direction and guidance it is easy, even for experienced professionals, to lose their way in the *reflective processes* (O'Donovan 2006). Sometimes when using models of reflection only part of the reflective cycle is completed (Timmins and Dunne 2009) or the process may not be completed at all.

Support for reflection such as mentor, supervisor or facilitator is very useful and not having such support can be a barrier to reflective practice. Additionally, if staff either using reflection or supporting other staff to use it are unfamiliar with reflection or reflective processes this too causes challenges (O'Donovan 2006). After a time the benefits (or lack of) of reflection are limited and people may start to give up. Many will not complete the reflection even if they are supposed to (Timmins and Dunne 2009). Not attributing importance to reflective practice such as assigning a grade to reflective writing accentuates this issue, as people may not see the value of it and/or realize that there is no penalty for not doing it.

There are also cultural (Joyce-McCoach et al 2013) and logistical barriers such as time (Constantinou and Kuys 2013, Manning et al 2008). Joyce-McCoach et al (2013) assert that Asian cultures find the notion of open and public disclosure more difficult than do Western counterparts.

When becoming a reflective practitioner or being encouraged to use reflection it can sometimes be difficult to know what to reflect on. *Critical incidents* are one useful prompt for reflection, suggesting that issues that stand out or cause concern should form the basis of reflection; however, there are times, perhaps due to the particular professional context, that seeking out circumstances that are suitable for reflection can be difficult. There are various approaches to reflection and reflective practices, many of which provide prompts including probing questions that could get you started on processes. If you are required to reflect for learning or professional purposes and yet cannot think of specific suitable experiences or critical incidents, it might be helpful to think of the key elements of Johnson et al's (2007) cultural web model (below) to assist you to identify situations to reflect upon. Although it is more global in its approach than critical incidents, you can choose to reflect either on global matters or specific ones.

Think about the following in relation to professional practice:

- Stories and myths that may exist
- Rituals and routines
- Symbols
- Organizational structure
- Power structures (Johnson et al 2007)

Stories in the form of *narratives* are becoming increasingly popular as a mechanism for exploring practice. You can see from this that your reflection and use of reflective models does not have to be confined to incidents but rather multiple elements of your professional practice may be explored.

Davies (2012) outlined doctors' reasons for non-engagement with reflective practice as follows:

- Lack of understanding of the reflective process
- Staff feel uncomfortable challenging and evaluating their own practice
- Reflection is perceived as time-consuming
- Staff are unsure which experiences/problems to reflect on

implications for reflective practice
Given the impetus towards the use of reflection and reflective practice among many modern professions it is important that barriers are identified and addressed in order to facilitate reflective practice. It is best to be honest and open about the existent barriers, seeing them as challenges, and aim to find solutions where possible. If you are engaging with reflection or models of reflection or supporting staff to do so (as mentor, facilitator or supervisor) it is important that barriers are tackled otherwise it is likely that compounding

barriers (for example time, organization and motivation will be barriers for many) will adversely affect success. Although reflection and reflective practice do not conform to scientific principles, and as such do not need to follow a rigorous process, emerging opinion is that instructive guidelines and support are required.

KEY TEXTS
- Constantinou, M. and Kuys, S. S. (2013) 'Physiotherapy Students find Guided Journals Useful to Develop Reflective Thinking and Practice During Their First Clinical Placement: A Qualitative Study', *Physiotherapy*, 99 (1): pp. 49–55.
- Davies S. (2012) 'Embracing Reflective Practice', *Education in Primary Care* 23 (1): pp. 9–12.
- Hargreaves, J. and Page, L. (2013) *Reflective Practice* (Cambridge: Polity Press).

benefits

SEE ALSO **awareness; barriers; facilitator; mentor; models; reflection; reflective practice; reflective processes; supervision.**

While *barriers* to the use of *reflection* have been identified, there are also many benefits that have been elucidated. Constantinou and Kuys (2013), for example, found very rich learning among physiotherapy students who are guided to reflect on their clinical practice. Through reflection on practice students learn from their experiences and to develop *reflective practice*. Using reflection helped to raise students' *awareness* of thoughts and feelings. It also helped them to critically analyse situations and begin to see new perspectives (Constantinou and Kuys 2013). Similarly among GPs, Davies (2012) identified potential benefits as follows:

- Increases learning from an experience or situation
- Promotes deep rather than superficial learning
- Identifies personal and professional strengths and weaknesses
- Identifies educational needs
- Results in the acquisition of new knowledge and skills
- Facilitates practitioners to understand their own beliefs, attitudes and values
- Encourages self-motivated and self-directed learning

- Acts as a source of feedback
- Improves personal and clinical confidence (Davies 2012)

Oelofsen (2012) points out that reflection and reflective practice can be useful in preventing staff burnout and stress as it allows the exposure of difficult situations and feelings before they reach crisis point.

implications for reflective practice
While not exhaustively researched, there is some emerging evidence that reflections and reflective practice can have beneficial effects on personal development, self-awareness and professional practice. If implementing or engaging in *reflective processes*, it might be useful to open up reflective conversations about the perceived benefits. Importantly, if this evaluation yields negative commentary and identifies barriers to reflective practice, then steps need to be taken to address these so that the potential benefits will ultimately come to light. It is important if you are using reflective processes yourself, or supervising someone who is, that you provide feedback to the organizing authority about what worked and what did not. This type of feedback is especially important in an area that relies on non-scientific evidence and where sparse evidence of benefits exists.

KEY TEXT
- Oelofsen, N. (2012) *Developing Reflective Practice: A Guide for Students and Practitioners of Health and Social Care* (Banbury: Lantern Publishing).

c

codes of practice

SEE ALSO consequences; critical friend; critical incident; critical reflection; criticality; diary; ethical issues; facilitator; learning log; mentor; reflection; reflective practice; reflective processes.

Many professions are guided by regulations or codes of conduct and as such are bound by ethical and legal codes that guide practice (Gardner 2014, Oelofsen 2012). Modern professions are increasingly becoming regulated, which requires the individual professional to adhere to rules about practice that permit standardization of practice and safeguard the public (Hargreaves and Page 2013). This regulation usually permits complaints about professional conduct to be dealt with by the profession, through fitness-to-practise mechanisms. At the very least as a professional or employee you are accountable to criminal law, civil law, your employer and possibly your profession (if registered or licensed) (Hargreaves and Page 2013). Practices of *reflection* and *reflective practice* need to be mindful of the requirements of these codes and legal/*ethical issues* where relevant. In nursing, for example, the nurses' and health-care support workers' codes of conduct (DOH 2013, NMC 2008) emphasize that matters such as service-user autonomy, dignity, respect and honesty need to be considered at all times (DOH 2013, ICN 2012, NMC 2008). It is important that the reflective practice does not compromise these in any way.

If your reflections or reflective practice require the explicit discussion of a client case, for example, client consent must be sought. It would be a breach of confidentiality to discuss this client, for example, on an online *learning log*. Clients are in a vulnerable position with regard to consent, so this must also be done in a way that does not force the client to take part. They ought to be very clear that they can choose to be part of your learning or not. Obviously reassurance would need to be given to the client regarding matters of confidentiality and clear explanation about who might see the work. Professions usually aspire to do the client no harm and to do good and this should be at the forefront of all reflective activities.

Similarly if you choose to analyse local policy or power relationships as part of your reflection, your organization may not necessarily wish to see the results of such an endeavour made public, at least in the first instance. While the analysis might centre on elements of practice that could be within the public domain, or potentially within that domain (by virtue of freedom of information), it would be more ethical for employers to be the first to know about your findings, particularly if there is cause for concern. This enables you to clarify the confidentiality or otherwise of the work and the employer can begin to respond and act accordingly. At the same time were your reflections and reflective practice to raise ethical issues, these need to be reported and managed in an appropriate way. Not to do so might contradict your professional code of practice or regulatory body requirements or contravene legal obligations in the matter. At the same time if you are working with a *mentor*, supervisor or *facilitator*, they may have similar professional obligations.

implications for reflective practice

Before embarking on *reflective processes* it is important to clarify your own personal responsibilities in terms of personal and professional codes of conduct, your responsibility to your employers and your legal responsibilities. Reflection and reflective practice are ultimately action oriented and require changes in thinking, behaviours and practices. Reflective practice is not merely a conceptual journey, and as such you need to be aware of your limitations and obligations in the professional sphere with regard to any action that you may take, or any inaction on your part as a result of your reflections.

KEY TEXTS

- Department of Health (DOH) (2013) *Code of Conduct for Healthcare Support Workers and Adult Social Care Workers in England.* Aavailable at http://www.skillsforhealth.org.uk/about-us/news/code-of-conduct-and-national-minimum-training-standards-for-healthcare-support-workers/, accessed April 14, 2014.

- Gardner, F. (2014) *Being Critically Reflective* (Basingstoke: Palgrave Macmillan).
- Hargreaves, J. and Page, L. (2013) *Reflective Practice* (Cambridge: Polity Press).

competence

SEE ALSO **barriers; critical incident; critical reflection; diary; facilitator; journals; knowledge; learning logs; lifelong learning; mentor; models; reflection; reflective practice; reflective processes; reflexivity; supervision; work-based learning; writing.**

Broadly speaking, competence refers to whether or not a person has the requisite skills and *knowledge* to perform their professional role. In some professions the guidance for this required competence emerges directly from the requirements of the professional regulatory bodies (for example NMC 2008), and universities that provide the requisite education are regularly assessed to ascertain the extent to which they are providing sufficient systems that guide both the development and accurate measurement of competence. As a result, competence assessment now forms a large component of overall assessment within many professional educational programmes, for those people both in preparatory programmes and in post-qualifying courses. Many modern professions have embraced the notion of *lifelong learning* by means of a process (either mandatory or voluntary) of continued professional development (CPD) (Ruch 2009b).

The transition to competence-based approaches from more traditional and often informal approaches has influenced the introduction of a variety of assessment tools. Those working in the professional practice sphere may be familiar with these competence assessment tools that serve to monitor the professional's performance and are generally marked and graded by a *mentor*, supervisor or *facilitator*. Indeed, in keeping with the principles of lifelong learning, the professional's competence is no longer seen as static and unchanging, but rather professionals are expected to continuously update their own competence and, increasingly, mechanisms for doing this are being developed. *Reflection* and *reflective practice* are among a variety of approaches that can be used to develop and maintain professional competence.

Competence is considered using three main approaches: firstly the behaviourist *model*. This is where the measurements of the performance of specified behaviours or tasks are observed and measured as core components of competence. An overt focus on tasks and behaviours as the main components can lead to the belief that practice placements are dominated by the focus on task achievement rather than students gaining a holistic experience of learning (Dolan 2003).

Competence may also be considered in a more generalized way symbolized by a cluster of generalized abilities required to achieve competence. Holistic competence is more comprehensive and far-reaching and includes many domains of practice including cognitive, psychomotor and affective domains of learning (Timmins 2008). Contemporary approaches ultimately aim for a consistent, objective, rigorous approach to the assessment of competence, and competence-based approaches are inherently complex. The use of reflection to support professional health-care practice is advocated by many national and international agencies. Consequently, the skill of developing reflective practice is a key competence requirement of today's practising health-care worker.

implications for reflective practice

If you are a professional you might either have a personal concern or a professional requirement in maintaining your competence to practise. This professional competence is made up of the requisite knowledge, skills and behaviour of your particular discipline that are usually monitored at point of entry, and in some cases on an ongoing basis, to ensure that your competence skills match the requirements of the profession. While there are multiple and complex approaches to the development and monitoring of professional competence, many of which are beyond the scope of this book to explore, it is worth noting that for many professions reflection and reflective practice serve as key mechanisms to develop this competence. For most professionals, competence is required in both technical and practical aspects of the role; while reflection on all aspects of the role is important, reflective practice has an important part to play in developing social wisdom. It is only by interacting with others in the professional environment that the social skills of the professional develop. As many of these are learned in the practice domain, and not directly out of textbooks, having a mechanism to turn this *work-based learning* into new knowledge is useful. When using a model of reflection to reflect on personal competence it is possible to focus on a *critical incident*, on extracts from a *diary* or *journal* that you might keep, or you can focus directly on the specific competence that you are developing. For example, nurses are expected to have competence in the following domains of practice:

- Professional values
- Communication and interpersonal skills
- Nursing practice and decision making
- Leadership, management and team working (NMC 2010b)

The professional nurse might therefore choose then to focus on any one of these four elements and to choose critical incidents, work experiences or cultural aspects of the working environment as the basis for reflection and reflective practice, using models of reflection and *critical reflection* to unpack important elements of the situations.

KEY TEXTS
- Ruch, G. (2009) 'Introduction – Developing Holistic Social Work practitioners' in G. Ruch (ed.), *Post-Qualifying Child Care Social Work*. Developing Reflective Practice (London: Sage): pp. 3–7.
- Timmins, F. (2008) *Making Sense of Portfolios: An Introduction to Portfolio Use for Nursing Students* (Glasgow: Open University Press, McGraw Hill Education).

confidence

SEE ALSO **analysis; andragogy; awareness; contracts (*learning contract*); critical incident; critical reflection; facilitator; lifelong learning; mentor; models; reflection; reflective practice; reflective processes.**

Although not regarded as a key feature of *reflection* and *reflective practice*, confidence is required in order to develop and increase self-awareness and to reflect on professional practice. Confidence is:

the feeling that someone knows how to do something, has the power to make things happen, and knows that one's efforts will be successful; it is the belief that knowledge, skill, experience, and potential will result in success. (Davidhizar 1993:218)

Developing confidence, reflection and reflective practice can be difficult due to existent barriers such as lack of experience, lack of guidance and time restrictions. These barriers can lead the professional to either lack confidence from the outset of the *reflective process* or to develop a lack of confidence having embarked on it – one begins to lack the belief in one's power to make things happen or achieve success.

Although confidence can be related directly to the situation (for example reflective practice) overall it is taken that a person can possess an innate confidence. This is an intrinsic feeling of self-worth and self-respect. Bandura (1977) introduced the term 'self-efficacy' as the belief that one can carry out an activity successfully. 'Self-efficacy' as a term is used interchangeably with the term 'confidence' (Hecimovich and Volet 2009). Self-efficacy is based on four major sources of information: performance accomplishments, vicarious experience, verbal persuasion and physiological states. Self-efficacy levels can enhance or impede motivation. People with high self-efficacy choose to perform more challenging tasks (Bandura 1977). They set themselves higher goals and stick to them. Actions are preshaped in thought, and people anticipate either optimistic or pessimistic scenarios in line with their level of self-efficacy. Once an action has been taken, high self-efficacious people invest more effort and persist longer than those who are low in self-efficacy. When setbacks occur, they recover more quickly and maintain the commitment to their goals. Self-efficacy also allows people to select challenging settings, explore their environments, or create new ones. From this you can see that some individuals embarking on reflection and reflective practice will be more daring and more tenacious as they have a high self-efficacy. Others with perhaps lower self-efficacy may give up more easily, particularly when barriers to reflective practice exist. It is important therefore as a professional that you have a level of self-awareness when embarking on reflection and reflective practice. By performing self-awareness *analysis* you can come to know whether or not you feel confident in reflection, and if you do not you as an adult learner can seek out learning opportunities and support that can improve this confidence.

While reflection offers individuals an opportunity to evaluate their experiences and thought processes, this will not necessarily improve personal confidence, even in the face of apparent success (Bandura 1986). Thus reflection alone is not sufficient to improve performance. It could indeed have a negative effect. This is because deeply held beliefs about your capabilities powerfully influence the ways in which you will behave (Bandura 1986). Your personal confidence is an important consideration during reflection and reflective practice. If you are considering a *critical incident*, for example, and something did not go well, your feelings and description of the incident might point to an underlying lack of confidence in the area. This is something that can be addressed, but not necessarily through the reflective processes themselves but by actively seeking out learning experiences and support that is taking action on the deficits.

implications for reflective practice
Being aware of personal confidence is an important consideration for both embarking on and the success of your reflections and reflective practice. Confidence is about your belief in your ability to do something and this is influenced not only by your experiences but by your personally held beliefs about your ability. Reflection and reflective practice require confidence and you ought to explore your personal confidence with reflective processes before starting off. As an adult learner, if you perceive gaps in your confidence, once you have identified these needs you can seek out learning opportunities to improve and increase your knowledge, experience and thus your confidence. Similarly if reflection and/or reflective practice reveal to you a gap in your professional skills and/or knowledge, or a negative belief that is affecting your confidence, then seek to address these in a similar independent way. While reflection and reflective practice will perhaps highlight gaps in confidence, the reflective processes will not necessarily address these deficits. Using a learning contract, for example, might enable you to set specific goals to improve your learning in a specific area.

Take, for example, the qualified nurse working in critical care dealing with life-supporting technology. Despite specialist education and training in the field, and experience, the nurse finds through reflection that they are very nervous using a particular intervention. This nervousness is not related to their skills, knowledge or experience but rather to a heightened *awareness* of potential risks involved with the intervention (if not performed correctly) and deep-rooted, yet unfounded, fears of doing harm. By recognizing this inappropriate fear through reflection the nurse is able to work with a colleague, developing a learning contract that identifies their needs, and learning activities that will improve confidence. Gradually, under the supervision of the *mentor*, practice under laboratory conditions and reading up on the intervention the nurse's confidence improves. They realize that while it is natural and human to feel afraid, in the context of good professional training, skill, knowledge and experience, these instinctive reactions need to be set aside, and thus confidence grows.

KEY TEXT
• Davidhizar, R. (1993) 'Self-confidence: A Requirement for Collaborative Practice', *Dimensions of Critical Care Nursing*, 12: pp. 218–222.

consequences

SEE ALSO **analysis; critical action; critical friend; critical reflection; criticality; ethical issues; facilitator; mentor; models; reflection; reflective practice; reflective processes; reflexivity; supervision; writing.**

Another important issue in the use of *reflection* and *reflective practice* is the potential for consequences from these *reflective processes* (Timmins and Duffy 2011). It is important that you are prepared for what might emerge from your reflections (Duffy 2008). It is important to consider the question: 'Can I manage the consequences of this ... reflection?' (Duffy 2008:335) As many of the *models* of reflection prompt you to outline your feelings, consequences that could arise include the emergence of strong feelings. You might feel quite sad or angry having reconsidered a difficult situation.

In terms of preventing negative consequences it is important to choose an appropriate model for your reflections (Timmins and Duffy 2011). Boud et al (Boud et al 1985, Boud and Walker 1990, 1993) invite you to attend to the feelings, taking note of them, but not dwelling on them for too long. Others (such as Johns 2013 and Gibbs 1988) ask for an outline of how you felt. For some this exposure of feelings is unwarranted and seems like an invasion of privacy (Johns 2013). Depending on the situation, and how much you wish to explore your feelings, a suitable model can by chosen that suits your situation best. Interestingly this focus on analysing feelings is very much a component of health and social care reflection, and doesn't necessarily feature in the reflections of professions such as engineering. The extent to which this exploration contributes to the reflective processes is unclear as limited testing of models of reflection has taken place.

It is also very important to complete the reflective processes. Very often when using models of reflection people tend to get 'stuck' in certain phases, particularly the 'description' or feelings phase. Concentrating too much on describing the situation and/or your feelings rather than moving on to *analysis* and action is more likely to result in exposing negative feelings. Finally, even when feelings are being uncovered, the reflection ought to be objective and focused on improving and developing your professional practice. This means that the purpose of reflection is not primarily personal development, although this too can occur (Timmins and Duffy 2011). As such the focus ought to be on the service user and the work-based or environmental context rather than too much concentration on self.

Structured, objective, focused reflection is best. If a *mentor*, supervisor or *facilitator* is on hand to assist with this structure, this will hopefully deter or support negative consequences that could occur. This is also helpful should you become particularly upset about a reflective experience, as the mentor, supervisor or facilitator will be able to talk to you about this or refer you to someone else for support. The notion of *supervision* for reflection is one that is frequently discussed (Johns 2013). It is often thought best for reflection to occur with the support of others, preferably in a one-to-one situation, although group reflection is also useful (Johns 2013). This allows support for keeping reflection structured and objective, ensuring the full cycle is complete and dealing with any negative consequences or feelings that arise. For those reflecting alone without this support it is important that support is sought if negative consequences arise.

Another consequence of reflective practice is the necessity to take action. This places a professional requirement on a person to act in order to remedy, rectify or improve the situation. It is important to take steps towards action, otherwise another consequence arises: inaction. At the very least, inadequate or lack of learning might arise if inaction occurs. Additionally if the required actions would improve or benefit your practice then both your practice and presumably the experiences of those in your care might suffer if the action is not taken. If your reflections expose poor or inadequate practices, it would be of utmost importance for the relevant action to be taken. The consequences of not taking action in this case include potential harm to clients; but professional negligence is also possible by omission or complicity. You will need to seek advice on the relevant procedures for taking action in these cases. Most professional employers will have outlined procedures for dealing with this, which for the most part would confer a supportive element to the complainant. Stress is also likely to be a consequence of this action and additional support in the form of counselling would also be recommended in these cases.

It is important that reflections have a *critical* perspective. So rather than just personal introspection you consider the whole practice milieu, take others' viewpoints into consideration, consider policy/knowledge and procedures, and take action (where required) within the practice environment. This is rather more complex than simple personal reflection, but it is a requirement of many professions.

However, it is important to remember when reflecting on professional clinical practice that reflective practice is maintained both within one's scope of practice and, where possible, scope of responsibility. It is possible within situations while taking stock of what is going on (that is, context) to focus more closely on one's own circle of influence and/or zone of responsibility. For example, if you are reflecting on your own hand-washing practices you can confine your action (if relevant) to improving your own personal practices rather than attempting to change that of the whole organization, which may be (a) beyond your scope of responsibility and (b) a challenging task for one person without direct responsibility.

It is also important to remember that if your reflections are not private, then you are exposing yourself in a very public way. Documents submitted to a university or other authority could be subject to legal disclosure depending on the nature of the circumstances, and there could be other legal ramifications of *writing* about other people. For this reason Jasper (2013) suggests caution when writing about others. Reflection and reflective writing are primarily concerned with oneself and one's own learning. This is the first advice, to keep the description to your own experiences rather than broadening these to others' experiences. However, there will be times when others may need to be discussed particularly in order to contextualize the reflection and develop a greater understanding and awareness of context. The following advice is recommended:

- Consider the effect of this reflection (and reflective writing) on others
- Gain consent from others involved
- Consider confidentiality and protecting this
- Ensure anonymity
- Ensure that others are informed of your discussion about them
- Consider the consequences of your disclosure
- Work within professional codes of practice and understand the implications of this
- Consider the implications of misconduct/malpractice/negligence
- Develop a greater understanding of others and their professional role (Jasper 2013)

implications for reflective practice
It is important to be prepared firstly for what might emerge from your reflections (Duffy 2008). It is important to consider the question: 'Can I manage the consequences of this ... reflection?' (Duffy 2008:335). As many of the models of reflection prompt you to outline your feelings, consequences that could arise include bringing up strong feelings. It is important where possible to have a *critical friend* or mentor, supervisor or facilitator to support you while you are developing your reflections (reflection) and using models of reflection. In addition to providing support with your learning and reflections, increasing your awareness and providing you with support, they will be able to assist you to deal with consequences should they arise. It is important as a professional that you keep in mind your own professional responsibility with regard to reflection, reflective practice and reflective writing and that you prevent and deal with consequences and *ethical issues* as they arise.

KEY TEXT
- Johns, C. (2013) *Becoming a Reflective Practitioner* (Oxford: Wiley-Blackwell).

contracts

learning contracts

SEE ALSO **analysis; andragogy; awareness; reflection; reflective practice; reflective processes.**

Suggested initially by Knowles (1989) as an outcome of *andragogy*, learning contracts foster and encourage independence in learning. Rather than learning according to prescribed outcomes, the learning contract facilitates the negotiation of student-led objectives. A contract is drafted between professional and mentor/facilitator/supervisor whereby the professional identifies the learning objectives, the experiences that will form part of the contract and the evaluation method to be used (to ensure objectives have been met). As such, the learning contract contains the four core components of the diagnosis of learning needs.

Where *reflection* and/or *reflective practice* or self-awareness reveal to you a gap in your professional skills and/or knowledge, or a negative belief that is affecting your practice, instead of seeking out a formal learning opportunity, or if none is available to you, a learning contract is one mechanism for addressing these gaps. As the professional you are an adult learner and one that is required to be committed to lifelong learning, and the general responsibility for achieving your learning lies with you (rather than the organization or employer, for example).

Once you have identified a gap in your knowledge or skills, thus identifying a learning need, you can then set objectives for your learning. These need to be explicit, focused and straightforward goals for your learning and should demonstrate clearly those skills, attitudes and behaviours that you need to achieve, and are documented within the learning contract (Jones-Boggs 2008). The learning contract is usually a written document, either electronic or hard copy, and it is useful to have easy access to it for your record.

If you have learned through reflection and reflective practice that you find it difficult to manage your anger in certain situations, for example, then your learning objectives would identify specific learning goals relative to this, indicating those behaviours, skills and attitudes that you would like to achieve in this regard. An example of learning objectives might be as follows:

- To be able to recognize signs of personal anger early
- To be able to manage and deal with anger that arises during departmental meetings
- To be able to discuss feelings of anger with the team without acting upon these

As a learning contract is usually arranged between yourself and one other person, using the learning contract in the context of a mentorship, supervisory or facilitative relationship is more useful than simply trying to attend to your learning independently. You can brainstorm your ideas for learning objectives with this person, and also seek their advice on possible learning activities that you might need to do to achieve the objectives. Examples might be:

- To attend weekly team meetings with Roger to observe his behaviour and reactions to difficult conversations
- To read textbooks and research related to anger management (these can be named)
- To undertake an online anger management course (this can be named)

Following this you will have the task, with your mentor/supervisor/ facilitator, of demonstrating that you have achieved your goal, and the method of evaluating your learning to be agreed in advance (Jones-Boggs 2008). You might like to keep a learning log which can be evaluated by self-assessment to ascertain whether or not you have achieved your learning objectives. You might specify that your learning log must identify reflection on responses to difficult conversations and must demonstrate reflective learning in dealing with anger. You could be more specific in your plans for assessments, suggesting that at least two episodes of managing your own anger are reported in your learning log. Demonstrating a task is another method of assessment using a learning contract, and for the given example you might like to ask your mentor/supervisor/facilitator to accompany you to the meetings while you aim to demonstrate in two meetings or more that you have controlled your anger.

implications for reflective practice

Learning contracts are useful to foster independence in learning (Jones-Boggs 2008) and may be used as a scaffold to support future learning (Timmins and Duffy 2011). As contemporarily self-directed learning and lifelong learning are gaining increasing popularity it is important to explore mechanisms for achieving learning goals independently. People often make the mistake of thinking that learning just happens, particularly in the context of adult learners; however, increasingly, it is being recognized that structure and guidance are important in all learning situations, including independent learning. As such the learning contract may be useful to you in structuring your learning for a given task, situation or behaviour that you require to develop. Developing a learning contract usually occurs within a mentorship, supervisory or facilitative relationship and a record of the learning contract, objectives, learning activities and methods of evaluation are developed. This approach offers both structure and flexibility and the prospect of flexibility in creating learning opportunities and solutions.

KEY TEXT
- Jones-Boggs, K. (2008) 'Perceived Benefits of the Use of Learning Contracts to Guide Clinical Education in Respiratory Care Students', *Respiratory Care*, 53 (11): pp. 1475–1481.

critical action

SEE ALSO **analysis; awareness; critical incident; critical reflection; critical thinking; criticality; knowledge; models; reflection; reflective practice; reflective processes; reflexivity.**

Critical action involves four elements: critical skills, *reflexivity*, refashioning of traditions and transformatory critique (Barnett 1997). Critical action is a tangible rather than conceptual activity and occurs in the practice or professional work environment. Barnett (1997) emphasizes the 'world' as the most crucial and neglected area of *reflection*. He believes *criticality* needs to be emphasized here in relation to practice environment. He describes the domain of the world as the 'dominant mode(s) of reflection'. Barnett (1997:99) believes strongly that the self-reflection of metacompetence (reflection on competence and skills within the discipline), *reflective practice* and active problem solving used within this domain could act as a 'self-monitoring' of one's performance in the real world and ultimately improve the practice of the discipline.

Critical action allows the individual to act as a reflective practitioner and perform reflective practice. It encompasses metacompetence (reflection on skills at an organizational level), the actions of a reflection ultimately as a social formation, and is informed by *critical reflection*; it requires *critical thinking* to problem-solve initially. Later it requires advancement to reflexivity and reflective practice. In the final stages refashioning of understandings commences through mutual understanding and development of traditions and finally transformation occurs through critique-in-action and collective reconstruction of the professional world of practice.

Transformation means making a complete change into something new. Fundamental to reflective practice and critical action is the notion of taking something (practice experiences) and making them into something new (practice theory). Thus transformation is the aim of critical action and a key component, one of the most important, of reflective practice (Oelofsen 2012). By taking a closer look at practice and the practice environment persistently and over time, it is anticipated that new ways of knowing and operating can be developed. By developing an openness to examine one's own contribution to matters when things did not go quite right, one can take the important step of practice development, thus self-transforming. When organizations commit to reflective practice and begin to examine systems and organizations in a holistic and honest way, transformation can occur (McCray 2007).

implications for reflective practice
Critical action facilitates reflective practice. Rather than merely thinking about professional practice, transformatory actions are taken. This requires self-awareness, critical thinking skills, reflexivity and reflective practice. In the final stages, refashioning of understandings commences through mutual understanding and development of traditions, and finally transformation occurs through critique-in-action and collective reconstruction of the professional world of practice. *Models* of reflection and reflection on *critical incidents* are useful *reflective processes* to facilitate this action in the world of professional practice. Transformation is the ultimate aim of critical

action and a key component of reflective practice (Oelofsen 2012). By taking a closer look at practice and the practice environment persistently and over time, it is anticipated that new ways of knowing and practising can be developed.

KEY TEXT
• Barnett, R. (1997) *Higher Education: A Critical Business* (Bristol: The Society for Research into Higher Education).

critical friend

SEE ALSO **analysis; awareness; critical incident; critical reflection; criticality; diary; ethical issues; facilitator; mentor; models; reflection; reflective processes; supervision; values**

A critical friend is someone who is chosen to guide and assist with your reflective practice and developing self-awareness. This is someone who is known to you, usually appointed by you (at your request) and in whom you trust. Their role is to be honest with you about your development and *reflections*, to be blunt, but not to be hurtful. They act in the capacity of an informal and friendly *facilitator* of reflection and reflective practice.

Taylor (2006) suggests that a critical friend is a useful construct perhaps in a setting where there is no formalized structure for reflection. Their role is not to criticize, but rather to support and also to challenge your thinking and assumptions. They might be encouraged to ask the following prompt questions:

• What happened?
• Who was involved?
• What was your role?
• How did you feel when..?
• How do you explain the situation to yourself?
• What alternative views were there in the situation?
   (Oelofsen 2012)

Being prepared for critique and critical feedback requires maturity, openness, self-awareness skills and an *awareness* of your personal strengths and weaknesses (Timmins and Duffy 2011). Some of these may be negative. You might find that you hold negative stereotypes of people that you were unaware of, and you need to be honest about this in a safe, confidential environment where you will not be judged. Developing self-awareness requires an honesty – a confrontation of self. Realization or finding out negative things about ourselves is not a bad thing. Facing up to them and taking action as a result of this is a good thing. When we hide these negative feelings or prejudices, or don't own up to our part in situations, this leads to more difficult situations. It is also deemed useful in contemporary professional settings for practitioners to be in touch with their emotions, naming them and reflecting on them, in order to avoid developing defence mechanisms to avoid them (Bolton 2010).

Guided sessions of reflection can take place when you and your critical friend will probably be quite informal (Timmins and Duffy 2011). Generally it is helpful to use a *model* of reflection to structure some of your thoughts. Being willing to be open and non-defensive is generally the best place to start, and if both the friend and reflector work towards mutual understanding, the process generally will go well (Timmins and Duffy 2011). Guided reflection is not always easy, especially if the critical friend is not aware of the whole situation or the sometimes hidden issues that may have led you to your decision. It is important that the critical friend is aware that any unsafe, illegal or unethical revelations may need to be reported.

implications for reflective practice

If you are not in a situation whereby you are appointed a *mentor*, supervisor or facilitator, then seeking out a critical friend to share reflections with is an important consideration. This person, who you will have chosen, and with whom you feel comfortable, will be able to guide and assist with your reflective practice. This is someone who you trust and who will be honest with you about your development, and guide your reflection and reflective practice by asking probing questions and providing regular follow-up and support.

KEY TEXTS

- Oelofsen, N. (2012) *Developing Reflective Practice. A Guide for Students and Practitioners of Health and Social Care* (Banbury: Lantern Publishing).
- Taylor, B. (2006) *Reflective Practice a Guide for Nurses and Midwives* (Buckingham: Open University Press).

critical incident

SEE ALSO **analysis; awareness; critical action; critical reflection; criticality; models; reflection; reflective practice; reflective processes; reflexivity.**

The practice of using critical incidents as a focus for *reflection* has been used in social work and health-care professions for a number of years (Gardner 2014, Knott and Spafford 2007). Critical incidents are issues that practitioners come across that leave them puzzled or concerned in some way (Gardner 2014). They are often situations that prompt ethical or moral dilemmas (Gardner 2014). Reflection serves a purpose when critical incidents arise to enable professionals to develop practice knowledge by unpacking these events that occur in everyday practice. This was first espoused by Dewey (1933:100), who suggested that reflective thought can turn situations of 'obscurity, doubt [and] conflict' into situations that are 'clear, cohesive, settled [and] harmonious'. Clearly disharmony was the prompt for reflection (Dewey 1933) and issues such as 'disequilibrium and perplexity' continue to serve as foundation prompts for contemporary reflection (Boud 2006, Miller et al 2012:51,). For Brookfield (1995) a critical incident is an essential prompt for reflection.

Critical incident *analysis* might mean using a *model* of reflection to analyse the situation, breaking it down into its component parts. This helps to work out what happened, what feelings were occurring and what was going on in the particular context. Using reflection in this way can be very useful for practitioners, as it prevents an overfocus on the negative and demonstrates the learning from the experience (Asselin and Fain 2013). Without this there can be a tendency to keep quiet about disturbing events and even to harbour guilt about what more could have been done (Asselin and Fain 2013). Exploring the critical incidents can serve to harness this guilt into meaningful learning for future practice whereby new and better approaches might be established. An example of an outline of a critical incident in clinical health-care practice can be found in McBrien (2007).

It must be borne in mind that while critical incidents refer often to issues that cause problems, ethical dilemmas, puzzlement or confusion (Gardner 2014), these incidents do not need to be confined to negative or serious issues. While there is certainly learning in all practice, it is important that reflections are used to challenge the ordinary as well as the big issues. It is also important to remember that in many critical incidents there may be other procedural avenues (of complaint, for example) that need to be explored, and it is important that reflection on practice does not supersede these. Certainly, reflection may trigger further action of course and is useful in this regard.

It is helpful then in this context if the use of the term 'critical incident' is broadened out. Benner's (2000) identification of critical incidents can be helpful to trigger *reflexivity* and situations to reflect upon:

- Where interventions really made a difference
- Those that went unusually well
- Those in which there was a breakdown of some description
- Those that were ordinary and typical
- Those that captured the essence of nursing
- Those that were particularly demanding (Benner 2000)

The following may be considered critical incidents:

- When you felt you had done something wrong
- When you made the wrong decision
- When something went better than expected
- When you lacked confidence
- When you made a mistake
- When you really enjoyed working with someone or a group
- When you had a feeling of pressure
- When you found it difficult to accept or value a service user
- When you felt unsupported
- When you were worried about a service user
- When you took a risk and it paid/didn't pay off (Knott and Spafford 2007)

When using critical incidents as the focus of reflection the following steps are useful:

- Provide a brief outline of the incident
- Explore why the incident had a particular impact on you that made it critical

- Examine the theoretical concepts that informed your response and intervention
- Consider what has been learned from the incident (Knott and Spafford 2007)

Alpers et al (2013) describe a useful exercise of asking nursing students to create an assignment based on a critical incident. This assessment asks students to think about clients in their care and consider an 'event, incident, encounter, or experience they have had [recently]' (Alpers et al 2013:33). They prompt the students towards reflection by suggesting that the situation must have been one that 'elicited an emotion in the nursing student such as fear, anger, joy, relief, and others'. They are asked to describe it, providing details about context and why this particular incident had this effect on their emotions. After this they are to think about what they learned from the situation. Using Borton's model of reflection and three key prompts the students were asked to include the following:

WHAT? A brief description and context of the encounter/event.

SO WHAT? How has this experience informed/transformed/ changed your nursing practice?

NOW WHAT? What are the specific lessons learned from this service user care encounter, and what would you do differently if the situation could be repeated?

The teachers reported that these reflections were sensitive and insightful and allowed students to explore their innermost thoughts and feelings about emotive situations in practice (Alpers et al 2013:33).

Branch (2010:328) similarly used critical incident technique with medical students. The students were prompted to 'write a story about an important event that you experienced in medicine'. When the researchers analysed these critical incidents they found that they served to document an 'acculturation into medicine'. Medical students frequently documented challenges to their personal values of caring and they highlighted how they resisted becoming indoctrinated into prevailing cultures that in some cases placed less value on caring and were rather 'dispassionate' (Branch 2010:328).

An interesting perspective on critical incident is provided by a study of eight occupational therapists in Canada (Vachon and

LeBlanc 2011). Participants were recruited to participate in a group reflection (12 meetings held over a 15-month period) that utilized critical incident technique as a mode of reflection. The prompt for the critical incident reflection was to think of 'difficult or surprising past clinical situations' (Vachon and LeBlanc 2011:897). The study results indicated that the reflection on critical incidents provoked strong emotions, and overall reflection on very recent critical incidents rather than episodes from the distant past was more valuable (Vachon and LeBlanc 2011). Reflection on past episodes appeared to bring maximum frustration and negative emotion, whereas current events could be analysed, shared and worked upon in real time.

One important thing to remember about reflection is that it doesn't always have to relate to a specific incident. Reflection is often considered as being a one-off event, perhaps associated with *incidents* or often referred to as *critical incidents* in practice, whereby you thought back over negative or positive experiences, in order to glean learning from these events and to understand what you could do differently or similarly the next time you encounter a comparable incident. However, reflection is much broader than this:

> a specific incident is not in question but rather the need to reflect upon cumulative experience and products and processes of learning over time. (Timmins 2008:63)

It can serve to create a barrier to your reflection and *reflective practice* if you focus too much on seeking out critical incidents particularly when they are not readily available to you. In these circumstances broader issues in the professional environment can be used to trigger reflection.

implications for reflective practice
Critical incident analysis provides a useful focus for your reflections and reflective practice. Having determined a critical incident using the criteria outlined above, you are able to use a model of reflection to analyse and make sense of the situation. This approach helps you see the situation more clearly, understanding your contribution to it and recognizing what needs to be changed for the future. It is important to remember that critical incidents encompass the ordinary and the extraordinary.

KEY TEXTS

- Alpers, R. R., Jarrell, K. and Wotring, R. (2013) 'Toward a Reflective Practice: Using Critical Incidents', *Teaching and Learning in Nursing*, 8 (1): pp. 33–35.
- Gardner, F. (2014) *Being Critically Reflective* (Basingstoke: Palgrave Macmillan).

critical reflection

SEE ALSO **analysis; awareness; critical action; criticality; diary; models; reflection; reflexivity; reflective practice; reflective processes.**

In addition to the popularity of *reflection* and *reflective practice* the acknowledged complexity of the world of practice in professional fields such as health and social care means an increasing and recommended use of critical reflection within disciplines. Rather than simply terming this 'reflection', increasingly the disciplines refer to what is known as *critical* reflection. While reflection may be considered to be an *analysis* of situations and incidents, critical reflection takes a wider look at these situations and takes into account the context and situation within which they took place (Gardner 2014). While the two terms ('reflection' and 'critical reflection') are often used interchangeably (Fook and Askeland 2006) the key added dimension of critical practice is that the reflection includes a more substantive analysis of personal beliefs, how these fit within social settings and how these social settings influence and affect situations (Fook and Askeland 2006). In particular, power differences in social settings are taken into consideration (Fook 2012, Brookfield 1995). Critical reflection is not necessarily better or more in-depth than reflection, rather it takes a different form (Brookfield 1995).

It is commonly accepted that reflective practice 'is more than the examination of personal experience; it is located in ... political and social structures' relevant to the profession that one is in (Bolton 2010:11). Critical reflection is:

> the process by which adults identify the assumptions governing their actions, locate the historical and cultural origins of the assumptions, question the meaning of the assumptions, and develop alternative ways of acting. (Fook et al 2006)

One criticism of reflection has consistently been that it can become overly personal and individual (Boud 2010); this means that a person might think mostly about themselves in the situation, what they did and how they reacted without considering the wider context of the practice environment (Høyrup and Elkjaer 2006, Boud and Walker 1998). Critical reflection is 'the questioning of contextual aspects that are taken-for-granted – social, cultural and political – within which the task is situated' (Høyrup 2004:444). It also involves questioning of meanings of situations with regard to our roles and relationships (Høyrup 2004). Høyrup (2004:444) argues that while reflection can result in new knowledge, critical reflection:

> may imply changes in the very psychological mechanisms that constitute the basis of our interpretations of the world.

Critical reflection involves a close examination of underpinning beliefs and values and a questioning of previously held assumptions (Høyrup and Elkjaer 2006). In a rapidly changing environment it is suggested that taking account of the whole picture is better, in order to have a more accurate account and to develop a greater understanding of factors that contribute to actions or inactions in particular contexts (Gardner 2014). Specifically critical reflection is 'to be reflective and to understand how that reflection is influenced by social context' (Gardner 2014:23).

Critical reflection is both a theory and a process (Gardner 2014). It involves a deeper look at the underpinning reasons why situations occur and consideration of all the elements that contribute to it (Gardner 2014). It permits understanding and engaging with the interaction between:

- Experiences
- Emotions, thoughts and reactions
- The social context

Critical reflection involves:

- Recognizing and affirming differences
- Openness and creativity

- Considering opposing beliefs
- Thinking about the context in which experiences take place (Gardner 2014)

Gardner (2014) suggests that critical analysis requires a two-stage approach:

1. Analysis/exploration/deconstruction
   a. Exploring the experience and why it is significant
   b. Exploring the background and context of the experience
   c. Identifying assumptions, hidden theories and meanings
   d. Exploring where assumptions and theories originate and whether they fit with personal and professional values
2. Change/reconstruction
   a. Exploring how practice or actions require changing
   b. Exploring mechanisms for change

Models for reflection may be used as a structured framework for critical reflection. However, it is important to remember that the particular context – social, environmental, political and personal – is taken into account for the reflections to be truly critical.

Critical reflection requires a practitioner to look over events that were puzzling, difficult or new and think about these. For real learning to occur with reflection it is best if a model or framework is used for this. A practitioner who visits a client, for example, and discovers that they have not adhered to the required practices may wish to question themselves about the reasons for this. A baseline reflection might consider the practitioner's approach (to education, to the relationship, as examples) whereas critical reflection would lead the practitioner to consider the context more carefully. At a basic level, during this reflection one might consider factors such as age, gender, social status and the service user's understanding of their condition or situation. More considered reflection might take account of income factors (such as whether these are affecting adherence to a regimen or required actions), their beliefs (for example, about health, religion, family values) and the social environment. If as a health-care worker you have advised a client to exercise, for example, there may have been religious and/or social reasons why this was not undertaken. A greater understanding of these reasons can be developed through critical reflection that would help to develop a plan of care that incorporates these.

implications for reflective practice
Critical reflection entails looking deeper within one's own thinking and questioning taken-for-granted assumptions. One might, for example, suggest preferences for others based on our own particular likes and needs. For example, being an exercise enthusiast, one might advocate exercise and become surprised when the client doesn't share the same enthusiasm. Or one's own religious and cultural beliefs might limit understanding of the religious and cultural beliefs of others. Using our example of suggested exercise – a suggestion of using a gym or walking in the local area may not suit a female Muslim client. If you are not from this faith you may not have previously considered this aspect of your client's care. You may realize through critical reflection that you should have taken this into account. Following your critical reflection you decide to work with your client to find the best exercise that is feasible within her religious and social context.

KEY TEXTS
- Bolton, G. (2010) *Reflective Practice. Writing and Professional Development* (London: Sage).
- Fook, J. and Askeland, G. A. (2006) 'The "Critical" in Critical Reflection' in S. White, J. Fook and F. Gardner (eds), *Critical Reflection in Health and Social Care* (Berkshire: Open University Press): pp. 40–53.
- Fook, J., White, S. and Gardner, F. (2006) 'Critical Reflection: A Review of Contemporary Literature and Understandings', in S. White, J. Fook and F. Gardner (eds), *Critical Reflection in Health and Social Care* (Berkshire: Open University Press): pp. 3–20.
- Gardner, F. (2014) *Being Critically Reflective* (Basingstoke: Palgrave Macmillan).

critical thinking

Critical thinking is the cognitive process of analysing information and breaking it down into its component parts. It may involve reflecting upon the meaning of things, examining the evidence behind something, and judging the veracity of the facts. Reflection and reflective practice require critical thinking as analysis forms the basis of most reflective processes and models. Critical thinking generally involves evaluation, which is weighing up the benefits and drawbacks and identifying strengths and weaknesses. Even identifying your own strengths and weaknesses requires this type of thinking. Critical thinkers gather information from observation, experience, reasoning, and/or communication, and by exploring your professional practice through reflection, critical reflection and reflective practice you will gradually develop critical thinking skills.

Critical thinking involves identifying the most relevant or salient points of the situation. It involves an understanding of the complexities of situations and underpinning assumptions. All of these are features of critical reflection and criticality. Critical thinking means that you can examine a situation from several aspects rather than accepting it as one-dimensional, and seek to uncover new understandings. Critical thinking involves (Ennis 2010):

- Being capable of taking a position or changing a position depending on the evidence
- Remaining relevant to the point
- Seeking information as well as precision in information
- Being open-minded
- Taking the entire situation into account
- Keeping the original problem in mind
- Searching for reasons
- Dealing with the components of a complex problem in an orderly manner
- Seeking a clear statement of the problem
- Looking for options
- Exhibiting sensitivity to others' feelings and depth of knowledge
- Using credible sources

A critical thinker also:

- Raises vital questions and problems, formulating them clearly and precisely
- Gathers and assesses relevant information, using abstract ideas to interpret it effectively
- Comes to well-reasoned conclusions and solutions, testing them against relevant criteria and standards

- Thinks open-mindedly within alternative systems of thought, recognizing and assessing, as needs be, their assumptions, implications and practical consequences
- Communicates effectively with others in figuring out solutions to complex problems (The Critical Thinking Community 2014a)

implications for reflective practice
Critical thinking is an important skill for the world of professional practice. By exploring your professional practice through reflection, critical reflection and reflective practice, you will gradually develop critical thinking skills that will enable you to see situations in their complexity while at the same time finding salient points within these situations to focus on, develop or learn from.

KEY TEXTS
- Fook, J. and Askeland, G. A. (2006) 'The "Critical" in Critical Reflection' in S. White, J. Fook and F. Gardner (eds), *Critical Reflection in Health and Social Care* (Berkshire: Open University Press): pp. 40–53.
- Gardner, F. (2014) *Being Critically Reflective* (Basingstoke: Palgrave Macmillan).
- Hargreaves, J. and Page, L. (2013) *Reflective Practice* (Cambridge: Polity Press).

criticality

SEE ALSO **analysis; awareness; critical action; criticality; diary; models; reflection; reflective practice, reflective processes; reflexivity.**

Rather than merely reflecting internally on events (at a personal level), *criticality* allows individuals to act as critical beings. Thus self-reflection is extended to thinking about the influence of the wider surroundings, and information that informs this. Criticality also moves beyond thinking to taking action. Barnett's (1997:70) classification of criticality extends beyond *reflection* and allows the individual to 'act critically in the wider world, or to evaluate critically theories produced within bodies of thought or, indeed to understand (oneself) critically'. This criticality comes about as a result of critical reflection and *reflexivity* ultimately results in new knowledge being constructed by reflective and empirical means; it recognizes multiple perspectives and serves to challenge dominant paradigms and involves action (Fook 2012). As a result of ongoing critical reflection, reflexivity and the development of criticality, the professional becomes a critical practitioner (Fook 2012) capable of engaging with knowledge that is:

> obtained empirically and through reflection in a way that recognises the processes by which this knowledge (and thus power structures and relations) is maintained. (Fook 2012:47)

Through ongoing critical reflection this knowledge is further deconstructed so that ultimately the professional develops:

> their own practice in inclusive, artistic and intuitive ways which are responsive to the changing ... contexts in which they work. (Fook 2012:47)

The ever-changing contexts of modern societies in which professionals practice are an important consideration for criticality and being a critical practitioner. Learning from experience in changing contexts can be challenging (Fook 2012). However, maintaining this criticality and continuing to reflect on practice yields positive results in terms of becoming aware of personal emotions (and their contributions to situations), understanding and challenging power differences and taking the required action (Fook 2012). Where criticality is present among staff in organizations the following benefits occur:

- Better staff morale
- Increased ability to tolerate ambiguity
- Increased sense of professionalism
- Commitment to holistic attention to service users
- Increased accountability and creativity
- Increased openness to multiple perspectives and diversity

implications for reflective practice
Through the developing *awareness* that comes about as a result of self-analysis, reflection/*reflective practice* and critical reflection, a growing sense of criticality emerges within the professional. According to Barnett (1997) criticality is a crucial aspect of modern

professional lives by virtue of their increasing complexity, advancing technological requirements and continuous human interaction. Criticality permits useful *analysis* of the situations and background information and also informs *critical action*. Rather than focusing on oneself, criticality fosters actions that are other-centred, responsive to environments and committed to service improvement.

KEY TEXT
- Barnett, R. (1997) *Higher Education: A Critical Business* (Bristol: The Society for Research into Higher Education).

d

decision making

SEE ALSO codes of practice; experiential learning; reflection; reflective practice; reflective processes; work-based learning.

Decision making is about making a logical choice from available options (Jasper et al 2013). For many, decision making is part of everyday life. Simple decisions are taken each day regarding dress and diet. These are usually logical and draw on available clothes and/or food. In the same way the world of work and practice is filled with decisions to be made. Some of these are minor and some are major. In certain circumstances, such as health and social care, the person is not only making personal decisions and organizational decisions, but they are often making decisions either on behalf of the service user or that could affect the service user. A professional's decision can affect others (either positively or negatively) and also may have financial consequences. As such, the nature and manner of decision making in many spheres of practice has undergone considerable scrutiny.

Within health and medicine, for example, decision making can be complex and involve a range of personnel and conflicting evidence (Hunink et al 2001). When considering available options there is range of conflicting demands – from service user requirements to resources. A practitioner therefore needs a great deal of skill and knowledge to effectively make decisions on a regular basis. Decision making can be difficult. It requires confidence and often requires support from others. Once the decision is made the person needs to be determined to see it through.

When making complex decisions that are not immediately urgent, it is important to involve key personnel (or their spokesperson) who have an interest in or concern about the topic. Although it may seem a lengthy process it is important to involve as many stakeholders as possible. At one level, making a decision might be quite straightforward; however, at another level if this decision involves change in practice it will be extremely difficult to implement without buy-in from the personnel involved. It is also important to consider the whole environment and how the multitude of elements within it might be affected by the decision.

As a first step it is essential to identify and be clear about the actual nature of the problem (Hunink et al 2001). It then needs to be reframed in the context of how it is viewed from other perspectives, and objectives should be set for courses of action (Hunink et al 2001). All relevant information needs to be collected and possible outcomes from various actions explored. A competent practitioner is able to make decisions in practice guided by experience, skills and policies/procedures. Previous experience guides problem solving and decision making and allows practitioners to have a focused analysis of problems and solutions (Jasper and Mooney 2013).

Jasper et al (2013) differentiate between intuitive decisions (ones that come instantaneously, naturally and easily) and analytical ones (those which require logical step-by-step thinking to resolve). Decision making in clinical practice also differs from personal decision making (Jasper et al 2013). While inevitably the core skills (of decision making) may overlap in a person, so that someone who is a poor decision maker in their personal life is likely to find similar difficulty in the work situation (and vice versa), however, decision making in working environments is infinitely more complex. There are often multiple parties involved including a customer or service user and often legal, ethical and moral variables to take account of. In health-care, for example, *codes of practice* guide decision making. Ultimately accountability for practice and for service users' care is a paramount consideration underpinning decision making in health (Jasper et al 2013).

There are also many decision-making *models* available to guide thoughtful, logical decision making in practice (Jasper et al 2013). Jasper et al (2013) suggest a process model, the '5WH Cues' to guide decision making, that is both analytical and intuitive. This approach to decision making asks you to consider the following questions in relation to the decision ahead:

1. What is the problem; what decision is required?
2. Why is the decision required; why is there a problem?
3. Who will the decision affect; who is experiencing the problem?

4. When is the decision required; when is the problem occurring?
5. Where will the decision take place; where is the problem?
6. How will the decision be implemented; how will a decision that best suits be found?

implications for reflective practice

Decision making and *reflective practice* are inextricably linked in terms of developing as a professional (Jasper et al 2013). Reflective practice can serve to provide the models and structure necessary to reframe problems and explore solutions in order to facilitate good decision making. They also permit observation of the problem from multiple perspectives which is essential to inform the analysis required for good decision making. Experience forms the basis of making decisions; reflective practice serves to build up this *experiential learning*. This is particularly useful for students who may have only limited exposure to professional practice before qualifying and therefore are required to maximize the learning from situations encountered. Reflective practice is not designed specifically with decision making in mind but it can foster and engender skills that will enable the individual to be confident, knowledgeable and informed when making decisions.

KEY TEXTS

- Hunink, M., Glasziou, P., Siegel, J., Weeks, J., Pliskin, J., Elstein, A. and Weinstein, M. (2001) *Decision Making in Health and Medicine: Integrating Evidence and Values* (Cambridge: Cambridge University Press).
- Jasper, M., Rosser, M. and Mooney, G. (2013) *Professional Development, Reflection and Decision-Making in Nursing and Healthcare.* 2nd edn (Oxford: Wiley-Blackwell).
- Jasper, M. and Mooney, G. (2013) 'The Context of Professional Development' in M. Jasper, M. Rosser and G. Mooney (eds), *Professional Development, Reflection and Decision-Making in Nursing and Healthcare.* 2nd edn (Oxford: Wiley-Blackwell).

diary

SEE ALSO **autobiography; codes of practice; consequences; critical friend; critical incident; critical reflection; criticality; reflection; reflective practice; reflective processes; reflexivity; writing.**

It's a good idea to keep field notes, perhaps in a diary, because our memories often don't recall incidents exactly as they happened, and sometimes you may not be able to take time out to reflect following a *critical incident*. A diary is quite open in terms of what it might contain. People often write their personal thoughts and confidences in their diary or it can act as a pseudo confessional (Bolton 2010). Generally the diary contains:

> stories of happenings, hopes and fears, memories, thoughts, ideas, and all attendant feelings. They also contain creative material: drafts of poems, stories, plays or dialogues, doodles and sketches. (Bolton 2010:128)

It may actually be a while before you have a chance to return to the incident. Field notes can be documented in your diary. There is value in using a diary to record personal experiences. This can include free-flowing *writing* and thoughts that can be very useful to monitor your progress. *Autobiography* is also possible with this approach. There is great value and learning in the narrative approach (Benner et al 2011). A diary is often kept on a chronological basis (recorded according to dates).

Diaries are also useful tools for learning in organizations. This learning has been displayed at one school of English in the UK where undergraduates kept diaries during project work (Beal 2012). By using this method students were facilitated to reflect on their employability skills and learn together as a group. Similarly, diary use with design engineers has had productive results (Babapour and Rahe 2013). Recent use by one UK GP (Miller 2014:119) provides useful insights into the practical benefits of keeping a reflective diary:

> At first I was a little resistant to the imposed requirement of documenting my *reflections* ... I didn't feel that I had the time and I felt that I wasn't being trusted to regulate myself. However, having found the experience of reflective writing effective in embedding new learning in my everyday practice, I have taken ownership of the process for myself. I now keep a reflective diary that I use for my own self-supervision when I have found something particularly difficult. At other times I write straight into my electronic appraisal folder. Writing helps me stand back and

take a critical stance. Often there are surprises and prejudices that I uncover and the process of writing actually reinforces my new learning. When I notice gaps in knowledge I am quicker to fill them than I used to be. I am less defensive and I am better able to respond to feedback constructively. Like many other professionals I learn much from conversations with others and find that I often reinforce this learning when I write about it.

However, one needs to be mindful at all times of the potential *consequences* of writing about others. One needs to be careful to operate within one's own professional *code of practice*; although the diary may seem to be a personal one, as you are ultimately writing about clinical practice, both the organization and the clients in your care have a direct involvement in it. Remember that if the diary contains personal information it must be kept safe, whether it is electronic or a paper version.

implications for reflective practice
Diaries are also useful tools for learning in organizations. A diary is quite open in terms of what it might contain. People often write their personal thoughts and confidences in their diary or it can act as a pseudo confessional (Bolton 2010). As time may elapse between an event (e.g. a critical incident) and when you are able to reflect upon it or write out the details, keeping a diary, with perhaps shortened entries, serves as an aide-memoire. Field notes can be documented in your diary. There is value in using a diary to record personal experiences. This can include free-flowing writing and thoughts that can be very useful to monitor your progress. Autobiography is also possible with this approach. There is great value and learning in keeping a diary and developing a narrative approach to your practice.

KEY TEXT
- Bolton, G. (2010) *Reflective Practice: Writing and Professional Development* (London: Sage).

e

ERA cycle

SEE ALSO critical action; critical reflection; reflection; reflective practice; reflective processes.

The experience-reflection-action (ERA) cycle (Jasper 2013) summarizes the processes required for *reflective practice*. For reflective practice to occur there needs to be an *experience*, something that happens to a person. This is followed by the *reflective processes* that allow you to learn from the experience. Finally, for true reflective practice to be carried out, action must be taken. All three elements need to have taken place for reflective practice to have occurred. In fact there is a possibility for all three elements to happen in isolation, but it is the unique synergy of these three parts that enables both the learning and the engagement in practice that are required for reflective practice. Guidance with these elements specifically is found within the models of *reflection* that guide practice.

The notion of experience in the ERA cycle can be looked at in many different ways (Jasper 2013). This can be simply one single experience, a set of experiences or indeed the totality of experiences that a person has had (Jasper 2013). Experiences can be further classified into personal, psychological, physical, spiritual, religious and social, among others (Jasper 2013).

implications for reflective practice
The experience-reflection-action (ERA) cycle (Jasper 2013) provides an outline summary of the processes required for reflective practice. The first requirement of reflective practice is an experience. After this the reflective processes that follow allow you to learn from this experience. The final stage in reflective practice is doing something with your learning from experience by taking some necessary action. All three elements need to have taken place for reflective practice to have occurred.

KEY TEXT

- Jasper, M. (2013) *Beginning Reflective Practice*. 2nd edn (Hampshire: Cengage Learning).

ethical issues

SEE ALSO **consequences; facilitator; group reflections; mentor; models; reflection; reflective practice; reflective processes; reflexivity; supervisor; writing.**

Reflective practice has the possibility to not only address ethical issues (Gardner 2014) but also raise ethical issues (Knott 2007). Four fundamental ethical principles underpin most modern professional practice codes and guidelines; these are:

- Autonomy – respecting the right of others to make decisions and choices
- Non-maleficence – not doing any harm to others
- Beneficence – doing good for others
- Justice – fairness towards others (Oelofsen 2012)

Professionals who witness breaches in these ethical rights might wish to reflect on the situation in order to make sense of it, analyse what happened and take action and change behaviours for the future. Situations that evoke concerns about ethical considerations are often complex, and straightforward guidelines and regulations may not uniformly apply. This is why reflecting on these situations using a *model* of *reflection* can be very helpful as a guide to sorting out your feelings, actions and knowing what to do to improve the situation if possible. If the situation concerns many people in your workplace there may already be in place facilities for *group reflection* where the team can learn together from the situation and take appropriate action.

Reflection can re-awaken painful feelings or memories and this in itself has ethical connotations (Knott 2007) and may have *consequences* for the individual. It is important that no harm come to the participant in reflection, and as such the notion of guided reflection is a useful consideration as the *mentor, supervisor* or *facilitator* can identify the potential for harm early on. If a person is affected negatively by their reflections, then they should seek support (Knott 2007). If supportive mechanisms are not in place, then it is questionable ethically whether or not active reflective practice should be encouraged (Knott 2007). It is likely that a certain level of distress may emerge when engaging in reflection and this ought to be explained to participants by the facilitator, or in guidelines for staff and students (Knott 2007).

In some cases the reflection may have unearthed poor practice, which needs reporting through the official systems of the organization. Any potential harm to service users or clients in care needs to be addressed immediately. A practitioner may feel a sense of relief when sharing a situation with a group or facilitator, but this does not negate their responsibility to utilize the appropriate reporting mechanisms. *Reflective process* ought not to be used as a proxy reporting mechanism. While it is acknowledged that there are many organizational, personal and cultural reasons why reporting may be difficult, this does not negate the responsibility for the requirement to do so (Hargreaves and Page 2013).

Similarly, the *writing* of reflections may incur ethical issues. Naming of service users and staff within written reflections is not generally permitted. Hargreaves and Page (2013:85) advise that 'anything written down has legal status'. Good practice indicates that a third party ought not to be included in written reflections without their explicit permission; at the very least you ought to write 'with the expectation that the person will see what you have written' (Hargreaves and Page 2013:85). You are advised to anonymize your entries (names and distinguishing characteristics), or convert your writing to a fiction piece to draw out the key points without naming people (you would need to explain that it is fiction) (Hargreaves and Page 2013). Writing about incidents in practice, whether they involve named individuals or not, may require action by the recipient (e.g. a university or organization) if poor practice is outlined. Staff therefore need to be mindful that written reflections are a public record. They ought not to harm individuals or organizations, and are not the appropriate mechanisms for reporting. They are a mechanism of personal and professional development. Their focus ought to be primarily the self, with an awareness of context (including procedural, legal, political and ethical). Issues of concern in practice ought to be addressed using appropriate local and national procedures. The major ethical principles that need to be adhered to are:

- Trust – in the process
- Self-respect – in our belief and actions
- Responsibility – for our reflections, writing and actions
- Generosity – by giving time for reflection
- Positive regard – for others that we refer to in our reflections (Bolton 2010)

Another ethical issue that can arise with the use of reflection and reflective practice is lack of truthfulness. This particularly applies to narratives that form the basis of reflections that are submitted as part of an assessment or for viewing by a facilitator (Knott and Spafford 2007). There is usually no way that assessors can verify whether or not the story is authentic and, to an extent, each iteration of a story can have deviations from the actual lived experience (Knott and Spafford 2007). Ethically, one would expect truthfulness and authenticity in reflections and ways to perhaps ensure authenticity could be included within reflective processes and procedures. These include the use of others' testimonies and other objective evidence within the reflections. Where an inauthentic written reflection has potential to do harm, is if it is a misrepresentation of reality – perhaps an accusation of poor practice – which could have consequences for other staff members.

At the same time, professionals have a responsibility to respond to ethical and moral dilemmas which might be raised during reflective processes (Gardner 2014). It is suggested that strategies need to be in place to deal with such issues and that staff need to be active in 'speaking up, building support networks and developing policies' (Gardner 2014:129). This may take courage and in some cases a policy change. However, it is important to recognize reflection as a mechanism to engage with ethical issues (Gardner 2014). This allows sharing of issues, perhaps with a mentor, supervisor or facilitator or within group reflection, which can lead to an openness and problem-solving approach.

implications for reflective practice

Reflective practice has the possibility to not only address ethical issues (Gardner 2014) but also raise ethical issues (Knott 2007). Reflection can re-awaken painful feelings or memories and this in itself has ethical connotations (Knott 2007) and may have consequences for the individual. In some cases the reflection may have unearthed poor practice, which needs reporting through the official systems of the organization. Any potential harm to service users or clients in care needs to be addressed immediately. Professionals have a responsibility to respond to ethical and moral dilemmas which might be raised during reflective processes (Gardner 2014). It is suggested that strategies need to be in place to deal with such issues and that staff need to be active in seeking support networks and addressing these issues (Gardner 2014:129).

KEY TEXTS

- Bolton, G. (2010) *Reflective Practice: Writing and Professional Development* (London: Sage).
- Gardner, F. (2014) *Being Critically Reflective* (Basingstoke: Palgrave Macmillan).
- Hargreaves, J. and Page, L. (2013) *Reflective Practice* (Cambridge: Polity Press).
- Knott, C. (2007) 'Reflective Practice Revisited' in C. Knott and Scragg (eds), *Reflective Practice in Social Work* (Exeter: Learning Matters): pp. 3–12.
- Knott, C. and Spafford, J. (2007) 'Getting Started' in C. Knott and Scragg (eds), *Reflective Practice in Social Work* (Exeter: Learning Matters): pp. 13–29.
- Oelofsen, N. (2012) *Developing Reflective Practice: A Guide for Students and Practitioners of Health and Social Care* (Banbury: Lantern Publishing).

experiential learning

SEE ALSO **reflection; reflective processes.**

Kolb's (1984) framework for learning from experience is often termed 'experiential learning' (Jasper 2013). Experiential learning generally means that the learner is engaged in some type of active learning. Drawing upon the work of Kolb (1984), Gibbs (1988:46) further describes experiential learning methods for the classroom followed by a 'structured debriefing' exercise, commonly referred to as a model of *reflection*. The later model became popular for use within classroom settings.

The notion of this debriefing is that in order to learn from the structured activities students need to actively reflect on the process and seek out the meaning and learning from the experience. Without this debriefing the experiential learning is thought to be of minimal use. Thus the concrete experience (in the classroom) is maximized and accentuated by reflections on the process. It is often thought to be a simple process (Brackenreg 2004) but its value ought not to be underestimated. It is generally held as a six-stage approach with detailed pre-planning. Later there is an introduction, followed by the learning activity, debriefing, summary and evaluation (Brackenreg 2004). The experiential model described (Kolb 1984) considers four stages of learning. Firstly the concrete experience, followed by reflective observation, abstract conceptualization and finally active experimentation.

This debriefing or reflection that has become part of classroom experiential learning is thought to be vital. Without this planning for, and skilled use of, debriefing and reflection after the action stage, students are, at best, left with doubtful learning outcomes or, at worst, vulnerable to unresolved, emotional unfinished business. Without effective debriefing the facilitator has no way of finding out about the effects and outcomes of the action stage and students are left to their own devices to explore meaning (Brackenreg 2004:267). Consequently, experiential learning occurs not from undergoing the experience but from subsequent meaningful reflection. Thus the reflection (debriefing) that is required for experiential learning to have taken place means that the:

> role of the teacher is to provide a cognitive 'bridge' so that the student is more likely to refine affective and cognitive outcomes from the raw affective and cognitive experience. (Brackenreg 2004:267)

This debriefing exercise is a reflective one and its use has transformed within the education setting into reflective model use. As such, the term 'debriefing' is not commonly used with these models. Drawing upon the work of Kolb (1984), Gibbs (1988:46) describes experiential learning methods for the classroom followed by a 'structured debriefing' exercise, commonly referred to as a model of reflection. The later model became popular for use within nurse education settings (Rolfe et al 2011) and is widely used for educational purposes in the Republic of Ireland (O'Donovan 2006). Gibbs' (1988) model, while primarily an educational framework (Rolfe et al 2011) for use in teaching environments for debriefing purposes, is widely regarded as a reflective cycle or framework for reflection.

implications for reflective practice
Experiential learning generally means that the learner is engaged in some type of active learning. Drawing upon the work of Kolb (1984), Gibbs (1988:46) further describes experiential learning methods for the classroom followed by a 'structured debriefing' exercise, commonly referred to as a model of reflection. The later model became popular for use within classroom settings.

KEY TEXT
- Rolfe, G., Jasper, M. and Freshwater, D. (2011) *Critical Reflection for Nursing Generating Knowledge for Care.* 2nd edn (Basingstoke: Palgrave Macmillan).

f

facilitator

SEE ALSO **group reflections; reflection; reflective practice; reflective processes; supervision.**

While *reflection* and *reflective practice* are often isolated individual activities there is also room for others within personal reflections. Firstly, for those who are in employment there is the possibility of *group reflections*. There is also potential and scope to share reflections with another person on a one-to-one basis (or in a group), and this person is often referred to as a facilitator. The facilitator is generally a person assigned to the area with a key role in either educational or work-based support. The role of the facilitator is to help to structure and organize individual or group reflections, listen actively to participants and assist with productive outcomes. The facilitator generally should be able to entice and encourage discussion as well as cease it when necessary. A good facilitator requires a good understanding of the principles of reflection and reflective practice. Personal attributes such as genuineness, openness and a sense of humour are useful. The facilitator needs to be a good listener and also needs to be able to challenge assumptions when necessary (Moon 1999). While many of these attributes are natural personal qualities, it is also seen as very beneficial if the facilitator has received specific training for this task, and cases where training has been provided to staff have proved successful (Gardner and Taalman 2013).

In general the attributes of a good facilitator are as follows:

- Openness and curiosity
- Flexible yet consistent and reliable
- Supportive and attentive
- Non-defensiveness
- Approachable and trustworthy

- Shows empathy and concern
- Is self-aware and capable of relevant self-disclosure (Rogers 1969)

In the context of group reflections the facilitator might take the responsibility of organizing regular group sessions. They need to ensure consistency of approach and follow up on issues from meeting to meeting. Ensuring equitable participation and good timekeeping are also important (Johns 2013). Most importantly they would create a safe, supportive environment for others to share and learn from their experiences. Facilitator behaviours that enable and enhance reflection are as follows:

- Ensuring that everyone in the group has an opportunity to contribute
- Being non-defensive about actions and reactions
- Supporting the issues that members raise
- Being open and analytical
- Listening effectively
- Adopting a challenging but constructive approach
- Valuing individual contributions
- Motivating and encouraging the group
- Encouraging the less vocal to share
- Being creative in facilitating possible insights and solutions (Carter 2013)

The facilitator also acts within a group as:

- Teacher
- Instructor
- Interpreter (of facts)
- Confronter/devil's advocate
- Compatriot/discloser
- Consultant
- Neutral chairperson
- Participant
- Manager (Bolton 2010)

implications for reflective practice
A good facilitator requires a good understanding of the principles of reflection and reflective practice and is useful for either personal or

group reflections. Personal attributes such as genuineness, open-ness and a sense of humour are helpful to support learning and encourage development of the other. The facilitator also needs to be a good listener and needs to be able to challenge assumptions when necessary (Moon 1999).

KEY TEXTS

- Bolton, G. (2010) *Reflective Practice: Writing and Professional Development* (London: Sage).
- Carter, B. (2013) 'Reflecting in Groups' in Bullman and S. Schutz (eds), *Reflective Practice in Nursing* (Oxford: Wiley Blackwell): pp. 93–120.
- Gardner, F. and Taalman, E. (2013) 'Critical Reflection and Supervision' in J. Fook and F. Gardner (eds), *Critical Reflection in Context: Applications in Health and Social Care* (Oxon: Routledge).

g

generating practice knowledge

SEE ALSO analysis; knowledge; reflection; reflective practice; reflective processes; wisdom; work-based learning.

Reflection and *reflective practice* have the ability to assist you to generate practice knowledge. Through using models of reflection, the information gained through examining experiences and actions can be transformed into working knowledge for practice. Although *knowledge* is gleaned traditionally from reading, studying and taking examinations, there is powerful learning to be had in the practice setting. Boud (2006) uses the phrase 'workplace learners' who, by reflection on practice, can identify knowledge and evidence that is useful in future practice. Reflection opposes the dominant discourse of positivism. It generates theory from experience and personal reflection on that experience (Schön 1983), whereas traditional scientific methods require objective observation and systematic recording of events (Freshwater and Rolfe 2001).

Reflective practice can uncover hidden knowledge and *wisdom* that practitioners in practice may have (Benner et al 2011). It is often not until situations are reflected upon that motivations, assumptions and reasons for behaviour are understood. Practitioners develop *theories in use* which differ from espoused theories (protocols and other directives that underpin practice) by continuously reflecting on practice, re-evaluating and making changes to approaches (Howatson-Jones 2010). However, Howatson-Jones (2010) asserts this knowledge obtained from practice does not develop into professional knowledge and evidence unless it has been reflected upon to analyse and deduct its meaning and significance.

implications for reflective practice
Reflective practice can uncover hidden knowledge and wisdom that practitioners in practice may have (Benner et al 2011). Through

using models of reflection the information gained from examining experiences and actions can be generated into working knowledge for practice. There is powerful learning to be had in the practice setting. Workplace learners can, through reflection, identify knowledge and evidence to inform practice. Reflection provides an opposing knowledge base to positivism. It generates theory from practice experience, which develops professional wisdom. Although barriers exist to reflection and reflective practice, it is important for professionals to strive towards reflective practice in order to provide a more holistic evidence base for practice that is responsive to complex changing environments.

KEY TEXT
- Howatson-Jones, L. (2010) *Reflective Practice in Nursing* (Exeter: Learning Matters).

group reflections

SEE ALSO **analysis; awareness; codes of practice; consequences; critical incidents; critical reflection; generating practice knowledge; knowledge; models; reflection; reflective practice; reflective processes; work-based learning; writing.**

Group reflection may be formal or informal (Carter 2013) whereby two or more colleagues meet together, or online, to discuss their work experiences (Carter 2013, Boud 2006). While formalizing the process can inhibit creativity and *reflection*, possibly making it more of an exercise than a meaningful contribution to *work-based learning*, providing time and space for group reflections can be important in both demonstrating a commitment to this and encouraging reflection. It also allows for formal *models* of reflection to be used among the group. Using models of reflection provides a useful structure for the group and it is helpful if this model is chosen for its suitability to the workplace in terms of both language and organizational goals (Fook 2013). For group reflection to be effective there needs to be a culture of reflection developed in the particular workplace or organization (Gardner 2014).

Critical incidents can be used as a catalyst for group reflections, and each colleague contributes their own *knowledge* and experience to the discussion. In this context, and particularly where several different professions are involved, rich collective learning can take place (Breidensjö and Huzzard 2006). As such, group reflection may be directly related to an event or disturbance, but it can also be used to manage change and develop new innovative ideas in the absence of change and/or critical incident (Breidensjö and Huzzard 2006). The underpinning principle is that by bringing people together in the workplace to brainstorm and think together, valuable collective learning is possible (Breidensjö and Huzzard 2006). Key functions of group reflections are problem solving and solution development. While exposing thoughts and feelings in this public way can be daunting, the benefits of sharing with colleagues are as follows:

- Others might take a more objective stance on issues that you raise
- Others might ask questions that you had not thought about
- Others may see things differently or from a different perspective
- Others may act as a sounding board
- Others can validate your thoughts and ideas
- Others might bring different knowledge and experiences
- Others might come up with solutions that you had not thought about (Jasper 2013)

Indeed, contemporarily, it is suggested that in health-care settings professionals need to do much more to work together on issues related to practice, and reflection forms an important component of this (WHO 2010). Many clinical practice areas in health undertake group reflections and these are generally very positive experiences (Sweeney and McCormack 2013, Gardner and Taalman 2013, Bailey and Graham 2007). It enables a diverse group of opinions to gather, and sharing others' expertise on events can prove invaluable (Johns 2013). It can be useful to less vocal participants who might shy away from one-to-one supervision (Johns 2013). Practitioners in groups can support one another (Hargreaves and Page 2013, Johns 2013). Overall, the contribution of group reflection within the workplace appears to have a positive benefit on individuals, groups and teams but rather less is known about the organizational impact (Fook 2013). It is advisable that, in order to develop reflective practitioners, organizational culture needs to change to reflect a commitment to reflection and *reflective practice* (Gardner 2014). However, this aspect of many organizations is often underdeveloped (Gardner 2014). At the same time though, even when individuals or groups begin to engage in reflection or group reflection, this can begin to make small changes to people, and, as a result, the organization (Gardner 2014). However, for many, the changes required through reflection and *critical reflection* were not perceived as possible due to barriers within their organization and lack of organizational support (Gardner 2014). So for some, while individual changes may be possible, effective reflective practice is not entirely possible and more organizational support would be required for this to occur (Gardner 2014).

Using a suitable model of reflection which can enable critical *analysis* of the situation is important. It is important to realize that reflections with others may not always proceed smoothly (Duffy 2008); thus, facilitators of the group reflections must be prepared to manage the challenges that may arise. Some opening questions for reflective activity are as follows:

- What was the problem?
- Who was involved?
- Who was affected and how?
- What was the impact on team functioning?
- What was the impact on service delivery? (Oelofsen 2012)

Overall the key guiding questions are:

Success or failure?
Challenging assumptions?
What do we do now?
What do we do differently? (Breidensjö and Huzzard 2006)

Group reflections are often difficult to begin with, but with effective commitment, ground rules and management ought to yield successful results. An important factor for success is openness and transparency (Stebbins et al 2006). Choosing a suitable venue is one of the key first steps (Hargreaves and Page 2013). It is also important where possible to ensure a consistent attendance at the group (Fook 2013).

Suggested stages of group reflection are outlined as follows (Stebbins et al 2006):

- Participants explore their vision and goals
- Participants explore theory, methods and practices
- Explicit links between theory and practice are considered
- Participants are encouraged to explore meanings of events
- Participants' learning from experiences is facilitated
- Future designs for work-place practices may be explored and uncovered

Key factors in group reflections are (Høyrup and Elkjaer 2006):

- Learning from mistakes
- Vision sharing
- Challenging groupthink
- Asking for feedback
- Experimentation

It is also important to speak clearly about issues when among groups of different types of professionals as each can develop their own particular phrases, acronyms or words that are unfamiliar to others (Hargreaves and Page 2013). Remaining non-judgemental, providing time for others to talk (while you listen), being present emotionally and opening up and contributing are also important features for successful group reflection (Hargreaves and Page 2013). It is important to remember that groups may have hidden agendas, and *awareness* of this possibility is needed (Bolton 2010). Individuals each bring along their own hopes, fears and expectations and these need to be explored, acknowledged and managed (Bolton 2010).

In group reflective sessions ground rules are imperative (Hargreaves and Page 2013). It is also important that professional practice codes or guidelines are upheld and reporting mechanisms are known to all. The ground rules should include issues related to reflector confidentiality, mutual respect for members of the group, time limits per reflection, agreed mechanism for taking records and discussions to allow the expression of emotions. Rotating some of these roles can be a useful mechanism (Gardner and Taalman 2013).

In order to facilitate group reflections, guides or facilitators should be self-aware, and know when to gently encourage the reflector to express their views. Ground rules that could be observed are as follows:

- Specific allocated time is required
- Staff should be respectful towards each other
- It is best to have a plan of discussions or an agenda, which is agreed in advance
- People take responsibility for their own learning
- Each person should have equal opportunity to speak (Timmins and Duffy 2011)

It is often difficult to find the time or space in the workplace or a college for such reflections, and in practice people often perform these group reflections informally, such as in the car on the way home or when a team are involved in a project together (Boud 2006). Boud (2006) suggests that reflection requires both formality and informality. Indeed Boud (2006) goes so far as to say that merely scheduling in official time for reflection at work is a 'naive' view; as such it is important for reflections to also happen naturally and spontaneously among groups. On the other hand, structured group reflections can be a powerful way of dealing with work-related problems (Boud 2006). This approach requires a skilled facilitator, time commitment and investment in a long-term successful outcome. Having a good facilitator is a key element of success (Gardner and Taalman 2013). The following are important principles for the group:

1. Responsibility – over personal reflections and *writings*
2. Trust – in each other and the process
3. Self-respect – for beliefs, thoughts and actions
4. Generosity – giving freely of self within the group
5. Positive regard – acting positively towards all others
6. Valuing diversity – valuing differences among the group (Bolton 2010)

It is also important to establish group boundaries and ground rules and to ensure that everyone knows each other by name

(Bolton 2010). The function and purpose of the group needs to be clearly outlined and the life of the group decided (Bolton 2010). At least three meetings are suggested to be able to tackle any issue, and six is the recommended number (Bolton 2010). Group reflection may be used to:

- Address blocks in practice
- Develop knowledge relevant to practice
- Empower practitioners
- Facilitate staff to work with uncertainty in changing environments
- Understand assumptions that are made about practice and the impact that these have
- Assist in making workplace transitions
- Develop skills of reflection
- Develop a critical consciousness
- Assist in integrating practices, theories and values (Fook 2013)

Reports of group reflection indicate that it has a mainly positive effect (Dawber 2013). One exploration of this found that shared reflection in a group setting was beneficial to permit talking about difficult clinical situations, which perhaps would not otherwise be spoken about (Dawber 2013). It permitted staff to express and work through their thoughts and feelings while reviewing their actions with the support of their colleagues, who then were able to provide challenges to this, different perspectives and shared solutions as appropriate (Dawber 2013). Participants in this group reflection also found that the sessions improved communication among the team and improved team performance as a result (Dawber 2013). A skilled facilitator also emerged as an important component of a successful group reflection meeting (Dawber 2013). Benefits of group reflection are outlined as follows:

- It can encourage democratic sharing of ideas
- It can encourage more ideas to develop and flourish
- It can foster imagination and creativity
- New solutions can emerge
- It can strengthen group identity
- It can lead to new insights

- It may be less threatening than one-to-one approaches
- It can improve team work
- It provides opportunities to listen to one another (Carter 2013)

Disadvantages include that it can cause anxiety or it can be uncomfortable, and skilled facilitation is required to combat these possibilities (Carter 2013).

implications for reflective practice
Group reflection has the potential to generate practice knowledge and there are reports of positive effects with this approach (Dawber 2013). Although less common than individual reflection there is also a practice of reflection in a group (Hargreaves and Page 2013); group reflection involves uncovering and making explicit what was observed or achieved in practice and reconstructing its meaning to contribute usefully to the group's activities (Stebbins et al 2006). This can be very useful in professional practice situations to reflect on events that involve several members of a team. Having many perspectives can aid understanding. Learning occurs through active engagement with peers and colleagues.

KEY TEXTS
- Bolton, G. (2010) *Reflective Practice: Writing and Professional Development* (London: Sage).
- Carter, B. (2013) 'Reflecting in Groups' in Bullman and S. Schutz (eds), *Reflective Practice in Nursing* (Oxford: Wiley Blackwell): pp. 93–120.
- Hargreaves, J. and Page, L. (2013) *Reflective Practice* (Cambridge: Polity Press).
- Fook, J. (2013) 'Implementing Critical Reflection in Health and Social Care' in J. Fook and F. Gardner (eds), *Critical Reflection in Context: Applications in Health and Social Care* (Oxon: Routledge): pp. 233–241.

h

history of reflection

SEE ALSO reflective practice; reflection; reflective processes,

The origins of *reflection* have their roots in the seminal work of Dewey (1933), Kolb (1984) and Schön (1983). From a historical perspective Dewey (1933) first began to articulate the need to think reflectively in order to solve problems (Rolfe et al 2011, Høyrup and Eltjaer 2006). However, it wasn't until the 1980s that reflection began to emerge as a popular mechanism for professional development (Mackintosh 1998, Høyrup and Elkjaer 2006). Schön (1983) in particular, concerned with professionals' development of skills and knowledge, outlines reflection *in* and *on* action. Schön's (1983) conceptualization of reflection has been influential within healthcare, engineering and teaching professions, suggesting less reliance on traditional and scientific forms of enquiry and encouraging practitioners to learn from reflecting both within practice and on their practice (Rolfe et al 2011). Opposed to the dominance of positivism, Schön (1983) proposes reflection as an alternative method of practice theory generation. Schön's (1983) seminal work subsequently underpinned many structured models of reflection (Rolfe et al 2011).

implications for reflective practice
The popularity of reflection first emerged in the late 1980s and early 1990s (Jasper 2013, Boud 2010). The seminal writings of Donald Schön (1983) were very influential to this end, as he described how professionals used reflection as a method of ongoing or continuous learning. Reflection could either be of an immediate reflexive nature, referred to as reflection in action, or you could reflect by looking back over practices – this was known as reflection on action. Many embraced reflection as something that could be of benefit in terms of developing insight into professional practice through

developing self-awareness. As a result, the use of Schön's (1983) work is evident throughout the health and educational literature since this time.

KEY TEXT

- Rolfe, G., Jasper, M. and Freshwater, D. (2011) *Critical Reflection for Nursing Generating Knowledge for Care*. 2nd edn (Basingstoke: Palgrave Macmillan).

i

individuality

SEE ALSO **critical reflection.**

Reflection has been predominantly incorporated within professions as a mechanism for the development of the individual professional in his or her own practice (Boud 2010), largely influenced by Schön's (1983) notion of reflection *in* and *on* action. Models such as Kim (1999) and Taylor (2000, 2006), though emphasizing *critical reflection*, retain this notion of individual professional self-development (Rolfe et al 2011). Similarly aimed at self-development is Johns' (1999, 2004) model, influenced by Schön (1983) but drawing comprehensively upon Carper's (1978) ways of knowing.

However, although not specifically referring to particular theorists (other than Schön 1983), contemporary authors raise concern with the individualized perspective that these models utilize (Boud et al 2006), suggesting instead a greater focus on the context within which learning takes place. A criticism of these individual focused models of reflection is that they lack this critical perspective (Barnett 1997). Their orientation is overtly personal, often resulting in personal knowledge gain rather than seeking to challenge the particular context and instigating the wider change that is required for critical reflection, critical action and reflexivity. While context may be referred to within particular models such as Taylor (2006), the focus is predominately self-development rather than taking action within a particular context.

Ronald Barnett, a professor of education at the Institute of Education, University of London, is highly critical of this personalized self-reflection for professional practice (Barnett 1997). Barnett (1997) suggests that it is limited in its scope and application. He is critical of the current use of self-reflection within disciplines, stating that it is often performed at a superficial level that he says can 'hardly be termed *critical* self-reflection' (Barnett 1997:101, emphasis author's own). Furthermore, he suggests that the use of reflection *in* action, espoused in professional practices, lacks both effective action and sufficient theoretical context as it over-relies on personal reflection in the knowledge domain, thus paying little attention to the domain of the world in which the action takes place. In particular, he criticized Schön's (1983) narrow interpretation and application of reflection, which avoids the context of the wider world of practice. Although consideration of the world may seem over ambitious, this doesn't refer to the whole world, but rather the world as it applies to an individual. This may be a community of learning (Wenger et al 2002) or local organization (Høyrup and Elkjaer 2006:39).

In one chapter, 'Taking it Beyond the Individual', Høyrup and Elkjaer (2006:29) further explore the limitations of the individual approach to reflection, suggesting instead the use of a 'critical perspective' that takes into account social, political and cultural influences, thus expanding the notion of reflection into critical reflection (Høyrup and Elkjaer 2006).

Boud et al (2006) concur with Barnett's (1997) views, suggesting that:

> reflection must be re-thought and re-contextualised so that it can fit more appropriately within group settings. It must also shift from its origins in concerns about individuals to learning within organisations. (Boud et al 2006:3)

implications for reflective practice
The individual approach to reflection, which is ultimately about personal growth and development, is limited in its social contextual consideration and also lacks an overt action perspective (Barnett 1997).

KEY TEXTS
- Høyrup, S. and Elkjaer, B. (2006) 'Reflection: Taking It Beyond the Individual' in D. Boud, P. Cressey and P. Doherty (eds), *Productive Reflection at Work* (Oxon: Routledge): pp. 3–10.
- Taylor, B. (2000, 2006) *Reflective Practice a Guide for Nurses and Midwives* (Buckingham: Open University Press).

j

journals

SEE ALSO **critical reflection; diary; facilitator; group reflections; learning logs; mentor; models; reflection; writing.**

Journals are frequently used as a vehicle for reflective writing among professionals (Bolton 2010, Williams et al 2002). The term 'journal' is often used interchangeably with terms such as 'learning log' or 'diary' but there are differences. The description of these three in the literature is often significantly overlapped or interchanged even within a single study (Henter and Indreica 2014). The *learning log* is a listing of events as they occur. The *diary* records personal experiences, thoughts and actions. The journal records experiences thoughts and actions for the purpose of learning.

Journals are described as:

> Records of experiences, thoughts, and feelings about particular aspects of life or specific structures. A journal can record anything, and in any way, relative to the issue to which it pertains. These documents (some virtual), might be intended for a wide audience ... but most are written for [individuals], supervisors etc. (Bolton 2010:128)

Journals involve the *writing* out of personal *reflections* in a relatively unstructured way (Bolton 2010). It can include writing (handwritten or electronic) or the development of drawings or maps about experiences (Oelofsen 2012). Even the mere fact of putting words onto paper or into electronic format can bring about learning as you are better able to see and recognize your thoughts (Stephens and Winterbottom 2010). Increasingly blogs, which serve as online journals, are being encouraged for reflection (Muncy 2014). For student groups this has the advantage of demonstrating to the teacher exactly when entries were made and prevents dishonesty in this regard (Muncy 2014). It also saves time on paperwork. Blogging is increasingly being used for reflection journaling (Yang 2009, Muncy 2014), and although limited research evidence exists on its effectiveness (Ali et al 2013), there is some evidence that the ability to reflect increases with increasing time spent blogging, and solitary blogging was more influencing in developing reflective ability than discussion and peer feedback on the journal (Xie et al 2008), and students find it easy to use (Ali et al 2013). A blog is an 'online journal with dated entries, presented in reverse chronological order providing an archive of posting with the newest post at the top of the page' (Ali et al 2013).

A journal generally requires that you enquire into:

- What you and others did on a particular occasion
- What you thought and what others might have thought on this occasion
- What you felt and what others might have felt
- What you believe and how these beliefs are manifested in practice
- Consideration about how your actions, thoughts, feelings and beliefs may affect yourself and others (Bolton 2010)

When keeping a journal it is important to remember the following:

- The journal is for you – write somewhere private and keep the journal private
- Date your entries to remind yourself of context
- Make your entries as soon as possible after events to keep memories clear
- Try writing in different forms, for example, in an explorative way; playing devil's advocate; in poetry form; using reflection and lists (Bolton 2010)

A journal can be very useful for you to keep a written record of reflection. It provides an opportunity to document the situation, initial reactions and feelings which might otherwise be forgotten over time (Gardner 2014). Brookfield (1995) reports encouraging students to keep a learning journal to record their learning.

Entries were recorded weekly. He insists (Brookfield 1995) for these to be successful there must be:

- Clear guidelines on the structure and function of the journal
- Convincing and sufficient rationale and motivation for students to complete the journal
- Some acknowledged reward of achievements

Support for the students during the process is also important (Brookfield 1995).

Physiotherapy students, for example, might be asked to keep a reflective journal while attending clinical placements. Williams et al (2002:7) described using such an intervention with the following instructions:

Reflective journals should include observations, impressions, and reactions to what you have learned in the academic portion of the semester and how you are applying it to clinical practice. How does the clinical experience change what you thought, felt, or did in the past, and how you may respond in the future? You are expected to write at least one journal entry per week during your clinical placement.

Fifty-six physiotherapy students kept these journals and reflected on at least one learning event each week during their clinical placement. They were asked to describe each learning event, their reactions to it, and its value, and to discuss the new learning and what they might do differently in the future. Researchers then read, coded and categorized the events and reflections. The following themes emerged from the data collection: (1) process of making clinical decisions; (2) complexity and richness of interactions with service users; (3) effects of the practice environment on learning and care of service users; (4) acquisition of clinical and administrative skills; (5) value of clinical experiences in validating and integrating previous learning; and (6) acknowledgment and evaluation of different learning methods. Most (n=42) demonstrated a new understanding as a result of their reflections, and journal writing emerged as a valuable source of reflection that was instrumental in developing the students as reflective practitioners. The findings showed how valuable reflection can be in the real world of practice where nothing is as straightforward as in the classroom. Students found that their decision-making processes were continuously being challenged and enhanced. They also gained an understanding of the complexity of interacting with clients in their care.

Reflective journals have also been reported to have been used among general practitioners (GPs) undertaking a post-graduate certificate in primary care (Baldwin and Lucas 2012). Participants found that the journal challenged their thoughts and provided a critical perspective:

[I] Think it is very powerful for this [professional practice] as you are often your harshest critic. (participant 2)

It also was found to enhance reflective practice:

I have learned through theory, that reflection fosters a number of attributes such as professionalism and life-long learning, so I will try to reflect more and hope other things follow! I feel that others in my profession do not share these views and that reflective practices are open to ridicule amongst non-believers and it feels a bit geeky to promote it formally. (participant 7)

However, time to complete journals can be an issue for some, and some participants expressed concerns about the personal nature of reflection and whether or not this should be used within course assessments (Baldwin and Lucas 2012).

Similarly Constantinou and Kuys (2013) reported journal use among first-year undergraduate physiotherapy students. Students completed the journal during a two-week placement with older people and daily journal entries, according to specific criteria, were required. A survey of the students (n=90) revealed that most (88%, n=79) of the respondents found the journal useful in assisting them to learn from their experiences, and to develop reflective practice. Many (54%, n=49) stated that they would continue to use the journals. When the researchers analysed the reflective journals they found evidence of emerging awareness of thoughts and feelings, critical analysis of situations and developments of new perspectives (Constantinou and Kuys 2013). Time emerged as a significant issue with journal use (44%, *n*=40). Students also thought that twice-weekly, rather than daily, journal entries would suffice.

Henter and Indreica (2014) reported the use of reflective journals by second-level students whereby students were encouraged to record their learning and positive and negative experiences on a weekly basis during a course. Some questions and prompts were also given. Results of the study did not demonstrate any grade difference in those who used the journals compared with those who did not, but the journals fostered independent learning.

implications for reflective practice

Journals are regarded by some as the cornerstone(s) of reflective practice and critical reflexivity (Bolton 2010:136). However, it must be borne in mind that this type of writing takes time and practice and does not come easily to everyone (Bolton 2010). Knowing what to write about can be challenging, and to begin with it is useful to write about situations that interested you. Remember that a journal is primarily for the writer; as such, it is an internal dialogue for your own reflexivity, reflection, and therefore development (Bolton 2010:139). Journals can also facilitate *critical reflection* (Gardner 2014). Having a *mentor*, supervisor or *facilitator* to assist you can be useful and discussing your journal entries in groups can provide powerful learning; however, careful facilitation is required.

KEY TEXTS
- Baldwin, K. and Lucas, B. (2012) 'Promoting Reflective Practice Skills for Postgraduate GPs: Do Journals Aid Journeys?' *Education for Primary Care*, 23 (3): pp. 213–216.
- Oelofsen, N. (2012) *Developing Reflective Practice: A Guide for Students and Practitioners of Health and Social Care* (Banbury: Lantern Publishing).
- Williams, R. M., Wessel, J., Gemus, M. and Foster-Seargeant, E. (2002) 'Journal Writing to Promote Reflection by Physical Therapy Students During Clinical Placements' *Physiotherapy Theory and Practice*, 18: pp. 5–15.

k

knowledge

Knowledge refers to the facts and information received through experience or formal education. Knowledge is socially constructed in so far as those facts which are considered to be the truth are passed on within societies in particular cultural and time contexts. Humans' understanding of facts, thus their knowledge, has changed considerably over time. Importantly, since the Enlightenment there has been a greater reliance on scientific facts derived from experiment and science as a form of ultimate truth. However, increasingly there are considerations of different types of knowledge other than that generated by scientific enquiry.

Habermas (1971) was also critical of the dominance of positivistic science as the basis of all knowledge. Habermas explored the roots of knowledge (24) and revealed them to be embedded in the socio-cultural form of life (McCarthy 2002:26). He developed an alternative theory of knowledge suggesting three categories of human knowledge: rational/empirical, historical/hermeneutical and emancipatory. It was his belief that people strive for liberation through emancipation. He suggested three general orientations guiding modes of enquiry. In sciences of nature (concerned with predicting and controlling events), this is technical interest. That which is rooted in securing and expediting possibilities of mutual and self-understanding of life was termed 'practical interest'. The third mode he termed 'critical reflection', which was grounded in emancipation. Thus *reflection* has a key role to play in the development of human knowledge. While the dominant world view lends more credence to positivism and the technical/rationale approach, for some disciplines reflection is proposed as the 'radical alternative to technical rationality, with the promise of revolutionizing the way in which ... knowledge [is] conceptualized, generated, taught and applied to practice' (Rolfe 2002). Increasingly, reflection is being used and promoted across professional disciplines such as engineering, nursing, occupational therapy, physiotherapy and social work to develop professional knowledge.

Wenger et al (2002) outlined a knowledge development strategy for within practice communities which entailed developing strategic goals, developing required core competencies, maintaining business processes and key activities.

Wenger et al (2002:8–10) outlined the following premises:

- Knowledge lives in the human act of knowing
- Knowledge is tacit as well as explicit
- Knowledge is social as well as individual
- Knowledge is dynamic

knowledge lives in the human act of knowing

To describe this, Wenger et al (2002) give the example that surgeons performing operative procedures do not 'blindly apply knowledge they have gleaned from books' but rather 'consider the patient's medical history, monitor vital signs, look at tissues, draw conclusions and possibly revise the plan ...' (Wenger et al 2002:8). They suggested 'engaging their expertise in this way is an active, inventive process that is just as critical as their store of knowledge itself' (Wenger et al 2002:8). In order to develop this expertise they suggested that the practitioner needs to actively engage with others who face similar situations: 'The knowledge of experts is an accumulation of experience – a kind of "residue" of their actions, thinking and conversations ...' (Wenger et al 2002:9). A similar situation exists with practitioners working in nursing; as Thompson et al (2001) noted, nurses relied on the expertise of others to guide them and such is the way often in practice. Nurses learn from conversations and observations with each other.

knowledge is tacit as well as explicit

Wenger et al (2002:9) suggested that not all knowledge can be '... codified as documents or tools'. Tacit knowledge exists within communities and is a valuable source of knowledge that is diffi-cult to replicate. It consists of 'embodied expertise – a deep under-standing of complex, interdependent systems that enables dynamic responses to context specific problems' (Wenger et al 2002:9). Tacit knowledge is shared through interaction and informal learning, for example storytelling, conversation and apprenticeship.

Other writers have described tacit knowledge. Baumard (1999) highlighted that tacit knowledge may be passed directly from one person to the other within professional practice. Sternberg (1999:231) described tacit knowledge as

> procedural knowledge that guides behavior but is not readily available for introspection ... often ... takes the form of rules of thumb for what to do under what circumstances.

Tacit knowledge is largely acquired from experience, preferably in the environment where the knowledge is required.

In his delineation of knowledge, Baumard (1999) draws upon the work of the Greek philosophers who differentiate between four forms of knowledge:

- Episteme (abstract generalization)
- Techne (capability, capacity to accomplish tasks)
- Phronesis (practical and social wisdom)
- Mètis (conjectural intelligence)

He described episteme as universal knowledge that is shared and general. Episteme according to Aristole is knowledge about which we can be certain and it equates to scientific knowledge (McGee 2005). Phronesis is the opposite, that is, personal and meaningful to the individual. It is 'non-scientific, practical, contextual knowl-edge ... generated in the intimacy of lived experience' (Baumard 1999:53). Techne is the application of technical knowledge; mètis is the combination of explicit and tacit knowledge, the collective and individual and thus the implementation of the four forms of knowledge.

Interestingly Flaming (2000) suggested the use of phronesis 'instead of "research-based practice" as the guiding light for nurs-ing practice'. The author suggested that the use of phronesis takes consideration of the context within which nursing takes place. Drawing on Aristole's writings, she suggested that the goal of phronesis is eudaimonia, that is 'genuine happiness' or 'human flourishing', thus suggesting that nursing practice should be guided by a 'desire for patients' genuine happiness'.

Polanyi (1974:64) also referred to tacit knowledge in the development of skills: 'The aim of a skilful performance is achieved by the observance of a set of rules which are not known as such to the person.' He proffered the example of a swimmer who isn't necessarily aware of every movement that contributes to the performance. Polanyi (1974:64) explored the nature of knowledge and 'entered on an analysis of the arts of skilful doing and skilful knowing' and found

> in the exercise of skill and the practice of connoisseurship, the art of knowing is seen to involve an intentional change of being: the pouring of ourselves into the subsidiary awareness of particulars, which in the performance of skills are instrumental to a skilful achievement, and which in the exercise of connoisseurship function as the elements of the observed comprehensive whole.

the challenge of tacit knowledge

Baumard (1999:208) suggested that organizations can 'dismantle' tacit knowledge by 'enforcing over codified knowledge to communities of practice'. Baumard (1999:208) (refering to Wenger's 1998 definition of communities of practice) questions how durable communities of practice are particularly where organizations rely upon 'umbrellas of codified knowledge' and wherein the community of practice is suppressed. The community itself can become isolated if it is so enmeshed in practice that it is unable to articulate its knowledge and develop a collective wisdom.

Polanyi (1969:144) suggested that tacit knowledge and explicit knowledge are not 'sharply divided'. While it is possible to possess tacit knowledge alone, it is not possible to have explicit knowledge without this being tacitly understood and applied: 'All knowledge is either tacit or rooted in tacit knowledge. A wholly explicit knowledge is unthinkable' (Polanyi 1969:144). (For example, an explicit physiological understanding of balance and engineering understanding of the mechanism of a bicycle are not sufficient to enable one to cycle; one must absorb this knowledge tacitly in order to perform the skill.)

Boud and Middleton (2003) investigated how learning from others at work takes place. They aimed to identify ways in which participants in different organizations learn from others. In their paper they also consider whether the framework of communities of practice (Wenger et al 2002) is a useful framework for discussion of informal learning at work. These researchers interviewed four distinct groups of workers in Sydney. Analysis of the interviews revealed three common patterns of learning across the organizations: mastery of organizational processes, negotiating the political (including local relationships) and dealing with the atypical.

Dealing with the atypical generally involved direct liaison and conversation with individuals. Rather than reliance on documents, policy or precedents, the approach to atypical situations was similar to the construct of work-process knowledge noted in other studies (Boreham et al 2002). This knowledge is embedded in the workplace and draws upon both theoretical knowledge and direct experience of the work and is resolved by the workers themselves

knowledge is social as well as individual
Wenger et al (2002:10) also asserted that knowledge is social as well as individual. Thus a body of knowledge is developed through a 'process of communal involvement'. Thus knowledge is not necessarily the prerogative of individuals (although they have knowledge); knowledge within communities needs to be shared.

knowledge is dynamic
Wenger et al (2002) also asserted that knowledge is dynamic, thus requiring constant update 'by people who understand the issues and appreciate the evolution of their field'. They cited an example of a community that keeps up to date by sending different representatives to conferences who each report back, thus improving and changing the knowledge within the community. They emphasized that the challenge of managing knowledge is that it 'is not an object that can be stored, owned and moved around like a piece of equipment or a document. It resides in the skills, understandings, and relationships of its members as well as in the tools, documents, and processes that embody aspects of this knowledge.'

implications for reflective practice

Increasingly, reflection is being used and promoted across professional disciplines such as engineering, nursing, occupational therapy, physiotherapy and social work to develop professional knowledge. Wenger et al (2002) outlined a knowledge-development strategy for use within practice communities which entailed developing strategic goals, developing required core competencies, maintaining business processes and key activities.

Wenger et al (2002:8–10) outlined the following premises:

- Knowledge lives in the human act of knowing
- Knowledge is tacit as well as explicit
- Knowledge is social as well as individual
- Knowledge is dynamic

Within the context of reflection and *reflective practice* it is important to remember that this critical reflection and *reflexivity*, while having some impact on personal *awareness* and development, is primarily aimed at developing practice knowledge and *wisdom* rather than personal self-development itself. As such, the documentation and codifying of individual reflections, perhaps using *models* of reflection, *journals* or *learning logs*, ought to ultimately inform practice. Gathering all these reflections and other learning into a *portfolio* is one useful way of collating and summarizing results and emerging knowledge and wisdom.

KEY TEXTS

- Baumard, P. (1999) *Tacit Knowledge in Organizations* (London: Sage Publications).
- Herbig, B. Büssing, A. and Ewert, T. (2001) 'The Role of Tacit Knowledge in the Work Context of Nursing', *Journal of Advanced Nursing*, 34 (5): pp. 687–695.

1

leadership

SEE ALSO **reflective practice; reflection.**

Up until recently, leadership has not been considered directly in the context of *reflective practice*. However, Jasper (2005) highlighted the requirement for leaders to think and operate within complex, rapidly changing circumstances and more recently began to explore the notion of reflective leadership (Jasper et al 2012). It was found that where leaders are taught to use *reflection* and when they engage and support reflection, they are more likely to have increased positive service user outcomes (Jasper et al 2012). Additionally, reflective leadership is viewed as fundamental as a process for facilitating change and development in service user care and outcomes (Jasper et al 2012). A reflective leadership style increases confidence, team work and promotes effective change. Previous studies of nurses and social workers identified the use of group reflections as a key component of collaborative working and effective leadership (McCray 2007).

Johns' most recent version of his well-cited text, *Becoming a Reflective Practitioner* (2013), also alludes to the notion of reflective leadership, including a fully dedicated chapter for the first time. He asserts that an effective leader must primarily be a reflective one. Reflectiveness and mindfulness are the hallmarks of leadership. Other characteristics of reflective leadership are as follows:

- Having a vision
- Developing shared vision and values
- Acting with integrity towards a common goal
- Consistency in purpose despite obstacles
- Perception of being in service to (rather than in control of) others
- Emotional intelligence
- Authenticity
- Inspiration and energy

implications for reflective practice

Leadership involves the ability to bring others along. In a modern context it generally means creating positive, nurturing environments that aim to get the best out of people. It means creating a vision and aiming towards that vision even though sometimes the path ahead is not clear. It involves believing in people, investing in people, getting to know their strengths and weaknesses and maximizing their strengths. It involves patience and understanding and avoids the use of aggressive, forceful or manipulative tactics. Communication is key to success and reflective practice is becoming an increasingly important part of modern leadership.

KEY TEXT

- McCray, J. (2007) 'Reflective Practice for Collaborative Working', in C. Knott and Scragg (eds), *Reflective Practice in Social Work* (Exeter: Learning Matters): pp. 130–142.

learning logs

SEE ALSO **andragogy; critical reflection; models; portfolios; reflection; reflective practice; work-based learning.**

Learning logs are:

> Straightforward, record[ed] events, calculations or readings as aide memoires, like ships' logs. (Bolton 2010:127)

One example of using a learning log is to document experience, reactions and learning gained by attending academic conferences (Brookfield 1995). This is a good example of how the recording of straightforward events can be useful. Brookfield (1995) suggests in these situations to note:

- The event (briefly describing it)
- Whether the experience was positive or negative
- Any thoughts that you have on the event
- Any lessons that you may have learned

There is also a use for a 'teaching log' that is a weekly record of 'the events in a teacher's life that have impressed themselves most vividly on his or her consciousness' (Brookfield 1995:72).

Usage of learning logs by the Open University (Macdonald and Hills 2005) provided a good example of how straightforward data can be entered into a log and used for reflective purposes. Forty Open University tutors were asked to report on their teaching activity and student support (such as receiving and sending student emails) using an online system supported by the university. A structured pro forma was provided within which tutors could enter their supports as they occurred. They later shared these logs with their colleagues during a virtual conference. While there was some perception of extra work with this task, there were perceived benefits in terms of observing patterns and trends in support and highlighting to tutors themselves the amount and type of support given to students. Tutors were able to reflect on these and through sharing with other tutors at the conference they were able to identify patterns in behaviours and brainstorm ways to deal with this (for example, where students did not respond). The log served as an objective basis for in-service learning for university tutors.

Stephens and Winterbottom (2010) used learning logs with biological sciences high school students. A structured format was provided, with a tick-box approach, to enable students to document their learning after each class. Interviews with students found that the log prompted them to reflect, highlighting the learning outcomes to them and improving their learning overall.

There are, however, explanations of a more detailed and explicit learning log. Carrington and Selva (2010) described the use of *reflection* logs with teachers in training. These entailed documenting reflecting on learning from practice using a *model* of reflection during an eight-week period of teaching practice. An analysis of 13 of these logs found that it helped students to integrate theory and practice, to learn about practice and to develop an awareness of cultural issues (Carrington and Selva 2010). Similarly, the University of Hull (2015) describes learning logs as:

> [a] record or journal of your own learning ... It is a personal record of your own learning ... [which] helps you to record, structure, think about and reflect upon, plan, develop and evidence your own learning.

These logs provide for recording of a series of reflections which are encouraged after each new learning experience. Using a modified model of reflection, students are asked to consider and elucidate on the following:

- What you did
- Your thoughts
- Your feelings
- How well (or badly) it went
- What you learnt
- What you will do differently next time (University of Hull 2015)

Although essentially this learning log is recording a catalogue of events (University of Hull 2015), in this case these events are reflective cycles and encourage *critical reflection*. This learning log is an active living document and expects changes in skills and behaviours as a result of ongoing reflection in the log (University of Hull 2015). For example, by reflecting, the students are expected to experience changes in approach such as becoming self-aware, questioning rather than accepting and reflective rather than reactive (University of Hull 2015). These students were encouraged to use blogs to support their learning logs (University of Hull 2015), and online uses of resources for reflection are becoming increasingly popular (Muncy 2014). Blogging has been found to encourage reflection (Yang 2009, Muncy 2014). A model of reflection is also used to develop a learning log for GPs (Miller 2014); thus the overlap between a simple outline recording of events and the more detailed reflection required in a journal are common in the literature.

implications for reflective practice
Learning logs are usually straightforward accounts of events that record events, calculations or occurrences, although a more in-depth usage has been reported. A learning log can be used to document experience, reactions and learning gained by attending academic conferences (Brookfield 1995) or to document support given to a client or student and can be useful as both an aide-memoire and a learning device (Macdonald and Hills 2005).

KEY TEXT
- Bolton, G. (2010) *Reflective Practice. Writing and Professional Development* (London: Sage).

lifelong learning

SEE ALSO **andragogy; reflection; reflective practice; work-based learning.**

Lifelong learning refers to the capacity to continue to learn through-out a person's lifetime, rather than simply obtaining the knowledge and skills that one needs to know at second- or third-level education (Howatson-Jones 2010). It challenges the assumption that many people obtain formal knowledge and skills through educational systems such as schooling, university or job training and once this stops, formalized learning ceases. While at one time exiting from university with a degree and entering the workplace, or a profession, meant the end of formal studies for many, increasingly it is being recognized that even outside of formalized educational settings individuals can become lifelong learners.

While the notion of independent learning is not new, the notion of achieving recognition for this is increasing. More and more value is being placed on the usefulness of *work-based learning*, and systems for documenting and recording this are of increasing importance. An emphasis on lifelong learning through the acquisition of formal education beyond initial qualification is also prevalent in health-care professions such as UK social work, whereby requirements and standards for these courses are monitored by an independent regulatory body (the General Social Care Council (GSCC)) within the context of a post-qualification (PQ) framework (Ruch 2009b). This serves to standardize approaches to lifelong learning to ensure that practitioners are achieving broadly the same level. In keeping with principles of lifelong learning and work-based learning, these post-qualifying courses (such as post-graduate diploma and master's degree) would usually entail professionals in this field working in the practice sphere, and *reflection* on this practice, as a part requirement of the programme. One benefit of a framework such as this is that it serves to formalize and document individuals' continuous professional development (CPD) and lifelong learning and give recognition and advancement for this (Tunney 2009). Professionals such as nurses are required to continuously keep up to date with their knowledge and skills and to document evidence of this (NMC 2011). In keeping with the principles of lifelong learning there is no set requirement for the type of CPD that a nurse undertakes (NMC 2011) so long as documented evidence of the rationale, content and outcome of that learning is evident. The preparation for this lifelong learning begins at undergraduate level (NMC 2010a).

implications for reflective practice
Reflection can contribute to both the practice and documentation of lifelong learning within professions. As such, it provides a tool for continued learning from work-based learning and practice and a means of formalizing and documenting this. Such reflections could be retained in a portfolio that could be used for interview or self-development purposes.

KEY TEXTS
- Ruch, G. (2009) 'Introduction – Developing Holistic Social Work Practitioners' in G. Ruch (ed.), *Post-Qualifying Child Care Social Work. Developing Reflective Practice* (London: Sage): pp. 3–7.
- Tunney, G. (2009) 'The PQ Framework, PQ and CPD Developments: Consolidation Unit, Introduction' in G. Ruch (ed.), *Post-Qualifying Child Care Social Work. Developing Reflective Practice* (London: Sage): pp. 8–17.

m

mentor

SEE ALSO assessment; confidence; consequences; critical friend; critical incident; critical reflection; diary; facilitator; journals; models; reflection; reflective practice; reflective processes; supervision; writing.

A mentor denotes a 'formal supervisory role and is used to describe the role of a qualified [professional] who facilitates learning and supervises ... in the practice setting' (Saarikoski et al 2007). The use of *reflection* is firmly rooted within the context of adult- and student-centred learning. In keeping with this philosophy students or practitioners reflecting either in the classroom or in practice ideally require a *facilitator*. For students in health and social care practice this role is often undertaken by the mentor. For others a facilitator may be used. In either case this person provides a supportive relationship to aid *reflective practice*. The mentor (for example, in the *supervision* of nursing students) may also take on other roles in this context such as role modelling best practice, teaching clinical skills and student *assessment*.

The mentor's role as a facilitator of reflective practice needs to be formalized, and the role needs to have clear parameters and boundaries (Hull and Redfern 2005). It is also important that facilitators are adequately prepared to undertake this role as they may find it difficult to support reflective practice if they lack knowledge and *confidence*.

This supportive relationship requires partnership and mutual respect. Both of these latter factors are in keeping with the definition of a mentor. It is important that both mentor and student agree common understandings of the term 'reflective practice' so that there are no misunderstandings (Edwards 2007). Where students are concerned, a mentor may assist with using a range of tools to support reflection such as *critical incident* analysis or *diary*. It is important to agree when and how reflective practice will take place. The mentor in this context can perhaps prompt reflections on critical incidents and lead the reflective discussion with questions such as:

- How did you feel during that?
- What skills did you think that you used well?
- What theories have you learned that you think might apply to this situation?
- Are there issues now apparent that you hadn't considered before?
- What did you learn from this?
- How can you relate this to future practice? (Edwards 2007)

There is some impetus within the literature to suggest that the student should have choice regarding selection of mentor, however, in practical terms this is often not possible. Students respect mentors who appear to have good knowledge and skills within their own profession, who are friendly and approachable and who have a good sense of humour. Characteristics as prerequisites of a 'good' mentor also include effective interpersonal skills, adopting a positive teaching role, paying appropriate attention to learning and providing supervisory support.

implications for reflective practice
A mentor is a formal supervisory role used to support students and staff in professional settings. Professionals engaged in reflection and reflective practice ideally require a facilitator and this role is often undertaken by a formal mentor, who receives training and support for their role. The mentor's role needs to have clear parameters and boundaries and is a supportive relationship based on mutual respect. A mentor is useful to seek guidance about reflection and reflective practice, how to use the *models* of reflection, deciding on critical incidents, and dealing with *consequences* and ethical issues as they arise. They may also assist with reflective *writing* or formal or informal assessment of your reflection.

KEY TEXT
- Edwards, C. (2007) 'Reflective Practice on Placement', in C. Knott and Scragg (eds), *Reflective Practice in Social Work* (Exeter: Learning Matters): pp. 102–113.

models

SEE ALSO **andragogy; autobiography; critical action; critical friend; critical incident; critical reflection; diary; journals; reflection; reflective practice; work-based learning.**

Models of *reflection* are commonly used to structure reflective thinking processes. Overall they serve to assist us generally to document our experiences and reflections on these. They generally take the form of:

- Description of the experience
- Evaluation
- Analysis
- Future action (Howatson-Jones 2010)

These models simply serve to formalize and make sense of the thinking process. They have an important use in assisting us to make sense of situations (Bolton 2010). Not all situations follow a linear path and many are complex. However, it is very helpful in our learning and dealing with situations effectively if we can structure situations into meaningful units. Models of reflection help us to do this.

It is suggested that you have someone who will guide you through your reflection (Johns 2013, Timmins and Duffy 2011). Your supervisor, facilitator, mentor or *critical friend* could assist you with this, thus your model and your approach form the framework for reflection. Regardless of framework chosen it is important to progress through each stage and complete the cycle. Although these models are not meant to be used in a technical, robotic way and movement between phases is natural (Johns 2013), it is also important not to simply stop at the description or outlining of feelings. For *reflective practice* to occur there needs to be a move towards *critical action*.

In particular, models help us to complete the reflective cycle. What we mean by this is that when left to our own devices there may be a tendency to rehash the situation (either mentally or verbally to others) repeatedly without coming to any concrete solution. However, by using a model of reflection you are enabled to systematically think through the event and consequently are provided with opportunities to embrace new learning from the experience. This interpretation is only possible of course if the model is used in its entirety. Sometimes, the temptation when using a model or framework is to use it only in part, such as the students in Timmins and Dunne's (2009) study, many of whom when prompted to use Gibbs' (1988) model of reflection never moved beyond the descriptive phase.

Examples of models are as follows.

Kolb

Kolb's work helped to lay the foundations of our understanding of the power of learning from experience (Jasper 2013). Quite simply, in order to learn from that which has occurred (our experiences) it is necessary in the first instance to call these to mind once again and think over them. Kolb (1984) describes a model for experiential learning within the classroom that is widely used in education. This model (Kolb 1984) considers four stages of learning. Firstly the concrete experience, followed by reflective observation, abstract conceptualization and finally active experimentation (Figure 2).

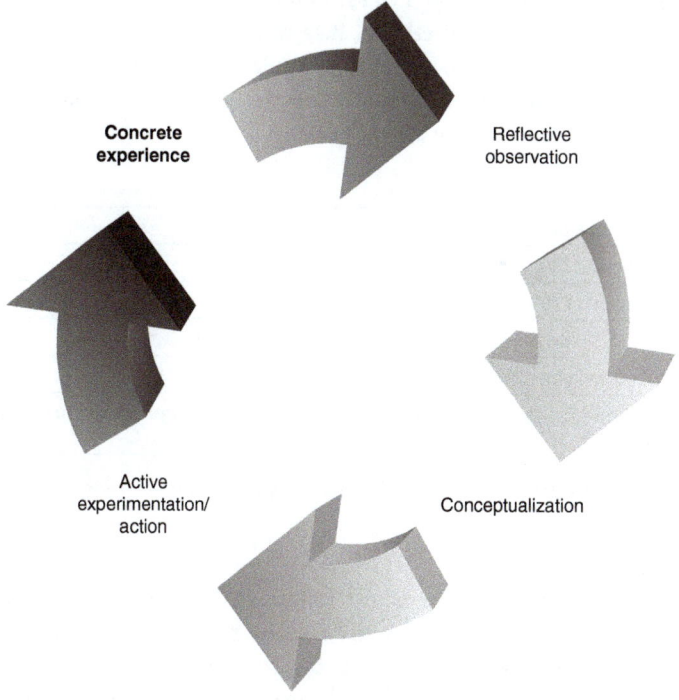

FIGURE 2   *Learning cycle*

Source: Kolb (1984)

It has been used as a framework for the stages or phases in the planning and implementation of experiential learning (Brackenreg 2004).

Kolb (1984) suggests that in order to derive meaningful learning from events we need to recall these and observe our reactions to them (Jasper 2013). This thinking back over experiences can transform our learning and make it more meaningful (Jasper 2013). Indeed it is suggested in terms of learning from concrete experiences that without this reflection and thinking back over events the learning is not captured effectively (Brackenreg 2004). Jasper (2013) replaces the phrase 'active experimentation' with 'action' as a more fitting word for the clinical practice environment.

Gibbs

Gibbs' (1988) model of reflection has its origins in the work of Kolb (1984) and started out as a classroom debriefing exercise as part of experiential learning methods. It is widely used in practice-based educational courses to encourage students to reflect on practice and to encourage reflection and reflective practice in assignments. It involves the following steps (Table 1):

1.	Describe the event
2.	How does it make you feel? (as a nurse)
3.	Evaluate this situation (What was good and bad about the experience?)
4.	Analyse the situation (What sense can you make of it?)
5.	Conclude this situation
6.	Action plan (What would you do differently in this situation or in your future practice?

TABLE 1   *Stages of Gibbs' (1988) model of reflection*

Borton

Borton's (1970) framework for reflection (What? So what? Now what?) provides a framework and cues for reflection. This approach has been widely used in health-care practice and underpins approaches to reflection such as those suggested by Driscoll (2007) and Rolfe et al (2011). This checklist approach also provides for a quick approach to reflection.

Boud

Boud et al (Boud et al 1985, Boud and Walker 1990, Boud and Walker 1993) developed a framework for reflection specifically designed to enhance *work-based learning* (Table 2).

I.	**Return to the experience** (brief acknowledgement, full description not needed)
2.	**Attend to the feeling** (just take note of the feelings)
3.	**Association** (new information from the reflection is associated with existing knowledge and attitudes)
4.	**Integration** (new conclusions and insights from the information towards the piecing together of new understandings)
5.	**Validation** (use evidence to test these assumptions to ascertain whether there are contradictions or inconsistencies between the new understandings)
6.	**Appropriation** (making knowledge one's own)

TABLE 2   *Boud et al's (Boud et al 1985, Boud and Walker 1990, Boud and Walker 1993) model of reflection*

Using this framework, people are prompted to re-evaluate the experience. To do so, *association* is used whereby new information from the reflection is associated with existing knowledge and attitudes and the relationships are observed (Boud and Walker 1990, 1993). This is followed by *integration*, thus identifying the nature of the relationships that have been observed in the association phase and drawing new conclusions and insights from the information towards the piecing together of new understandings (Boud and Walker 1990, 1993). Assumptions are tested by *validation* to ascertain whether there are contradictions or inconsistencies between these new understandings. You incorporate your new understandings into your knowledge base for practice. Reading and understanding such work often forms the basis of more up-to-date developments in reflective practice and despite the primary work on reflective practice appearing quite dated now, it is still in general use and considered seminal work in the field (Johns 2013).

Validation involves determining the authentication of ideas (Boud and Walker 1990, 1993). Within the context of reflection these authors suggest that some validation is required at the end of the process to confirm the ideas and knowledge that have been generated. This means using evidence to test these assumptions to ascertain whether there are contradictions or inconsistencies between the new understandings. Although this is not widely suggested it is a useful approach to counteract issues of honesty and authenticity within written reflections. It might also serve to confirm or disprove ideas that you have had about the situation, perhaps forcing you to seek alternative views on matters. Validation could involve service user or colleague testimony, photographic evidence or reference to the published literature.

Appropriation is making knowledge one's own (Boud and Walker 1990, 1993). It is important once reflections are complete that new perspectives are integrated within one's own understanding. Only in this way can knowledge be generated that can inform future practice. Rather than merely learning from experience, appropriation means that the learning becomes personally embraced and part of who you are (Boud et al 1985). 'Appropriation' is a key term used in approaches to reflection espoused by Boud et al (1985) – key authors who have extensively explored reflection over a 20-year period. This is not to say that this term is widely used in reflection. However, this notion is useful in moving reflection beyond merely following a recipe approach where the learning can be limited (Boud and Walker 1998).

Johns

Johns proposed a structured model of reflection (see below) using key 'cue' questions. Johns' (1996) early versions categorized this reflection according to Carper's ways of knowing (1978), with the added component of reflexivity.

Aesthetics

- What was I trying to achieve?
- Why did I respond as I did?
- What were the consequences of that for:
  - the service user
  - others
  - myself?
- How was this person feeling? (or these persons?)
- How did I know this?

Personal

- How did I feel in this situation?
- What internal factors were influencing me?

Ethics

- How did my actions match with my beliefs?
- What factors made me act in incongruent ways?

Empirics

- What knowledge did or should have informed me?

Reflexivity

- How does this connect with previous experiences?
- Could I handle this better in similar situations?
- What would be the consequences of alternative actions for:
  - the service user
  - others
  - myself?
- How do I feel about this experience?
- Can I support myself and others better as a consequence?
- Has this changed my way of knowing? (Johns 1996)

Johns has updated this model a number of times (Johns 1999, 2004, 2013) including the most recent model 'bringing the mind home' (see below), which is now on its 16th iteration (Johns 2013). Johns has been vociferous in this view that effective reflection requires the support and mentorship of another, and as such ought to be supervised in clinical professional practice.

Johns' Cues for Reflective Practice:
Preparatory Phase

Bring the mind home

Descriptive Phase

Focus on a description of an experience that seems significant in some way

Reflective Phase

What issues are significant to pay attention to?

How are others feeling, and what made them feel that way?

How was I feeling, and what made me feel that way?

What was I trying to achieve, and did I respond effectively?

What were consequences of my actions on the service user, others and myself?

To what extent did I act for the best and in tune with my values?

How does this situation connect with previous experiences?

What assumptions govern my practice and what factors influence the way I feel, think and respond to the situation?

Anticipatory Phase

How might I reframe the situation in order to respond more effectively?

What would be the consequences of responding differently for the service user, others and myself?

What factors might constrain my responding in new ways?

How do I NOW feel about this experience?

Insight Phase

What insights have I gained? (Johns 2013)

Brookfield

Brookfield (1995) suggests the use of four lenses of reflection. These have been used extensively for reflection within the teaching professions. He suggests the use of these lenses to consider who we are and what we are about in order to refocus our thinking. He suggests that a specific focus on a critical incident is required to permit us to explore our deeper understandings and assumptions.

These lenses are:

- The autobiographical lens
- The student lens
- The colleague's lens
- The theoretical lens

Brookfield's (1995) original model was developed for use among teachers. Within the autobiographical lens the teacher is encouraged to consider their own *autobiography* in relation to teaching. This has particular relevance as teachers' experiences of being taught often informs their teaching practice in a much more powerful way than learned teaching pedagogies. For example, an early teacher may have inspired their approach. This may not be conscious and through autobiographical work, perhaps using a *journal* or diary, the hidden values and assumptions can be uncovered.

Following this, to discover oneself as a teacher one needs to consider what the students think. This can be done by seeking direct feedback from them or by means of student evaluation,

critical incident technique

Although not originally designed as a model for reflection, Hargreaves and Page (2013) adapted this technique for use as a model of reflection suited to the exploration of critical incidents. The steps are as follows:

- Identify a critical incident
- Describe what is critical about this incident for you
- Analyse the incident – why is it critical? What are the key components of the incident?
- What conclusions can you draw from this? Ask whether or not this incident challenges your professional understanding. What gaps exist in your knowledge, understanding and skills that you could work on?
- What does your analysis suggest you should do differently or should change?

the autobiographical lens

Brookfield (1995) suggests that investigating our autobiographies as teachers is a logical first reflective step. This often begins by developing a personal philosophy of teaching, drawing on what it is we believe about teaching. Keeping a learning journal or *diary* of teaching and your reflections on this are also important.

the student lens

Collecting information about the audience (the student) is an important step in reflective practice. Seeking student feedback by means of discussion, commentary or evaluation surveys permits teachers to see from the students' perspective. Seeking student feedback on teaching approaches provides valuable feedback as to the impact of the teaching.

the colleague's lens

Fostering critical conversations about our teaching with trusted colleagues can yield useful insights. It helps break down the silence that can accompany teaching practice experiences, which unlike disciplines such as health-care are often solo ventures rather than shared experiences of a group. Often their experiences are similar in ways and this can be helpful to us in exploring alternatives and opening new ways of seeing and thinking about practice.

the theoretical lens

While it can be challenging for some (Ainsworth 2005), collecting literature and theory on our teaching can often equip us with an enlarged vocabulary to describe and understand our practice. It offers multiple perspectives on familiar situations. According to Brookfield (1995:378), consulting the literature can become 'a psychological and political survival necessity' by which teachers can come to understand the link between their reflections on critical incidents and the wider social, environmental and political context. Exploring the literature on relevant topics to your teaching or student/peer feedback provides alternative viewpoints that can be used to explore and question the assumptions that underpin our teaching in order to reach a different understanding of what we do (Ainsworth 2005). Using the literature to write and present papers about teaching practice is a useful exercise in this reflective phase which permits your insights on your teaching to develop through interaction with peers in a more public sphere (Ainsworth 2005).

Where models of reflection are used by practitioners they prove very useful in practice. Asselin and Fain's (2013) exploration of nurses' use of a model of reflection in the USA found that participants had changed their approach to practice as a result of using the model. Nurses used the model to look back over difficult situations, and it helped relieve a feeling of guilt for some. Having used the structured model, the nurses felt after the study was over that they would continue to use it in their practice and suggested keeping a copy close to hand (Asselin and Fain 2013). Some nurses felt that if left to their own devices they tended to think too negatively about situations, whereas focusing their reflections and learning using a model helped them to be more positive. It also helped staff to 'gain insights and resolve situations' (Asselin and Fain 2013).

implications for reflective practice
Models serve to formalize and make sense of the thinking process. They have an important use in assisting us to make sense of situations (Bolton 2010). Not all situations follow a linear path and many are complex. However, it is very helpful in our learning and dealing with situations effectively if we can structure situations into meaningful units. Models of reflection help us to do this. In order to assist you with choosing a suitable approach there are numerous models of reflection available within nursing textbooks and articles. Rolfe et al (2011) and Jasper (2013) provide several good examples.

Models of reflection are also commonly referred to as frameworks (Jasper 2013). A framework is simply a way of organizing things and giving them structure. Overall the choice of model for use for reflection is a personal one, and may be guided by the underpinning theory of the model or how consistent its philosophy is with yours or that of your professional environment. There is not much advice about how to choose a model, but it needs to be appropriate to your needs (Rolfe et al 2011), consistent with your personal or professional philosophy, relevant to your professional practice and clear and straightforward to use.

KEY TEXTS
- Hargreaves, J. and Page, L. (2013) *Reflective Practice* (Cambridge: Polity Press).
- Rolfe, G., Jasper, M. and Freshwater, D. (2011) *Critical Reflection for Nursing Generating Knowledge for Care*. 2nd edn (Basingstoke: Palgrave Macmillan).
- Hargreaves, J. and Page, L. (2013) *Reflective Practice* (Cambridge: Polity Press).

n

narratives

SEE ALSO diary; facilitator; journals; learning logs; models; reflection; reflective practice; reflective processes; writing.

Relationships are central to professional practice. Within the context of these human relationships a range of narratives occur. Narratives are conversations between and among individuals that are either spoken or written. Some professions, such as health and social care, are heavily reliant on these conversations to share information and knowledge (Frost 2006). Through this dialogue others come to know what is accepted and what may be rejected (Frost 2006). As such, narratives are a strong mediator of social behaviour. Narratives feature strongly in relationships with service users too. Narratives may serve as a basis for *reflection* and are now being used more frequently (Frost 2006). Through the exploration of people's stories and by reflecting on these we can come to know and understand practice more. Narratives such as client records, meeting minutes and recordings (Frost 2006) can be analysed using *models* of reflection in order to learn from events. Professionals can create their own narratives using a *diary* or *journal*. It is important to remember that in the context of reflection and *reflective practice* there is a focus on making sense of situations. This sense making taps into what it means to be human as:

> To be human is to care for the meaning of things, events and experiences for personal life. Such sense making involves an impetus or motivation to bring things together, to find significance and to make wholes out of parts. Within this context, we are story makers and storytellers. (Todres et al 2009:72)

In professions that interact with the public it is very valuable to begin to use reflection as a means of making sense of situations, and uncovering the deeper meanings of events. Not to do this and to see one's professional role as a series of tasks serves to dehumanize individuals (both colleagues and service users (Todres et al 2009)).

implications for reflective practice
It must be noted that while written narratives are often accepted as 'what really happened' these are more likely to have been reconstructed and reshaped, and they may only be a reflection of what actually took place (Knott and Spafford 2007). Knott and Spafford differentiate between the story (what actually happened) and narratives (the recounting of the story). Including actual dialogue, such as direct quotations, film or recordings, within narratives can increase authenticity (Knott and Spafford 2007).

KEY TEXTS
- Frost, S. (2006) 'Recasting Individual Practice Through Reflection on Narratives' in S. White, J. Fook and F. Gardner (eds), *Critical Reflection in Health and Social Care* (Berkshire: Open University Press): pp. 107–117.
- Knott, C. and Spafford, J. (2007) 'Getting Started' in C. Knott and Scragg (eds), *Reflective Practice in Social Work* (Exeter: Learning Matters): pp. 13–29.

p

portfolios

SEE ALSO **reflective practice; reflection.**

A portfolio provides evidence of the attainment of learning or achievement of learning outcomes (Timmins 2008). It is a collection of items that attest to learning. However, in reality, issues arise with this as the portfolio becomes little more than a receptacle, with little connection between items and no explanation (to the reader) of the learning achieved. Portfolios are used for both personal and professional reasons. Nurses, for example, are encouraged to keep a portfolio (NCNM 2008).

Whether or not the portfolio is used for personal or professional reasons, applying a clear structure to it is important. There needs to be a consistent theme (or themes) running throughout, clear signposting and use of an organizing framework. Discussion within the portfolio is important. This can introduce the portfolio, explain items, explain linkage and context and importantly draw out key learning.

Reflection is often a component part of a portfolio and sometimes the whole purpose of a portfolio is to develop reflective skills (Hull and Redfern 2005). Certainly documentation of reflections and *reflective practice* often form the basis of the portfolio.

A good practice model for the use of the portfolio as an assessment tool would include:

- A portfolio of evidence-based learning
- An exemplar of reflection on practice using a model of reflection (Johns 2013)
- A record of clinical learning

implications for reflective practice

Many professionals today are encouraged or required to develop a professional portfolio. Using a framework to structure the portfolio is very useful; for example, there is one derived from core require-ments of the role of *clinical nurse specialist* (Coffey 2005). These are clinical focus, service user advocate, education and training, audit and research and consultant (Coffey 2005). Using this type of framework permits the key themes to be used as subheadings to structure and develop the portfolio. Reflection and reflective prac-tice are then integrated within these themes.

KEY TEXTS
- Coffey, A. (2005) 'The Clinical Learning Portfolio: A Practice Development Experience in Gerontological Nursing', *Journal of Clinical Nursing*, 14 (8b): pp. 75–83.
- National Council for the Professional Development of Nursing and Midwifery (2009) *Guidelines for Portfolio Development for Nurses and Midwives*. 3rd edn (Dublin: National Council for the Professional Development of Nursing and Midwifery).
- Timmins, F. (2008) *Making Sense of Portfolios: An Introduction to Portfolio Use for Nursing Students* (Glasgow: Open University Press, McGraw-Hill Education).

procrastination

SEE ALSO **reflection; reflective practice; writing.**

Procrastination entails putting something off. This is a common experience for people as there is always a tendency to want to get to the task later, particularly when there are more desirable tasks to be done in the meantime. However, one of the greatest chal-lenges within *reflective practice* is getting started. We all have the tendency to put off this daunting task, or procrastinating about getting started. Procrastination can become long term, and even-tually the task is put aside never to be thought about again. A lack of structure for *reflection* can encourage this procrastination. This happens when you are asked to produce a piece of written reflec-tion but are provided with no guidelines or structure for this. This is becoming less and less common as departments and organiza-tions familiarize themselves with reflective processes. However, being as prepared as possible will assist you to get started. Find out what the guidelines are and the recommendations for structure. In the absence of guidelines, examine core texts such as Jasper (2013) for advice.

Procrastination is common; indeed Nagayda and her colleagues (2005) devote a whole chapter in their book on professional portfolios in occupational therapy to this very topic, entitled 'overcoming procrastination'. Students who are facilitated in their reflections while either attending a clinical practice area or within the classroom setting will find this structure helpful to avoid procrastination. It might be useful to agree times/dates in advance and set aside protected time to meet.

implications for reflective practice
Planning class time to facilitate students' progress, allow for individual and group discussion and offer feedback have been offered as practical suggestions to overcome some of the difficulties that students face (Serembus 2000). Nurses in Jasper's (1999) study suggested that reflective *writing* needed a commitment and personal motivation. These are key elements to resisting procrastination.

KEY TEXTS
- Jasper, M. (2013) *Beginning Reflective Practice.* 2nd edn (Hampshire: Cengage Learning).
- Nagayda, J., S. Schindehette, et al. (2005) *The Professional Portfolio in Occupational Therapy Career Development and Continuing Competence* (Thorofare, NJ: Slack Incorporated).

r

reflection

SEE ALSO analysis; awareness; critical incident; critical reflection; diary; experiential learning; facilitator; journals; knowledge; learning logs; mentor; models; reflective practice; reflective processes; reflexivity; supervision; wisdom.

Reflection is a natural human thinking process of looking back over our actions, or situations that we have encountered that either caused us concern or even satisfaction (Fook and Askleland 2006). We mull these over and try to make sense of experiences in order to learn from them and understand them. Indeed the need to make sense of situations is a fundamental human reaction (Todres et al 2009), and mechanisms like reflection enable us to do this effectively. Reflection means 'that thoughts of significant aspects of an experience are reconsidered and other explanations are contemplated' (Howatson-Jones 2010:1). At one level this human propensity towards reflections is a survival mechanism (Jasper 2013). This enables us to learn from life's experiences so as not to repeat mistakes or to better our circumstances. However, in the context of learning formally from experiences, reflection is understood as a 'conscious, volitional process' (Boud 2006:159) whereby the individual usually uses a structured *model* of reflection as a guide. Based on the original work of Schön (1983), scholars in the field generally refer to two types of reflection:

- Reflection-on-action

This is retrospective reflection; thinking about the experience after it has passed, aiming to make sense of it through consideration of theories, guidelines, experience and *knowledge*.

- Reflection-in-action

This means thinking in the moment. While we are actively practising within our professional lives we are using our existing knowledge and experience to modify thoughts, actions and responses as the situation is occurring (Oelofsen 2012). Reflection is used to learn about and improve professional practice, to develop practice-based theory, to link theory and practice, or to improve or change practice (Fook et al 2006).

Johns (2013) describes reflection as mindfulness, an *awareness* of self, either during or after an experience. It acts like a mirror so that the practitioner 'can view and focus self within the context of a particular experience' (Johns 2013:2). Reasons for reflecting within the professions are as follows:

- To develop and embed good practice
- To record valuable thinking processes
- To develop new skills
- To improve practice
- To deal with difficult situations effectively
- To apply theory to practice
- To deal effectively with human situations (Hargreaves and Page 2013)

Reflection seeks to identify meaning from events and situations in educational settings and practice in order to learn from experience. Reflection is a systematic step-by-step process, which invites the person to structure their thoughts and experiences in a specific way targeted at learning from experience using models for reflection. It can be broken down into three levels:

- Identifying the salient features of a situation upon which you wish to reflect
- Drawing conclusions from observations and considering solutions
- Appreciation of the wider social, environmental and political influences on the situation at hand (Oelofsen 2012)

Among many professions the popularity of reflection dates back to the 1980s (Jasper 2013). The seminal writings of Schön (Schön 1983) are notably influential (Jasper 2013) and Schön's (1983) work informs the literature of many professional disciplines since this time. Indeed many models of reflection are underpinned by his theories. Schön (1983) described how professionals used reflection as a method of ongoing or continuous learning about their practice. Reflection was described as being of an immediate nature, referred to as 'reflection in action'. Or it was suggested that you could reflect by looking back over situations; this was known as 'reflection on action'.

The use of reflection and models of reflection are popular contemporarily among many health-care professionals and across other practice-based disciplines such as teaching and engineering (Thomsen and Chraudin 2013, Beal 2012). Schön (1983) can be seen to be influential in many respects with regard to this increasing practice of encouraging reflection. His work gave credence to the necessity to develop knowledge and theory from practice and experience rather than just from empirical measurement.

Reflection is a structured form of learning from experience that either occurs during the experience or by thinking back and analysing situations later. Thus reflection can be conceived as:

> a complex and deliberate process of thinking about and interpreting experience in order to learn from it. (Boud et al 1985:135)

Reflection is considered an 'effective tool for recognizing formal and informal learning and development through practice' (Pearce 2003:20).

One important thing to remember about reflection is that it doesn't have to relate to a specific incident. Reflection is often considered as being a one-off event, perhaps associated with *incidents* or often referred to as '*critical incidents*' in practice, whereby you thought back over negative or positive experiences, in order to glean learning from these events, in order to understand what you could do differently or similarly the next time you encounter a comparable incident. However, reflection is much broader than this:

> a specific incident is not in question but rather the need to reflect upon cumulative experience and products and processes of learning over time. (Timmins 2008:63)

Critical incidents are also useful to target reflection and learning in one key area (Jasper 2013). However, it is important to interpret *critical* as significant and important to you (and your learning) rather than its more common interpretation as life-threatening or serious. It is a common feature in education for students to focus on matters such as reported errors that were dealt with in the practice situation and with which they had some experience. While there is potentially some learning in these situations these are usually ultimately so complex and require some systemic investigation that they are beyond the capabilities of a student. Furthermore, the student is often new to the practice situation and unable to comprehend all the relevant contextual factors. Benner (1984) suggests a focus on the ordinary aspects of practice. If you are working in health-care or practice with service users you could consider:

- Situations that went particularly well
- New experiences, such as your first time in the field
- Your first exposure to the language (for example, the reporting system) of the discipline – did you understand it?
- Your first experience with a service user
- An unusual experience or event
- Situations that you were placed in on your own for the first time
- Sad situations – what were these like?
- Situations that made you feel uncomfortable
- A communication difficulty that you had

The most important point here is to focus on issues that are meaningful for you. While recent recollections are easy to recall, and perhaps that which was most distressing is often uppermost in mind. Usually students working with service users have a huge range of potentially valuable experiences to reflect upon but often have difficulty isolating these as they seem commonplace.

Reflection is said to occur in different ways and at different levels (Jasper 2013). Freshwater and Rolfe (2001) identify three distinct 'types' of reflection:

Type 1: Reflection on the process of reflection 'deeper level and largely introspective metareflection'

Type 2: Reflection beyond 'introspection' that considers the wider social and political context.

Type 3: Reflection in action in which practice is reflected upon and modified as it is happening

In order to move towards *reflective practice* type 3 reflection needs to occur (Freshwater and Rolfe 2001).

Things that can enable successful reflection to occur are as follows (Driessen et al 2005):

- **Mentoring and feedback** – can provide a guide to the process of reflective practice and facilitate the identification of learning needs as well as enhancing motivation for the overall process
- **Provision of structure and guidelines for reflection** – professionals may need a structure to guide reflective activities
- **Materials for reflection** – professionals may need templates to structure their reflections, *journals*, diaries or *learning log*

implications for reflective practice
Reflection is a natural human thinking process of looking back over our actions (Fook and Askleland 2006). Indeed the need to make sense of situations is a fundamental human reaction (Todres et al 2009). Reflection in the context of reflective practice means a structured and thoughtful recounting of significant experiences using a model for reflection. As well as making sense of a situation, the *analysis* of a situation by means of reflection enhances self-awareness and develops practice-based *wisdom* and knowledge. Overall, reflection is a valuable source of learning for professionals in practice.

KEY TEXTS
- Fook, J. and Askeland, G. A. (2006) 'The "Critical" in Critical Reflection' in S. White, J. Fook and F. Gardner (eds), *Critical Reflection in Health and Social Care* (Berkshire: Open University Press): pp. 40–53.
- Fook, J., White, S. and Gardner, F. (2006) 'Critical Reflection: A Review of Contemporary Literature and Understandings' in S. White, J. Fook and F. Gardner (eds), *Critical Reflection in Health and Social Care* (Berkshire: Open University Press): pp. 3–20.

reflective practice

SEE ALSO **critical reflection; facilitator; knowledge; leadership; reflection; reflective processes; reflexivity; understanding.**

It is determined that reflective practice gained popularity within health-care professions in particular due to limitations in the scientific paradigm's contribution to our *understanding* of complex human and health-care situations (Ruch 2009a). As such, *reflection* on our practice and developing and integrating new insights and new ways of working within practice as a result (reflective practice) provide an alternative evidence base for practice (Ruch 2009a). It can be described as:

> Paying critical attention to the practical values and theories which inform everyday actions, by examining practice reflectively and reflexively. This leads to developmental insight. (Bolton 2010:ix)

It involves:

- Developing a sense of the problem at hand
- Enriching that sense with observations of the relevant conditions
- Elaborating a conclusion
- Testing that conclusion in practice (Oelofsen 2012)

While the terms 'reflection' and 'reflective practice' are often used interchangeably (Ruch 2009a) the main difference between reflection and reflective practice is that reflection is the straightforward analytical thinking about practice using a model or framework for reflection whereas reflective practice is putting this reflection, and insights/knowledge gained from it into action in practice (Gardner 2014). Reflection is an:

> In-depth consideration of events or situations: the people involved, what they experienced, and how they felt about it. This involves reviewing or reliving the experience to bring it into focus, and replaying from diverse points of view. Seemingly innocent details might prove to be key; seemingly vital details may be irrelevant. (Bolton 2010:xix)

Reflective practice is one of the most important ways of learning from experience (Jasper 2013). Many professions are now adopting reflective practice as a tool for learning from practice as a component of continued professional development (CPD) (Ruch 2009b). Indeed reflective practice is a key element of practice within professions such as nursing (NMC 2010b) and social work (Ruch 2009b).

Reflective practice allows you to learn from experience, increase *knowledge* and skills and grow as a practitioner (Jasper 2013). Reflective practice means 'taking our experiences as a starting point for learning' (Jasper 2013:1). It is through the purposeful act of reflection that reflective practice is achieved. Reflective practice is a 'concept for learning' (Jasper 2013:3). As practitioners when we think about our experiences in practice, examining them in a new way, and take action as a result, this is reflective practice. It emphasizes a 'thoughtful approach to understanding experience, whether in real time or retrospectively' (Boros 2009:23). Jasper (2013) summarizes this as the experience-reflection-action (ERA) cycle.

Reflective practice allows practitioners to develop a greater self-awareness about the nature and impact of their performance. This awareness increases professional growth and development. For students, reflective practice serves to 'make the links between theory and practice' (Jasper 2013:1). The purposes of reflective practice are outlined as follows:

- To identify learning needs
- To identify new opportunities for learning
- To identify the ways in which we learn best
- To identify new courses of action
- To explore alternative ways of solving problems
- For personal development
- To escape routine practice
- To be aware of the consequences of our actions
- To demonstrate our competence to others
- To demonstrate our achievements to ourselves and others
- To build theory from observations
- To helps us make decisions or resolve uncertainty
- To empower or emancipate ourselves as individuals
  (Jasper 2013:6)

Developing reflective practice in a service requires institutional support (Oelofsen 2012). This may be in the form of *facilitators*, education and training or allocated time for reflection. However, it also needs to be practised by many and supported by *leadership* (Oelofsen 2012). This means an increasing space for reflective leadership in organizations. Taking action is an important component of reflective practice which may happen naturally during your actions, or it may need to occur afterwards. A reflective practitioner needs to consider:

- What do you want to achieve as a result of your action?
- How will you do it?
- When will you do it?
- Where will you do it?
- Who will be part of the action? (Jasper 2013)

Atkins and Schutz (2013) have identified attributes of the reflective practitioner which include:

- Possessing a repertoire of experience
- Being able to frame problems and experiment in practice
- Having an ability to articulate your reflective practice

implications for reflective practice
Over-reliance on the scientific paradigm to inform professional knowledge limits our understanding of complex human situations (Ruch 2009a). As such, reflection on our practice and developing and integrating new insights and new ways of working within practice as a result (reflective practice) provide an alternative evidence base for practice (Ruch 2009a). Reflective practice allows you to learn from work-based experience to increase knowledge and skills as a professional (Jasper 2013). Reflective practice therefore suggests that experiences directly inform your learning (Jasper 2013).

KEY TEXTS
- Atkins, S. and Schutz, S. (2013) 'Developing Skills for Reflective Practice' in Bullman and S. Schutz (eds), *Reflective Practice in Nursing* (Oxford: Wiley Blackwell): pp. 23–52.

- Ruch, G. (2009a) 'Reflective Practice and Reflective Spaces' in G. Ruch (ed.), *Post-Qualifying Child Care Social Work:* Developing Reflective Practice (London: Sage): pp. 19–30.
- Ruch, G. (2009b) 'Introduction – Developing Holistic Social Work Practitioners' in G. Ruch (ed.), *Post-Qualifying Child Care Social Work.* Developing Reflective Practice (London: Sage): pp. 3–7.

reflective processes

SEE ALSO **critical reflection; journals; learning logs; models; reflection; reflective practice; reflective processes.**

Jasper (2013) described the term 'reflective processes' as one of the three phases of *reflective practice* outlined in the experience-reflection-action (ERA) cycle. *Reflective processes* are all those frameworks and *models* that permit individuals to learn from experience. This is a broad conceptual term that pertains to the overarching principles employed across reflective cycles, models and frameworks. In general these reflective processes involve re-examining the experience using a structured framework for *reflection*. These processes will also differ depending on the model used.

Reflective processes help us to see the work in alternative ways by enabling us to focus on different aspects of our experiences. Reflective processes [means] ... the stages of thoughtful activity we go through when we consciously decide to explore an experience. (Jasper 2013:12)

These processes involve outlining the experience, identifying feelings, outlining the learning that occurred and providing for action. Fundamental stages of the reflective process, which are implicit in most recommended models of reflection, are outlined as follows:

Stage 1: selecting an experience to reflect upon

Stage 2: observing and describing the experience

Stage 3: analysing the experience

Stage 4: interpreting the experience

Stage 5: exploring alternatives

Stage 6: taking action (Jasper 2013)

These reflective processes may be carried out in a continuous and evolving fashion and are not necessarily confined to one set of thought processes (Jasper 2013). Reflective practice is reliant on information. It is the information about events, actions, feelings, consequences and new perspectives that provides the rich material for learning from practice. Reflective practice is reliant upon further thinking, which is what using reflective processes such as models stimulates. In the practice environment the information is not contained, it does not reside in one specific place such as a textbook. Rather the information is the practice itself – the visual cues that the practitioner receives, the oral information received, the written information read, the interventions performed. Many of these latter are complex, interchanging and interdependent. It can be a challenge to simply outline the information about a situation in a concise way. This is especially true if you have an emotional reaction to a situation as it is all too easy to become preoccupied with either thinking or talking about this element.

As a result of this complexity, and to an extent due to the invisibility of many elements of practice (such as subtle gestures that encourage trust and relationship building), reflective practice encourages practitioners to elicit key information about practice by using cues. Questioning forms a key part of this process and most models and frameworks of reflection entail some form of questioning that prompts the practitioner to uncover and re-examine key information. Borton's framework (1970) consists entirely of questions. Facilitators too are encouraged to use this questioning approach to focus practitioners towards providing key essential information.

In teaching practice, for example, where reflection has taken on an increasingly important role in recent decades, reflective practice for university teachers is encouraged to focus on questions: 'questioning why we do something rather than how, and most important of all, learning by this process' (Kuit et al 2001, 130–131).

implications for reflective practice
Reflective processes are all those frameworks and models that permit individuals to learn from experience. This is a broad conceptual term that pertains to the overarching principles employed across reflective cycles, models and frameworks. In general these reflective

processes involve re-examining the experience using a structured framework for reflection. These processes will also differ depending on the model used.

KEY TEXT
• Jasper, M. (2013) *Beginning Reflective Practice*. 2nd edn (Hampshire: Cengage Learning).

reflexivity

SEE ALSO **awareness; critical reflection; criticality; reflection; reflective practice.**

Reflexivity requires a practitioner who is self-aware in their practice. It may be defined as 'reflecting on the specifics of the situation, as well as the conditions from which they arise, and how we might be implicated in those conditions' (Howatson-Jones 2010:79). It means the growth of an *awareness* to recognize our own personal influence, and those of the social context, on situations (Fook and Askeland 2006). A key feature of reflexivity is seeing your own personal contribution to situations and acting on this awareness (Laing and Humphries 2013). It comprises:

[Finding] a way of standing outside the self to examine, for example, how seemingly unwittingly we are involved in creating social or professional structures counter to our espoused values. It enables becoming aware of the limits of our knowledge, of how our own behaviour is complicit in forming organisational practices, which for example, marginalise groups or exclude individuals ... It requires being able to stay with personal uncertainty, critically informed curiosity, and flexibility to find ways of changing deeply held ways of being: a complex, highly responsible social and political activity. (Bolton 2010:ix)

Reflexivity concerns being aware of and examining the conditions around you. Reflexivity enables thinking about and reflecting upon practice in a continuous manner (Jasper 2013) and 'continuous review' of personal actions (Howatson-Jones 2010:79). It requires the person to be fully engaged, self-aware, questioning personal assumptions and values on a continuous basis (Brechin 2000).

The main difference between the act of *reflection* and reflexivity is this continuation in so far as there are continuous repetitive cycles of reflection or *critical reflection* (Jasper 2013) accompanied by a growing awareness of self and one's contribution to the professional context. Key to this is a critical awareness of the professional environment, and critical reflection on this to understand that there are many factors influencing conditions that can influence behaviours and actions (Howatson-Jones 2010). As such, reflexivity is a means of professional development (Lipp 2004).

implications for reflective practice
Reflexivity as a means of professional development has important implications for many modern professions. Complex practice situations often involve interplay between human factors and the professional intervention, and as such, elements of human relationships often form the basis of those critical incidents about which we wish to reflect. Situations that are confrontational, challenging or difficult often inspire us towards reflection and it is crucial as we develop as practitioners that this is done with awareness and emerging reflexivity.

KEY TEXTS
- Bolton, G. (2010) *Reflective Practice. Writing and Professional Development* (London: Sage).
- Fook, J. and Askeland, G. A. (2006) 'The "Critical" in Critical Reflection' in S. White, J. Fook and F. Gardner (eds), *Critical Reflection in Health and Social Care* (Berkshire: Open University Press): pp. 40–53.

S

supervision

SEE ALSO confidence; critical incident; critical reflection; facilitator; knowledge; reflection; reflective practice; reflexivity.

Supervision is a common concept across modern professional practice. Many students and practitioners work under the auspices of a supervisor or mentor either during their initial educational preparation or in early-stage career. Indeed lifelong mentorship is becoming more common and, depending on the nature of the professional role, a supervisor might continue to be a feature of your career throughout. This supervisor generally oversees your work and practice and ensures that this complies with the required competencies and the organizational procedures and goals. Supervision can be either on a one-to-one basis, or you may be supervised in a group (Johns 2013). Depending on your level of attainment or seniority the supervisor might have overall responsibility for the enactment of your professional role, or may provide feedback and guidance to you on your role, while you take the responsibility. Supervisors have a useful role in assisting a person with their own personal *reflection* (Johns 2013). They may have direct responsibility for helping you to learn the work of your profession (formative supervision); or they may support on aspects of your role that relate to policies, procedures, guidelines or ethical practices (normative supervision); or they may provide a supportive relationship for participants that supports their emotional needs (restorative supervision) (Oelofsen 2012).

Their role incorporates various elements including:

- Developing practitioner competence
- Safeguarding standards of care
- Developing reflective skills (in self and others) (Johns 2013)

Reflection with a supervisor is usually facilitated individually. It is important for supervisors and participants to take cognisance of the issues that surround facilitated reflection such as confidentiality, credibility and honesty. Clear guidelines regarding these issues also need to be in place in addition to a pathway for disclosure should participants reveal items during reflective writing or discussions that may warrant reporting within the health service or elsewhere. These guidelines ought to be developed locally in a partnership arrangement with health service providers. The role of a supervisor with regard to reflection is very much supportive in terms of listening and guiding (Hull and Redfern 2005).

Once a decision is reached to reflect upon a particular learning situation, the participant may bounce ideas off the supervisor in relation to the critical analysis that may precede this *reflexivity*, and the supervisor may indeed provide guidance as to whether a student may access the relevant policies. With regard to different levels of analysis the student may summarize and describe local policy, for example, and also describe findings from an international perspective. The mentor may also provide *confidence* and encouragement to a participant to begin to write.

Crucial phases in the supervisor relationship have been outlined as follows:

The Beginning phase

- Clarifying the relationship with the supervisor
- Establishing ways of working
- Developing required competencies and practices together

The Mature phase

- Increasing individual nature of the relationship, becoming more flexible and less role bound with supervisor
- Increasing self-confidence and independence
- Confronting personal issues as they relate to professional practice

The Termination phase

- Decreasing need for supervision
- Clear understanding of professional practice role (Freshwater 2005)

As the participant develops from the process of reflection to becoming a critical practitioner, they, through discussion with the mentor, come to new understandings about practice. Students are often concerned and embarrassed about showing reflective work to a mentor. However, this may be due to the overly personal and ultimately self-development approach to many models, that may in fact be for personal and maybe internal use (Jasper 2013). With the critical practice approach, the description and analysis is broader in terms of practice, and a mentor is important to facilitate student learning in this regard. It is important to remember that in many professions the supervisor will support a student in work-based settings that involve clients and service users. As such the relationship of supervision is three-dimensional and may have input from service users too. While service users may not have direct access to personal reflections, the reflection in action that takes places in the working environment may occur in the presence of the public who may have a contribution to make to the dialogue (Oelofsen 2012).

Supervision is of course also useful for qualified staff in many situations (Johns 2013). In the context of reflection, supervisors in clinical practice may serve to support and guide this. There are many considerations with this, not only in relation to choice of model of reflection but also choice of supervisor. This can be a line manager or senior staff, however, peer supervision is recommended as a very useful basis for reflection as both persons are equal in the relationship and better able to support an open and honest dialogue (Johns 2013). Johns (2013:222) suggests a nine-step process to supervision in this context:

1. Preparation – creating the best possible environment for successful supervision of reflection.
2. Pick up – ensuring continuity from session to session – picking up where you left off last time.
3. Listening – active listening to pick up important points of the practitioner's story.
4. Clarifying – ensuring that you have heard correctly.
5. Understanding – facilitating the practitioner to gain insight into their feelings and reactions.
6. Options – enabling the practitioner to explore alternative options.

7. Taking action – guiding the practitioner to draw conclusions from their reflections and consider possible actions.
8. Empowering – facilitating the identification of possible barriers to action and how to address these.
9. Wrap up – summarizing each session and ensuring that the participant feels comfortable with the closure.

Important qualities of a supervisor are as follows:

- Sharing a similar purpose and vision
- A good listener
- Being able to challenge
- Being trustworthy
- Being authentic and honest
- Being open and transparent
- Being committed to the supervisory relationship
- Concerned and compassionate
- Experienced in reflection
- Understanding (Johns 2013)

implications for reflective practice
Although not uniform or widespread, supervision is a common approach to reflection and *reflective practice* across modern professional practice. Many students and practitioners work under the auspices of a mentor, supervisor or *facilitator* either during their initial educational preparation or in early-stage career. Indeed lifelong mentorship is becoming more common and, depending on the nature of the professional role, a supervisor might continue to be a feature of your career throughout. This supervisor generally oversees your work and practice and ensures that this complies with the required competencies and the organizational procedures and goals. This can assist with developing your reflective practice, confidence, *knowledge* and awareness.

KEY TEXTS
- Johns, C. (2013) *Becoming a Reflective Practitioner* (Oxford: Wiley Blackwell).
- Oelofsen, N. (2012) *Developing Reflective Practice: A Guide for Students and Practitioners of Health and Social Care* (Banbury: Lantern Publishing).

u

understanding

SEE ALSO analysis; andragogy; assessment; awareness; confidence; critical action; critical reflection; diary; facilitator; journals; learning logs; mentor; models; reflection; reflective practice; reflective processes; reflexivity; supervision; values.

Understanding means gaining an insight into how something works. This is a key component of the *reflective processes* as we seek to understand ourselves, others and the practice/work environment. Understanding requires an appropriate level of cognitive function and *awareness* in order to be able to interpret ourselves and the world around us. Understanding is something that develops over time and as our life experience develops so does our understanding. Understanding is a mental process of interpreting, analysing, rationalizing and accepting facts. Through understanding we get to know ourselves and the world and ascribe meaning to certain activities, characteristics and events. With this store of knowledge about the meaning of events we are able to interpret and react to future events in appropriate or improved ways. *Reflection, critical reflection* and *reflective practice* increase our understanding of ourselves, our professional environments and our service users.

Understanding generally occurs at a personal level, although as a child growing in maturity this understanding may be supported by parents and other concerned adults. Increasingly as adults this understanding is a sole occupation. When we experience events, we interpret them based on our senses, react to them and store facts about this experience for the next time. Personal understanding is important to personal survival. You might know, for example, that stepping onto a pedestrian crossing obliges the cars to stop, but when you get a fright when you experience a car not stopping one day you gain the understanding that there is a chance that a car may not stop and that you must take additional time before stepping out and look very carefully. This may save your life or at least protect your health.

However, there are limits to this personal understanding. Understanding is enriched and developed if we are able to seek feedback from others. To an extent feedback is ever present in the environment. The car speeding by on the pedestrian crossing is an example of feedback. Your bosses frown when you are late for work. We are constantly receiving verbal and nonverbal cues from the environment about our behaviour and actions and the effect that this may have on others. However, there are still limits to this as the thinking and interpreting are limited to one person only, you. You have certain *values*, past experiences and hidden aspects of self that all affect your interpretation of events and thus potentially influence understanding.

Reflection and reflective practice allow for personal understanding to grow beyond personal to a greater awareness of the environment and its influence on events. Working with another person such as a *mentor*, supervisor or *facilitator* may illuminate and clarify your understanding of events, thus helping you to grow as a person and professional. Developing your self-awareness will also assist you to see what influences your current understanding. Through discussions with your mentor/supervisor or facilitator you might find that your interpretation of their frowning during the activity as negative was actually quite the opposite, as your mentor often frowns when deep in thought and was actually thinking what a good job you were doing. Your understanding of your own actions, thoughts and feelings will also be enhanced by using the tools of the reflective processes, such as *learning logs, journals* and diaries. These modalities along with *models* of reflection, which may be used in conjunction with these or independently, all assist you to analyse situations, and your reaction to them uncovers meanings and contextual contributions which serve to improve your understanding of events.

If you are a student taking a course your understanding will also develop through continuous feedback received on exams, assignments and practical components. It is important to remain open to this commentary as it will assist you to gain more insight into how to perform better. Feedback in terms of how you are progressing, the context of reflection and reflective practice is very important to build skills and *confidence* and also to improve your practice by assisting and supporting you with *critical action*. Working with a mentor/supervisor or facilitator is one of the most useful mechanisms of seeking feedback to gain a greater understanding of situations, and how your reflection is progressing, particularly in the absence of formal feedback, for example, by *assessment*.

implications for reflective practice
Reflection and reflective practice allow for personal understanding to grow. Working with your mentor, supervisor or facilitator may illuminate and clarify your understanding of events enabling greater understanding and professional development. Your own understanding of events will also be further enhanced by using the tools of the reflective processes, such as learning logs, journals, diaries and models of reflection. Developing an increased understanding improves your self-awareness and your ability to become a reflective practitioner.

KEY TEXT
• Jasper, M. (2013) *Beginning Reflective Practice*. 2nd edn (Hampshire: Cengage Learning).

V

values

SEE ALSO analysis; awareness; mentor; models; reflection; reflective practice; reflective processes; supervisor

When developing self-awareness it is important to develop an understanding of your personal values (Jasper et al 2013). Values arise from our upbringing and life experiences and the socialization process that occurs as a result (Jasper 2013). Cooper (2009) suggests that it is important for professionals to reflect on their values by considering what values are, how to identify them and why they are important. Values are worthy standards or qualities deemed important by a person or social group (Butts and Rich 2013).Values held by people guide what is important for them (Horton et al 2007). It drives them, sometimes unconsciously, to activities, actions and behaviours that are deemed worthwhile and worth working for (Horton et al 2007). Values are both socially and culturally determined. As a result, items such as ideals, beliefs, customs, modes of conduct and qualities are highly prized by an individual, group or society (Horton et al 2007). Values motivate and guide your behaviour and can influence life choices (Horton et al 2007). Self-analysis using the Johari window exercise or the SWOB can provide useful insights into your underpinning values and beliefs.

Values are not concrete. They are constantly developing and are influenced by changing peer groups, work environments, experiences and so on. As a result they can change during our lives. We are often unaware of our values until they are challenged (McCabe and Timmins 2013). When our values contradict with others', this can be a source of conflict for us. For example, if you value hard work and your friend does not and wishes to take a short cut by looking at your work, this may cause you to be angry. Similarly for those working in the helping professions there will be times when your own personal values conflict with those in your care. Those who value honesty may find it difficult to understand the dishonesty of others such as offenders.

However, as professionals, often a new set of values is embraced – those of the profession. As such we are no longer guided by our own values, but rather, those of the professional are subsumed and prioritized within our hierarchy of values. Honesty and compassion, for example, are common values required across those involved in health-care practice and are specifically required for registered professions such as nurses (ICN 2012, NMC 2008). Overall when identifying your values you must ensure that you protect the interests and dignity of your service users, irrespective of your own values related to factors such as gender, age, race, ability, sexuality, economic status, lifestyle, culture and religious or political belief (NMC 2008).

implications for reflective practice
When developing self-awareness becoming aware of your personal values is important (Jasper et al 2013). Values are worthy standards or qualities deemed important by a person or social group (Butts and Rich 2013). Values arise from our upbringing and life experiences and the socialization process that occurs as a result (Jasper 2013). It is important to reflect on your values by considering what values are, how to identify them, and how they are important to helping professions. This can be done through self-awareness techniques, *reflection* or specific *analysis* of values. It is helpful during *reflective processes* to carry out a values clarification exercise (such as that provided free by Fleming 2014). This will help to solidify and clarify your personal values and contribute to your growing self-awareness.

KEY TEXTS
- Fleming, A. (2014) *Values Clarification Exercise.* Available at www.amandafleming.co.nz/, accessed April 14, 2014.
- Jasper, M. (2013) *Beginning Reflective Practice.* 2nd edn (Hampshire: Cengage Learning).

W

wisdom

SEE ALSO **knowledge; reflection; reflective practice; reflective processes; reflexivity; supervision.**

Wisdom refers to the ability to make correct judgments and decisions. It is a quality gained through experience. It relates to practical know-how, experience and underlying *knowledge*. Benner and her colleagues uncovered much information about the wisdom required in professional practice by demonstrating that critical care nurses develop and demonstrate wisdom in practice (Benner et al 2011). This wisdom is developed by understanding situations, observing clinical situations repeatedly in practice, and *reflection* on these events. Some of this wisdom is not captured in textbooks or science, but rather develops within the professionals to a point where they can observe subtle differences in service user conditions that warrant attention despite contradicting clinical signs (Benner et al 2011). Reflection is thought to contribute to the development of wisdom and being reflective is a component of wisdom (Moon 1999). Johns (2013:5) describes practical wisdom as the 'ability to mindfully weigh up any situation and consider how best to respond given the likely consequences'. The outcomes of reflection and *reflective practice* ultimately aim to develop local and personal wisdom among professionals. This type of wisdom is valued highly in many disciplines and is beginning to be respected in the same way that traditional forms of knowledge (such as science and research) are. It is very important in health-care disciplines such as social work and nursing that practice wisdom is fostered and developed through *reflective processes*, reflection and reflective practice as dealing with the complexity of the human condition requires a wisdom developed in practice that is sensitive to human needs and requirements in addition to the science and research that informs care.

implications for reflective practice

Developing practice wisdom through reflection and reflective practice and use of models of reflection has important implications for many professionals, especially the caring professions or those that deal closely with the public. At the same time those requiring technical skills, such as engineering, would still benefit from reflection on the technical know-how to develop practice wisdom as part of knowledge development.

KEY TEXT

- Johns, C. (2013) *Becoming a Reflective Practitioner* (Oxford: Wiley Blackwell).

work-based learning

SEE ALSO **analysis; assessment; awareness; barriers; critical incident; critical reflection; criticality; diary; ethical issues; experiential learning; facilitator; group reflections; journals; learning logs; lifelong learning; mentor; models; procrastination; reflection; reflective practice; reflective processes; reflexivity; supervision.**

Powerful knowledge is gained through experience (Boud and Walker 1993). Dewey (1933) first highlighted the importance of the rich learning that is possible from experience. Learning from experience is a key component of *reflective practice*. Experiences, all the things that happen to us, serve to inform and form the person that we are. However, re-examining experiences is thought to have useful benefits for growing and developing as a professional. How we are influenced as a person through our experience can be moulded and shaped depending on the context.

Rather than experiences just happening and just continuing to move forward in life, it is suggested that in order to learn from experiences they must be reflected upon. Moreover, it is possible for groups and organizations to also learn from experiences (Boud et al 2006). By examining events in a new way, we can come to new understandings that are aimed at improving future performance and developing *criticality*. Importantly, without learning from experience we are likely to repeat similar poor practices, perhaps without knowing it.

Although it is noted that while *reflection* has become of growing importance during the education of professionals, and for ongoing continuous professional development of these, formal reflection in the workplace as a standard practice is unusual (Boud 2006). However, while it is not common practice across educational institutions, public bodies or industry to formally reflect on practice, there are many instances where learning takes place through informal reflection, such as conversations with colleagues (Boud 2006). While these opportunities are not always recognized and valued as work-based learning they are powerful contributors to our learning at work (Boud 2006). We learn through our experiences all of the time and sharing these with others can help to tease out important issues and receive feedback on them that further contributes to our learning (Boud 2006).

However, creating space for reflection may be a useful *facilitator* of work-based learning, and if no natural spaces occur (for example, in the drive home or in the cafeteria) then less reflection will take place. In order to maximize the benefits of learning from working practice, formalized *group reflection* is a useful structure but it can serve to impede reflection too (Boud 2006). Organizing a group reflection provides dedicated space and time for people to share their work experiences and ideas together and learn from these. Individuals within this group can share incidents and experiences that are problematic or puzzling in order to learn and share with the group. As reflection may not necessarily be a priority in the workplace, and conflicts with many other high demands, it is useful to give a particular purpose to that reflection in order to encourage engagement within these reflective groups. The group purpose could be to improve a specific area of practice, develop a product or presentation or reflect on and analyse difficult situations in the workplace. Keeping a *journal* can form part of this reflective learning in the workplace (Boud 2006). Based on the work of Boud (Boud et al 2006) and others, work-based learning is established as an important field internationally (Linehan 2008). Reflection and reflective practice form a central component of this type of learning.

'Productive reflection' is a term used to denote deliberate group reflections in the work context that aim to result in better performance and outcomes. Boud et al (2006) consider that in the modern context reflection ought to occur more frequently in the workplace and less at an individual level. Central to productive reflection is an acknowledgement of the learning potential of work (Boud et al 2006). Productive reflection aims to encourage workers to reflect on work experiences in order to learn from them. It engages within individuals but also takes consideration of the worker's needs. It means viewing the worker as a valuable commodity who has an active say in organizational management. It is a useful mechanism for dealing with difficult or ambiguous situations (Boud et al 2006).

implications for reflective practice
Work-based experiences hold opportunities for rich learning experiences. In the context of *lifelong learning*, increasingly professionals will be expected to learn from their working environments. While reflection, *critical reflection* and reflective practice are useful mechanisms to explore learning in the work context through the use of *models* of reflection, diaries, journals, *learning logs* and *assessments* it is important that the working environment is one which fosters reflection and reflective practice and seeks to overcome *barriers*. Learning in groups can also be very useful in this context as can informal conversations with peers. Overall, time and space for *reflexivity* is required in the workplace.

KEY TEXTS
- Boud, D., Cressey, P. and Doherty, P. (2006) 'Setting the Scene for Productive Reflection at Work' in D. Boud, P. Cressey and P. Doherty (eds), *Productive Reflection at Work* (Oxon: Routledge): pp. 3–10.
- Boud, D. (2006) 'Creating the Space for Reflection at Work' in D. Boud, P. Cressey and P. Doherty (eds), *Productive Reflection at Work* (Oxon: Routledge): pp. 157–169.

writing

reflective writing
SEE ALSO **analysis; assessment; awareness; critical incident; diary; ethical issues; experiential learning; facilitator; journals; learning logs; lifelong learning; mentor; models; procrastination; reflection; reflective practice; reflective processes; supervision.**

When using *reflection* it may be a matter of choice as to whether you write down your reflections or not (Jasper 2013). Sometimes if the reflection forms part of course work or an assignment you will be obliged to write at least some of it down (Hargreaves and Page 2013). Using a *model* provides a useful framework for an essay or assignment, and it can be helpful when planning and developing your essay (Hargreaves and Page 2013). Writing out experiences provides a perspective that we would not otherwise achieve (Bolton 2010).

Reflective writing differs from contemplative or verbal refection (Jasper 2013). Reflective writing is a purposeful activity that is a means of communication. It is a particular form of writing that is performed for the purposes of learning (Jasper 2013). It is a means of ordering your thoughts. Reflective writing can be categorized within two main domains: analytical and creative (Jasper 2013). Analytical writing involves analysing situations using a structured approach. Creative writing is freer, including activities such as storytelling, poetry or keeping a *journal* (Jasper 2013). When using analytical writing techniques you need to avoid being overly descriptive and aim to be reflective (Jasper 2013). Most models of reflection provide for *analysis* of the situation under consideration and within this component it is often useful to explore the literature or textbooks on the topic (Hargreaves and Page 2013). This will help you to support your emergent ideas within the reflection or to challenge your ideas or practice (Hargreaves and Page 2013). It will also provide a more theoretical component to your assignment and prevent you spending too much time on describing the incident. While reflective writing is most commonly done for these purposes (academic assignment) it is becoming increasingly popular among professionals for personal and professional reasons. This means that you might write down your reflections, in the same way, but their use will be for your own personal and professional development, *lifelong learning* or continuous professional development. You might use a *diary* or journal for this purpose, however, *ethical issues* in relation to the storage of this and its contents need to be borne in mind.

Benner et al (2011) supported the notion of reflection and strongly supported the need to either verbalize or write about clinical situations as a powerful form of learning. From their research, they concluded that *experiential learning* requires a narrative approach to experiences. Indeed writing, rather than being a means to an end, is learning in itself. One can learn by writing (Jasper 2013). Bolton (2010:47) suggests that the following 'ethical principles' ought to apply to ethical writing:

1. Trust – in the processes, in your ability to write. Trust that it will lead to personal insight. Writing about our experience cannot be wrong; it is our perception of our own experience and is therefore correct.
2. Self-respect – in our own beliefs, feelings, values and identity. We communicate respectfully with ourselves, opening up to fears, prejudices, mistakes and avoiding the destructive inner critic.
3. Responsibility – we maintain an *awareness* of what we need to take responsibility for. We have full authority over our writing at all stages. We take full responsibility for our actions that arise as a consequence of writings.
4. Generosity – we willingly give time, energy and commitment to our personal and professional development through the means of writing. This allows us the time and space to receive inspiration.
5. Positive regard – unconditional positive regard is maintained towards others. Feelings are noted and contained within the writing. Feelings are aired in the writing for reasons of catharsis and to understand our actions and reactions. The intention is not to harm others as a result of these emotions.

Writing can be difficult to get started (Bolton 2010). People often lack confidence at first; it can be difficult to do this alone. Bolton (2010) suggests that a *mentor* or supervisor can be useful in this regard, particularly for students taking courses who simply may not know where to start. This person can simply encourage and support the writer and encourage them to use and develop their own voice (Bolton 2010). It is best not to be too perfectionistic when writing. It is suggested to simply write out your thoughts, as they occur, without giving consideration at first to spelling, grammar and punctuation (Bolton 2010). If the writing is to be submitted as part of course work, errors can be picked up in later drafts. The use of a reflective framework is encouraged (Bullman 2013, Timmins and

Neill 2013) as this is known to provide more structure to the writing. It also ensures that you get down to the important analysis and action stages of *reflective practice*, as otherwise, without this structure, you could become preoccupied with describing the situation.

Bolton (2010) suggests this four-stage approach:

1. Write an account of an experience
   a. Allow the event to surface in your mind
   b. Think of something ordinary, or puzzling, don't necessarily focus on *critical incidents*
   c. Write about your experience describing it in as much detail as you can
   d. Give your writing a title, as if it were a story or a film
2. Re-read all that you have written and question yourself by asking the following:
   a. What strikes you about this story?
   b. Have you missed out any details? If so, add them
   c. How do you feel now reading it? How did you feel back then?
   d. What thoughts come to your mind now reading it? What were you thinking then?
   e. What assumptions have you made?
   f. What does the story say about your values?
   g. What do you find challenging?
3. Write another more detailed account, attempting to gain more depth and a wider perspective
   a. Write the story again from the viewpoint of another
4. Re-read your writing after a time period (of days, weeks, months) and question yourself in the following way:
   a. Where has this story taken you?
   b. What patterns can you see, for example, repeated behaviours?
   c. What do you notice about the dialogue you are using?
   e. Is there a destructive self-critical voice in your writing? If so try to make it constructive

Reflective writing takes practice. Using a diary or journal can help to get you started. There are some acknowledged challenges to diary use. Rushton and Duggan (2013) noted in their interviews with post-graduate business students that the ability to write reflectively can be inhibited by both cultural and language issues. International students, although experienced in reflective writing, struggle with exactly how and what to write. A very important finding of Rushton and Duggan's (2013) study is that students need clear direction and support with reflective writing, and that it is all too easy to make assumptions that people know instinctively how to write. Brookfield (1995) previously noted that students are often expected to be able to reflect although minimal instruction may have been received. Where either students or qualified professional staff are expected to use reflection, models of refection or to write reflectively, then some basic training and support in these modes is required, and where this support and education is provided results are very successful (Redmond 2006).

implications for reflective practice

Reflective writing can take many forms. It may be used as part of an *assessment* if you are undertaking a preparatory professional course or ongoing professional development. It might form part of your *learning log*, diary or journal or it may be required for your use of reflective frameworks. Knowing how to structure the writing can be problematic, and it is important to simply get started. Bolton (2010) suggests some guidance for this in the form of a four-stage approach, and once your writing begins it is important to get down to the important analysis and action stages of reflective practice, as otherwise, without this structure, you could become preoccupied with describing the situation. Writing is a useful exercise that enables you to see the situation more clearly and gain a new perspective on it. It also serves as a useful aide-memoire. Cultural and language issues can present challenges and it is important to seek advice and support from your mentor, supervisor or *facilitator*.

KEY TEXTS

- Bullman, C. (2013) 'Getting Started on a Journey with Reflection' in Bullman and S. Schutz (eds), *Reflective Practice in Nursing* (Oxford: Wiley Blackwell): pp. 201–224.
- Hargreaves, J. and Page, L. (2013) *Reflective Practice* (Cambridge: Polity Press).

bibliography

Ainsworth, S. (2005) 'Becoming a Relational Academic', *Synergy*, 22, 5–14. Available at http://www.itl.usyd.edu.au/synergy/article.cfm?articleID=263, accessed January 21, 2015.

Ali, I., Byard, K., Jülich, K. and Kommunuri, J. (2013) 'Student Perceptions on Using Blogs for Reflective Learning in Higher Educational Contexts' in S. Frielick, N. Buissink-Smith, P. Wyse, J. Billot, J. Hallas and E. Whitehead (eds), *Research and Development in Higher Education: The Place of Learning and Teaching*, 36 (1–10). New Zealand: Auckland, July 1–4, 2013. Available at: http://www.herdsa.org.au/wp-content/uploads/conference/2013/HERDSA_2013_ALI.pdf, acccesed January 21, 2015.

Alpers, R. R., Jarrell, K. and Wotring, R. (2013) 'Toward a Reflective Practice: Using Critical Incidents', *Teaching and Learning in Nursing*, 8 (1): pp. 33–35.

Asselin, M. E. and Fain, J. A. (2013) 'Effect of Reflective Practice Education on Self-reflection, Insight, and Reflective Thinking among Experienced Nurses: A Pilot Study', *Journal of Nurses in Professional Development*, 29 (3): pp. 111–119.

Atkins, S. and Schutz, S. (2013) 'Developing Skills for Reflective Practice' in Bullman and S. Schutz (eds), *Reflective Practice in Nursing* (Oxford: Wiley Blackwell): pp. 23–52.

Babapour, M. and Rahe, U. (2013) *Bridging the Discrepancy between Reflective Practice and Systematic Form Generation Approaches*. E&DPE 2013 15th International Conference on Engineering and Product Design Education 5th & 6th September 2013, Dublin Institute Of Technology, Dublin, Ireland, pp. 778–783.

Bailey, M. and Graham, M. (2007) 'Introducing Guided Group Reflective Practice in an Irish Palliative Care Unit', *International Journal of Palliative Care*, 13 (10): pp. 550–560.

Baldwin, K. and Lucas, B. (2012) 'Promoting Reflective Practice Skills for Postgraduate GPs: Do Journals Aid Journeys?' *Education for Primary Care*, 23 (3): pp. 213–216.

Bandura, A. (1977) 'Self-efficacy: Toward a Unifying Theory of Behavioral Change', *Psychological Review*, 84 (2): pp. 191–215.

Bandura, A. (1986) *Social Foundations of Thought and Action: A social cognitive theory* (Englewood Cliffs, NJ: Prentice Hall).

Barnett, R. (1997) *Higher Education: A Critical Business* (Bristol: The Society for Research into Higher Education).

Bates, C. (2009) *Malcom Knowles (1913–1997)*. Available at http://web .utk.edu/~start6/knowles/malcolm_knowles.html, accessed April 10, 2014.

Baumard, P. (1999) *Tacit Knowledge in Organizations* (London: Sage Publications).

Beal, J. (2012) *Assessing Employability Through Reflective Diaries on Teamwork*. Available at http://www.shef.ac.uk/lets/cpd/conf/conf/conf12-m3, accessed April 14, 2014.

Benner, P. (1984) *From Novice to Expert: Excellence and Power in Clinical Nursing Practice*. (London: Addison-Wesley).

Benner, P. (2000) *From Novice to Expert: Excellence and Power in Clinical Nursing Practice* (London: Prentice Hall).

Benner, P. E., Kyriakidis, P. H. and Stannard, D. (2011) *Clinical Wisdom and Interventions in Acute and Critical Care: A Thinking-in-action Approach*. 2nd edn (New York: Springer).

Bleakley, A. (2000) 'Writing with Invisible Ink: Narrative, Confessionalism and Reflective Practice', *Reflective Practice*, 1 (1): pp. 11–24.

Bolton, G. (2010) *Reflective Practice: Writing and Professional Development* (London: Sage).

Boreham, N., Samurcay, R. and Fischer, M. (eds), (2002) *Work Process Knowledge*. (London: Routledge).

Boros, S. (2009) *Exploring Organisational Dynamics* (London: Sage).

Borton, T. (1970) *Reach, Touch and Teach* (London: McGraw Hill).

Boud, D. (2006) 'Creating the Space for Reflection at Work' in D. Boud, P. Cressey and P. Doherty (eds), *Productive Reflection at Work* (Oxon: Routledge): pp. 158–169.

Boud, D. (2010) *Relocating Reflection in the Context of Practice* (URI: http://hdl. handle.net/10453/14325). Available at http://www.leeds.ac.uk/educol/ documents/155666.pdf, accessed January 20, 2015.

Boud, D., Cressey P., (2006) 'Setting the Scene for Productive Reflection at Work' in D. Boud, P. Cressey and P. Doherty (eds), *Productive Reflection at Work* (Oxon: Routledge): pp. 3–10.

Boud, D., Keogh, R. and Walker, D. (1985) 'Promoting Reflection in Learning: A Model' in D. Boud, R. Keogh and D. Walker (eds), *Reflection: Turning Experience into Learning* (London: Kogan Page): pp. 18–40.

Boud, D. and Middleton, H. (2003) 'Learning from Others at Work: Communities of Practice and Informal Learning', *Journal of Workplace Learning*, 15 (5): pp. 194–202.

Boud, D. and Walker, D. (1990) 'Making the Most of Experience', *Studies in Continuing Education*, 12 (2): pp. 62–80.

Boud, D. and Walker, D. (1993) 'Barriers to Reflection on Experience' in D. Boud, R. Cohen and D. Walker (eds), *Using Experience for Learning* (Buckinghamshire: Society for Research into Higher Education and Open University Press).

Boud, D. and Walker, D. (1998) 'Promoting Reflection in Professional Courses: The Challenge of Context', *Studies in Higher Education*, 23 (2): pp. 191–206.

Brackenreg, J. (2004) 'Issues in Reflection and Debriefing: How Nurse Educators Structure Experiential Activities', *Nurse Education in Practice*, 4 (4): pp. 264–270.

Branch, W. T. (2010) 'The Road to Professionalism: Reflective Practice and Reflective Learning', *Patient Education and Counselling*, 80 (3): pp. 327–332.

Brechin, A. (2000) 'Introducing Critical Practice' in A. Brechin, H. Brown and M. Eby (eds), *Critical Practice in Health and Social Care* (London: Sage Publications): pp. 25–47.

Breidensjö, M. and Huzzard, T. (2006) 'Reflecting on Workplace Change', in D. Boud, P. Cressey and P. Doherty (eds), *Productive Reflection at Work* (Oxon: Routledge): pp. 157–169.

Brookfield, S. (1995) *Becoming a Critically Reflective Teacher* (San Francisco, CA: Jossey Bass).

Bullman, C. (2013) 'Getting Started on a Journey with Reflection' in Bullman and S. Schutz (eds), *Reflective Practice in Nursing* (Oxford: Wiley Blackwell): pp. 201–224.

Businessballs.Com (2014a) *Johari Window.* Available at http://www.businessballs.com/johariwindowmodel.htm, accessed March 24, 2014.

Businessballs.Com (2014b) *SWOT Analysis.* Available at http://www.businessballs.com/swotanalysisfreetemplate.htm, accessed March 24, 2014.

Butts, J. B. and Rich, K. L. (2013) *Nursing Ethics: Across the Curriculum and into Practice* (3rd edn). (Burlington MA: Jones & Bartlett Learning).

Carper, B. A. (1978) 'Fundamental Patterns of Knowing in Nursing', *Advanced Nursing Science*, 1 (1): pp. 13–23.

Carrington, S. and Selva, G. (2010) 'Critical Social Theory and Transformative Learning: Evidence in Pre-service Teachers' Service-learning Reflection Logs', *Higher Education Research & Development*, 29 (1): pp. 45–57.

Carter, B. (2013) 'Reflecting in Groups', in Bullman and S. Schutz, S. (eds), *Reflective Practice in Nursing* (Oxford: Wiley Blackwell): pp. 93–120.

Chien, W.T., Chan, S. W.C. and Morrissey, J. (2002) 'The Use of Learning Contracts in Mental Health Nursing Clinical Placement: An Action Research', *International Journal of Nursing Studies*, 39 (7): pp. 685–694.

Coffey, A. (2005) 'The Clinical Learning Portfolio. A Practice Development Experience in Gerontological Nursing', *Journal of Clinical Nursing*, 14 (8b): pp. 75–83.

Constantinou, M. and Kuys, S. S. (2013) 'Physiotherapy Students Find Guided Journals Useful to Develop Reflective Thinking and Practice During Their First Clinical Placement: A Qualitative Study', *Physiotherapy*, 99 (1): pp. 49–55.

Cooper, L. (2009) 'Values Based Mental Health Nursing Practice', in P. Callaghan, J. Playel and L. Cooper (eds), *Mental Health Nursing Skills* (Oxford: Oxford University Press).

Critical Thinking.Net (2014) Available at http://www.criticalthinking.net/index.html accessed April 14, 2014.

Dalmau, M. C. and Gudjónsdóttir, H. (2002) 'Framing Professional Discourse with Teachers: Professional Working Theory' in J. Loughran and T. Russell (eds.), *Improving Teacher Education Practices Through Self-Study* (London: Routledge Falmer): pp. 13–29.

Davidhizar, R. (1993) 'Self-confidence: A Requirement for Collaborative Practice', *Dimensions of Critical Care Nursing*, 12: pp. 218–222.

Davies, S. (2012) 'Embracing Reflective Practice', *Education in Primary Care*, 23 (1): pp. 9–12.

Dawber, C. (2013) 'Reflective Practice Groups for Nurses: A Consultation liaison Psychiatry Nursing Initiative: Part 2 – the Evaluation', *International Journal Mental Health Nursing*, 22 (3): pp. 241–248.

Department of Health (DOH) (2013) *Code of Conduct for Healthcare Support Workers and Adult Social Care Workers in England.* Available at http://www.skillsforhealth.org.uk/about-us/news/code-of-conduct-and-national-minimum-training-standards-for-healthcare-support-workers/, accessed April 14, 2014.

Dewey, J. (1933) *How We Think: A Restatement of the Relation of Reflective Thinking to the Educative Process* (Boston: DC Heath).

Dewey, J. (1938) *Experience & Education.* (New York: Kappa Delta Pi).

Dolan, G. (2003) 'Assessing Student Nurse Clinical Competency: Will We Ever Get It Right?' *Journal of Clinical Nursing*, 12 (1): pp. 132–141.

Driessen, E., Tartwijk, J., Overeem, K. et al. (2005) 'Conditions for Successful Reflective Use of Portfolios in Undergraduate Medical Education', *Medical Education*, 39: pp. 1230–1235.

Driscoll, J. (2007) *Practising Clinical Supervision: A Reflective Approach for Healthcare Professionals.* 2nd edn (Edinburgh: Bailliere Tindall Elsevier).

Duffy, A. (2008) 'Guided Reflection: A Discussion of the Essential Components', *British Journal of Nursing*, 17 (5): pp. 13–26, 334–339.

Edwards, C. (2007) 'Reflective Practice on Placement' in C. Knott and Scragg (eds), *Reflective Practice in Social Work* (Exeter: Learning Matters): pp. 102–113.

Ennis, R. H. (2010) 'Definition of Critical Thinking: Reasonable Reflective Thinking Focused on Deciding What to Believe Or Do', *Critical Thinking.Net*, Available at http://www.criticalthinking.net/definition.html, accessed April 14, 2014.

Facilitating Reflective Practice (2014) Available at http://learning.cf.ac.uk/peerreview/prlt-facilitating-reflective-practice/ accessed 10th April 2014.

Farren, M. (2004) *The Transformative Potential of Individuals' Collaborative Self-Studies for Sustainable Global Networks of Communications American Educational Research Association Annual Conference.* April 12–16, 2004, in San Diego.

Field, J. (2011) 'Researching the Benefits of Learning: The Persuasive Power of Longitudinal Studies', *London Review of Education*, 9 (3): pp. 283–292.

Field, J. (2012) 'Transitions in Lifelong Learning: Public Issues, Private Troubles, Liminal Identities' *Studies for the Learning Society*, 2–3. ISSN 1736–7107, available at: http://dspace.stir.ac.uk/bitstream/1893/7380/1/SLS%20fulltext.pdf, accessed 20 January 2015.

Flaming, D. (2000) 'Using Phronesis Instead of "Research-based Practice" as the Guiding Light for Nursing Practice', *Nursing Philosophy*, 2 (3): pp. 251–258.

Fleming, A. (2014) *Values Clarification Exercise.* Available at www.amandafleming.co.nz/, accessed April 14, 2014.

Fook, J. (2012) *Social Work: A Critical Approach to Practice.* 2nd edn (London: Sage).

Fook, J. (2013) 'Implementing Critical Reflection in Health and Social Care' in J. Fook and F. Gardner (eds), *Critical Reflection in Context. Applications in Health and Social Care* (Oxon: Routledge): pp. 233–241.

Fook, J. and Askeland, G. A. (2006) 'The "Critical" in Critical Reflection' in S. White, J. Fook and F. Gardner (eds), *Critical Reflection in Health and Social Care.* (Berkshire: Open University Press): pp. 40–53.

Fook, J., White, S. and Gardner, F. (2006) 'Critical Reflection: A Review of Contemporary Literature and Understandings' in S. White, J. Fook and F. Gardner (eds), *Critical Reflection in Health and Social Care* (Berkshire: Open University Press): pp. 3–20.

Freire, P. (1970) *Pedagogy of the Oppressed* (London: Penguin Press).

Freshwater, D. (2005) 'Reflexivity and Intersubjectivity in Clinical Supervision: On the Value of Not-knowing' in C. Johns and D. Freshwater (eds), *Transforming Nursing Through Reflective Practice*, 2nd edn (Oxford: Blackwell Publishing): pp. 99–113.

Freshwater, D. and Rolfe, G. (2001) 'Critical Reflexivity: A Politically and Eethically Engaged Research Method for Nursing', *NT Research*, 6 (1): pp. 526–538.

Frost, S. (2006) 'Recasting Individual Practice Through Reflection on Narratives' in S. White, J. Fook and F. Gardner (eds), *Critical Reflection in Health and Social Care* (Berkshire: Open University Press): pp. 107–117.

Fulton, Y. (1997) 'Nurses' Views on Empowerment: A Critical Social Theory Perspective', *Journal of Advanced Nursing*, 26 (3): pp. 529.

Gardner, F. (2014) *Being Critically Reflective* (Basingstoke: Palgrave Macmillan).

Gardner, F. and Taalman, E. (2013) 'Critical Reflection and Supervision' in J. Fook and F. Gardner (eds), *Critical Reflection in Context: Applications in Health and Social Care* (Oxon: Routledge).

Gibbs, G. (1988) *Learning by Doing: A Guide to Teaching Learning Methods* (Oxford: Oxford Brookes University).

Habermas, J. (1971) *Knowledge and Human Interests* (Boston: Beacon Press).

Hargreaves, J. and Page, L. (2013) *Reflective Practice* (Cambridge: Polity Press).

Hartog, M. (2004) *A Self Study of a Higher Education Tutor: How Can I Improve My Practice?* Unpublished Ph.D. Thesis University of Bath. Available online at http://people.bath.ac.uk/mnspwr/doc_theses_links/m_hartog.html, accessed February 14, 2014.

Hecimovich, M. D. and Volet, S. E. (2009) 'Importance of Building Confidence in Patient Communication and Clinical Skills among Chiropractic Students', *The Journal of Chiropractic Education*, 23 (2): pp. 151–164.

Henter, R. and Indreica, E. S. (2014) 'Reflective Journal Writing as a Meta-cognitve Tool' *International Conference of Scientific Paper Afases*. Brasov, 22–24 May 2014: pp. 547–553. Available at http://www.afahc.ro/ro/afases/2014/socio/henter_indreica.pdf, accessed January 25, 2015.

Herbig, B., Büssing, A. and Ewert, T. (2001) 'The Role of Tacit Knowledge in the Work Context of Nursing', *Journal of Advanced Nursing*, 34 (5); pp. 687–695.

Horton, K., Tschudin, V. and Forget, A. (2007) 'The Value of Nursing: A Literature Review', *Nursing Ethics*, 14 (6); pp. 716–740.

House of Commons, Children's, Schools and Families Committee (2009) *Training of Children and Families Social Workers. Volume 11: Seventh Report of Session 2008–2009* (London: TSO, The Stationary Office).

Howatson-Jones, L. (2010) *Reflective Practice in Nursing* (Exeter: Learning Matters).

Høyrup, S. (2004) 'Reflection as a Core Process in Organisational Learning', *The Journal of Workplace Learning*, 16 (8): pp. 442–454.

Høyrup, S. and Elkjaer, B. (2006) 'Reflection: Taking It beyond the Individual' in D. Boud, P. Cressey and P. Doherty (eds), *Productive Reflection at Work* (Oxon: Routledge): pp. 3–10.

Hull, C. J. and Redfern, L. (2005) *Profiles and Portfolios a Guide for Health & Social Care* (Basingstoke: Palgrave Macmillan).

Hunink, M., Glasziou, P., Siegel, J., Weeks, J. Pliskin, J. Elstein, A. and Weinstein, M. (2001) *Decision Making in Health and Medicine: Integrating Evidence and Values* (Cambridge: Cambridge University Press).

International Council of Nurses (2012) *Code of Ethics*. Available at http://www.icn.ch/about-icn/code-of-ethics-for-nurses/, accessed April 15, 2014.

Jasper, M. (2005) 'The Challenges of Healthcare Leadership in Britain Today' in M. Jasper and M. Jumaa (eds), *Effective Healthcare Leadership* (Oxford: Blackwell).

Jasper, M. (2013) *Beginning Reflective Practice*. 2nd edn (Hampshire: Cengage Learning).

Jasper, M. A. (1999) 'Nurses' Perceptions of the Value of Written Reflection', *Nurse Education Today*, 19 (6): pp. 452–463.

Jasper, M. and Mooney, G. (2013) 'The Context of Professional Development' in M. Jasper, M. Rosser and G. Mooney (eds), *Professional Development, Reflection and Decision-Making in Nursing and Healthcare*. 2nd edn (Oxford: Wiley-Blackwell).

Jasper, M., Rosser, M. and Mooney, G. (2013) *Professional Development, Reflection and Decision-Making in Nursing and Healthcare*. 2nd edn (Oxford: Wiley-Blackwell).

Jasper, M., Timmins, F., Curtis, E., O'Sullivan, K. Rolfe, G. and Cromie, S. (2012) 'Exploring Contemporary Debates in Reflection and Reflective Practice in Nursing', *NET 2012 23rd International Participative Conference for Education in Health Care*, September 4–6, 2012, (Cambridge: Robinson College, 5).

Johns, C. (1996) 'Visualizing and Realizing Caring in Practice Through Guided Reflection', *Journal of Advanced Nursing*, 24 (6): pp. 1135–1143.

Johns, C. (1999, 2004, 2013) *Becoming a Reflective Practitioner* (Oxford: Blackwell Publishing Ltd.).

Johns, C. (2006) *Engaging Reflection in Practice* (Oxford: Blackwell Scientific Publications).

Johnson, G., Scholes, K. and Whittington, R. (2007) *Exploring Corporate Strategy*. 8th edn (Harlow: Prentice Hall).

Jones-Boggs, K. (2008) 'Perceived Benefits of the Use of Learning Contracts to Guide Clinical Education in Respiratory Care Students', *Respiratory Care*, 53 (11): pp. 1475–1481.

Joyce-McCoach, J. T., Parrish, D. R., Andersen, P. R. and Wall, N. (2013) 'Unlocking Reflective Practice for Nurses: Innovations in Working with

Master of Nursing Students in Hong Kong', *Nurse Education in Practice*, 13 (5): pp. 388–392.

Kim, S. H. (1999) 'Critical Reflective Enquiry for Knowledge Development in Nursing Practice', *Journal of Advanced Nursing*, 29 (5): pp. 1205–1212.

Knott, C. (2007) 'Reflective Practice Revisited' in C. Knott and Scragg (eds), *Reflective Practice in Social Work* (Exeter: Learning Matters): pp. 3–12.

Knott, C. and Spafford, J. (2007) 'Getting Started' in C. Knott and Scragg (eds), *Reflective Practice in Social Work* (Exeter: Learning Matters): pp. 13–29.

Knowles, M. S. (1989) *The Adult Learner: A Neglected Species*. 3rd edn (Houston: Gulf Publishing Company).

Kolb, D. A. (1984) *Experimental Learning* (London: Prentice Hall).

Kuit, J. A., Reay, G. and Freeman, R. (2001) 'Experiences of Reflective Teaching', *Active Learning in Higher Education*, 2 (2): pp. 128–142.

Laing, L. and Humphries, C. (2013) *Social Work & Domestic Violence* (London: Sage Publications Ltd.).

Laming, L. (2003) *The Victoria Climbié Inquiry*. Presented to Parliament by the Secretary of State for Health and the Secretary of State for the Home Department by Command of Her Majesty. Available at https://www.gov.uk/government/uploads/system/uploads/attachment_data/file/273183/5730.pdf.

Levett-Jones, T. (2007) 'Facilitating Reflective Practice and Self-assessment of Competence Through the Use of Narratives', *Nurse Education in Practice*, 7 (7): pp. 112–119.

Linehan, M. (2008) *Education in Employment. Work Based Learning Graduating Through the Workplace* (Cork: CIT Press).

Lipp, A. (2004) 'Reflexivity: A Method of Research and Professional Development', *Journal of Advanced Perioperative Care*, 2 (2): pp. 55–58.

Lowry, M. (1997) 'Using Learning Contracts in Clinical Practice', *Professional Nurse*, 12 (4): pp. 280–283.

Lyons, N. (2010) 'Reflection and Reflective Inquiry: Critical Issues, Evolving Conceptualizations, Contemporary Claims and Future Possibilities' in N. Lyons (ed), *Handbook of Reflection and Reflective Inquiry: Mapping a Way of Knowing for Professional Reflective Inquiry* (New York: Springer): pp. 3–24.

Macdonald, J. and Hills, L. (2005) 'Combining Reflective Logs with Electronic Networks for Professional Development among Distance Education Tutors', *Distance Education*, 26 (3): pp. 325–339.

Mackintosh, C. (1998) 'Reflection: A Flawed Strategy for the Nursing Profession', *Nurse Education Today*, 18 (7): pp. 553–557.

Manning, A., Cronin, P., Monaghan, A. and Rawlings-Anderson, K. (2008) 'Supporting Students in Practice: An Exploration of Reflective Groups as a Means of Support', *Nurse Education in Practice*, 9 (3): pp. 176–183.

McBrien, B. (2007) 'Learning from Practice – Reflections on a Critical Incident', *Accident and Emergency Nursing*, 15 (3): pp. 128–133.

McCabe, C. and Timmins, F. (2013) *Communication Skills for Nursing Practice*. 2nd edn (Basingstoke: Palgrave Macmillan).

McCray, J. (2007) 'Reflective Practice for Collaborative Working' in C. Knott and Scragg (eds), *Reflective Practice in Social Work* (Exeter: Learning Matters): pp. 130–142.

McCarthy, T. (2002) 'The Critical Theory of Jürgen Habermas' in D. M. Rassmussen and J. Swindal (eds), *Jürgen Habermas*. Vol. 1 (London: Sage Publications): pp. 3–31.

McCauley, V. and McClelland, G. (2004) 'Further Studies in Self-directed Learning in Physics at the University of Limerick, Ireland', *International Journal of Self-Directed Learning*, 1 (2): pp. 26–37.

McGee, C. M. (2005) *Phronesis in the Habermas vs. Gadamer Debate*. Available at http://www.mcgees.net/fragments/essays/archives/Phronesis.in.the.Habermas.vs.Gadamer.Debate.html, accessed August 30, 2005.

Mezirow, J. (1981) 'A Critical Theory of Adult Learning and Education', *Adult Education*, 32: pp. 3–24.

Miller, L. (2014) 'Reflective Practice for Appraisal and Revalidation in General Practice: Towards New Learning and Improved Patient Safety?' *Education in Primary Care*, 25 (2): pp. 119–121.

Miller, L., Divall, S. and Maloney, A. (2012) 'Using the Learning Log to Encourage Reflective Practice', *Education in Primary Care*, 23 (1): pp. 50–55.

Moon, J. (1999) *'Reflection in Learning and Professional Development Theory and Practice* (London: Kogan Page).

Muncy, J. A. (2014) Blogging for Reflection: The Use of Online Journals to Engage Students in Reflective Learning', *Marketing Education Review*, 24 (2): pp. 101–113.

Nagayda, J., Schindehette, S., et al. (2005) *The Professional Portfolio in Occupational Therapy Career Development and Continuing Competence* (Thorofare, NJ: Slack Incorporated).

National Council for the Professional Development of Nursing and Midwifery (2009) *Guidelines for Portfolio Development for Nurses and Midwives* (3rd edn). (Dublin: National Council for the Professional Development of Nursing and Midwifery).

National Council for Nursing and Midwifery (NCNM) (2008) *Code of Conduct*. Available at http://www.nmc-uk.org/Publications/Standards/The-code/Introduction/, accessed April 15, 2014.

Nelson, S. (2012) 'The Lost Path to Emancipatory Practice: Towards a History of Reflective Practice in Nursing', *Nursing Philosophy*, 13 (3): pp. 202–213.

Nursing and Midwifery Council (NMC) (2008) *Standards to Support Learning and Assessment in Practice*. 2nd edn (London: Nursing and Midwifery Council).

NMC (2010a) *Standards of Proficiency for Pre-registration Nursing Education* (London: NMC). Available at http://www.nmc-uk.org/Publications/Standards/, accessed January 22, 2015.

NMC (2010b) *Standards for Competence for Registered Nurses* (London: NMC). Available at http://www.nmc-uk.org/Publications/Standards/, accessed January 22, 2015.

NMC (2011) *The PREP Handbook* (London: NMC). Available at http://www.nmc-uk.org/Documents/Standards/NMC_Prep-handbook_2011.pdf, accessed January 22, 2015 and http://www.nmcuk.org/Documents/Standards/nmcStandardsToSupportLearningAndAssessmentIn Practice.pdf.

O'Donovan, M. (2006) 'Reflecting During Clinical Placement – Discovering Factors That Influence Pre-registration Psychiatric Nursing Students', *Nurse Education in Practice*, 6 (3): pp. 134–140.

Oelofsen, N. (2012) *Developing Reflective Practice. A Guide for Students and Practitioners of Health and Social Care* (Banbury: Lantern Publishing).

Pearce, R. (2003) *Profiles and Portfolios of Evidence* (Cheltenham: Nelson Thornes).

Polanyi, M. (1969) *Knowing and Being Essays by Michael Polanyi* (London: Routledge & Kegan Paul).

Polanyi, M. (1974) *Personal Knowledge Towards a Post – Critical Philosophy* (Chicago: The University of Chicago Press).

Redmond, B. (2006) 'Starting as We Mean to Go on: Introducing Beginning Social Work Students to Reflective Practice' in S. White, J. Fook and F. Gardner (eds), *Critical Reflection in Health and Social Care* (Berkshire: Open University Press): pp. 211–227.

Roberts, P. (2003) 'Emerging Selves in Practice: How Do I and Others Create My Practice and How Does My Practice Shape Me and Influence Others?' Unpublished Ph.D. Thesis University of Bath, UK.

Rogers, C. R. (1969) *Freedom to Learn* (Columbus, OH: Merrill Publishing Company).

Rolfe, G. (2002) 'Reflective Practice Where Now?' *Nurse Education in Practice*, 2 (1): pp. 21–29.

Rolfe, G., Jasper, M. and Freshwater, D. (2011) *Critical Reflection for Nursing Generating Knowledge for Care*. 2nd edn (Basingstoke: Palgrave Macmillan).

Ruch, G. (2009) 'Introduction – Developing Holistic Social Work Practitioners' in G. Ruch (ed.), *Post-Qualifying Child Care Social Work: Developing Reflective Practice* (London: Sage): pp. 3–7.

Ruch, G. (2009a) 'Reflective Practice and Reflective Spaces' in G. Ruch (ed.), *Post–Qualifying Child Care Social Work: Developing Reflective Practice* (London: Sage): pp. 19–30.

Ruch, G. (2009b) 'Introduction: Developing Holistic Social Work Practitioners' in G. Ruch (ed.), *Post-Qualifying Child Care Social Work: Developing Reflective Practice* (London: Sage): pp. 3–7.

Rushton, D. and Duggan, C. (2013) 'Impact of Culture on Reflective Writing in Masters Level Students', *Procedia Social and Behavioral Sciences Journal*, 93: pp. 956–963.

Saarikoski, M., Marrow, C., Abreu, W., Riklikiene, O. and Ozbicakçi, S. (2007) 'Student Nurses' Experience of Supervision and Mentorship in Clinical Practice: A Cross Cultural Perspective', *Nurse Education in Practice*, 7 (6): pp. 407–415.

Schön, A. (1983) *The Reflective Practitioner: How Professionals Think in Action* (London: Temple Smith).

Schutz, S. (2013) 'Assessing and Evaluating Reflection' in Bullman and S. Schutz (eds), *Reflective Practice in Nursing* (Oxford: Wiley Blackwell): pp. 201–224.

Serembus, J. F. (2000) 'Teaching the Process of Developing a Professional Portfolio', *Nurse Educator*, 25 (6): pp. 282–287.

Shulman, L. S. (2005) 'Signature Pedagogies in the Professions', *Dedalus*, 134 (3): pp. 52–59.

Smith, R. (1995) *Derrida and Autobiography* (Cambridge: Cambridge University Press).

Stebbins, M., Freed, T., Rami Shami, A. B. and Doerr, K. H. (2006) 'The Limits of Reflexive Design in a Secrecy-based Organisation' in D. Boud, P. Cressey and P. Doherty (eds), *Productive Reflection at Work* (Oxon: Routledge): pp. 81–92.

Stephens, K. and Winterbottom, M. (2010) 'Using a Learning Log to Support Students' Learning in Biology Lessons', *Journal of Biological Education*, 44 (2): pp. 72–80.

Sternberg R. J. (1999) 'What Do We Know about Tacit Knowledge? Making the Tacit Become Explicit' in R. J. Sternberg and J. A. Hovarth (eds), *Tacit Knowledge in Professional Practice Researcher and Practitioner Perspectives* (Mahwah, NJ: Lawrence Erlbaum Associates, Inc.): pp. 231–236.

Sweeney, B. and Mc Cormack, D. (2013) *Caring for the Dying: Can we do it Better?* 32nd Annual International Nursing & Midwifery Research & Education Conference, February 20–21, 2013: p. 4. Available at http://www.rcsi.ie/files/facultyofnursingmidwifery/20130725040938_Book%20of%20Abstracts%202013.pdf.

Tarnas, R. (1991) *The Passion of the Western Mind* (New York: Ballantine Books).

Taylor, B. (2006) *Reflective Practice: A Guide for Nurses and Midwives* (Buckingham: Open University Press).

The Critical Thinking Community (2014a) *Our Concept and Definition of Critical Thinking*. Available at http://www.criticalthinking.org/pages/our-concept-and-definition-of-critical-thinking/411, accessed May 5, 2014.

The Critical Thinking Community (2014b) *Critical Thinking and Nursing*. Available at http://www.criticalthinking.org/pages/critical-thinking-to-think-like-a-nurse/834, accessed April 14, 2014.

The Mid Staffordshire NHS Foundation Trust (2013) *Report of the Mid Staffordshire NHS Foundation Trust Public Inquiry Executive Summary* (London: HMSO The Stationery Office). Available at http://www.mid-staffspublicinquiry.com/sites/default/files/report/Executive%20summary.pdf, accessed January 13, 2014.

Thompson, C., McCaughan, D., Cullum, N., Sheldon, T., Mulhall, A. and Thompson, D. R. (2001) 'The Accessibility of Research-based Knowledge for Nurses in United Kingdom Acute Care Settings?' *Journal of Advanced Nursing*, 36 (1): pp. 11–22.

Thomsen, B. D. and Chraudin, M. (2013) *A Reflection Model for Sensing And Development of Experience*. E&DPE 2013, 15th International Conference on Engineering and Product Design Education, September 5– 6, 2013, Dublin, Ireland: Dublin Institute of Technology, pp. 560–565.

Tierney, A. J. (1998) 'Nursing Models Extant Or Extinct?' *Journal of Advanced Nursing*, 8 (1): pp. 77–85.

Timmins, F. (2008) *Making Sense of Portfolios: An Introduction to Portfolio Use for Nursing Students* (Glasgow: Open University Press, McGraw-Hill Education).

Timmins, F. and Duffy, A. (2011) *Portfolio: A Guide for Nurses in Practice* (Glasgow: Open University Press, McGraw-Hill Education).

Timmins, F. and Dunne, P. (2009) 'An Exploration of the Current Use and Benefit of Nursing Student Portfolios', *Nurse Education Today*, 29: pp. 330–341.

Timmins, F., Howe, R., Dennehy, C. and Murphy, M. T. (2013) '*I Hate GIBB's Reflective Cycle 1988* (Facebook© 2009): Registered Nurses Experiences of Supporting Students' Reflective Practice in the Context of Nursing Students' Public Commentary', *Procesia Social and Behavioral Sciences Journal*, 93: pp. 1371–1375.

Timmins, F. and Neill, F. (2013) 'Teaching Communication and Reflection to Undergraduate Nursing Students: An Audit of Student Performance', *Procesia Social and Behavioral Sciences Journal*, 93: pp. 1368–1370.

Timmins, F. and Nicholl, H. (2005) 'Stressors Associated with Nurses Undertaking Part-time Degree Programmes – Some Implications for Managers to Consider', *Journal of Nursing Management*, 13 (6): pp. 477–482.

Todres, L., Galvin, K. T. and Holloway, I. (2009) 'The Humanization of Healthcare: A Value Framework for Qualitative Research', *International Journal of Qualitative Studies on Health and Well-being*, 4: pp. 68–77.

Tunney, G. (2009) 'The PQ Framework, PQ and CPD Developments: Consolidation Unit, Introduction' in G. Ruch (ed.), *Post-Qualifying Child Care Social Work: Developing Reflective Practice* (London: Sage): pp. 8–17.

University of Cumbria (2014) Jack Whitehead. Available at http://www.cumbria.ac.uk/Courses/SubjectAreas/Education/Meetthestaff/CPDResearch/JackWhitehead.aspx, accessed April 10, 2014.

University of Hull (2015) *Tips for Writing a Reflective Learning Log for an Assignment*. Available at http://www.google.ie/url?sa=t&rct=j&q=&esrc=s&source=web&cd=1&ved=0CCAQFjAA&url=http%3A%2F%2Fvle.westking.ac.uk%2Fpluginfile.php%2F41761%2Fmod_folder%2Fcontent%2F0%2FEssay%2520and%2520report%2520writing%2FTips%2520for%2520writing%2520reflective%2520logs.pdf%3Fforcedownload%3D1&ei=QUzFVL_yHOvV7Qb9s4GwBw&usg=AFQjCNH2sooJVTJBs1RDyco plTl6d8SrFA&bvm=bv.84349003,d.ZGU,accessed January 21, 2015.

University of Leicester (2014) David Kolb. Available at http://www2.le.ac.uk/departments/gradschool/training/eresources/teaching/theories/kolb, accessed March 21, 2014.

University of Nottingham (2014) Driscoll (by Borton). Available at http://www.nottingham.ac.uk/nmp/sonet/rlos/placs/critical_reflection/models/driscoll.html, accessed April 10 2014.

University of Technology, Sydney (2014) David Boud. Available at http://www.uts.edu.au/staff/david.boud, accessed April 14, 2014.

Vachon, B. and LeBlanc, J. (2011) 'Effectiveness of Past and Current Critical Incident Analysis on Reflective Learning and Practice Change', *Medical Education*, 45 (9): pp. 894–904.

Watson, S. (2002) 'The Use of Reflection as an Assessment of Practice. Can You Mark Learning Contracts?' *Nurse Education in Practice*, 2 (3): pp. 150–159.

Wenger, E. (1998) *Communities of Practice: Learning Meaning and Identity* (Cambridge: Cambridge University Press).

Wenger, E., McDermott, R. and Synder, W. M. (2002) *A Guide to Managing Knowledge Cultivating Communities of Practice* (Boston: Harvard Business School Press).

Whitehead, J. (1999) How do I Improve my Practice? Creating a Discipline of Education Through Educational Enquiry Unpublished Ph.D. Thesis Vol 1 University of Bath available online at: http://www.actionresearch.net/writings/phdok.pdf accessed 10th May 2015.

Whitehead, J. (2004) *Jack Whitehead's Ontological Commitments in Self-study: The Transformative Potential of Individuals' Collaborative Self-studies for*

Sustainable Global Educational Networks of Communication. A contribution to the AERA 2004 Symposium of the Self-Study in Teacher Education Practices, Special Interest Group on in San Diego on the 16th April, 2004.

Williams, R. M., Wessel, J., Gemus, M. and Foster-Seargeant, E. (2002) 'Journal Writing to Promote Reflection by Physical Therapy Students During Clinical Placements', *Physiotherapy Theory and Practice*, 18: pp. 5–15.

World Health Organization (WHO) (2010) *Framework for Action on Interprofessional Education and Collaborative Practice* (Geneva: WHO). Available at: http://www.who.int/hrh/resources/framework_action/en/, accessed January 22, 2013.

Xie, Y., Ke, F. and Sharma, P. (2008) 'The Effect of Peer Feedback for Blogging on College Students' Reflective Learning Processes', *The Internet and Higher Education*, 11: pp. 18–25.

Yang, S.-H. (2009) 'Using Blogs to Enhance critical Reflection and Community of Practice', *Educational Technology & Society*, 12 (2): pp. 1–21.

index

- the need to remove staff from their normal working environment (to free them from day-to-day work-related distractions; to help them think more creatively, in a different setting)
- the wish to reward staff by holding the event in an attractive location, usually with leisure elements added
- the need to keep proceedings confidential, when, for example, sensitive topics are under discussion.

The purpose of most corporations is to make money. They hold meetings to increase the chances for profit. Training executives and motivating sales people, for example, are carried out by companies because they believe that these activities will help make the company more profitable.

Corporate meetings events may take a number of different forms, including the following.

Annual general meetings: publicly owned companies invite their shareholders (or stockholders) to these events, at which the company's annual results are presented. Shareholders are usually asked to approve the dividend and to endorse a certain number of resolutions, which will determine the company's activities in the year ahead. Every shareholder who wants to take part in the decision-making process of his company can attend such meetings and vote personally.

Sales meetings: a sales meeting is a regular forum used by management to impart information, enthusiasm and team spirit to those selling their products and services 'out in the field'. Sales figures for a particular period are generally reviewed, and the achievements of particularly high-performing sales staff are recognized and praised. The type of information imparted generally concerns the company's market share, competitors' activities or new legislation that affects the selling process. Such meetings also give those present the opportunity to share their experiences, positive and negative, of selling.

Staff training: it is generally recognized that, in order to keep their skills and knowledge up to date, company management and staff must regularly attend training sessions in subjects such as information technology, customer relations skills and employment law. Frequently, these are held in seminar rooms that are situated off-site, bringing business to suppliers such as hotels and management training centres.

Retreats: A term used, until very recently, only to signify a temporary withdrawal from everyday life for the purpose of religious contemplation and meditation, the word 'retreat' is now commonplace in corporate language, meaning an off-site, usually residential, board meeting. But such events differ from regular off-site board meetings in a number of ways:

- Instead of moving quickly through a rigid agenda, board members spend their time at a retreat concentrating on specific long-term issues or thinking more broadly and strategically about the future of their organization
- Retreats are designed to spark creative thought
- Retreats can be an effective way to teach new members of staff about a company's goals and customs
- Retreats often make use of outdoor settings that are conducive to walking and reflecting on what is happening during the event
- Time for social interaction is a vital element: teambuilding activities are often requested. Outside facilitators may be used.

Product launches: introducing a new product or service to the market is an important stage in the marketing process. A new car, new perfume, new type of medical insurance … whatever the product, companies often use an off-site event as a way of presenting it and explaining its properties and features to those who will be selling it, who may be buying it, and to journalists in the specialist press who may write about it for their readers. Such events are usually short but with high production levels, using special effects, sound and vision, in order to make the maximum impact on the audience.

Incentive trips: it is widely recognized that an extremely effective way of motivating and rewarding staff is by offering them the opportunity to participate in an incentive trip, as the prize for exceptional achievement in their work. This exceptional achievement may take the form, for example, of selling more of the company's products than other colleagues during a particular period. These trips, often held in exotic and lavish locations, may look like holidays, and indeed they are designed to be highly enjoyable and memorable; but they are firmly considered to be business events, since they are in essence a management tool, designed to elicit higher levels of performance from the company's employees.

When incentive trips are combined with a work element – usually one or more meetings that take place during the trip – such events may be known as 'concentives' – a combination of a conference and an incentive trip.

Association buyers

Among the largest and the longest conferences held throughout the world are association events. The several million different associations, clubs, federations and societies that exist throughout the world constitute another major segment of demand for conference services. These are generally non-profit groups, whose members affiliate with one another because they share a common profession, trade, or interest in a specific cause. Many of these organizations are trade associations and professional bodies and one of their functions is to help their members maintain the professionalism of the business or industry to which they belong. Associations may draw their members locally, regionally, nationally or internationally – and the geographical spread of their membership will determine the location of their meetings events.

Almost all associations hold regular meetings for a variety of purposes, but most often these are training/information sessions or the association's annual conference, offering members the opportunity to meet for one or more days in order to discuss matters of importance to their profession or their common cause. Meetings by trade unions would be included in this sector of demand.

One major difference between the corporate market and the association market for conferences is that while, for company buyers, conferences and meetings represent a cost to the company, for associations, conferences normally represent a source of funds. This is because – again, in contrast to the corporate meetings market – they charge their members for attending events. Many associations depend on the income from their annual conference to pay for many of the ongoing costs of running the association – staff salaries, headquarters rental, and so on.

Government and public sector buyers

Governments at all levels, from local municipalities to the international, intergovernmental scale, as well as public sector bodies such as those administering national health services, are also an important source of demand for conference facilities and services. The development of effective policies through consultation and negotiation is a key function of political activity, and conferences are often used as the medium for carrying out this process, bringing together the various stakeholders concerned by the proposed legislation.

At the international level, many of these conferences are high-profile events, with extensive media coverage – such as the European Union's Intergovernmental Conferences, at which the member states negotiate in order to reform the founding treaties of the EU; or the conferences sponsored by the United Nations and its agencies – for example, the World Summit on Sustainable Development held in Johannesburg, South Africa in 2002.

Once created, governments' new policies and measures have to be launched, in much the same way that companies' new products and services are launched, and this also generates regular business for the conference industry. One of the objectives of such events is to attract the attention of the media, in order to publicize new government measures. A typical example of such an event was the launch, in March 2005, of the UK government's new sustainable development strategy, 'Securing the Future'. To coincide with the publication of the strategy document, an official launch event was held at the Imagination Gallery in London, at which the Prime Minister and several other government ministers were present.

SMERF buyers

SMERF is the name given to conferences held in the Social, Military, Educational, Religious and Fraternal sectors. Often included in the association sector, as not-for-profit organizations, SMERF buyers are occasionally recognized (in North America in particular) as a discrete category of demand for conferences. SMERF meetings occur when groups travel and congregate for a wide range of purposes such as reuniting, fraternizing, or simply to share their common memories, experiences or faith. A random sample of SMERF events from around the world demonstrates that there is practically no limit to their variety in terms of size and themes:

- The 3000-person assembly of the Presbyterian Church (US): to be held in San Jose in 2008
- The 'Battle for Malta' Veterans' Reunion with 600 attendees, all of them veterans of the military campaign: in Malta over a 7-day period in September 2006
- The annual convention of twins, triplets and quadruplets, with 2000 attendees: held in the town of Pleucadeuc in the French region of Brittany
- The National Barbie Doll Collectors' Convention, with over 1000 collectors: in Boston 13–16 July 2005.

Given the very different characteristics of each of the conference market segments discussed above, it is clear that each segment requires different marketing strategies to be adopted by the destinations and venues targeting its buyers.

The key characteristics of these four principal market segments are summarized in Table 1.1.

Delegates

With the notable exception of those attending corporate meetings – for whom participation is usually obligatory – most people who are invited to conferences have the choice between attending or not attending. Delegates, also known as attendees, participants and guests, are therefore the ultimate buyers, or end consumers, of the conference product. Without the continuing participation of delegates, the conference

Table 1.1 Characteristics of the different market segments

Corporate	Association	Government	SMERF
The process of deciding where to hold events is relatively straightforward	The process of choosing a destination can be prolonged	Considerable variety in terms of length of event and budgets available	Price-sensitive, regarding accommodation rates and venue rates; but more recession-proof than corporate meetings
But the actual corporate meeting buyer may be difficult to identify within the initiator's organization: secretaries, personal assistants, marketing executives, directors of training and many others may book corporate meetings	A committee is usually involved in the choosing of the destination; and the organizers may be volunteers from the association's membership	However, budgets are usually scrutinized, since public money is being used	Held by organizations that are run by volunteers – so the task of identifying them can be challenging
Attendance is usually required of company employees	Attendance is voluntary. The annual convention may be booked many years in advance	High security measures are indispensable: these meetings are frequently accompanied by demonstrations and disruption	Frequently held over weekends and in off-peak periods
Lead times can be short.	Events typically last 2–4 days		Often held in 2nd-tier cities, using simple accommodation and facilities
Events typically last 1–2 days	A lower budget per delegate, since for some attendees, price is a sensitive issue and they may be paying their own costs		Attended by delegates who bring their spouses/families and are likely to extend their trips, for leisure purposes
A higher budget per delegate			
Venues used: hotels, management training centres, unusual venues	Venues used: conference centres, civic and academic venues		
Delegates' partners are rarely invited, except in the case of incentive trips	Delegates' partners frequently attend		

industry cannot function, and it is therefore vital that delegates' experience of the conference product is a satisfactory one.

But the experience of the individual delegate is largely dependent on choices made by other stakeholders, notably the initiators of the event and the intermediaries working on their behalf. These are the stakeholders who select the destination, the venue, the accommodation and other key features of the conference product such as the speakers and the social programme. Thus, delegates' level of satisfaction with a conference usually depends on their response to a range of individual elements that have been 'packaged' together for their purchase and over which they have little control.

Most conference buyers and organizers understand the importance of satisfying the end consumer of their events, and for that reason, post-conference evaluation, using questionnaires for example, is frequently carried out. It is clear that delegates' needs from conferences must be satisfied if they are to return to such events in the future and recommend others to attend. This is an ongoing challenge for the entire conference industry.

The suppliers

Supply-side stakeholders are those who supply the facilities and services that are essential to the effective operation of a conference. For each type of supplier specified below, the marketing function is vital to business success. Responsibility for the marketing of these suppliers' services and facilities can range from one person who undertakes all of the marketing tasks discussed in this book, to an entire department managed by a marketing director with specialized staff such as market researchers and sales staff working for him/her.

Venues

Conferences, at the most basic level, require closed space in which the event can be accommodated and seats for the delegates. The meetings venues that provide these facilities are, therefore, an essential element of the conference market. Several types of venue have already been mentioned in this chapter. Purpose-built conference centres are the most visible type of venues, and indeed most conferences of several hundred or more delegates are held in such locations. But in fact by far the vast majority of meetings are still held in seminar rooms and conference facilities within hotels. These can range from small independent establishments with a single 'function room' to a venue such as the Hilton-Americas Houston, that city's largest convention hotel, with over 1200 guest rooms and 92000 square feet of meeting space.

In addition, meetings are increasingly hosted by a growing variety of venues, for many of which, conferences are a secondary, but nevertheless important, commercial activity. These include universities, museums, theatres and cruise ships as well as a whole range of tourist attractions such as theme parks that offer their facilities for meetings of all kinds. The term 'unusual venues' is often used to describe some of the more exotic locations used for meetings events. Product launches and team-building events, in particular, often seek unusual venues to make the events more attractive and memorable.

In the supply of venues, public sector as well as private sector operators are important stakeholders. National, state-level, regional and municipal governments throughout the world are involved in the construction and operation of conference facilities; while the private sector, from family-run hotels to multinationals such as Starwood, Marriott International and Accor, are also key players in the provision of meetings space.

Accommodation providers

Residential conferences and other business events lasting more than one day require some form of accommodation for delegates, speakers and organizers. In many cases, the venue itself may be equipped to provide the accommodation – as in the case of hotels, residential conference centres, universities and cruise ships, for example.

But when venues without on-site accommodation are used, the conference organizer must ensure that an adequate supply of lodging – of the appropriate standard – is available. In that case, organizers may identify a single 'conference hotel' or may provide delegates with a list of local, approved, hotels or guest houses that they recommend.

Organizers may book a 'block' of rooms with a particular hotel or hotels, to ensure that their delegates can be accommodated close to the actual conference. By undertaking to fill a substantial number of a hotel's rooms for several days, conference organizers may avail themselves of a valuable negotiating tool with which to discuss rates for the rooms themselves as well as the conference facilities if they are within the same hotel. However, this approach assumes that:

- the organizer is able to determine with some degree of accuracy how many rooms will be required, and
- that delegates will book the rooms in the hotel in which the 'block' has been reserved.

Organizers as well as providers of accommodation are becoming increasingly aware that these two conditions cannot be taken for granted. In particular, the phenomenon of delegates 'booking outside the block' (often using the Internet to find lower hotel rates) is becoming more prevalent.

Other suppliers

A number of other support services can contribute to the successful operation of conferences.

Transport providers are responsible for carrying delegates to and from the conference destination and for providing transport services within the destination, notably through venue/hotel transfers. Rail and coach operators, taxis and limousines can all be involved in providing these services. For international events, air travel is usually the chosen means of transport for most delegates and this can raise the challenge, for both organizers and transporters, of dealing with groups: determining in advance the size of the group booking and the names of the passengers. For corporate groups, and in particular for incentive events, this information may not become available until the last minute, therefore some degree of flexibility is required of the airline.

Caterers play a key role in providing delegates with food and beverages (F&B). The quality (and quantity) of F&B is often a talking point between delegates during and after the event, and can be a serious source of delegate dissatisfaction if it falls short of expectations. Conference meals and refreshment breaks serve a number of purposes beyond sustaining the delegates. For example, they provide opportunities for them to network with each other in a more relaxed setting; or they supply the context for entertainment or the participation of celebrity speakers, as in the case of the conference gala dinner, for example.

Technical services such as the provision of audio-visual equipment and expertise are vital to the effective functioning of most modern conferences. Sophisticated sound, lighting and data-projection equipment are essential elements of meetings events, and these must either be supplied by the venue or, increasingly, leased by the organizers from specialized conference equipment hire companies. Indeed, the pace of technological progress is now so rapid that many venues and organizers prefer to hire technical equipment and support, to ensure that they always have access to the most up-to-date material. Conference video production companies may also be used, to film the proceedings, then edit and produce a video that can be used as an effective way of extending the scope of the event.

The range of other suppliers is extensive, and can include the conference interpreters who make international conferences accessible to all, regardless of their linguistic abilities; the companies that hire out interpreting booths; and the florists who decorate the conference stage, the gala dinner tables, and who provide 'thank you' bouquets for VIPs and guest speakers.

The intermediaries

While some buyers in the conference market deal directly with suppliers – for example when a secretary calls a hotel to book a seminar room for a one-day meeting for managers in his or her company – a vast proportion of all conferences take place with the involvement of some form of intermediary or intermediaries. These are the stakeholders who form a link between buyers and suppliers, and the effective functioning of the conference market depends on their specialist skills and knowledge.

It is useful to consider intermediaries in two categories: those working on behalf of suppliers and those working for buyers.

Intermediaries working on behalf of suppliers

Destination marketing organizations

Although most suppliers of facilities and services for the conference industry actively market themselves directly to potential buyers – either individually or through marketing consortia – they usually understand that the success of their own business is partly dependent on the image and reputation of the destination in which it operates. In a highly competitive world, with no shortage of suitable locations for meetings, it is generally easier to attract conferences and other business events to a well-marketed destination. The responsibility for promoting individual destinations to potential buyers lies with the destination marketing organization (DMO). In general, DMOs are responsible for attracting not only business events but also leisure tourists to the destination, and hence the term 'tourism' or 'visitor' is often included in the names of individual DMOs.

DMOs fall into one of the following categories:

- National Tourism Authorities (NTAs) or National Tourism Organizations (NTOs), responsible for the management and marketing of tourism at a national level
- Regional, provincial or state DMOs (Regional Tourism Organizations), responsible for the management and/or marketing of tourism in a geographic region defined for that purpose, sometimes but not always an administrative or local government region such as a county, state or province
- Local DMOs, responsible for the management and/or marketing of tourism based on a smaller geographic area or city/town.

The structure of these bodies changes from country to country and from city to city. In particular, how DMOs relate to governments and where they find their funding varies considerably. A worldwide survey of DMOs (WTO, 2004) found that, for the 250 DMOs surveyed:

> *The simplest status models exist at the NTO and NTA level, where 88% of organizations are either a department of National Government or an agency accountable to National Government. Four of the NTOs/NTAs are not for profit public–private partnerships.*
>
> *At a regional level the status of organizations is more varied. The majority are accountable to regional, provincial or state government, either as an agency or in fewer cases (18%) as a department of local government. However, 37% have private sector involvement (21% within a public–private partnership), which is much higher at the regional level than the national level.*
>
> *39% of City DMOs have regional, provincial or local government accountability, and the percentage of public private partnerships (33%) and profit driven companies (6%) is highest in this sector.*

At all levels, DMOs may have a dual function of promoting their destinations to the leisure market, as well as the market for conferences and other business events. The proportion of DMO resources devoted to attracting conferences varies considerably from destination to destination. However, it is extremely rare for any destination to ignore the conference market entirely.

Convention and Visitor Bureaux

The use of the term Convention and Visitor Bureau (CVB), which originated in the US, is becoming widespread throughout the world. In this book, this term will be used to refer to the type of not-for-profit destination marketing organization that is responsible for stimulating interest in the destination, so that conference buyers may choose to hold their events there, or so that intermediaries may recommend them to their clients. (It should be pointed out, however, that those responsible for marketing their destination for conferences may work in tandem with colleagues whose role it is to market the same destination for leisure: holidays, short-breaks, day-trips, etc.)

As well as being responsible for promoting a favourable image of their destination, CVBs can also serve as the focus to unify the marketing efforts of the various suppliers operating in the area they cover and provide a shared sense of direction and unity to a range of individual marketing programmes.

With this function in mind, Harrill (2005) describes CVBs as 'umbrella' marketing or promotional agencies, under which the extensive collection of businesses that promote their own products and services stand. This is often referred to as a 'consolidated' approach to marketing, the principle being that consolidated efforts provide greater strength and unity and therefore enhanced results; while segmented, fragmented individual marketing programmes yield less impact and success.

The CVB function may be undertaken at any geographic level: a country, a region within a country, or a specific town or city. Although, as stated at the beginning of this chapter, the original CVB concept was created in the US at the end of the 19th century, the first *national* CVBs were founded in Europe many years later. The German Convention Bureau, established in 1973, and the Finland Convention Bureau, established in 1974, were, for example, two of the first national convention bureaux in Europe.

However, the vast majority of CVBs operate at the level of the individual city or town, operating on behalf of the suppliers there, to attract conference business to that locality, thus filling the meetings venues, bringing guests to hotels and attracting clients for local restaurants, shops and the other service providers discussed above. It is difficult to estimate the number of CVBs that exist around the world, and their numbers are constantly growing as more and more cities market themselves as new conference destinations. But the trade body Destination Marketing Association International (previously known as the International Association of Convention & Visitor Bureaus) counts over 500 CVBs in its membership.

In some cases, individual CVBs join forces to market a particular region that is considered to be recognized as a single destination for the purposes of tourism and conferences. For example, the French Riviera Convention Bureau operates in concert with the CVBs of Antibes, Cannes and Nice to promote the Côte d'Azur as a conference destination.

Whatever the geographical scope of their responsibilities, CVBs derive their funding from one or more of the following sources:

- public sector contributions
- hotel (or lodging) transient occupancy taxes

- membership fees (from members, such as venues, accommodation providers, transport operators, etc.)
- contributions from members participating in joint commercial activities
- commission charged to venue members in return for conference business placed with them, by the CVB.

Most published surveys on this issue primarily reflect the situation of CVBs in the US, which has by far the largest numbers of bureaux in the world. However, there are fundamental differences between continents with regard to how CVB operations are financed.

Research undertaken by Koutoulas (2005) reveals a number of key comparisons between bureaux based in and outside the US:

- Both US and non-US CVBs achieve similar average revenue. The average annual budget of CVBs based outside the US is €5380188 as compared to €5315615 (US$6.4 million) of US-based bureaux.
- Non-US bureaux receive less public funding and tax income than their US counterparts (67.5% of total income for non-US, compared with 84% for US-based bureaux). The share of private sources is therefore twice as high in the case of non-US bureaux than US-based CVBs (32.5% as opposed to 16% of total income, respectively). Private sources of funding include membership dues, advertising, promotional participation, print and jointly-funded advertising, donated (non-cash) services, interest etc.
- Bureaux in the US and elsewhere spend about the same share of their budget for marketing purposes (56.4% by non-US bureaux vs. 53% by US-based CVBs).
- Non-US bureaux employ an average of 23.6 full-time staff members. The average staff size of US-based CVBs is 18 full-time employees.
- 60% of non-US bureaux accept individual businesses as their members, compared with 51% of US-based CVBs.

The major source of public income of US-based bureaux is the local transient tax, a tax that can be imposed upon visitors, with one of its specific objectives being to fund the marketing of the destination to future visitors. Revenue collected in this way either can go directly to the relevant CVB or can be included in its funding provided by local authorities. Such hotel room taxes have been used since the 1950s to fund both the construction and operation of conference centres as well as the activities of CVBs in the US. The importance of this tax for CVB funding in the US becomes clear when surveys show that, on average, 88% of US CVBs receive around three-quarters of their funding from hotel occupancy taxes (Gehrisch, 2004).

US-based CVBs receive, on average, a 54% share of locally collected room taxes. The mean hotel tax rate in the US is 12.2%. Other taxes that may be used to finance bureau operations and/or tourism promotion include car rental taxes (with an average rate of 9.4%) and restaurant taxes (with an average rate of 7.9%) (Koutoulas, 2005).

While the concept of being funded by a tax dedicated to subsidize the costs of destination marketing may be attractive for some CVBs, the system of collecting transient occupancy taxes has not been widely adopted outside the US. Koutoulas (2005) suggests one reason for this:

> *It would be quite challenging to persuade local tourism associations that the benefits of introducing a tax outweigh any costs such as becoming a more expensive destination. Even when stakeholders and legislators agree with its introduction, it would be challenging to establish an efficient mechanism to enforce and collect the tax.*

Private sources of funding are therefore likely to remain imperative for most CVBs operating outside the US, for the foreseeable future.

The marketing activities on which CVBs spend their funding are a major theme of this book, and will be considered in detail in later chapters.

Intermediaries working on behalf of buyers

Although some associations and companies use their own staff to organize events, most buyers rely on the expertise and experience of a range of professional intermediaries. This is partly the case when the conference to be organized is large and complex, when it demands technical knowledge, or when it is to be held far from the company's or association's office – notably overseas.

In these cases, buyers are able to draw on the specialist skills and knowledge of a range of intermediaries who can work on their behalf.

Professional conference organizers (independent meetings planners)

Professional conference organizers (PCOs) are independent, specialist meetings planners who work on a consultancy basis, being temporarily hired by associations and companies to organize a specific event or series of events. In return for a fee, they can offer a very comprehensive range of services, including:

- Venue selection, booking and liaison
- Reservation and management of delegate accommodation
- Event marketing, including the design of conference programmes and promotional materials, PR and media co-ordination, presentations to organizing committees and boards
- Conference programme planning, speaker selection and briefing
- Provision of an administrative secretariat, handling delegate registrations, recruitment and briefing of conference staff
- Co-ordinating of delegates' travel arrangements
- Organization of exhibitions, including sales and marketing functions
- Advising on and co-ordinating audio-visual services and the production of the event, including the provision of multilingual interpretation and translation services
- Arranging social events, tour programmes and technical visits
- Arranging security cover and advising on health and safety issues
- Recording, transcribing and producing the proceedings of meetings for publication, arranging poster sessions, processing of abstracts
- Preparation of budgets, managing event income and expenditure, generating revenue through sponsorship, exhibitions and satellite meetings, handling VAT and insurance issues
- Preparation of contracts with venues and other suppliers.

Venue-finding services

VFSs – sometimes known as conference placement agencies – provide a much more limited service, yet one that is extremely valuable to any buyer who simply needs a few suggestions of where their meeting could be held. They therefore save their clients (most commonly, companies) time and effort by finding them suitable venues for their events.

VFSs generally begin by asking their client specific questions regarding their requirements for the event being planned: its date, location, the number of delegates and the budget for the event. They then undertake the necessary research and produce a number of options for venues that match the client's requirements, followed by a quotation and possibly a brochure for each venue short-listed by them. The VFS may also set up viewing appointments for their client.

In the majority of cases, this service is provided free to the client, as the VFS derives its commission from the venue booked. Many conference venues obtain the major part of their business from VFSs, who can be a valuable source of repeat business for them.

Association management companies

Managing an association involves undertaking a considerable number of tasks: attracting and maintaining members, financial management, public relations and lobbying on behalf of members, providing educational and training opportunities for members, publishing the annual report and association newsletters, and organizing the annual conference and other events. Traditionally, these activities have been undertaken either by volunteer staff drawn from the association's own membership or, in the case of large associations, by full-time salaried staff based in the headquarters.

However, in the past few decades, many associations have become aware of the limitations of both of these models of association management. On the one hand, volunteer staff appear to have less and less time available for association-related duties – and in some cases lack the experience and expertise necessary to carry out their tasks effectively; on the other hand, maintaining full-time staff and office facilities can result in a major investment in overheads for associations.

As the need for the effective and professional management of associations has become increasingly recognized, many of them have turned to an alternative concept of association management – the association management company (AMC).

An AMC is a firm of skilled professionals whose goal is to provide management expertise and specialized administrative services to trade associations and professional societies in an efficient, cost-effective manner. Based on the concept of shared resources, an AMC provides volunteer organizations with the expertise they need when they need it, usually assigning specific executives and administrators to conduct each client association's day-to-day operations.

An AMC also provides a centralized office that serves as the client association's headquarters, and the overhead costs for these offices are shared by all of the AMC's client associations and societies. In this way, the need for individual associations to make major capital investment in their own headquarters and staff is obviated.

One of the key tasks undertaken by AMCs on behalf of their association clients is the organizing of their annual conference and other events for members. In this respect, AMCs must employ staff with similar professional expertise and experience to that required by PCOs. AMCs are growing in importance as intermediaries between association buyers of conferences and those who supply the facilities and services that make such events possible.

Destination management companies

Most organizers of large, complex conferences could not do their jobs effectively without using the skills and knowledge of a destination management company (DMC) – particularly when the conference is being held in a destination with which the organizer is unfamiliar. Also known as 'ground handlers', these intermediaries are agencies that are based at the destination in which the event takes place, and their valuable contribution to the conference planning process derives from their in-depth knowledge of the destination including their familiarity with local suppliers of conference-related services and their knowledge of the language and customs of the destination. DMCs act, therefore, on behalf of PCOs, AMCs and other event planners, as the prime local contractor for logistical services. They can provide assistance with a range of services, including:

- Creative proposals for special events within the meeting
- Pre-and post-conference tours
- VIP amenities and transportation
- Shuttle services
- Staffing within the conference centre
- Entertainment, such as after-dinner speakers
- On-site registration services
- Accommodation services.

Conference production companies

For high-profile events requiring advanced specialist technical facilities and expertise, conference organizers often use the services of conference production companies. These intermediaries are valuable sources of the ideas and inspiration necessary to making meetings memorable – particularly important in the case of events such as product launches, awards ceremonies and other motivational events.

Creativity and technical knowledge are the qualities that production companies bring to the successful operation of conferences and they are particularly valued for the services they provide in the fields of:

- design and printing of conference materials
- lighting, sound, projection, stage/set design
- script writing
- video production
- web-streaming.

It is clear from the above list of professionals that an extensive range of specialist knowledge and skills is available to buyers of conference and other business events.

However, three important points arise from the preceding description of intermediaries' roles:

- The roles of these intermediaries are not always as clearly delineated and differentiated as outlined above. As will be seen in Chapter 11, terminology in the conference sector is still far from precise, and this is nowhere more evident than in the titles used by the different intermediaries. In most countries, all of these professions are unregulated, and this fact, coupled with a lack of firm demarcations for most conference-related occupations, means that there is considerable scope for agencies to offer their clients services that go beyond their specific field of expertise. For example, many venue finding services, destination management companies and conference production companies will readily offer to undertake tasks more commonly associated with a PCO, such as managing the budget for the conference and dealing with matters such as protocol and insurance.
- In many cases, two or more of these intermediaries are working together to make the conference a success. In particular, PCOs need to draw upon the expertise of DMCs and conference production companies for certain events. In those cases, the PCO becomes a subcontractor, assigning certain aspects of the event planning and production process to other agencies.

- Although some buyers may go directly to venues and other suppliers, this is the exception rather than the rule. The planning of most conferences involves the participation of one or more intermediary working on behalf of the buyer. As a consequence, suppliers very often have to market to, and negotiate with, a range of intermediaries as well as the actual buyers of the event. The next section examines the particular challenges of marketing in the conference sector.

Marketing destinations and venues

It is clear from the preceding section that the effective functioning of the conference, convention and business events market depends on the interaction of two forces, demand and supply, where the demand-side stakeholders are represented by the buyers of conferences and the supply-side stakeholders are those offering the facilities and services required for the successful operation of such events.

If the conference market is the process of interaction between these buyers and sellers, then what is marketing itself? The Chartered Institute of Marketing gives a broad definition as follows:

> *Marketing is the management process responsible for identifying, anticipating and satisfying customer requirements profitably.*

A number of key points may be developed out of this definition.

Marketing is considered to be a process (not just a particular marketing technique or series of techniques) that is concerned with satisfying customer (buyer) needs. This particular philosophy – based on the belief that those suppliers who anticipate customers' needs and respond to them first and/or best will be those that succeed – is often referred to as the 'marketing orientation' that characterizes the approach taken by most modern suppliers of products and services.

However, the conference industry, in common with many other sectors of the economy, has evolved through at least two earlier marketing stages before adopting a marketing orientation. That evolution, related to the changing supply and demand relationships and the competitive conditions prevailing during earlier stages of capitalism, is summarized below.

Production orientation

This level is characterized by a shortage of supply, when suppliers' priority is to produce maximum volumes by increasing output. Such an approach only works effectively when a business operates in very high growth markets when goods and services sell easily, in other words, a sellers' market. It is generally accepted that, for Europe and the US, the production orientation was the dominant manufacturing business philosophy from the beginning of capitalism until the mid 1950s, during which time there was a shortage of manufactured goods relative to demand.

For the conference industry in Europe and the UK, this era lasted longer as the demand for conference venues and other services continued to exceed supply into the 1980s.

Sales orientation

A sales orientation tends to be used when supply out-paces demand, leading to a buyer's market, in which there may be a downward pressure on prices. In these market conditions, businesses concentrate on persuading customers to buy the available stock, using selling, pricing and promotion strategies. However, little attention is paid to customers' needs and wants. Economists trace the beginning of the sales orientation era for the manufacturing sector to the mid 1950s, by which time supply was starting to outpace demand in many industries. This arose as a consequence of converting industrial plant from wartime production to the production of consumer goods at the end of the Second world war.

But it may be argued that the supply of conference facilities and services did not exceed demand until the beginning of the 1990s, when a global recession coincided with the first conflict in the Gulf. These events dealt a severe blow to venues of all types, who found themselves with an enormous amount of spare capacity at the same time as buyers were negotiating from a position of power not previously witnessed in the conference market.

Marketing orientation

In the 21st century, the marketing orientation firmly prevails in most sectors of the economy in most parts of the world – including the world-wide conference industry. This is an approach that allows the wants and needs of customers and potential customers to drive all of an organization's strategic decisions, so that its entire corporate culture is systematically committed to creating customer value. This is also an approach that requires the full support of the entire organization – not only its marketing department.

The rationale behind adopting a marketing orientation is that the more an organization understands and meets the real needs of its consumers, the more likely it is to have satisfied customers who bring it repeat business and/or recommend the organization's products and services to others. In this way, this process can entail the fostering of long-term relationships with customers. In order to determine customer wants and needs, the organization usually needs to conduct market research, which, if carried out correctly, may provide the company with a sustainable competitive advantage.

Recognizing the way in which marketing had evolved, the American Marketing Association in 2004 announced a new definition of marketing (this was only the second time that the AMA's official definition had been changed by the association since 1935):

> *Marketing is an organizational function and a set of processes for creating, communicating and delivering value to customers and for managing customer relationships in ways that benefit the organization and its stakeholders.*

The conception of marketing as a process (or set of processes) is maintained, as is the emphasis on delivering customer satisfaction and on the benefits to the organization undertaking the marketing. But there is a new emphasis on the use of marketing to manage customer *relationships*, as well as the need to bring benefits to the organization's *stakeholders* more broadly.

Customer relationship management is an important theme of this book, and it will be considered in detail in Chapter 5. But the question of bringing benefits to stakeholders is particularly relevant to the destination marketing that is undertaken by CVBs.

It has been stated earlier in this chapter that CVBs work on behalf of the suppliers in the city or region or country. However, as bodies in receipt of public funding, they also have a wider responsibility to the host community – those who live and work in the territory covered by the CVB – as well as to the natural environment of the destination. All members of the host community, therefore, may be regarded as important stakeholders whose general well-being should be taken into account by the organization that is responsible for the marketing of the place where they are located.

When a CVB, a venue, or indeed any organization, accepts this wider responsibility to the welfare of the community and to the protection of the natural environment and takes these into account in its approach to its marketing, it may be said that it is adopting a *societal marketing orientation*, a fourth level in the hierarchy of the evolution of marketing approaches. Kotler *et al.* define this concept as:

> *The idea that an organization should determine the needs, wants and interests of target markets and deliver the desired satisfactions more effectively and efficiently than competitors* in a way that maintains or improves the consumer's and society's well-being.
>
> (2003: 882; emphasis added)

Clearly, for organizations adopting a societal marketing orientation, the marketing orientation, as described above, is maintained; but a new, broader, responsibility to stakeholders is introduced at this fourth level.

Pike (2004: 13) elaborates on this definition of societal marketing and emphasizes its relevance to the tourism (and, by association the conference) sector. He states that the societal marketing approach adheres to a marketing orientation

> *but [is] operationalized in a way that also considers the well-being of society and the environment. DMOs, as representatives of a host community and natural environment as well as commercial tourism services, have such a wider societal obligation.*

However, even when the societal marketing orientation is, explicitly or implicitly, adopted by a CVB or by an individual venue in its programme of promotional activities, there is no guarantee that all stakeholders at the destination will benefit from the positive impacts that the conference industry can bring to a destination. Neither is this approach to marketing a way of ensuring that all stakeholders will be protected from the negative impacts that can be created by conference activity.

These positive and negative impacts are the subject of the final section of this chapter.

The impacts of the conference industry

All industries and all human activities have impacts, which can be positive or negative. These impacts may be seen primarily in changes to the state of the economy, to the natural and built environment, and to people's quality of life and the culture of society in the widest sense.

For each impact, a number of different stakeholders may be affected, positively or negatively. In this section, the principal impacts of the conference industry are reviewed.

Economic impacts

One of the primary motivations for a community developing any industry are the economic benefits expected to result from that industry. It is generally accepted that the conference sector is a high-yield, year-round market, and it is the possibility of reaping substantial economic gains that represents the main motivating factor that has spurred so many destinations to pursue proactively the conference market. However, as well as economic benefits, there may be also considerable costs incurred by any community targeting this sector.

Many commentators have acknowledged that a continuing problem for conference destinations is that of *quantifying* the benefits and costs associated with this market. For example Dwyer (2002: 21) points out that:

> little hard data are available upon which to estimate the precise magnitude of these effects. This is unfortunate because decisions about resource allocation by both private and public sector stakeholders greatly depend on accurate information regarding potential gains.

Nevertheless, a number of government statistical agencies, tourist boards, CVBs and industry associations are engaged in the attempt to estimate the economic impacts of the conferences that are held within the territories they cover. One such attempt to quantify the economic contribution of the conference industry is undertaken on an annual basis by the Convention Industry Council, in the US (see Figure 1.1).

The main economic impacts are reviewed below.

Positive economic impacts

Foreign exchange earnings

Smith (1990: 68) quotes a US city mayor who extols the economic benefits of the conference industry as follows:

> When we have a convention in town, it is as if an airplane flew overhead dropping dollar bills on everyone.

When these conference dollar bills are spent by visitors to the city, this means that 'new' spending is coming into local businesses such as shops, restaurants, entertainment centres and taxis. Furthermore, when a proportion of the delegates originate from abroad, their spending represents a boost in foreign exchange earnings for the destination.

For nations dependent on attracting foreign income, a single international conference can make a substantial impact on the national economy. For example, the six-day International Bar Association Conference, an event attended by international lawyers, held in New Zealand in 2004, injected almost $NZ20 million into the economy, according to a report by Horwath Asia Pacific Ltd. The report also shows that 65% of delegates participated in pre- or post-tour options, spending $NZ407 each per day during this time.

Contribution to government revenues

Conference-related spending results in benefits, not only for individual companies, but also local and national governments. Government revenues from the conference sector can be categorized as either direct or indirect contributions. *Direct* contributions are generated by taxes on incomes from employment in the conference industry, taxes on the profits of businesses operating in this sector, and by direct levies on conference delegates such as airport departure taxes. *Indirect* contributions are those originated from taxes and duties levied on goods and services supplied to delegates, such as VAT (value added tax) charged on the champagne consumed at a conference reception.

In the US, the Convention Industry Council (CIC) has as its members over 15 000 companies and venues involved in the conference and business events industry. Formed in 1949 to provide a forum for member organizations seeking to enhance the industry, the CIC has as one of its roles the educating of the general public on the economic impact of this industry.

The CIC's 2004 Economic Impact Study, which provides a macroeconomic analysis of the industry's direct spending and contribution to employment in the US, claims that the conference and business events industry generated $122.31 billion in total direct spending in 2004, making it the 29th largest contributor to the US gross national product. That situated the industry above the pharmaceutical and medicine manufacturing sector and only slightly below the US nursing and residential care facilities industry.

The impacts from the industry's spending and tax revenue were felt in many sectors of local economies, from restaurants and transportation to retail stores and other services, and supported 1.7 million jobs in the US. According to the CIC Study, the conference and business events industry generated more than 36% of the hotel industry's estimated $109.3 billion in operating revenue, and its attendees accounted for nearly 17% of the air transportation industry's operating income.

The industry's total direct spending in 2004 was $122.31 billion. Direct Employment Impact, the number of full-time equivalent (FTE) jobs supported by the direct spending of the industry, was 1 710 000 jobs. And Direct Tax Impact rose to $21.40 billion.

Association-sponsored events accounted for two thirds, or $81.94 billion, of the direct spending industry total. Corporate-sponsored events (including incentive travel) accounted for the remaining one third, or $40.37 billion.

The largest share of the spending on conferences and business events (35%) was spent in hotels and other facilities. The rest was widely distributed throughout local economies. After air transportation (24%), the next principal beneficiaries of spending were: restaurant and outside catering food and beverage outlets (14%) and business services (12%).

Source: CIC, 2005

Figure 1.1 The Convention Industry Council's 2004 Economic Impact Study.

Employment generation

A wide range of employment is created by a thriving conference industry. As a service-sector, this industry can be labour-intensive, and is responsible for sustaining a significant proportion of the jobs found in the hotel and transport sectors, for example, as well as the specialist conference-related professions represented by all of the suppliers and intermediaries discussed earlier in this chapter. Although conference-related employment is often amalgamated, in statistical analyses, with the jobs generated by tourism and leisure, it tends to demonstrate slightly different patterns, notably in its less seasonal nature.

Stimulation of investment

The development of a conference industry can induce national and local governments to make infrastructure improvements such as better water and sewage systems, roads, electricity supply, telephone and public transport networks, all of which can improve the quality of life for residents as well as facilitate the expansion of the conference industry at the destination. Other industries may also be attracted by the improved infrastructure, leading to the type of inward investment so desired by many economies.

Negative economic impacts

While the positive economic impacts of conferences are generally visible – and increasingly proclaimed by the conference industry itself, there can also be significant hidden costs to developing and operating a conference industry, which can have a number of unfavourable economic effects on the host community.

Infrastructure costs

The development of the infrastructure necessary for the operating of a significant conference industry can cost national and local governments (and, by extension, taxpayers), a great deal of money and can require a substantial outlay of funds long before the first conference arrives in the destination. In order to equip the destination to receive large numbers of delegates, governments may have to improve airports, roads and other elements of the infrastructure. They may also have to provide tax breaks, investment incentives and other financial advantages to conference centre and hotel developers, for example.

This type of government spending may bring with it a significant 'opportunity cost', since public resources spent on subsidised infrastructure or tax breaks can reduce government investment in other critical areas such as education and health.

Promotional costs

In a competitive world, destinations must vie with one another to attract conferences and other business events. Promotion is generally undertaken by the types of destination marketing organizations discussed earlier in this chapter. A destination promoting itself to conference buyers and intermediaries may do so in tandem with its promotion of itself as a leisure destination; or it may create a separate entity. Either way, the vast majority of countries and cities around the world have some form of tourism organization or convention bureau that undertakes this task.

The costs of establishing and maintaining such organizations can be a considerable drain on the public resources of some countries, particularly when, as is often the case, offices must be maintained in key overseas markets. The Netherlands Board of Tourism & Conventions, for example, promotes that country as a conference destination through its offices in London, New York, Paris, Brussels, Stockholm, Milan, Madrid, Cologne and Tokyo. For a developing country, supporting such a network of offices in foreign cities would be a significant financial burden, and yet many do exactly that, in their efforts to attract conferences to their cities.

Leakage

Developed nations are often better able to profit from being a conference destination than are poor ones. One of the reasons for this is the developed nations' ability to retain a high proportion of the expenditure arising from the conferences that take place within their territory.

Dwyer (2002) emphasizes the importance of recognizing that not all conference-related expenditure is retained within the destination hosting the conference. 'Leakage' is the term given to income that is lost to the host destination because it 'leaks out' to other regions or to other countries. This can take several forms. For example, a significant amount of the economic benefits arising from the spending of delegates attending international conferences can go to foreign airlines and to international hotel chains based outside the host nation, when delegates use these instead of locally owned accommodation and the national airline of the host country. Similarly, nations that need to import goods from other countries, in order to service their conference sector, also experience leakage of the economic benefits. For example, a country that needs to import building materials and hotel equipment and furnishings in order to build a conference facility is automatically losing some of the gains accruing from its conference industry.

Large, developed nations with advanced and varied economic sectors suffer least from leakage, as they are able to produce most of what is required to establish and maintain a viable conference industry. The consequence is that while the least developed countries may have the most urgent need for the income, employment and rise in the general standard of living that can be generated by the conference industry, they are often the destinations that are least able to realize these benefits.

Environmental impacts

The quality of the environment, both natural and man-made, is important to the successful functioning of the conference and business events industry. Delegates expect a clean, attractive locality, and this is particularly true when there is a motivational element to the conference, as in the case of an incentivized meeting. However, the conference industry's relationship with the environment is complex, bringing both positive and negative impacts.

Positive environmental impacts

At the most basic level, towns and cities hosting conferences need to ensure that the physical environment is maintained in a clean, tidy and healthy condition, in just the same way that certain standards of housekeeping are required when receiving guests in one's home.

Knowing that delegates expect conference localities that are at least as clean and attractive as they find in their home towns, no conference planner would knowingly choose to hold an event in a destination in which the environment was degraded and unhygienic.

Beyond creating the need for municipalities to maintain the quality of their built and natural environment, the conference industry also has the potential to create beneficial effects on the environment of destinations by contributing to environmental enhancement and conservation. For example, many urban regeneration programmes throughout the world have been based on the construction of new conference centres in neglected and often derelict areas. For example, the Edinburgh International Conference Centre, which opened in 1995, was the showpiece of the regeneration of that city's Exchange Business District, a previously run-down area of Edinburgh, now entirely revitalized with the iconic EICC as its flagship development. Similarly, the Hilton San Diego Convention Center Hotel, located across from the San Diego Convention Center, is built on the site of the former Campbell Shipyard, which fell into disuse and extreme contamination before being cleared for hotel development, as part of its regeneration programme.

The conference industry has also contributed in no small measure to urban conservation initiatives, notably through the re-conversion into conference centres of buildings that might otherwise have been demolished. From private mansions to palaces and factories, countless examples of architecturally valuable buildings have been saved by their conversion into conference facilities. Ottawa's Government

Conference Centre is an outstanding example of this type of conservation, being converted from that city's former Union Train Station, which was designed in the Beaux-Arts style with a former monumental waiting room that was copied from the great thermal baths of Rome.

Negative environmental impacts

On first impressions, the conference industry, as a modern 'knowledge industry', would appear to be one that makes very little negative impact on the environment. After all, it has no factory smokestacks, releases no chemicals into the water and soil, and only uses, for its functioning, machines such as computers and photocopiers that account for a relatively modest proportion of energy consumption.

But on closer examination it becomes clear that the conference industry can indeed have a number of adverse environmental effects. Some of these impacts are linked with the construction of the infrastructure necessary for the hosting of events, and there are examples throughout the world, from Niagara Falls Convention Center in New York State to the Spanish city of San Sebastian's Kursaal Conference Centre (see Chapter 5), of venues that have been controversial in their design or in their location, or both.

Conferences may also be criticized at times for their use of natural resources, notably paper. For example, the paper required in order to present each of 500 delegates with a conference pack of information (the conference programme, list of delegates, print-offs of presenters' notes, etc.) can represent a substantial use of natural resources. Aware of the potential for this, and other forms of wastage, some venues have taken the initiative of offering advice to conference planners on how to minimize this (see Figure 1.2).

However, the most damaging impact made by the conference industry on the natural environment is now widely believed to be the energy use and the emissions associated with travel to meetings, in particular to international events. Most travel to international conferences uses air transport, and the negative environmental impacts from movements in the upper atmosphere are considerably greater than for movements at ground level. Globalization of the economy has greatly increased the volume of travel to international corporate events, and this situation has been mirrored in the growth of international and regional associations whose annual events also contribute significantly to the amount of air travel mobility around the globe.

Høyer and Nœss (2001: 467) have expressed their concern over this issue in unambiguous terms:

> *The increase in travel to international meetings forms one of the environmentally most worrying changes in the mobility of post-industrial society. It is a paradox that the consequences to global environmental problems from local transport have gradually been put higher on the environmental agenda, while there is virtually no focus on the long job-related journeys. For the individual conference participant, one such trip usually represents an amount of transportation larger than the total mobility for all other purposes during a whole year.*

While it is certainly true that the volume of travel for leisure purposes, such as holidays and visits to friends and relatives, far exceeds business- and conference-related travel, this fact by no means absolves the international conference industry from being a major contributor to the current and growing threat to the state of the global climate.

As an indication of how public concern over the impact of conference-related travel on global warming has grown, the UK Government decreed that the G8 Summit held in Gleneagles, Scotland, in June 2005 would be 'climate neutral'. The

The EICC website offers conference planners a number of ideas through which they can make their events more environmentally-friendly:

Pre event
- When producing literature for your event, use recycled and chlorine-free paper. Ensure paper is genuinely made from recycled stock – check for the NAPM approved logo.
- Give delegates information on the most efficient routes to both the conference destination and venue.
- Give consideration to the transportation of delegates around the city – use public transport and, if possible, organize a low-emission bus.
- When planning exhibitions, give consideration to how exhibition materials can be reused or recycled.
- During the organization of your event, use environmentally friendly methods of communication and promotion, such as e-mail and websites.
- When planning your refreshments, consider offering drinks in aluminium cans or glass bottles. These can then be sorted and collected for recycling.
- EICC can also provide water in recyclable plastic cups.
- Consider offsetting the carbon dioxide emissions created by your event.

During the event
- Remember the 3Rs – Reduce, Reuse and Recycle.
- Consider your energy use in the building – for example, switch off lights when rooms are not in use.
- EICC can recycle your non-contaminated paper and cardboard waste. Please remember to ask your Event Planner about this.

Some ideas from your organizer's office
- Photocopy double sided
- Photocopy/fax on used paper
- Do not print out e-mails unnecessarily
- Print drafts and internal documents on used paper
- Make your own note pads using scrap paper cut up and stapled together
- Only print when necessary
- Ensure you have done a spell check to avoid printing mistakes
- Make sure you don't print blank pages by mistake
- Make sure there is a recycling box near the printer/photocopier
- Make sure you know how to stop a print run if you do make a mistake
- Ensure you know how to cancel a job on the photocopier if you make a mistake when copying, especially during a large run
- Use a smaller font size where possible if you are printing

Source: www.eicc.co.uk

Figure 1.2 Edinburgh International Conference Centre's tips for greening an event.

government undertook to compensate for all of the greenhouse gases produced by delegates' travel to the G8 by investing £50 000 in green projects in Africa, to offset the environmental cost of the Summit.

Reconciling the demand for air travel to international conferences with the need to conserve energy use and prevent the further deterioration of the global climate will undoubtedly continue to be one of the major challenges facing the conference industry in the years ahead.

Social and cultural impacts

By definition, most conferences involve the influx of groups of people from other localities to the destination where the event is held. During the conference, therefore, two populations may come into contact with each other: the 'host' population (the local residents) and the 'guests' (the delegates themselves). In many cases, the delegates may be indistinguishable from the local people in terms of their physical appearance, manner of dress and visible level of prosperity, as well as their beliefs and general level of education. In that case, the social and cultural impacts can be minimal. However, a considerable gulf often exists between the different ways of life of host and guest, leading to the possibility of both positive and negative effects on both sides.

Positive social and cultural impacts

The rich literature on the social and cultural impacts of tourism demonstrates that many benefits can arise from the encounter of two different populations, and the conference industry offers many of the same advantages. The open and equal interaction between 'hosts' and 'guests' can generate a useful exchange of ideas and greater mutual understanding. Exposure to different traditions can be a progressive and liberating experience when, for example, the inhabitants of developing countries see female delegates interacting on an equal basis with their male colleagues.

Moreover, the very nature of most conferences, at which ideas are presented and discussed by those in attendance, lends itself to the sharing of views and the production of new intellectual capital. These are among the important yet intangible benefits of this industry, which ought never to be taken for granted.

Negative social and cultural impacts

Nevertheless, the negative impacts of the influx of large groups of people into host communities are also well documented.

These problems tend to be most exacerbated when there is a marked contrast in the standard of living between host and guest. It must be remembered that many conferences and other business events take place in destinations where a significant proportion of the local population is living in relative poverty in close proximity to the luxury hotels and palatial conference centres that provide the venues for such events.

Local people may easily come to perceive delegates to be privileged incomers who throw their own deprivation and hardship into sharp focus. And this is particularly true when the group of delegates is large and visible. Incentive groups are particularly vulnerable to being observed in this way. Davidson and Cope (2003: 183) note that:

> In the case of travel for conference or trade fair attendance, visitors spend most of their time indoors, engaging in activities that are related to their work. By comparison, the lavishly funded and occasionally frivolous activities indulged in by incentive travel award-winners run the risk of contrasting severely with the lifestyles and values of those living in some of the destinations chosen for incentive trips.

Sharp inequalities between the host and the temporary guest populations can produce a climate in which crime and exploitation can thrive, for the duration of the event. In unfamiliar surroundings, delegates can be the victims of such crime, suffering at the hands of pickpockets, muggers and fraudsters, for example. They can also exploit their own superior financial status over local people, and the relative anonymity that being in a new destination for a few days offers. The link between

> **Sex pros get ready for party**
>
> *By Jose Martinez, New York Daily News, June 28, 2004*
>
> With thousands of Republicans set to invade the city this summer, high-priced escorts and strippers are preparing for one grand old party. Agencies are flying in extra call girls from around the globe to meet the expected demand during the Aug. 30–Sept. 2 gathering at Madison Square Garden.
>
> 'We have girls from London, Seattle, California, all coming in for that week,' said a madam at a Manhattan escort service. 'It's the week everyone wants to work.'
>
> Charging from $300 to upwards of $1000 for an hour of companionship and a whole lot more, escorts said they can always count on conventioneers for big business.
>
> Political conventions have long been a boon for the sex industry.
>
> While many escort agencies operating on the sly out of Manhattan hotels and apartment buildings welcome the influx of potential customers, others are wary of increased police attention.
>
> Tracy Quan, author of the autobiographical novel, *Diary of a Manhattan Call Girl*, said she worries cops will crack down on the most visible sex workers: 'I get depressed whenever there's a big political convention because I know the street girls are going to be hassled, arrested and treated like criminals. All in the name of "cleaning up" our city for these people from out of town.'
>
> The players on the legal end of the city's sex industry have no such worries – and strip club owners are salivating at the prospect of crowds equipped with bunches of big bills. Clubs have started booking private parties for delegates anxious to ogle topless beauties after a day of watching fully clothed politicians boast about family values.

Figure 1.3 New York prepares for the 2004 Republican Convention.

conferences and prostitution is well established and is at its most evident in the case of political conventions, as suggested in the press article reproduced in Figure 1.3.

Summary

This chapter has introduced the conference industry in all its complexity. It has been shown to be a relatively young area of economic activity, involving a complex and broad range of stakeholders, some of whom – such as transport operators – depend only partly on conference business for their income. The extraordinary diversity of demand for conferences and meetings is matched by a wide range of suppliers providing facilities and services for the hosting and organizing of these events. In many cases, a destination marketing organization takes responsibility for promoting the destination as a whole and bringing together suppliers with buyers.

Marketing techniques themselves change over time, and current practices include focusing on the well-being of consumers and of society as a whole, not only on suppliers and their shareholders. But the conference industry, like all sectors, has a range of negative as well as positive impacts on the economy, the environment and on the lives of those working and living at the destinations where such events take place. A truly successful conference industry is one that is managed in such a way that the needs of all stakeholders are satisfied to the greatest extent possible.

Case Study 1.1

Access 2005, Vienna

The Austrian capital, Vienna, is a well-established and highly successful destination for conferences. In the ranking of the world's most popular conference cities published in 2005 by ICCA (International Congress and Convention Association), Vienna was in second place, after Barcelona and before Singapore, Berlin and Hong Kong. According to the UIA (Union of International Associations) league table for the same year, Vienna also sat in second place – after Paris, but just before Brussels and Geneva. But Austria itself is successful as a conference destination it its own right, appearing in the world top ten countries in the league tables of both ICCA and the UIA in 2005. It is estimated that conference travel to, and within, Austria generates an added value, for that country, of about one billion euro a year. In 2004, in Vienna the conference industry counted 1633 events which generated 888 000 overnights, amounting to 10.5% of the total overnights in Vienna, and generated 456 million euro.

Against this background of success as an international conference destination, the annual trade show for the conference sector took place in the prestigious setting of the Hofburg Congress Centre in Vienna on 3 and 4 October 2005. This was the second year that this event had taken place, and it once again brought together thousands of key stakeholders in the Austrian and international conference and incentive travel industry.

The event held particular significance in 2005, as Austria was due to take over the EU Presidency in the first six months of 2006. Linked to Austria's holding of the EU Presidency, 130 conferences and workshops were expected to take place in Austria according to current planning (MTS, 2005).

The annual Access event is an initiative taken by five partner organizations with an obvious interest in Austrian cities and towns being selected as destinations for conferences:

- ABCN (Austrian Business and Convention Network), the business tourism branch of the Austrian National Tourism Office
- the Austrian Convention Bureau (ACB)
- Austrian Airlines
- the Round Table Conference Hotels marketing consortium (RTK)
- the Vienna Convention Bureau (VCB).

Bringing together, in one venue for two days, both buyers and suppliers in the conference sector, Access aims to provide corporate and association buyers with information on Austrian cities and venues that are in the market for the hosting of national and international meetings. As well as being a forum for the stimulating of new business transactions, this event also offers suppliers exhibiting at the event a unique setting for networking and establishing new contacts with other destinations and venues in the conference industry, as well as meeting new potential customers while nurturing more long-standing business relationships at the same time.

A wide range of stakeholders

At Access 2005, 189 Austrian exhibitors including conference centres, convention hotels, CVBs and other suppliers and intermediaries in the conference industry (such as interpreters, equipment providers, and destination management companies) met more than 1300 trade visitors. These buyers included international visitors from 17 countries. With 150 participants, the largest foreign visitors contingent came from the German market, which is highly important for the Austrian inbound conference industry.

Included in the 1300 trade visitors were more than 300 hosted buyers and media representatives from 16 countries, who travelled to Vienna as the guests of the trade show. Russia and Hungary were two countries participating for the first time in the hosted buyer programme in 2005.

For the purposes of Access 2005, a trade visitor was defined as a professional who:

- organizes
- plans
- consults on, or takes decisions

in the fields of:

- conferences
- conventions
- incentive trips/programmes
- international congresses
- product launches and presentations
- staff training
- business trips, special events, etc.

Acceptance on to the Access hosted buyer programme entitled buyers to an all-expenses-paid programme, including airfare (sponsored by Austrian Airlines), hotel accommodation in Vienna, education and networking sessions and meetings with a number of selected Austrian suppliers at the trade show.

An important and successful part of Access 2005, organized for the first time as a means of knowledge transfer within the industry, was the Access Academy, a series of presentations, seminars and workshops at which industry representatives, university professors and other experts discussed a range of stimulating ideas. Under the title of 'Brand not bulk – how to position events successfully', these speakers discussed the basic steps of the brand formation process from a practical point of view. The keynote speech by the Chief Organizing Officer of the World Economic Forum, Geneva and Davos, André Schneider, attracted particular acclaim.

A social and entertainment programme arranged around the trade show created an effective environment for networking between professional visitors and exhibitors. An 'Austrian Welcome' evening was held in the magnificent rooms of the Schönbrunn Palace and a sumptuous Austrian buffet awaited the guests at the Orangerie.

The lively 'Access night' at the venue Arcotel Wimberger had the guests dancing until the early hours to jazz entertainers Mat Schuh and the Max-Hagler Orchestra. The faultless planning of these two evenings clearly proved the efficiency of the domestic congress and event industry to Access 2005 visitors.

Following the success of the first two years of Access, this trade show will continue to be the leading event for national and international decision-makers in the Austrian conference industry.

Review and Discussion Questions

1 Discuss the main differences between how a convention and visitor bureau markets a destination and how a car manufacturer markets its automobiles.
2 London has been a recognized conference destination since the middle of the 20th century. What are the key differences between how a city such as London is marketed now, and how it may have been marketed 50 years ago?
3 Discuss the contention that the positive impacts that conferences can bring to the economic situation of a destination are sometimes outweighed by the negative effects that conferences can bring to other aspects of life at the destination.

Sources

Boone, LE and Kurtz, DL (1998) *Contemporary Marketing Wired*, Dryden Press

CIC (2005) *The 2004 Economic Impact Study*, Convention Industry Council

Davidson, R and Cope, B (2003) *Business Travel: conferences, incentive travel, exhibitions, corporate hospitality and corporate travel*, FT Prentice Hall/Pearson Education

Dwyer, L (2002) 'Economic contribution of convention tourism: conceptual and empirical issues', in Weber, K and Chon, K (eds), *Convention Tourism: international research and industry perspectives*, The Haworth Hospitality Press

Gehrisch, M (2004) *Emerging Meeting & Business Travel Trends for 2004*, DMAI

Harrill, R (2005) Fundamentals of Destination Management and Marketing, IACVB

Høyer, KG and Næss, P (2001) 'Conference tourism: a problem for the environment, as well as for research?', *Journal of Sustainable Tourism*, 9, 6

Kotler, P, Bowen J and Makens, J (2003) *Marketing for Hospitality and Tourism*, Prentice Hall

Koutoulas, D (2004) *Benchmark Survey of Convention & Visitors Bureaux*, Koutoulas Consulting

Lawson, F (2000) *Congress, Convention and Exhibition Facilities: Planning*, Design and Management, Architectural Press

MTS (2005) 'Access to success – successful meetings in Austria', press release from Marketing Tourismus Synergie GmbH

Pike, S (2004) *Destination Marketing Organizations*, Elsevier

Smith, GV (1990) 'The growth of conferences and incentives', in Quest, M (ed.), *Horwath Book of Tourism*, Macmillan

Spiller, J (2002) 'History of convention tourism', in Weber, K and Chon, K (eds), *Convention Tourism: International Research and Industry Perspectives*, The Haworth Hospitality Press

Weber, K and Chon, K (eds) (2002) *Convention Tourism: International Research and Industry Perspectives*, The Haworth Hospitality Press

WTO (2004) *Survey of Destination Management Organizations Report*, World Tourism Organization

Chapter 2

The Marketing Environment for Destinations

Summary of Chapter Contents

This chapter looks at a number of key issues and current trends impacting the marketing of conference and convention destinations.
  The chapter covers:

- Disintermediation
- Destination marketing or destination management?
- Product development and investment
- Funding
- Accessibility and disability
- Crisis communications and issues management

It includes case studies on:

- Kent Conference Bureau and Venuedirectory.com
- Liverpool City Region's Destination Management Plan for 2005–2008
- Perth Convention Bureau's 'Beyond Compliance' Programme
- Toronto's crisis management strategy in response to the threats posed by the 'SARS' outbreak

Learning Outcomes

On completion of this chapter, you should be able to:

- explain the concept of disintermediation and its impact on the conference and business events sector
- discuss the evolving role of DMOs and their responsibilities for destination marketing and destination management

■ **appreciate the need for, and the issues associated with, investments in a destination's conference and convention 'product'**
■ **understand the financial and commercial pressures faced by DMOs**
■ **comment on the ethics and opportunities of a positive approach to disability and accessibility issues**
■ **define the characteristics of an effective crisis management strategy**

Introduction

While it may be true to say that the broad principles of marketing remain more or less constant, apart from fine tuning and some changes given to the priorities attached to them, it is certainly the case that their practical application is extremely dynamic. It has to take account of the impacts of new legislation, for example those affecting customer relationship management and client database development (examined in more detail in Chapter 5). It must be sensitive and respond effectively to a plethora of political, social and technological developments. And, of course, it must highlight innovations and enhancements to the product or service, which is the focus of the marketing activity.

Some of these factors may be less critical if the 'product' to be marketed is a washing machine, a retail outlet, or the latest home insurance package, for example, where the product is clearly defined and relatively static. Yet they are all extremely pertinent when it comes to the marketing of a destination, a living and continuously changing entity. There are many issues, challenges and opportunities confronting those tasked with the promotion of a destination in the conference and business events sector, most of which have a universal resonance: no matter whether the destination is in the northern or southern hemisphere, or in a developed or newly developing country, the same types of issues apply and must be understood and addressed. And there is a sense in which such issues gain further importance simply because of the growing number of conference destinations joining the market. There are now more than two hundred countries world wide competing for their share of conventions and business events, and new destinations are now forcing their way up the rankings of the most successful cities. Statistics published by the Union of International Associations (UIA) and the International Congress and Convention Association (ICCA) (see Chapter 11) clearly reveal the emergence of new destinations, such as Cape Town, Shanghai and Santiago de Chile, a trend that seems likely to continue for some years to come.

This chapter, therefore, examines a number of the most important contemporary issues and trends confronting destinations that are marketing themselves to attract conferences (although discussion of the very topical issue of destination branding has been left until Chapter 4), issues and trends that confront them no matter whether they are established destinations or one of the more recent arrivals on the destination scene. Chapter 3 will then analyse the current marketing environment for conference venues.

Disintermediation

Disintermediation is very much a 21st century term; quite simply, it means 'cutting out the middleman (or intermediary)'. It is a phenomenon that has been especially noticeable when consumers are making travel arrangements or booking holidays, as they are now able to do much of this work for themselves from the comfort of their home or office via the Internet. The traditional role of high street travel agents has been reduced or certainly changed, as they have been to some extent taken out of the booking process, or disintermediated, with customers able to make immediate bookings and commercial transactions through appropriate websites. Business travel agencies have been required to review their operations and client services in the light of the impact of the Internet in order to turn this potentially negative development into a positive one for themselves and their clients. Davidson and Cope (2003: 62) state:

> It would, of course, be a mistake to regard e-commerce and business travel agencies as two separate and incompatible intermediaries in the business travel distribution chain. The larger agencies, in particular, have embraced the technology and put it to use to enhance the service they provide to their clients.

In a similar way to travel agencies, destination marketing organizations (DMOs), such as convention and visitor bureaux (CVBs) and conference desks, also play a role as intermediaries or middlemen. They act as brokers of business, seeking to bring together those who want services from a destination (such as a making a convention centre booking, obtaining local information and advice, negotiating civic support for an event from the municipality) with the suppliers of such services, e.g. the members of a convention bureau or destination marketing organization. This has been the role of the DMO, to act as an intermediary, to serve as a custodian of the destination's information, to be the official voice of the destination and the guarantor of impartial, high quality information on the destination's facilities, services and overall 'product'. But technology is changing much of this by enabling others to replicate what DMOs have been providing, and sometimes doing so more effectively and more efficiently. As a result, the DMO is increasingly at risk of being disintermediated.

The impact of technology is well illustrated in the provision of venue-finding services. Many DMOs base their core business on handling and converting enquiries, acting as the middleman or intermediary between the client (buyer) and the venue (supplier), brokering information and relationships to find a suitable match. While there may continue to be a need for such intermediary services in respect of large and complex events requiring a destination-level response, the demand will certainly reduce for the smaller meetings and events, which technology can handle with minimal human input (see Chapter 9 reference to systems in use by Boston Convention Bureau and Edinburgh Convention Bureau). Those DMOs that only provide this kind of service are likely to face disintermediation and their very survival will be under threat.

However, it is also possible for DMOs to collaborate with potential technology disintermediators for mutual benefit, as demonstrated by the partnership developed between England's Kent Conference Bureau and Venuedirectory.com (see case study).

Disintermediation is something that DMOs will face continually, not just through the impact of technology but also through the actions of those in the private sector

Case Study

Kent Conference Bureau and Venuedirectory.com

Kent Conference Bureau (www.conferencekent.co.uk) represents some 55 conference and meeting venues throughout the county of Kent in South-East England. Venuedirectory.com is an online venue search facility that holds perhaps the most comprehensive range of meeting facility data on hotels/venues around the world. With nearly 400 fields on which to search, browsers are able to look for a venue in a particular location with very specific and detailed requirements. In addition to its main website, Venuedirectory.com has established customized 'private label' websites for a number of destinations, hotel groups and conference industry suppliers.

Kent Conference Bureau is the first destination marketing organization in the UK to have a fully customized private label web link arrangement with Venuedirectory.com, to whom it pays an annual fee for this service. By integrating Kent Conference Bureau's website with the excellent operating benefits of Venuedirectory.com's data distribution technology, the Bureau offers browsers the ability to use a truly professional search facility covering its member venues. The search process was customized to fit with the personality of the Kent venues – for example, instead of searching in the 'South East' and selecting 'Kent', the customized process allows browsers to select a town or location within Kent. They can search not only by capacity but by a multitude of criteria.

The collaboration provides many benefits to Kent Conference Bureau. As a membership organization, the Bureau's 55-plus venue members gain from the entitlement to have their venue data stored and presented on the Kent Conference Bureau website in the same way as a full subscriber on the Venuedirectory.com website. The venues can also change and update their information online at any time and add special offers. If they choose, they can also subscribe to the full Venuedirectory.com service, but this is not mandatory. They also receive enquiries (requests for proposals or RFPs – see Chapter 9) from conference organizers via the website.

Kent Conference Bureau itself benefits from its ability to act as the group manager to overview site activity. It also eases the pressure on Bureau staff resources by placing the onus of responsibility on the venues to update their information and add their own special offers. Another benefit is the ability to access the full site operating statistics, including 0870 telephone numbers which track and report on calls made to members from the Kent Conference Bureau site link.

who develop the capacity to undertake, in a commercially viable way, services that have traditionally been the role of the DMO. In doing so, they often catch the eye of elected officials who are looking to make savings on public budgets, perhaps buying services that were previously subsidized to the local DMO but now can be outsourced more effectively or bought more affordably from elsewhere. Such services could include accommodation or housing reservations; the production of marketing collateral and destination guides; or the development of competing websites.

Rick Antonson, President and CEO of Tourism Vancouver, speaking at the annual convention of the British Association of Conference Destinations in 2003, said:

> One could say that the greatest threat to the roles of the bureau, in the future, comes to those bureaux that try to hold onto things the way they were, because they are not that way any longer. Not just technology but entrepreneurial approaches from many people have replaced the traditional mindset of what makes a bureau of value to its community.

Destination marketing or destination management?

One of the growing roles for DMOs is an increased responsibility for destination development and management. While there is still an important focus on destination promotion and on selling the destination product, this in itself is no longer sufficient. DMOs need to take a role in defining what that product is and what it will become, a role not only in marketing but also in managing the destination, in helping to develop new destination products and features to ensure that the destination is offering what the consumer needs. The DMO has to take to the marketplace what the client will want to buy, taking the destination's personality and products onto the national or world stage.

In the UK during the 1960s, 1970s and 1980s, many of the leading conference destinations were seaside resorts, often with convention halls and facilities built during the heyday of the Victorian era in the 19th century. During the 1990s and the early years of the 21st century, a number of these destinations pulled out of the conference market because they had failed to attract investment in their destination's hotels, attractions and general infrastructure to make sure that it kept pace with trends in the market and the changing demands and higher expectations of the consumer. They had lost substantial market share because of a failure to manage their destination and keep abreast of the market. Their destination product was no longer what the customer wanted to buy.

Destination management is not just a case of managing the physical product (i.e. the venues, hotels, transport systems, visitor attractions) but is also very much to do with building partnerships and collaboration across the destination (see Chapter 10). It is also to do with developing the education and training of the destination's workforce, equipping them with the skills and knowledge needed to service the business events visitor effectively and professionally. Destination management also has an important part to play in creating understanding and recognition across the community for the economic importance of the convention and business events sector. It can entail looking at local planning regulations to ensure that they facilitate rather than hinder appropriate product investment, as well as approaching proactively potential investors in order to stimulate and attract new investments. Management of the destination also means protecting the product and developing sustainable policies that balance visitor experiences with the need to minimize damage to the environment. Such policies often focus on transport issues, for example the promotion of 'park and ride' schemes which encourage visitors and local residents to park in specially designated car parks on the outskirts of cities and use public transport to transfer into the city centre. But this could equally embrace policies to encourage major event venues to introduce waste management and recycling initiatives. For example:

In Harrogate, England, the Harrogate International Centre (HIC) has introduced training programmes for front line staff, covering such issues as waste reduction, recycling and offering free advice to exhibition contractors and exhibitors. The Centre has also teamed up with a local waste management company, to explore recycling of waste. As a result, the volume of waste has been reduced and the Centre claims that now 95% is sent for recycling. A large amount of cardboard and paper is compacted on-site and then sent to Scotland for use in the manufacture of plasterboards. In November 2003 HIC received an accreditation award from The Institute of Energy for achievements in

Energy Efficiency. The award recognizes the excellent work undertaken by HIC staff in reducing energy consumption and the introduction of energy efficient systems.

Again in his speech to the BACD Convention in 2003, Rick Antonson gave the following practical example of destination management in Vancouver:

> We at Tourism Vancouver, a number of years ago, decided that our taxi service was not anywhere near what it should be. If any of you have had the pleasure of riding in a taxi in North America, you cannot leave the ride without a story! And they are not always good stories. And much like a wonderful meal that ends with a cold cup of coffee, you go away and you tend to remember the cold cup of coffee – a visitor experience is very similar: people can have a tremendous time in your destination and, on leaving, have a poor taxi ride to the airport and their visitor experience is marked by their final experience. The equivalent of a cold cup of coffee. We cannot afford to have any element of the visitor experience in our destination, nor can you in yours, sub-par. So we as the bureau got quite involved in what is now a programme called 'Taxi Host', that's had some 7,000 drivers through it. It has three levels: the second level as a minimum is required to be able to pick up at the airport in Vancouver. It was tough when we got involved in doing that because many people said: 'That's destination management, that's not the role of the bureau.' We looked around and no-one else was doing it. They were our visitors that were having disappointing experiences, so we inserted ourselves into destination management.

The role of a DMO can no longer be solely in the rather narrow field of sales and marketing. That role now needs to be, more than ever before, in ensuring that the product is relevant, that new products are coming on-line, that the destination is being managed and that anything which visitors say has spoiled their visitor experience is addressed and remedied. The initials DMO increasingly stand for 'destination management organization' as much as 'destination marketing organization'.

Case Study 2.1 (presented at the end of the chapter) shows the Destination Management Plan 2005–2008 for the Liverpool (England) City Region, and outlines how this destination is addressing its management and marketing needs. The Plan serves as an example of what all destinations could be doing in developing a longer-term strategy.

Product development and investment

The previous section referred to the importance of ongoing investment in a destination's physical product and infrastructure in order to keep pace with changing market trends and to retain and, hopefully, increase market share. For all destinations this poses a constant challenge, both in attracting appropriate investment and then in meeting the increased expectations for a return on their investment from investors.

Investment patterns and trends differ from country to country. In the UK over the past twenty years or so, much of the investment in the conventions and business events sector has gone to cities as they have worked to diversify their economies away from manufacturing and into the service sector.

Birmingham is now well established as one of the UK's top conference and business tourism destinations. The city's first major steps into the conference and business events market were taken in 1976 with the opening of the National Exhibition Centre adjacent to Birmingham's 'Elmdon Airport', now re-named 'Birmingham International Airport'. The change of airport name itself epitomizes the transformation and diversification of the city's economy, fully embracing the service sector, with business tourism acting as the catalyst for much of the investment in new hotels, visitor attractions, restaurants, retail, transport infrastructure, and other regeneration projects.

There is a delicate balancing act for all destinations in attracting the right kind of investment, in the right location, investment which is not only suitable for contemporary needs but which will also anticipate future market trends. Few countries, if any, have in place a national investment plan for the conventions sector to provide intelligence and direction for future investment projects. It is still left to individual destinations and the investment community to determine where money is spent and new facilities are developed. This can mean, and often does mean, that new venues are constructed that are not appropriate, or compete with existing local facilities in ways which create difficulties for both, displacing business rather than creating additional new business for the destination (see also Rogers, 2003: 72). Tress and Sacks (2004), referring to convention facilities built in a number of smaller US cities, state:

> These smaller cities are spending millions of dollars on new and expanded convention centres in a bid to reap the economic benefit from the national meetings market, but they are not meeting attendance targets. This is mostly because they have developed the centres in the belief that they will be an economic panacea rather than just a piece in the city's overall visitor package. They have often failed to consider that meeting planners don't merely want a large hall in which to hold their event; they also prefer that the host city offers desirable hotels, accessible restaurants and cultural facilities, plentiful transportation to and within the city, and even good weather. In short, a convention centre should be part of a city that is a legitimate destination for both business and leisure travellers, and one that will attract people because there are things to do there in addition to attending a meeting. Cities that build convention centres in the belief that they will be the foundation of economic prosperity are likely to be disappointed unless those facilities are part of a broader system to draw people to the city.

Destinations need to develop a balanced convention product, in line with the market segments being targeted for their main business. If the destination has a major purpose-built convention centre, say with a capacity of 2500 theatre-style seating in its main auditorium, it is likely to need a bedstock (assuming an average occupancy rate of 70% year-round) of around 8000 rooms as a minimum to provide sufficient availability for those events which will fill the centre. However, the quality and standard of accommodation also needs to be considered because some conventions will need budget-style accommodation (guesthouses, 2-star hotels, for example) whereas others will demand higher quality 3-star, 4-star and perhaps even 5-star hotels. Location of bedstock is also a factor, with proximity to the centre being advantageous from a delegate and organizer perspective, minimizing the time and costs of transfers between hotels and the centre itself.

In recent years there have been some suggestions of an over-supply of convention facilities, particularly in the United States, with convention and exhibition halls failing to attract sufficient business and, in effect, becoming 'white elephants'. Tress and Sacks (2004) quote the example of one city which:

> with a recently expanded convention centre, is expected to attract only 23 conventions this year – about 30 per cent fewer than in 2003 – with little improvement foreseen in 2005. Despite the US$75 million expansion, which was officially opened in May 2003, fewer than 10 per cent of last year's events were classified as conventions; the rest included consumer shows and cultural and sporting events, none of which generate as much fiscal and economic impact as a major meeting with its hundreds or thousands of overnight guests.

Tress and Sacks provide figures illustrating the growth in supply, quoting research from Tradeshow Week Research Inc.:

> *In 2003, the industry added 68 new or expanded venues in North America, down from 87 in 2002 and 96 in 2001, but still supplying the market with more than 9 million square feet of new exhibition space, or about 12 per cent of the total. By the end of 2003 there were 414 convention centres and exhibition halls in the United States and Canada. Meanwhile, demand has been slowing. The total number of US trade shows in 2003 was 3754, a slight increase from 2002 but about 7 per cent lower than in 2000. The average number of exhibiting companies dropped by almost 16 per cent over the same period, while the average number of attendees fell by nearly a quarter to 7099.*

A similar over-supply phenomenon has sometimes been apparent with cities that have hosted the Olympic Games or other major sporting events such as the Football World Cup. Once the event is over, the facilities themselves can remain little used and then become an expensive burden on the local community. An article by Philip Hersh in the *Chicago Tribune* on 13 August 2005, one year after the Olympic Games held in Athens, stated:

> *The Greek government finally has put out tenders for lease offers on many of the [Olympic] venues, now white elephants that will cost more than US$100 million a year to maintain.*

It is extremely difficult to measure whether there is a surfeit of convention centres because the market is constantly changing, and also experiences cyclical growth and decline, linked with economic, political and social factors. However, this issue does underline the need for a destination management plan that can take a longer-term perspective, and that includes an investment programme to ensure that the destination's product offering remains in tune with market demands. Tress and Sacks give an example of a US city that has successfully invested in its convention product and reaped the benefits:

> *San Antonio (Texas) has achieved a success with its Henry B. Gonzalez Convention Center, which was expanded in 2001 at a cost of US$200 million to cover a total of 1.3 million square feet, more than double the previous area. The Center complements the city's other well-known visitor assets such as The Alamo and the city-centre River Walk, a promenade lined with shops and restaurants, to offer an attractive package for meeting planners. Additionally, there are a number of quality hotels within a short walking distance, and the city is planning a headquarters hotel to accommodate the larger events in a single hotel. The number of attendees at San Antonio's CVB-hosted conventions rose to 424,951 in 2003 from 419,970 in 2001. Estimated total delegate expenditure in 2003 rose to US$382.8 million from US$378.3 million in 2001, and city-wide hotel occupancy increased to 64.6 per cent over the same period compared with the 2003 nationwide average of 59.2 per cent.*

Funding

Most, if not all, destination marketing organizations are established as not-for-profit entities. While they are required to trade profitably in order to survive, their primary *raison d'être* is service to their local community rather than maximization of profits. This inevitably means that, for many DMOs, the generation of funding and income streams to finance their destination marketing and management activities is a

Table 2.1 Funding sources for British DMOs in 2005

Source	Average % of total funding from this source
European funding	10
Local authority/municipality	47
Central government	5
Regional government/agency	5
Membership fees	9
Commercial activities	16
Private sector sponsorship	3
Other	4

Source: British Association of Conference Destinations 2005

constant challenge. A survey of British DMOs undertaken in 2005 by the British Association of Conference Destinations (BACD Membership Survey 2005) identified 'inadequate public sector funding' as the number one threat they faced. Funding is derived from a variety of sources, in both the public and private sectors. The BACD 2005 survey found, for example, seven different funding streams (see Table 2.1), although almost 70% of funding comes from the public sector in one form or another. Other international surveys of both national and city CVBs have also consistently shown that CVBs receive between 60 and 70% of their funding from public bodies (i.e. local and central government).

Those destinations that are particularly reliant on funding from their local municipality or other public sector agency may find that this helps them in their longer-term planning. Public bodies can commit to a strategy for the destination that will be implemented over a period of years, and they do not necessarily seek immediate returns and 'bottom line' benefits (i.e. specific business won) from their financial support. The downside, however, can be that tourism and business tourism are not necessarily statutory responsibilities (unlike education, housing, social services, for example) for a municipality and, if budgets need to be reduced, they are one of the easier targets for cost savings.

Some countries, led by the United States, have introduced a system of local tourist taxation. The Transient Visitor Tax (also referred to as a 'bed tax') is a system that surcharges the tourist directly at the point of consumption – their hotel bill. The tourist pays the tax to the hotel, which collects the tax and pays it to the local authority/ municipality, which then uses it for tourism promotion and for capital projects. In theory, such investments should result in more tourists, who pay more tax revenues, thus funding more promotion and investment and in turn producing more tourists – a truly virtuous circle. While the tourist industry in some countries may be starved of funds for destination marketing, the Transient Visitor Tax provides American cities and regions with finance, not just for tourism marketing but for the cost of constructing conference centres and arenas. However, the logic of this argument is sometimes undermined when cities do not ring-fence this tax income for ongoing investment in their tourism industry but opt to spend the money on what may be seen as more socially worthwhile (and politically beneficial) projects (such as education, health services, community housing).

Taxation is also, inevitably, a two-edged sword: its very existence may serve as a deterrent to visitors who, faced with many other destinations from which to choose, select one offering similar attractions and amenities but at a lower cost. McMahon and Sophister (1998) quote the following examples:

> *The experience of New York in 1990–94 should give cause for caution. In 1990 the state legislature brought into effect a 5% bedroom tax on hotel rooms costing over US$100 per night. An econometric study commissioned by New York State Hospitality and Tourism Association concluded that, by imposing the tax, New York gave up US$2 in related taxes for every US$1 it took in from the occupancy tax. In August 1994 the tax was repealed following a three-year battle by New York hoteliers.*
>
> *In the early 1980s the Irish Government increased Value Added Tax (VAT) on hotel accommodation to 23%. The effect of this was that more than 10% of hotels closed their doors. In 1985 the Irish Hotels Federation persuaded the Irish Government to cut VAT on room sales from 23% to 12.5%. In the period that followed, Irish tourism grew dramatically.*

Yet there is some evidence to suggest that bed taxes do not lead to major competitive disadvantage. The City of Vienna (Austria) has levied a bed tax of 2.8% since 1987, but still succeeds in regularly occupying a top-five place in the UIA (Union of International Associations) and ICCA (International Congress and Convention Association) rankings of international convention cities.

Destinations need constantly to be exploring new income streams, actively seeking new business partnerships and opportunities. At the same time, however, they must stay close to their local membership base and local tourism industry. They must avoid weakening such local community and local business links because this could lead to a loss of political sway. Local politicians can make a huge difference, not just to investment but also to public policy and support for the bureau or DMO. This reinforces the importance of effective lobbying by DMOs to their different constituencies and stakeholders, an activity which is explored more fully in Chapter 10.

Accessibility and disability

The past decade or so has seen a much greater public awareness of the needs of people with disabilities, combined with a growing recognition by governments that public policies and the infrastructure of our towns and cities should cater much more effectively for the 1 in 10 citizens possessing some form of physical, mental or emotional disability. In some countries legislation has been placed on the statute book to guarantee the rights of disabled people and give them proper access to events and to buildings.

Within the convention and business events field, much of the activity in the area of accessibility is at the level of the individual event venue. Venues are encouraged, as a matter of best practice, and required, by legislation, to provide appropriate signage, meeting space, bedrooms, equipment to ensure full accessibility for those with disabilities. Training courses are also being developed for event organizers to demonstrate what they need to do both to support and encourage disabled delegate participation in their events, and to minimize discriminatory practices.

To date, however, few initiatives have come forward at a destination level to maximize accessibility. There is great scope for destinations to address this gap, both as a moral imperative and also as a potentially lucrative market opportunity. The Australian city of Perth has led the way in this area, with its pioneering and innovative 'Beyond Compliance' programme (described fully in Case Study 2.2, presented at the end of the chapter), which serves as a model for other destinations to follow.

Crisis communications and issues management

One of the most important strategic decisions that communications professionals must make is how to handle an issue or a crisis. It is in the nature of DMOs that issues can arise regularly, and how they are handled will have a positive or negative effect on both the organization and the destination itself. Some of the common crises DMOs deal with are natural disasters as well as man-made occurrences such as violence against a visitor, terrorism and defective products. The first few years of the 21st century have already witnessed a number of major crises which, because of the immediacy of global communications and media coverage, have attracted the attention of the world community. Examples of such incidents include:

- The events of 9/11 in the United States
- The foot and mouth epidemic in the UK
- The SARS outbreak in Asia and elsewhere
- The Asian tsunami of 2004
- The war in Iraq
- Terrorist bombings in destinations such as Bali, Madrid, Casablanca, London
- The impact of Hurricane Katrina on the Gulf Coast of the USA.

The worst mistake is to think that 'it won't happen here'. Destinations should develop a crisis plan that covers the operations, communications and back-up systems, no matter how simple or complex. Once the plan has been prepared, it is advisable for it to be reviewed by an expert or an outside entity to make sure that it is complete and accurate. There will also need to be training sessions for the DMO team to ensure that the implementation of procedures is fully understood. Figure 2.1 summarizes advice on crisis management which has been produced by the media relations team of VisitBritain, the UK's national tourism organization, for use by tourism businesses.

The Canadian city of Toronto was faced with a major crisis in 2002/3 when cases of the SARS (Severe Acute Respiratory Syndrome) epidemic were experienced, leading to a sudden closedown in travel to and from the city, with a potentially catastrophic impact on conferences and business events. Toronto's response to the crisis demonstrated a highly professional and effective crisis management strategy, and is described in Case Study 2.3, which is presented at the end of the chapter.

The last few years have brought a number of crises in the tourism industry, from flooding to the foot-and-mouth outbreaks. Often such crises occur with little or no warning and many businesses can find themselves unprepared – not only for the incident itself, but also for media reaction. The media love nothing better than a crisis – often devoting acres of column-inches and hours of air-time to the issue. By keeping abreast of trends within the industry and economic and political factors, much can be done to identify potential crisis situations in advance and prepare yourself and your staff to deal with the resulting media attention.

Crisis checklist

Issues monitoring
- Identify the issues that could develop into a crisis as early as possible
- Attempt to diffuse situations before they develop into a crisis

Establish a crisis management team
- Select key members/staff
- Meet regularly
- Share information and ideas

Assess the crisis
- Gather relevant information
- Assess the type, extent and ramifications of the crisis
- Be aware of rumour and plan to counter it with fact

Choose a spokesperson
- Must be articulate, well briefed, confident
- Must appeal on a humanistic level, be compassionate and caring
- Chief executive/owner is preferable
- Must be available

Message delivery
- Media release
- Media conference
- Individual interviews

Dummy run
- Anticipate likely questions
- Draft responses
- Conduct a dummy run interview with your spokesperson

Dealing with the media
- Be available
- Be open
- Keep your cool
- Provide honest, factual comment, remember the truth always gets out!
- Establish who in your organisation is allowed to talk to the media and brief everyone accordingly

Log calls
- Log all media calls (useful for follow-up later)
- Record what was requested and the action taken

Cover all audiences
- Establish key audiences
- Allocate team member responsibility for each audience
- Keep your own staff well briefed

Post-crisis follow-up
- Assess what went wrong and why
- Formulate steps to prevent similar crises
- Assess the handling of the crisis
- Devise follow-up strategies

Figure 2.1 VisitBritain's guidelines on crisis communications and issues management.

Summary

It is clear that, over recent years, the marketing environment for destinations has undergone radical change. Coping effectively with rapid and constant change seems likely to be one of the major challenges facing DMOs in the years to come. No longer do DMOs carry out the relatively straightforward task of destination promotion but increasingly their role is one of managing the overall development of their destination to ensure that its product offering is one that is appropriate to the present and future needs of conference and convention organizers. DMOs need an awareness and understanding of the political, social and technological developments affecting the industry and wider society if they are to be successful in their endeavours. Such an understanding will inform their marketing strategies and activities, based on the models and examples of best practice outlined in later chapters of this book.

Case Study 2.1

Liverpool City Region's Destination Management Plan for 2005–2008

Liverpool (on Merseyside) is located in North-West England, and is famous in more recent times as the home of the Beetles (and other popular music bands) and of football teams Liverpool FC and Everton FC. In 2008, Liverpool will be European City of Culture, and huge investment is taking place in the city's tourism infrastructure.

The Destination Management Plan for the Liverpool City Region 2005–2008 runs to over 40 pages of text and covers both leisure and business tourism. This summary focuses on the structure of the Plan and its content specific to the convention and business events sector.

The structure of the Plan is as follows:

1 Preface
    What is a Destination Management Plan (DMP)?
    Why is the DMP important?
2 The Process and the Partnership
    How the DMP has been developed
    The Planning and Advisory Group
    The Partnership
3 Strategic Context
    Strategic framework
    The tourism vision
    Aims
    Targets
    Objectives
4 Industry Performance
    The national context
    The regional context
    Sub-regional performance, trends and context
    Destination performance indicators

****

1.1 What is a DMP?

The DMP is an action plan for the whole partnership of organizations involved in developing Liverpool and Merseyside[a] as an internationally important tourism destination. It is a key instrument to identify the actions and strategic relationships that will deliver the sub-regional tourism strategy. While it seeks to provide a context for decision-making regarding priority investments necessary to deliver the strategy, it should nevertheless be viewed as a distinct document from the business plan of The Mersey Partnership or the other partner organizations in Merseyside.

[a]Merseyside in this context includes Wirral, Sefton (including Southport), Knowsley, St Helens and Halton.

1.2 Why the DMP is important

The DMP is important because it provides a framework and rationale for investment in tourism, which is one of the major, growing sectors of Merseyside's and the North-West's economy. It provides the mechanism to reinforce existing partnerships as well as developing new relationships. It seeks to build commitment to a common goal based on a clear, shared understanding of the opportunities that exist, the resources that are available and the basis for the prioritization of the actions identified in the Plan.

3.2 The Tourism Vision for the Liverpool City Region – a Winning Brand for Tourism in England's North-West

The Shared Vision for 2015 places the Liverpool City Region amongst the top 20 European City Region Destinations, with an annual visitor spend of £2 billion supporting 30 000 jobs in the local economy. By 2015 the City of Liverpool has become a truly international destination for conference and leisure travel. The whole sub-region has benefited from increased tourism in the slipstream as a result of a sustained programme of tourism development based on a clear strategy of investing in specific opportunities for growth. The City Region is making a substantial contribution towards the tourism account for England's North-West – a key attractor of international and UK visitors.

3.5 Strategic Objectives

The Strategic Objectives for this Destination Management Plan are developed from Merseyside Tourism Sector Implementation Plan (February 2004) and are built around Liverpool's designation as European Capital of Culture in 2008 and the opportunities and challenges this provides over the next four years.

There are four key strategic objectives:

- To develop a class destination for conferences and business visits
- To promote the Liverpool City Region as a world-class destination for leisure tourism
- To develop the sub-region as a major events destination of international repute
- To deliver a warm Liverpool Welcome throughout the City Region

****

4   Destination Performance Indicators

Destination Performance Indicators for Case Study 2.1

Performance Measure	Performance in...					Target in 2008
	2003 (base)	2004	2005	2006	2007	
Core Measures						
1 No. of staying nights	9.7 m	9.3 m	9.1 m	9.4 m	10.2 m	11.0 m
2 No. of overseas visitor nights	2.4 m	2.4 m	2.4 m	2.5 m	2.7 m	3.05 m
3 Total staying tourism spend	£413 m	£415 m	£427 m	£463 m	£528 m	£598 m
4 Tourism-related employment	19 998	20 305	20 939	21 907	23 454	26 440
5 Average spend per staying night	£42.58	£44.62	£46.92	£49.26	£51.76	£54.34
6 Index of attractions	100	101	102	104	108	110
7 Room occupancy: Liverpool	70%	70%	70%	70%	72%	73%
Merseyside	60%	60%	60%	60%	62%	63%
8 % accommodation in QA	47%	47%	53%	65%	70%	75%
9 Bed spaces	22 517	21 517	21 177	21 877	22 977	24 377
Possible Additional Indicators						
10 No. of day visits	53.10 m	54.3 m	55.9 m	57.8 m	59.7 m	62 m
11 Total day visit spend	£448.98 m	£477.69 m	£506.39 m	£527.97 m	£570.97 m	£592.50 m

12 Nights spent in serviced accommodation	3.13 m	2.98 m	2.91 m	3.01 m	3.26 m	3.52 m
13 Total room nights sold in Liverpool	1.45 m	1.37 m	1.34 m	1.38 m	1.53 m	1.69 m
14 Index of customer contacts	100	105	110	115	120	125
15 No. of 250-delegate events held: Liverpool	N/A	110	135	170	218	280
16 No. of 250-delegate events held: Southport	25	42	40 (YTD)	24	24	24
17 No. of nationally accredited conference venues	10	12	15	18	21	25
18 No. of overnight study visits held	0	2	2	6	8	10
19 Position of Liverpool in top UK towns for international visitors	9	9	9	9	8	8
20 Destination benchmarking score for Liverpool: overall enjoyment/likelihood of recommending		4.28/4.60		4.40/4.65		4.59/4.77

****

6.1 The Four Year Plan – Focus 2008

As outlined in 3.5 Objectives, Merseyside's tourism priorities are closely linked to making the most of, and spreading the benefits of, Liverpool's Capital of Culture title. This gives a clear sense of focus to all partners.

Priority 1	**To develop a class destination for conferences and business visits**
Objectives	• To position Liverpool as a premier city conference destination for top tier associations, national and international MICE events and to secure 280 events of 250 delegates or more per annum by 2008
	• To further develop Southport as a premier resort conference destination for trade associations and events, in keeping with the coastal offer and to attract 24 events of 250 delegates or more per annum
	• To promote professionalism amongst conference venues in the Liverpool City Region to enhance reputation of the sub-region as a great place to hold meetings and to give Merseyside venues a competitive advantage
	• To promote the Liverpool City Region as an excellent best practice destination for study visits and to attract at least 8 overnight study visits per annum by 2008
Required Actions	• Develop a purpose-built conference/exhibition centre in Liverpool City Centre together with a robust subvention policy

- Build further on Liverpool's academic, medical, cultural, maritime and other key sector strengths to position the City as a premier conference destination
- Enhance Southport's conference product through additional exhibition and hotel space and a suitable subvention policy
- Secure further European funding for Southport and The Mersey Partnership to continue conference marketing campaign and sales activity building on successful track records
- Continue to improve conference venue quality and services throughout the sub-region to achieve more nationally accredited venues through Meetings Industry Association Hospitality Assured standard
- Ensure appropriate food, drink and hotel offering to support market growth
- Work with partners across the destination to develop and promote the market for education study visits

Rationale
- Business and conference tourism has accounted for much of the recent growth in UK tourism and is responsible for some 29.6m trips and £9249m spend in England. Conference delegates spend on average 2.5 times as much as leisure visitors and 40% indicate that they will return to a destination as a leisure visitor if an area has appealed to them. Approximately 49% of 4-star Liverpool city centre hotel trade is driven by the business market and 11% by residential conferences and meetings. The Liverpool City Region has over 50 conference venues catering for up to 1650 delegates in its largest venue (Southport Floral Hall) in a range of hotel and non-residential venues including some unusual venues

Regional Strategy Linkages
- A Region for Business/Celebrating Excellence/Make It Easy/Fantastic Food

****

8.0 Programme Summary

The programme summary is an outline of key strategic activity designed to prioritize work programmes and ensure a joined-up approach across Merseyside. It excludes capital investment in tourism facilities (major investments are included in 5.3 and a full schedule of proposed tourism developments is available as a separate annex from The Mersey Partnership – TMP). These priority work programmes are underpinned by a raft of support activity undertaken by local authorities and other agencies.

Priority 1: Class conferences: Year 1 (April 05–March 06)

Year 1 Activity	Lead Agency	Total Activity Cost Year 1	Tourist Board Funds	Other Public Funds	Other Funding/ Income	Notes
Product Development						
Quality Assured Venues	TMP	£20 000	£10 000		£10 000	Continuation of existing quality/skills activities
Subvention Policy: Liverpool	Liverpool City Council	£50 000				New for 2005 – not including any Kings Dock Conference Centre provision
Promotional Activity						
Conference Marketing Campaigns: city and coast thematics to appropriate markets	TMP/Sefton	£205 000	£75 000	£35 000 NWDA £30 000 Sefton	£65 000 (TMP private destination support programme)	Step up from previous years' DSP – TMP's destination support packages
Study Visit Programme development	TMP	£15 000			£25 000	New revenue-earning activity
Total Year 1 Spend		**£290 000**	**£85 000**	**£95 000**		
Years 2,3,4 (April 06–March 09)						
Product Development						
Quality Assured Venues	TMP	£60 000	£30 000		£30 000	Ongoing
Subvention Policy: Liverpool	LCC	£1.2m		£1m	£200 000	Not including Kings Dock subvented events
Promotional Activity						
Conference Marketing Campaigns: city and coast thematics to appropriate markets	TMP	£1.09m	£400 000	£300 000 NWDA £90 000 Sefton	£300 000 DSP	
Study Visit Programme	TMP	£45 000			£75 000	
Total Year 2, 3, 4 Spend		**£2.395m**	**£430 000**	**£1.390m**	**£605 000**	

Case Study 2.2

Perth Convention Bureau's 'Beyond Compliance' Programme

Perth Convention Bureau (PCB) in Western Australia has pioneered an initiative with the State's Disability Services Commission and a local university that aims to see Western Australia become the nation's leading convention destination for people with disabilities. Known as 'Beyond Compliance', the project seeks to bring about social change by rewarding tourism industry operators who are proactive in improving their accessibility.

It is a best practice example of how a convention bureau can partner with local organizations to help them achieve their objectives and, by so doing, directly stimulate more conference activity in their destination.

Perth is one of the most geographically isolated destinations in the world, and one of the last Australian cities to build a dedicated convention and exhibition centre. With the opening of the AU$220 million Perth Centre in August 2004, the city effectively doubled its meeting capacity but not its marketing budget. PCB continues to invest its limited marketing funding at home by developing a pool of committed local association executives and motivating them to develop or bid for meetings to be held in Perth (see also Chapter 7 for the Case Study on Edinburgh's Ambassador Programme).

Figure 2.2 The Perth skyline.

'Beyond Compliance' has developed as a component of the PCB's Customer Relationship Management Programme. Each of the PCB's 14 staff members, from the accountant to the managing director, is allocated a specific industry portfolio and charged with the responsibility of developing convention leads from that sector as part of their role. They also become experts in that field and follow trends, innovations, research grants and findings, and trade deals, as well as developing a network of industry relationships in the sector for which they are responsible.

When Scott Campbell, PCB's Research Manager, took on the disability sector portfolio in 2003, he was amazed at the sector's receptiveness and willingness to work in partnership with PCB. Initially, the programme involved researching the potential size and value of the disability sector and obtaining statistics demonstrating its impact on the State economy. This work was done in association with Curtin University (Perth) and undertaken by students as part of their curriculum training at no cost to PCB.

From this initial research it became clear that the disability sector organizations were quick to respond to new opportunities and, by facilitating business links between PCB's members (the tourism suppliers) and the State Government agency charged with representing the needs of the sector, the programme grew to the point where the State tourism body and Disability Services Commission formed a joint venture to work co-operatively in order to achieve social change.

Objectives

The objectives of the 'Beyond Compliance' programme are to:

1 Promote Western Australia as a leading tourism destination for people with disabilities
2 Improve accessibility and facilities for disabled visitors
3 Secure or create disability sector conferences to be held in Western Australia.

While objectives 1 and 2 are broader than PCB's business tourism charter, they form the methodology by which objective three, the Bureau's objective, is achieved.

PCB's primary target audience was the 96 associations within the sector that were represented in Western Australia and had possible links to national and international conferences. The initial objective was to create awareness of the project and motivate these associations to consider bidding or to create new meetings.

The method chosen to reach them was in association with their major funding source, the Disability Services Commission, utilizing strategic customer relationship management (CRM) techniques. In identifying its key partners, PCB researched the organization to determine its objectives and then the key contact or person responsible for running the organization, in order to ascertain their personal objectives and aspirations.

Curtin University's key objective is meeting the educational needs of its students. The key contact, Ruth Taylor, was also keen to establish industry connections and develop unique material for international presentations. She has subsequently presented on this project at conferences in Hong Kong and Boston.

To engage the lynchpin organization, the Disability Services Commission, PCB needed to develop a connection and it started by offering to circulate a new manual, created by the Commission for servicing the tourism sector, to PCB's 300 industry members, ensuring it was received and acknowledged. By demonstrating PCB's understanding of the Commission's objective to improve facilities within the tourism industry in order better to meet the needs of people with disabilities, the synergy came in jointly agreeing to use the conference sector as the catalyst for achieving change by:

1 Motivating the disability sector to pursue conferences and to encourage tourism operators to use part of the profits from the subsequent events to improve facilities.
2 Motivate the tourism industry to 'court' rather than simply 'cater' for the disability sector.

The initial sales target was to generate five convention bid leads from the disability sector and convert at least two of them for the destination within 12 months.

Campaign

Phase One of the campaign was undertaken over a 9-month period from November 2003 to June 2004 and consisted of the following elements:

1 Research and data preparation

Research findings on the extent and potential value of the sector were surprising, including the fact that in Australia:

- One in every five people has a disability.
- One in every ten people is a carer of someone with a disability.
- 70% of all assistance required by people with disabilities is provided by the informal network.
- 93% of people with a disability live in the community, either independently or with family or friends.

An average of 5–10% of people attending disability-related conferences actually have a disability requiring special facilities. The majority of attendees are able-bodied people.

The sector has traditionally been serviced rather than sought after and so is not used to being viewed or courted as a resource and opportunity. The association network, therefore, responded enthusiastically to the new opportunities presented to them and were keen to participate.

2 Direct mail campaign

A brochure outlining the programme was produced and an invitation to attend a launch function was distributed to 98 associations with links to the Disability Services portfolio.

The campaign achieved a remarkable 45% positive response rate to the launch event and 9% response requesting an immediate meeting to discuss a convention bidding opportunity.

3 Hosting a campaign launch function

The project was officially launched in February 2004 in front of 45 local associations within the disability sector, including representatives from Government and academia. The breakfast forum aimed to encourage support from the disability sector for the project and to motivate organizations to bid for their national and international conferences. Five of the organizations present made immediate requests for meetings after hearing about how the project was achieving social change, improving facilities and financially rewarding those in the tourism industry that were supporting the project.

Campaign budget

Funding and in-kind support for the programme was generated with the support of industry members. Event Edge, a professional conference management company, and the Esplanade Hotel, Fremantle, a newly expanded convention venue, each contributed as founding partners of the programme in return for marketing exposure to the meeting organizers. Curtin University provided in-kind support for the research programme. Marketing expenses included:

Date	Activity	Cost (Australian dollars)
November 2003 to February 2004	Research and data preparation in association with Curtin University	$5000
February 2004	Direct Mail Campaign	$950
14 February 2004	Campaign Launch	$2100
Ongoing	Media and public relations campaign	Nil
February–June 2004	Meetings with organizations and development of bids	$41 500
Total		$49,550

Results

By the end of 2004 PCB had sourced three international and seven national convention bidding opportunities in the disability sector, of which six were secured for Western Australia, one elected not to proceed to bid, and three were at the bid development stage.

Among those secured were the Disabled Artists International Conference, which was expected to attract 500 delegates in 2005, and the Congress of the International Federation of Disability Sailing with an estimated 700 delegates in 2006. These two conventions would generate AU$3.07 million in direct delegate expenditure. Together with the national conferences, the programme had so far generated in excess of 2800 delegates who would inject an estimated AU$5.36 million in direct delegate expenditure to the State economy.

The future

Phase 1 of the programme was such an outstanding success that the programme has received a funding boost and will be profiled internationally with the objective of generating international conference business from within Europe. Scott Campbell presented the campaign to an invited audience of disability organizations in London and Paris in November 2004. An alliance has been formed with the British equivalent (Disability Rights Commission) of the Disability Services Commission to encourage more conferences to consider Western Australia.

Disability awareness training programmes have been initiated for tourism employees, generating very positive publicity for PCB. PCB is also planning a 'Night of Recognition' for those tourism organizations that have improved their facilities and for those disability organizations that have undertaken to bid for a conference to be held in Perth.

The 'Beyond Compliance' programme won the Best Marketing Award at the International Congress and Convention Association's congress held in Cape Town in October 2004.

Case Study 2.3

Toronto's crisis management strategy in response to the threats posed by the SARS outbreak

This Case Study examines how one destination, Toronto, responded rapidly and effectively to a major crisis and, by so doing, successfully minimized its potential negative impacts and used the crisis as a platform for future growth.

Background on Toronto

Toronto is Canada's largest city, with a population of 4.7 million (in Greater Toronto), spanning more than 100 cultures. Its cultural diversity is reflected in the fact that, apart from the two official languages of English and French, other languages commonly spoken in the city include Chinese, Italian, Tamil, Portuguese and Spanish. Toronto's skyline incorporates CN Tower, one of the 'Modern Wonders of the World', together with miles of waterfront, beaches (on Lake Ontario) and a bustling central downtown. It can offer more than 35 000 hotel rooms in over 120 hotels, and has Canada's largest convention centre, which ranks among the top ten largest continuous space facilities in North America.

The economic impact of SARS

Severe Acute Respiratory Syndrome (SARS) originated in China. It has symptoms similar to a cold/flu, with most patients developing pneumonia. It is a very contagious disease but the full recovery rate from SARS in the world averages 85%. The case fatality rate varies by age group: for patients above 65 years of age, the death rate is over 50%, while the rate for those younger than 24 years of age is about 1%. The overall estimate of case fatality is 14–15% (*World Health Organisation Global SARS Conference, Malaysia, June 2003*).

The outbreak of SARS in Canada at the end of 2002 and through the first nine months of 2003 resulted in significant damage to the travel and tourism industry, especially in the Toronto area. The Conference Board of Canada's Canadian Tourism Research Institute (CTRI) analysed the economic impact of SARS on all aspects of business and leisure travel, and estimated a loss in economic activity for the City of Toronto of about $570 million in 2003 (a reduction of 0.5% in Gross Domestic Product). A more detailed breakdown of the impact is shown in Tables 2.2 and 2.3. However, it is important to note that, at this same time, the travel and tourism sector in Toronto was already suffering from fears and uncertainty surrounding the war in Iraq, making it difficult to identify precisely what percentage of the downturn in tourism business was due to SARS and how much to other factors.

In 2002 (pre-SARS year), convention business was estimated to have had an economic impact of $369 393 454 on the Greater Toronto area, and $136 057 175 on the rest of Ontario. By comparison, in 2003 convention business had an estimated economic impact of $231 241 717 on Greater Toronto, and of $89 970 252 on the rest of Ontario. In terms of employment, in 2003 convention business created a total of 4472 jobs in Greater Toronto, and another 1308 in the rest of Ontario. In 2002, convention business created 7449 jobs in Greater Toronto and 2031 in the rest of Ontario. These impacts are summarized in Table 2.4. In specific terms, nine city-wide conventions were lost in 2003, and some 307 000 convention- and meetings-related room nights.

It can be seen that a substantial decline in convention revenues and employment was experienced in 2003. However, a rapid improvement was achieved by 2004, when a total of 18.5 million visitors came to Toronto, 691 000 of whom were convention attendees. In 2003, 16.9 million people had visited Toronto, 606 000 of whom were attending a convention. These

Table 2.2 Impact of SARS on travel to Toronto

	Percentage change Q2 2003*	Percentage change overall 2003*
Overnight travel to Toronto (by market)		
Domestic	[−]15	[−]4.8
United States	[−]20	[−]9.1
Overseas	[−]40	[−]16.7
Same day travel to Toronto		
All markets	[-]25	[-]11.4

*Percentage change in real expenditures compared with previous year.
Source: The Conference Board of Canada

Table 2.3 Impact on economic activity at Toronto's Pearson International Airport and on the Toronto tourism industry due to SARS ($m)

	Q1 2003	Q2 2003	Q3 2003	Q4 2003	2003 overall
Impact	−40.5	−403.7	−203.6	79.2	−568.7

Source: The Conference Board of Canada

Table 2.4 Business convention economic impact in Greater Toronto

	2002	2003	% change
Total economic impact	$369 393 454	$231 241 717	[−]37
Employment	7449	4472	[−]40

Source: Statistics Canada and Ministry of Tourism (TREIM model)

figures suggest a stronger year-on-year recovery in convention business (14%) compared with total visitors (11%).

Toronto's Recovery Strategy

In order to counteract the negative publicity and damaging economic impacts of SARS, Tourism Toronto (the city DMO, www.torontotourism.com) put together a 'Recovery Strategy' in 2003 with the following aims:

- Reassure/demonstrate that Toronto is a safe travel destination
  - Primary Key: Rebuild local and global confidence immediately and sustain a programme of aggressive communication for the next 24 months. Generate 'grassroots' community enthusiasm, pride and engagement in *Toronto Campaign*

Table 2.5 Toronto's 'Recovery Roadmap'

1 May 2003 till all-clear	*Mid-May till 30 July 2003*	*Post all-clear and beyond*
Phase 1: Grassroots engagement and assurance	**Phase 2: Rally Toronto events and festival support**	**Phase 3: Marketplace outreach**
Assurance advertising	Festival/event support advertising and retail packaging	Recovery advertising
Convention damage control	Rally Toronto events	Convention sales development
Strategic media/trade relations focus groups	Trade relations/fam. trips/sales missions	Strategic media relations
Lifting the travel ban imposed by the World Health Organization (WHO)	Celebrity influencers' campaign and spokespeople	Media tours
Corporate outreach to key global organizations with Toronto offices	Lifting the travel ban imposed by the World Health Organization	Joint Marketing Agreements with trade partners
ALL CLEAR by WHO – announce Rally Toronto events	Trade development initiatives	Online marketing campaign
Ongoing research for travel attitudes and intentions	Ongoing research for travel attitudes and intentions	Fam. trips for all travel sectors
Corporate outreach to key global organizations with Toronto offices	Celebrity influencers' campaign	Ongoing research for travel attitudes and intentions

- Engage all stakeholders to support and drive the *Toronto Campaign* through a single, focused Plan.
- Preserve existing 2003 meetings/conference/incentive and leisure business to avoid a 'tourism meltdown'
- Position Toronto to recover lost market share in 2004 and use resulting marketplace momentum to springboard growth into 2005 and beyond.

The detailed implementation of the Recovery Strategy comprised a three-phase 'Recovery Roadmap', summarized in Table 2.5.

Crisis management and damage limitation

Toronto Tourism learned a number of key lessons from its experience of handling SARS, lessons that are applicable to other destinations facing a health-related crisis (many of which will be equally relevant to other forms of crises). These lessons may be summarized as follows:

Be prepared in advance: Educate yourself and become an expert by

- Working closely with local public health officials
- Liaising with embassies and consulates to ensure immediate access to their global communication networks

- Working with third party health organizations, such as national health bodies, the centre for disease control and the World Health Organization.

Educate your constituents and have a communication plan by:

- Identifying an accessible 'expert' health professional to work with and to use to support key tourism messages
- Appointing one designated tourism industry spokesperson and information channel for your enterprise, and make use of communication tools such as:
  - website
  - newsletters
  - conference calls/web casts.

Meeting planners/suppliers protect your meetings business

- Check your meeting plan
  - Financial sensitivity
  - On-site crisis response plan
  - Medical evacuation plan
  - First aid training for venue staff
- Check your contracts
  - *Force majeure* clause
- Check your relocation options
- Check insurance
  - Cancellation insurance
  - Liability insurance
  - Local health insurance
- Check your attitude
  - In a crisis, it is not about allocating blame or finding winners and losers. Work together to find solutions.

Damage control exercise

- Make sure you have a crisis before you engage in crisis management
- Assemble an information network and use it
- Prepare relevant and accurate information on a timely basis
- Identify high-impact stakeholders and cultivate those relationships throughout
  - Members
  - Host venue/community
  - Suppliers/sponsors
  - Media
- Define key messages
- Over-communicate
- Move to recovery fast: damage control is exhausting.

Summary: Guiding principles for success
Toronto Tourism recommends that destinations confronted by a major health scare or crisis should adhere to a number of guiding principles to steer them through it successfully. These are:

- FOLLOW public health officials' lead
  - Focus the crisis on the facts of the crisis – *not* on speculation about what might happen

- GET THE BEST
  - Get professional communication resources in place
- MOVE FAST – the crisis moves faster than you can imagine
  - Develop key messages and stick to them
  - Damage control
  - Recovery planning
- CHANNEL stakeholder energy
  - People will want to help. Find a way to use this interest rather than ignore it
- ONE SPOKESPERSON
- MOBILIZE networks
  - You will never be able to reach everyone who needs to know your messages as quickly as you need to
- RESEARCH aggressively
  - It is a fluid marketplace and you need to stay connected and current
- OVER-COMMUNICATE
  - Members
  - Clients/partner.

Review and Discussion Questions

1 Compare and contrast, from a customer or client perspective, the impacts of disintermediation on the conference and business events sector with its impacts on another service-based industry.

2 Examine two conference destinations: one enjoying a growing market share and one whose market share has declined. What have been the key factors in the marketing and management of these two destinations which have led to their relative success or failure over recent years?

3 'Public funding in support of conference destination marketing should only be provided to match contributions made by the private sector'. Discuss and illustrate with examples of:
   (a) publicly funded DMOs
   (b) public–private partnerships
   (c) fully private sector initiatives
   including return on investment (ROI) criteria.

4 Examine the response of a city conference destination to a major crisis, e.g. a natural disaster, terrorism or other violent disturbances, infrastructure failure, or other man-made crisis (but not healthcare-related). How successful has the city been in managing the crisis and recovering its market position? What lessons can be learned from the destination's response?

Sources

Davidson, R and Cope, B (2003) *Business Travel: conferences, incentive travel, exhibitions, corporate hospitality and corporate travel*, FT Prentice Hall/Pearson Education Ltd

Rogers, T (2003) *Conferences and Conventions: A Global Industry*, Elsevier Butterworth-Heinemann

Tress, B and Sacks, A (2004) *Convention Centers Alone Not an Economic Panacea*, Ernst & Young LLP (SCORE Retrieval File No. AL0055)

McMahon, M and Sophister, J (1998) Paper entitled 'Tourism Taxation: No Such Thing as a Free Lunch', University of Dublin

Chapter 3
The Marketing Environment for Venues

Summary of Chapter Contents

This chapter looks at a number of key issues and current trends impacting the marketing of conference venues.
The chapter covers:

- The growth in the supply of conference venues
- The changing design of conference venues
- Conference venues' use of technology
- Conference venues and the environment

It includes case studies on:

- Gaylord Palms Resort and Convention Centre
- The environmental management system of Tampere Hall

Learning Outcomes

On completion of this chapter, you should be able to:

- appreciate the reasons for the current increase in the supply of conference venues
- discuss the contention that there is an over-supply of conference venues
- understand the technological innovations that venues are using
- understand the measures being taken by some venues to minimize their negative impacts on the environment

Introduction

Just as those responsible for marketing destinations must understand and respond to important changes in the marketing environment over which they have little or no control, so too must the marketing staff of individual conference venues be aware of the various opportunities and threats created by changes in the context within which they operate. Some of these changes are slow and gradual, reflecting subtle variations in society as a whole; others, such as new laws and technological innovations, are more rapid in their impacts. But the fact remains that businesses and organizations that are slow to respond to changed conditions can quickly lose their competitive advantage in the market.

This chapter reviews some of the key elements in the market environment for conference venues.

Over-supply?

The early years of the 21st century have been witness to a rapid expansion of the supply of conference venues in the growing number of destinations that are active in this market.

Relatively new entrants to this market have made up for lost time by starting vast construction programmes in order to equip themselves with the hotel and conference infrastructure they believe will turn them into international meetings destinations.

Asian countries in particular have seen an explosion of new conference hotel and conference centre construction since 2000, and it shows no signs of abating. Much of the new build has come as the result of investment by multinational hotel companies. For example, by 2005, Marriott International had built 34 hotels in China, with plans to open eight more. Starwood Hotels and Resorts Worldwide, another international operator of upscale hotels in China, had 34 hotels open or under construction.

The first few years of the 21st century also saw substantial growth in Vietnam and Cambodia, aided by the development of direct air connections between these countries and the United States. Ho Chi Minh City planned to open, by 2007, a conference centre complex south of the city, including a 130 000 square foot conference centre and four- and five-star hotels. Cambodia was also in a hotel building frenzy, fuelled by the demand arising from its growing inbound business events market, including incentive trips to its capital Phnom Penh and to Siem Reap, near the ancient temples of Angkor Wat.

In the more established conference destinations, new venues are continuing to open their doors to meetings, large and small. While many of these are purpose-built conference centres, a growing number fall into the category of 'unusual venues', mentioned in Chapter 1: theatres, cinemas, museums and a host of other leisure facilities that either have surplus capacity available or find themselves with space to let at particular times of the day.

But it is perhaps in the North American market that the recent growth in the supply of meetings facilities has been greatest – and most controversial. Farmer (2005) states that the building of new meetings space in that region is reaching an unprecedented level, and that where there is no room for new construction, existing facilities are renovating and adding amenities and technology.

A typical case of this expansion – and a typical rationale for justifying it – is the Vancouver (British Columbia) Convention and Exhibition Center, which is to be expanded from 133 000 square feet to 500 000 square feet, at an estimated cost of CDN$500 million. The city will host the 2010 Winter Olympic and Paralympic Games, but this is reported to be only one of the factors behind the decision to expand. The vice-president of meetings and convention sales for Tourism Vancouver reports that the venue currently turns away CDN$150 million of business per year because of space limitations. According to projections, the expanded center will generate additional delegate spending of CDN$229 million per year, which translates into an additional CND$76 million per year in tax revenues. It is also estimated that 7500 new permanent jobs will be created with the completed project.

Can such optimism be justified by the actual facts concerning current and projected levels of demand?

In 2005, a controversial report from the Brookings Institution, entitled Space Available: The Realities of Convention Centers as Economic Development Strategy, was published (Sanders, 2005). Although the study focuses on the situation in the United States, it raises a number of questions that conference destinations and venues in any country need to address for themselves. Sanders argues that in the United States the convention marketplace is actually in decline (and has been even prior to the disruptions of 9/11) and therefore simply cannot support the ongoing proliferation of US venue development. Although the study focuses on trade shows, rather than conferences *per se*, there are serious implications for conference centres if its findings are valid, since these are the venues primarily used for such events. Sanders (2005: 1) argues that, despite this decline in the demand for conference centres,

> Nonetheless, localities, sometimes with state assistance, have continued a type of arms race with competing cities to hold these events, investing massive amounts of capital in new convention center construction and expansion of existing facilities. Over the past decade alone, public capital spending on convention centers has doubled to $2.4 billion annually, increasing convention space by over 50% since 1990. Nationwide, 44 new or expanded convention centers are now in planning or construction.

An important conclusion of the Brookings study is that, despite the immense amount of public funding invested in new venues in the United States, the benefits in terms of increased numbers of visitors and revitalization of the city centre through the stimulation of new private investment and development have not occurred in most conference destinations.

In response to the publication of the Brookings study, several industry associations issued statements rejecting its findings, including the Center for Exhibition Industry Research and the International Association for Exhibition Management. Both associations questioned Sanders' conclusion that the market was in decline, claiming that, in limiting his data to the 200 largest tradeshows in the United States and to conference centres, he had overlooked the expanding market for meetings-focused conventions and events held in hotels, where many fledgling meetings incubate (Minton, 2005).

Hazinski and Detlefsen (2005) also question whether Sanders paints an accurate picture of the state of the industry, claiming that in focusing on tradeshows, he relies on a 'small and unrepresentative sample of events', and that excludes consumer shows and other events that may occur in conference centres.

It is clear that further, objective, research is required, not only in the United States, but in any destination investing public funds in conference venues. Any assessment of the viability of new venues must be based on a realistic view of the future of the conference industry since it is this view that influences capital investment decisions and the fortunes of those who make a living in the conference industry.

Technology

It was once believed that new information and communications technologies heralded the certain decline of the conference industry, as these allowed people easily to communicate their ideas and messages without actually travelling to business events. However, rather than killing the industry, as was once feared, these communications technology solutions are now helping venues attract more business by providing the infrastructure needed to make all types of meetings more engaging and more effective for those who attend them. The application of the same technology has given venues a powerful – and now indispensable – tool for marketing themselves, namely their increasingly sophisticated websites.

But the accelerating pace of advances in information and communications technology have made the task of keeping up to date with emerging technology a continual challenge for those responsible for designing and operating conference venues. In the late 1990s venues were installing fibre-optic wiring systems to allow conferences to use high-speed communications such as web casting and reception of real-time video via the Internet; now they are busy equipping themselves with WiFi (short for Wireless-Fidelity) facilities to enable conference delegates', organizers' and speakers' wireless network connection.

It is widely predicted that RF (radio frequency) tags and RFID (radio frequency identification) will also have a significant impact on the meetings industry in general, and on venues in particular, in the next few years.

Ball (2005) describes RF tags as small computer chips that contain a string of identifying digits similar to a bar code. When the tag comes within range of a reader device, the information on the tag is captured via radio frequency waves. RF tags are faster and more reliable than bar code technology. RFID eliminates the need for line-of-sight reading that bar coding requires. An entire palate of products, for example, can be scanned automatically in a second compared to what would take minutes or hours to do manually with today's barcode scanners.

Since the applications of RFID technology to the meetings industry are numerous – particularly in situations where delegates' name badges are checked – venues are already preparing to equip themselves with RFID scanners. Once equipped, the venues will be able to offer the following services to conference planners and delegates:

- Access control: Scanners at the entrances to venues will be able instantly to verify that the person wearing the RFID-enabled badge has legitimate access to a specific room or rooms.
- Access to cyber-cafés will open by sensing delegates' identity from their badges. It will not be necessary for delegates to type in their names.
- Collection of registration materials will be more easily tracked.
- VIPs could be tracked to be given special service, for example by notifying staff when they have come 'within range' (Ball, 2005).

As the pace of change in technology accelerates and new products offering clear benefits to the conference industry are continually being developed, venues are constantly having to invest, in order to maintain their competitive edge.

Table 3.1 Percentages of venues making new technology investments

	2003	2004	2005
Website enhancement	81	83	85
Wireless technologies	48	66	67
Guest room technologies	55	65	56
New A/V equipment	55	62	58
Online booking/planning systems for meeting planners	54	59	52
Customer relationship management technologies	50	59	51
Registration technologies	40	47	45
Online travel and housing systems for bookings	48	47	42
Teleconferencing	35	29	28
Audience/attendee response tools	25	28	26
Virtual meetings/shows	24	24	20

Source: MPI/American Express Futurewatch Survey, 2005

The MPI/American Express Futurewatch Survey for 2005 asked venues (including hotels with meetings facilities) about their technology-related investment plans for the year ahead. The results showed that more than half of the venues responding expected to make some capital investment in new audio/video equipment, guest room technologies, online booking/planning systems and customer relationship management technologies in 2005. Eighty-five per cent of respondents planned to invest in website enhancements and sixty-seven per cent in wireless technologies, the two categories of technology investment which were expected to grow faster in 2005 than in 2004. Table 3.1 shows the detailed results of this question.

However, one ongoing debate among venues is currently the question of whether it is a better policy to outsource the technology management function or to continue to manage it in-house, using the venue's own staff.

There appear to be similarities between venues' current dilemma about technology investment and management and the earlier development of their audio-visual (AV) facilities and services. When AV facilities consisted of only slide and film projectors and screens, most venues owned their own equipment. But challenged to keep up with clients' rapidly changing demands and the increasing sophistication of AV, many venues eventually outsourced the service to specialist AV companies.

Supporters of the outsourcing of this function claim that it enables venues to take advantage of the latest technologies without capitalizing the costs, since the expense of purchasing the latest technology is borne by the specialist company to which the responsibility has been outsourced. For example, Walshak (1998) quotes the manager of technical services of the Washington State Convention and Trade Center, who speaks in support of outsourcing technology services:

> When you consider the speed at which technology is advancing and how the capital investment affects the bottom line, there is no way we could hope to keep up. As we see it, there is no reason to manage technology in-house ... and every reason to outsource it. By letting the experts do their job, we are able to provide the highest level of service to our customers. And save money in the process.

Opponents of outsourcing, on the other hand, maintain that since the contracting out of any service entails the risk of the venue losing control of the quality of that service, the preferable solution is to keep it in-house, where standards can be maintained more directly.

Case Study 3.1, at the end of the chapter, presents a US convention center, Gaylord Palms, that makes particularly effective use of the opportunities offered by information and communications technology.

Venue design

Design for the future

In cities across the world, beautiful, iconic buildings are the source of considerable civic pride for the local population and important attractions for visitors. The Gaudi Cathedral in Barcelona, the Coliseum in Rome and the Houses of Parliament in London are outstanding examples of buildings that have a timeless appeal and close associations with the cities in which they are situated. In many countries the legacy left to their inhabitants by the designers and builders of bygone eras are the imposing castles and palaces that still remain the centrepieces of cities such as Edinburgh, Prague, Bangkok and Stockholm. Built to celebrate the magnificence of the most powerful families in the world, royal palaces and castles are the consequences of an age in which the splendour and opulence of a prince or a people could be measured by the grandeur of a building, the extravagant decor of a salon, or the originality of a fountain.

It has been said that conference centres have the potential to be regarded as the 'castles of the future' – iconic buildings that, if well designed, can become the symbol of the city in which they stand. Indeed, part of the motivation for many local authorities commissioning the construction of a new conference centre is the desire to create a prestigious and magnificent 'signature' building for their city, rather than the somewhat unimaginative 'empty boxes' of yesteryear.

Some shining examples of iconic venues of renown are: the Colorado Convention Center, which has a 125 ft-high roof blade rising into the air above it, significantly altering the Denver skyline; the award-winning Hong Kong Convention and Exhibition Centre; and Manchester International Convention Centre.

The challenge of creating a building of a prestigious nature is naturally attractive to architects, and many such professionals generally enter the architectural competition for the design of the conference centre that usually heralds the beginning of such construction projects. However, architects need a very clear brief from their clients in order to guide them in their proposals. To prepare this brief effectively, the clients (usually local authorities) must first consult with a wide range of stakeholders with experience of using such venues. Meetings planners are key stakeholders in this process.

There is a growing body of evidence that suggests that the appearance and design of venues is a key factor in determining meeting planners' choice of where to hold their events. In terms of the design of the venue, flexibility in terms of layout is of ongoing importance to planners. But these stakeholders also increasingly understand the impact that physical features such as the presence of natural daylight and the comfort of the seats in the auditorium can have on the success of their conferences. Minton (2005) describes how meetings planners are increasingly choosing conference centres on the basis of which venues make the most strategic sense for their events: 'For planners, it's not what meetings they can bring to convention centres, but what those centres can bring to their meetings' (Minton, 2005: 65). In other words, they are increasingly expecting venues not only to accommodate their events, but also to enhance them.

Functionality, therefore, is a crucial feature of a successful conference venue. Meetings planners are usually a reliable source of information regarding their own operational needs from venues, and there is growing awareness of involving them (and even conference delegates, the end-users) in designing the brief that architects should follow. So, while the need to deliver an iconic building for the civic landscape is increasingly important, this should not be provided at the expense of careful attention being paid to the inner workings of the building. Indeed, some specialists in venue design believe that the design of a conference centre should always be driven from the inside out, not by the desire for an exceptional façade.

Design for flexibility

The Colorado Convention Center mentioned above represents another current development in conference centre design, the trend towards multi-use venues – venues that are flexible and customizable in their design and layout and which, as a result, hold appeal for a wider range of events.

Curtis Fentress, the architect whose company designed the expansion of the conference centre, created in that venue a 50 000 square foot multi-purpose space that can break out into 18 different permutations, making it suitable for use as an exhibition area, a ballroom or multiple meetings spaces. As part of the expansion scheme of the same venue, a new 5000-seat lecture theatre was built, capable of being sub-divided into three separate meeting rooms. As the only venue in Denver with 5000 seats, the Colorado Convention Centre has also hosted concerts by stars such as Bruce Springsteen and Alicia Keys, as well as a number of high-school graduation ceremonies.

As well as multi-purpose venues, mixed-use venues are also increasingly the choice of developers and city authorities. For example, the Washington State Convention & Trade Center in Seattle, in addition to its meetings facilities, also includes an office building, street-front retail and a museum. On the other side of the ocean, the new Dongqianu International Educational Forum Complex near Shanghai, designed by architects firm Denton Corker Marshall, and due to open in 2009, will include not only a conference centre and exhibition hall, but also a hotel and shopping facilities. The highly imaginative shape of the complex is designed to suggest dancing Chinese dragons.

Minton (2005: 74) quotes C. Andrew McLean, principal at TVS & Associates, an architectural firm that has built more than 50 convention centres during the past 30 years:

> We're asked pretty regularly to think about including retail space in [convention] buildings, usually on the edges so that it animates the street. There's always the concern that the building is a large inanimate structure [when it is not hosting events].

Design for security

Security has become an over-riding concern of those planning conferences and those attending them, and it is incumbent on all venues to ensure that the building in no way adds to the risks incurred, by delegates and visitors, in attending the events that

Table 3.2 Threats to the security of venues

Threat	Duty of the venue	Example
Petty crime	To combat casual vandalism and petty crime	Pickpockets infiltrating the event
Industrial security	To protect against industrial espionage during corporate conferences	Theft of delegates' laptops containing confidential company files
Public disorder	To protect delegates against demonstrations and similar, during sensitive events	Protests against high-profile summits: e.g. 2005 WTO trade talks in Hong Kong.
Terrorism	To protect the building and delegates during events which are attended by high profile terrorist targets	Personal attacks on scientists using animals for research

it hosts. Some venues will, by their very nature, attract many sensitive events, which will demand security on several levels, dependent on the threat assessment. The types of potential threat and the duty of the venue to counteract them can be categorized as in Table 3.2.

Venue designers, by taking account of the potential risk situations at the design stage, will help facilitate the task of the venue's managers when a high risk event is due to take place there. This is not merely altruistic – it is a positive contribution to the marketability and profitability of the venue.

Eric Rymer, a venue security specialist for the consultancy The Right Solution, makes the following observations about building in safety and security at the venue design stage:

> Operating a conference centre safely and securely can be made much easier if the initial design and construction of the building is done with these aspects in mind. It costs no more to design in safety and security. Furthermore, the venue operator will be grateful for a design which allows him to secure the building in as short a time as possible. If a high security conference requires an 'island site', the shortest time possible to achieve a secure perimeter means more time available for selling the space, as the centre will be closed down for a shorter period.
>
> Naturally, there are building regulations, which cover the statutory requirements, particularly for fire safety. These regulations vary from country to country – and some countries do not have regulations at all. The UK regulations are among the strictest in the world and consequently, they make a good minimum basis for design.
>
> Over and above the statutory requirements, the interior design and finishes can enhance delegate safety and security. For example, floor finishes that become slippery when wet should not be used, particularly by entrance doors. The designer should avoid dark corridors, or small corners hidden away from sight. Clear and airy foyers and circulation spaces not only make for a more pleasant environment, but for a safer one also. Even the simplest elements of design should be considered with security in mind. It is hard to believe, but convention centres have been designed with meeting room doors that do not lock!
>
> Circulation routes are particularly important in the design. Linear routes, with clear signposting, help to avoid confusion, especially in emergency situations. At the same time, natural control points should be built

into the routes. For example, stairs and escalators become control points, easily policed by one steward, to ensure only authorized delegates can go into a particular area.

VIP circulation routes should be carefully considered during design. A VIP may want to arrive or exit the building secretly, via a back-of-house route. There should also be a route from the main presentation area (typically an auditorium stage) to the exit, or a press interview room, without having to go through front of house areas.

In front of house areas, places of safety should be considered. For example, a concrete planter strategically placed can be used to shelter from bullets, should the need arise.

Early consideration of electronic security measures is beneficial. Intruder alarms, door entry indicators, electronic locking systems and CCTV (with both overt and covert cameras) all help towards a secure environment. Some electronic systems may not be required at all times, such as X-ray equipment or metal detectors. However, these will be needed for some events and consequently the building should have the ability to install such equipment on a temporary basis. This often just means the simplest of provision, such as power sockets by the entrance doors. If such measures are incorporated into the design at an early stage, it will avoid considerable disruption later on.

Design for accessibility

Case Study 2.2, focusing on Perth Convention Bureau's 'Beyond Compliance' Programme, underlined the importance of catering for delegates with disabilities.

Making sure that conferences are accessible for disabled people should be a key design consideration for any venue. In many countries, buildings must, by law, be designed so as to be accessible by disabled people. For example, in the UK, the 1995 Disability Discrimination Act gave disabled people equal rights to attend, participate in and enjoy events. This means that venues are required to make reasonable adjustments to their facilities and services, to make them accessible to people with disabilities. Moreover, it is not only conference delegates who are affected by the accessibility (or lack of it) of venues. Speakers, exhibitors and even some of the people employed by the venue can be disabled. There is, therefore, a compelling case for designing venues of all kinds for maximum accessibility.

But making venues accessible for disabled people is not just a legal requirement – it is an important commercial decision too. For instance, in the UK, there are around 10 million disabled people, with a combined annual spending power of £50 billion (DRC, 2004); and in the United States, there is also a strong disability travel market: more than 21 million adults with disabilities travelled for pleasure and/or business in 2004 and 2005. And of those who stayed in hotels, for example, 48% said they had problems with physical barriers (Anon, 2005).

A simple example of the type of problem disabled delegates can face – and a solution to the problem – is provided in the following example. A hotel conference suite has a policy of only providing a self-service buffet at lunchtime for delegates, who eat while standing, resting their drinks on small tables at waist height. But some disabled people with mobility impairments or visual impairments may find it difficult or impossible to help themselves to food from a buffet selection and to eat it without placing their plate on a table. It would be a reasonable adjustment for the venue to provide staff to serve people at the buffet and to carry food to a few tables provided for seated delegates. It would be good practice to reserve some places at these tables for disabled people who need this service.

Ultimately, the choice of which venue is used for their events is made by the events organizers. Aware of their own responsibilities under disability legislation, a growing number of meetings planners will only consider fully accessible venues: those that allow people to enter, exit and to move around the building with ease, that offer adapted toilet facilities and where, ideally, the event can take place on one floor only.

One of the most effective ways of establishing the impact that any building has on disabled people is to undertake an access audit, a technique being increasingly used by meetings planners when they are considering potential venues for their events. Increasingly, these audits are undertaken by independent, professional consultants, who inspect the venue and produce a report outlining existing access provision and recommending improvements. But for those meetings planners who wish to carry out their own access audit, a number of checklists are available.

Such checklists include the assessment of car parks, toilets, corridors, lifts, catering areas, plenary rooms, break-out rooms and entrance foyers. For example, if there are going to be exhibition stands and display cases, will there be ample room for safe and easy manoeuvre between the stands for everybody, including people using wheelchairs or guide dogs? The access audit will usually recommend changes such as installing accessible toilets, door opening mechanisms or simpler measures such as changing door handles and painting door and window surrounds in contrasting colours to assist people with visual impairments.

For new venues wishing to ensure that they are completely accessible to disabled people, or for established venues wishing to adapt their facilities for this market, there are many sources of advice and guidance. Venues should need no external pressure to compel them to undertake these measures. Making changes to the design of the physical environment not only makes venues more attractive to event organizers, it also makes them more accessible for people who are not disabled. Clearer signposting within the venue, for example, helps all delegates, not only the visually impaired.

Green venues

The need to observe high environmental standards in every aspect of human activity is now widely acknowledged. As was discussed in Chapter 1, the conference industry as a whole can have a range of impacts on the built and the natural environment, and stakeholders are increasingly accepting their responsibility for minimizing the negative effects of conference activity wherever it takes place.

Those who design and operate conference venues can also make a contribution to environmental protection. Purpose-built conference centres in particular have the potential to make a significant detrimental impact on the locality in which they are situated, through their use of resources such as energy and fresh water, and through the substantial amounts of waste they can generate.

Yet, as Bauer and Lam (2003) maintain, despite its worldwide importance, the environmental performance of the conference industry has received little attention by researchers. In their seminal research into this issue, the authors investigate the 'greening' practices of conference venues and evaluate the attitudes of venue operators, regarding green issues. Using questionnaires and in-depth interviews, they surveyed the 175 venue members of ICCA. Out of the 38 responses received, over 60% came from Europe (with Germany recording the highest response rate – five venues) and 15% from North America, leading the authors to conclude that environmental consciousness in this context is higher in western countries than it is in the Asia Pacific region. The results showed that 46.2% of venues already had an Environmental Management System in place; and 33.3% were planning to have one established. Such a system is defined as the setting of 'green' objectives and targets to improve environmental performance, and was found along with energy conservation and waste reduction programmes, to be one of the highest ranked measures identified by venues for conducting 'green' measures.

However, the inevitable conclusion of the authors is that many venues still do not recognize the need to be environmentally friendly. But:

> *If the environmental performance of venues would become a key selection criterion for organizations' meeting planners and convention organizers, the management of venues would no doubt be very quick in changing their ways to cater for a more environmentally friendly market.*

> (Bauer and Lam, 2003: 264)

Case Study 3.2 on Tampere Hall in Finland illustrates what can be achieved in the environmental management of a conference venue.

Summary

The number of new venues, and types of venues, opening their doors to conference delegates appears to be escalating, and there are increasing signs that demand for these facilities is not increasing at the same rate. Venues are not only changing in quantity, but also in their quality. Information and communications technology is rapidly changing the ways venues host their events, and design of new and converted venues is increasingly taking into account issues such as flexibility, security and accessibility. Regarding new-build conference centres, there is often a tension (not always creative) between the wish to commission or create a stunning, iconic building, and the more mundane, practical needs of those planning and attending conferences in such venues.

But perhaps the most over-riding concern is that venues should be constructed and operated in such a way that their negative impacts on the natural environment are minimal.

Case Study 3.1

Gaylord Palms Resort and Convention Center

Gaylords Palms Resort and Convention Center is a US venue that is widely recognized as making effective use of the opportunities offered by information and communications technology in the following aspects of its functioning:

Proposals

Meeting planners can use the Internet to solicit bids from Gaylord Palms Resort and Convention Center, through a central website, eliminating time-and-paper-consuming requests for proposals that generally rely on traditional written correspondence.

Connectivity

A full cabling system has been installed to meet the complex networking needs of conferences and exhibitions with the ability to create a secured, reliable and fast network (VLAN) including connections back to the Internet for corporate connectivity (VPN). The networks can be wired or wireless based on the customer's needs and may connect back to guests' rooms. Additionally, the venue has the flexible bandwidth to meet all needs.

In-house staff

Gaylord Palms Resort and Convention Center has a dedicated, on-site 'technology solutions representative' to accommodate clients' technology-related needs. The hotel's sales manager works closely with conference services and serves as the liaison between hotel and convention technological services and the hotel's clients.

HSIA

High Speed Internet Access is provided free to hotel guests, including a Gaylord Palms Resort and Convention Center specific portal that offers information and guest services. HSIA is also provided at the pool area and in the luxury cabanas that comprise some of the guest accommodation.

AV

The venue's audio-visual system includes a full-fly loft in the ballroom to accommodate large entertainment acts and complex shows and events. There are dedicated 'recording rooms' for audio recording and duplication of group sessions. All meeting and convention space is equipped with state-of-the-art audio and visual signal processing and a signal distribution network. A state-of-the-art lighting network offers individual control of all meeting rooms and pre-function zones.

Built-in power for major entertainment functions and an on-site audio-visual department serve both the ballroom and exhibition levels of the venue. There is a 40 ft × 100 ft permanent stage equipped with built-in sound and lighting, as well as a built-in infrastructure for routing signal feeds to exterior broadcast truck pedestals (for live satellite broadcast support). Boardrooms include built-in computer displays, tele-conferencing and video conferencing functionality.

Business centre

A full-service business centre includes: photocopy services, laser printing, secretarial services, document binding, network printing, off-site production, name badge creation, notary services, poster and banner printing, two-colour letterhead, pamphlets/brochures production, faxing, computer services and Internet connectivity, computer and small equipment rental.

Online registration

With a designated web address and password, delegates can register for accommodation in the venue via the Internet, eliminating the need for a manual rooming list. Guests may also request a particular room preference online.

Event boards

Meeting and marketing information is displayed on full-screen plasma displays in the large public space areas of the hotel and convention centre. Client logos can be screened behind event schedules and – since plasma and LED event boards are on the in-house local area network – information can be updated instantly.

Astrovision
Gaylord Palms Resort has its own jumbo-size Astrovision in the hotel atrium. On a screen reminiscent of that found in Times Square, important news of the day and information for meeting attendees and other guests may be displayed and updated daily.

Case Study 3.2

The environmental management system of Tampere Hall

Background
Tampere lies 170 kilometres north of Helsinki, the capital of Finland, and is located on an isthmus between two large lakes. It was the country 's leading industrial town in the 19th century, and the old factory buildings offer visitors a unique glimpse into the history of Finland's industrial heritage. Today, the city is a thriving centre of high-tech industries in many different fields. With its two universities, two polytechnics, a university hospital and numerous research institutes, Tampere is also an important centre of education and research.

In 1981, the City of Tampere set up a committee to plan and implement the construction of a conference and concert venue. An architectural competition was organized for the design of the facility in 1983, and the winning architects were Sakari Aartelo and Esa Piironen.

Tampere Hall was officially opened in September 1990 in the very heart of the city, opposite Tampere University and close to the railway station. A flagship development for the city, the venue has since then received over three million visitors in connection with various conferences and cultural events. Wholly owned by the City of Tampere, it is the largest concert and congress centre in the Nordic countries. In 2003, the venue's turnover was €3.8 million. Tampere Hall has twice been nominated as the best conference centre in Finland: in 1999 and in 2001.

The environmental programme
The idea that a venue should take every step possible to lessen the burden on the environment is an integral part of Tampere Hall's philosophy. For many years the Hall has played a pioneering role in preventative environmental protection. It was one of the first conference centres in the world to adapt its operations and services in order to conserve the environment. In addition to monitoring its own practices, Tampere Hall also considers itself to have an important duty to influence the environmental behaviour of its customers and other users of the venue.

Tampere Hall's environment-friendly measures concentrate above all on energy consumption and the elimination and recycling of waste created by its operations. Careful attention is also paid to the environmental friendliness of its acquisitions, the materials it requires for its own functioning.

Energy consumption: By means of an energy-saving programme Tampere Hall has managed to reduce its heating consumption by up to 30% and electricity consumption by 20–25% since the early years of its operation. The savings have been implemented mainly by means of accurate adjustments controlled by automation. These are principally connected with the air conditioning, heating and hot water systems and with the electricity consumption of office equipment. As an example of the measures routinely undertaken, the venue adjusts air-conditioning during concerts and meetings according to load levels. Staff responsible for air-conditioning circulate in the halls with carbon dioxide meters and increase or decrease air-conditioning as required.

Waste disposal: The burden on the environment is also reduced by eliminating the production of waste and sorting and recycling the waste that is produced, as much as possible. In addition to the staff's own day-to-day working facilities, waste sorting disposal points are also provided in conjunction with exhibitions, conferences and other events. This achieves cost saving by reducing the number of collections of mixed waste.

During events in its Exhibition Hall, Tampere Hall's 'Eco Guide' is circulated among exhibitors. This publication contains valuable advice about how exhibitors can sort their waste during and after the event. The House's 'Greencoats' (porters) and technicians are also available to provide advice to exhibitors.

In the Hall, the following materials are sorted:

- paper
- board
- energy waste
- mixed waste
- glass
- metal waste
- electronic scrap
- bio-waste
- fluorescent lamps
- hazardous waste.

Acquisitions: Tampere Hall's preference is for recyclable products that do not create hazardous waste.

Awards

In recognition of its efforts to protect the natural environment, Tampere Hall has received awards from a number of organizations, including:

- EIBTM (The European Incentive and Business Travel and Meetings exhibition) 1994
- Hämeen ympäristöpalkinto (Regional Environmental Award) 1994
- Green Globe 1997.

As one of the world's most renowned environmentally sensitive conference facilities, Tampere Hall markets itself as such, globally. As a result, it is successful in attracting a number of scientific events on themes relating to the environment. Two examples of international scientific conferences that it has hosted are the International Congress of Toxicology July 2004; and 'Ambience 2005', in September 2005. The latter event focused on intelligent ambience including intelligent textiles, smart garments, intelligent home and living environment.

Further reading

For more on the greening measures that Tampere Hall employs, see:

Anja Van Aerschot and Pekka Heikura (1995) 'Tampere Hall: an Environmentally Conscious Congress Venue in Finland', *Industry and Environment*, 18 (2–3), published by the United Nations Environment Programme

Review and Discussion Questions

1 Can the construction of any more conference centres be justified?
2 How might the design of a conference centre built this year be different from a conference centre built at the end of the 20th century?
3 What advice may be given to an entrepreneur who wishes to construct a new conference centre that is as environmentally friendly as possible?

Sources

Anon (2005) 'Do you overlook the disabled?', *Association Meetings International*, September

Bauer, TG and Lam, L (2003) 'The greening of convention venues', *Proceedings of 2003 Convention & Expo Summit*, Hong Kong Polytechnic University

DRC (2004) *Creating Accessible Events*, Disability Rights Commission

Farmer, RP (2005) 'The meeting industry's growth fuels a surge in renovations, expansions and new constructions', *The Meeting Professional*, August

Giannini, D (2004) 'WiFi, e-mail, war games, live streaming surgeries: technology raises the bar for the competitive convention host', *Hospitality Forum*, May

Hazinski, T and Detlefsen, H (2005) 'Is the sky falling on the convention center industry? A critical review of the Brookings Institution Research Brief on Convention Centers as Economic Development Strategy', *HVS Journal*, May

Minton, E (2005) 'What planners really want', *The Meeting Professional*, June

Sanders, H (2005) *Space Available: The Realities of Convention Centers as Economic Development Strategy*, The Brookings Institution

Walshak, H (1998) 'Great tech'xpectations: high-tech centers creating the next wave of convention networking', *Convene*, PCMA

Chapter 4

Marketing Planning for Destinations and Venues: Principles and Theories

Summary of Chapter Contents

This chapter examines the principles and theories underlying the planning strategies employed by venues and destinations to market their facilities and services.
  The chapter covers:

- The purpose of marketing plans
- The use of marketing research
- Market segmentation
- The positioning and branding of products
- The marketing mix
- The need for evaluation and monitoring of marketing plans

It includes case studies on:

- The branding of the Royal College of Physicians' conference facilities
- Canberra Convention Bureau Business Plan 2005/2006

Learning Outcomes

On completion of this chapter, you should be able to:

- appreciate the advantages offered by effective marketing planning
- understand the use of marketing research in the planning process
- understand the role of, and techniques used in, segmentation and positioning
- discuss how branding may be applied to the marketing of a destination or venue
- appreciate the use of the marketing mix
- understand the techniques that may be used to evaluate and monitor a marketing plan

Introduction

There can be no doubt that the success of any destination or venue depends on effective marketing planning. It is therefore essential that marketing managers devote sufficient time and energy to planning for the future. And the tangible manifestation of that planning process is the destination or venue's marketing plan.

An organization's marketing plan is a vital element of its corporate strategic plan or business plan. It is the fundamental tool that enables it to devise and execute successful marketing programmes. Gartrell (1994) describes marketing plans as a kind of 'navigational chart' for organizations; and, to continue with the nautical metaphor, it is clear that any convention bureau or conference centre, for example, attempting to market its facilities and services without a formal plan would risk going seriously adrift and directionless, obliged to rely on a series of *ad hoc* decisions and extemporized reactions to external events.

Middleton (2001: 194) emphasizes that the marketing strategy planning process 'is essentially proactive in the sense that it defines and wills the future shape of the organization as well as responding to changing industry patterns, technology, market conditions and perceived consumer needs'. A marketing plan, then, helps managers develop a clear direction for a set of complex, interrelated, activities to be carried out over the course of a specified period – usually one year.

There are further advantages offered by effective marketing planning. Kotler *et al.* (2003) list the purposes of a marketing plan as follows. It:

- provides a road map for all marketing activities … for the next year
- ensures that marketing activities are in agreement with the corporate strategic plan
- forces marketing managers to review and think through objectively all steps in the marketing process
- assists in the budgeting process to match resources with marketing objectives
- creates a process to match actual against expected results.

Components of the marketing planning process

An effective marketing plan is a working document that ultimately enables the destination or venue to instigate practical strategies in the form of a series of action plans. However, prior to the formulating of those strategies, a number of key steps must be taken.

The devising of marketing plans is a common theme of the marketing literature, and authors generally agree that the process includes following several interdependent steps in a logical progression. And although there is little agreement as to the number of actual components in the marketing planning process, or the terminology used for each one, several elements are almost universally recognized as being indispensable:

1 The conducting of marketing research
2 The selecting of target segments and the positioning of the organization

3 The establishing of objectives and action plans (what is to be done, when and by whom)
4 The monitoring and evaluation of the marketing plan.

The rest of this chapter will explore each of these elements in turn.

Marketing research

The planning process generally begins with the organization undertaking some form of research in order to evaluate its current and possible future position in the market. Commonly described as a *situation analysis* or *SWOT analysis*, this initial step involves a systematic assessment of the product (destination or venue) itself, as well as of the external market environment.

Product

This element of the marketing plan involves the destination or venue undertaking a detailed examination of where and how it stands in the marketplace, its market share and its relation to its competitors. It is clear that, in order to be effective, such an examination must be frank and comprehensive, and must be, in part, based on the organization's own internal, 'micromarket' information: sales figures, client profiles, post-event evaluations, studies of advertising/promotional effectiveness, and so on.

A rigorous review of both the strengths and the weaknesses of the product, in the widest sense, is a key part of this process. In Chapter 1, the interdependence of destinations and venues was emphasized. Accordingly, therefore, any venue's situation analysis must include a review of the destination's particular strengths and weaknesses, as well as its own – and vice versa.

Similarly, a 'competitor analysis' – a frank and full appraisal of the capabilities and limitations of competing venues or destinations – is indispensable at this point in the process. Genuine competitor analysis requires a recognition on the part of the destination or venue that true competitive advantages are limited to those factors that are recognized by meetings buyers and planners and influence their purchasing decisions.

Market environment

All organizations operate within a market environment over which they have little or no control. Marketers, therefore, need to undertake research in order to become fully aware of the principal environmental factors likely to affect their particular destination or venue. This can put them in a position to make the most of positive trends (opportunities) and to identify actual and potential obstacles to success (threats). This aspect of situation analysis is sometimes known as environmental forecasting.

Some of the opportunities and threats will inevitably be created as a result of the activities and business performance of the destination or venue's direct and indirect competitors. For example, if a conference hotel's closest rival in the same city plans to expand or refurbish its meeting facilities, this represents a potential threat that the hotel must take into account in its marketing plan. Whereas any conference destination affected adversely as a result of, for instance, repeated strikes by the local workforce or the national airline, will present business opportunities to its competitor destinations, that should be reflected in their marketing plans.

However, for all organizations the main element in their assessment of the external market environment will be a comprehensive review of all of those issues and trends that could have an impact on their future operation in general – and, in particular, on the level of demand for the facilities and services that the organization offers. It is precisely because that level of demand is rarely static that environmental forecasting is a vital step in the marketing plan.

For any destination or venue, this will comprise a careful consideration of all of the political, economic, social and technological (PEST) factors that were reviewed in Chapters 2 and 3 of this book – for example, new legislation limiting how much pharmaceutical companies may spend on sponsoring medical conferences; or a significant change in currency exchange rates; or new advances in the quality of teleconferencing technology; or new transport links. A broad analysis of all of these types of factors is a vital step for any organization systematically appraising its present position and identifying significant opportunities and threats.

Research into this aspect of situation analysis is generally undertaken using the relevant 'macromarket information' available to destinations and venues. This may take the form of 'big picture' research reports or surveys produced by national tourist organizations, industry associations, consultants, academics or the meetings and incentive industry press. The annual EIBTM Industry Trends and Market Share Report is an example of research that is commissioned and published by the organizers (Reed Travel Exhibitions) of a major conference trade show. Such macromarket information can comprise reports on general trends in conference demand and supply, economic forecasts, or the type of performance tables produced by ICCA (International Congress and Convention Association) or the UIA (Union of International Associations) for example.

Segmentation and positioning

Once an organization has conducted research to evaluate its marketing position, it can begin the next stage of its marketing plan: selecting its target segments and positioning the organization.

Segmentation

It is generally agreed that interest in market segmentation – or segmentation analysis – has been growing in importance over the past few decades, as its contribution to improving the effectiveness of destination and venue marketing has increasingly been recognized.

Kotler *et al.* (2003) define market segmentation as the sub-dividing of a market into homogeneous sub-sets of customers, where any sub-set may conceivably be selected as a market target to be reached with a distinct marketing mix. In other words, market segments are composed of customers who are alike in some way or another, and who may appear in the marketing plan as discrete targets for specific mixes of marketing activities undertaken by the destination or venue.

Fifield (1998: 130) notes that 'such a breaking up of … marketing into a number of different mixes is obviously much more costly in terms of marketing investment and control, but the argument goes that with a more relevant mix you would improve your penetration of a given market segment and the increased volume would pay off the additional costs incurred'.

A vital element of any marketing plan, therefore, is the analysis of available market segments and the selection of the most appropriate segments for targeting. The list of available segments will include segments currently targeted by the destination or venue, as well as newly recognized market segments. It follows that the task of selecting the most appropriate segments will inevitably require careful consideration of the information gleaned from the situation analysis stage of the marketing plan, since effective market segmentation presupposes an accurate understanding of where and how the organization stands in the marketplace, and of the principal forces shaping the market environment – some of which may generate new segments or exclude existing segments.

A well-conducted situation analysis is, therefore, a destination or venue's key to becoming aware of the market segments that are available, and understanding their own ability to satisfy those particular segments' specific demands.

There are a number of different possible bases for segmenting the market for conferences, conventions and business events:

- By geographical zones: for example, a conference venue may choose to target primarily regional and national events – such as the annual conferences of professional associations, and/or the business events of companies based in the region in which the venue is located.
- By industry sector: Vienna, for instance, specializes in attracting medical congresses to its many meetings venues.
- By price sensitivity: for example, given the ability of most UK university venues to offer genuinely competitive rates, they generally target market segments seeking value-for-money, such as youth groups or the SMERF market.
- By purpose of visit: the island of Mauritius, for example, with its image of luxury and exclusivity, targets primarily the incentive travel and incentivized meetings market.

But whatever the basis or bases used for segmenting the market, Yoram Wind's five principal rules for good robust segments are entirely relevant. According to Wind, a segment should be:

- measurable – how big it is and how it differs from the market at large. This shows whether the segment is growing or declining
- accessible – reachable by the organization's communication channels
- substantial – large enough to yield a profit, bearing in mind the need for the additional investment required in developing a specific marketing mix
- characterized by mutual exclusivity – a true segment will relate to marketing messages aimed at it, but will not relate to other messages aimed at other segments
- homogeneous in response to marketing variables – all people in the segment will respond in a uniform manner.

However, commentators are generally agreed that segments are not created by marketers, but, rather, *identified* by them. This is put most succinctly by Fifield (1998: 132), who states that:

> *Probably the most powerful aspect of … segmentation is that it forces the marketer to understand a fundamental truth about market segmentation, and that is that it is not the organization or the marketer who actually segments the marketplace; it is the marketplace which segments itself. People fit themselves into market segments. Our job is not to divide the marketplace – our job is to identify how the market divides itself up and then to package and present our marketing mix accordingly.*

Positioning

Following the identification and selection of their target segments, the next task for venues and destinations is to influence the ways in which their products are perceived by those segments. This is the process known as product positioning, or simply positioning – establishing a product's *position* in the minds of the targeted customers.

In a market characterized by an abundant over-supply of products that are broadly similar in many ways, the potential buyer's perception of particular venues and destinations plays a vital role in the decision-making process. Holloway's (2004: 77) observations on the importance of perception as a factor in leisure tourism decisions may be equally applied to the conference sector:

> *For those who have not actually visited a destination, perception is reality. Thus, building a distinct, positive and appealing image in the marketplace is critical. The image should not, however, be created through illusions. A product's image must be grounded in its unique and appealing attributes and developed through an intentional and systematic product positioning approach.*

Middleton (2001: 199) also stresses the importance of image, summarizing the important role of product positioning as follows: 'Positioning underpins product/market growth through creating and sustaining a long-term favourable image or perception among prospective customers and other key stakeholders.'

It is clear, therefore, that in order to increase their chances of succeeding in attracting business from their target market or markets, venues and destinations must first of all establish a clear position for themselves, and then effectively communicate this to buyers. Such products should be clearly positioned in relation to the actual and potential needs of the target market. Essential to this process, then, is the identifying of the product's benefits and demonstrating to the target markets how their needs are satisfied by these benefits. Once again, this information should have been gleaned from the situation analysis stage of the marketing plan.

Holloway (2004) outlines four different approaches that may be used in devising a positioning strategy:

1 Positioning by **product benefits**: showing how a product/service feature will produce benefit/value for customers. Marriott, for example, have positioned their Courtyard properties as a product catering for the business market, and use the slogan: 'Courtyard by Marriott: the hotel designed by business travellers'.
2 Positioning by **price and quality**: this strategy is generally easier to accomplish and more effective at the extreme ends of the pricing scale – high-priced luxury and low-priced economy products. The annual Luxury Travel Market trade show held in Cannes features a number of exhibitors representing meeting venues that

are clearly positioned at the top quality end of the market – chateaux and palaces, for instance, that offer opulent meetings facilities – at considerable cost.

3 Positioning relative to a **product class**: this approach involves emphasizing a particular class of products to which the venue or destination belongs. This may take the form of either *likening* the product to others in the same class (as in the case of Edinburgh, for example, positioning itself as a member of the BestCities consortium); or *disassociating* a product from others, in order to give it an enhanced position (as in the case of Mexico positioning itself as the only South American country to offer 0% VAT on conferences and exhibitions organized in their country by foreign companies).

4 Positioning relative to a **competitor**: sometimes known as 'head-on positioning', this positioning strategy takes direct aim at the product's own direct or indirect competition and draws them into the advertising campaign. For example, Eurostar has effectively positioned itself in the business travel market by favourably comparing its own services with those of the airlines flying to those destinations served by the Eurostar trains.

It is useful to make the distinction here between positioning and repositioning. In the sense that, by definition, a new product has no pre-existing image in the minds of buyers, an image must be created for it, in order to determine how it is perceived. Establishing a position for a new venue or destination is made somewhat easier by the fact that there are no pre-existing negative images to be counteracted.

The need for repositioning – changing the current position of an existing image – can arise due to different sets of circumstances, including the arrival of a new competitor. Most often, however, the need for repositioning derives from a change in the way the venue or destination relates to the market. For example, due to a lack of maintenance and product enhancement, conference venues in some UK seaside resorts have not been able to continue to satisfy the rising expectations of planners and delegates, and have, as a result, had to reposition themselves as centres for popular entertainment.

In a further example of how a product has been repositioned in response to changes in demand, Gartrell (1994) notes that many larger convention and visitor bureaux in the United States have attempted to redefine their destinations as small meeting or corporate meeting sites as a result of market pressures (the rise in importance of small- and medium-sized events), even though they have been traditionally known as major convention cities.

It is clear that even in the case of established venues and destinations, it is vital constantly to assess the validity of their image and consequently to decide either to maintain it or change it through a repositioning strategy.

Once the desired position has been established, the *positioning statement* may be written. Holloway (2004) describes a positioning statement as a document that is created for use within the organization – a concise theme/statement that is woven through all marketing communications. In essence, it is an internal document that helps the firm direct its marketing efforts by communicating a consistent viewpoint and a *unified* goal that can be shared by all members of the organization.

A marketing *slogan*, on the other hand, is an external marketing tool – often a phrase generated from the positioning statement that is designed to capture the attention of the target market and reinforce a product's image. It should indicate how the product is different from the others by highlighting the venue or destination's *unique selling proposition* (USP) and use words that produce a very distinctive image ('biggest, fastest, least expensive' …).

A slogan, then, may be seen as a proposition that helps to identify and position a venue or destination in the minds of prospective users, and differentiate it from all others. Such labels abound in both leisure tourism ('I love New York') and business events (the Polish city of Wroclaw has as its slogan 'The Meeting Place'). In the context of tourist destinations, Middleton (2001) considers the use of such slogans, noting that in order to be successful, they must:

• be based on genuine product values and attributes that can be delivered and that visitors recognize as authentic, not fake
• be readily understood by customers
• involve at least the leading players in the commercial sector
• be incorporated into the promotional efforts of a country's regions and resorts
• be sustained over several years (to overcome communication inertia, etc.)
• be systematically exploited in a range of sales-promotion and customer-servicing techniques designed to reach visitors on arrival at the destination, as well as prospective visitors in countries of origin.

Branding

Increasingly, the concept of branding is being linked with the positioning of all types of products, including venues and destinations.

The brand concept is best considered as simply a set of associations that is linked to a particular destination, venue or chain of venues, that resides in buyers' memory and helps them understand:

• What the brand is
• Why it is potentially relevant to them
• How it differs from other, competitor, brands.

Brand associations spring from various marketing actions undertaken by the supplier of the product, including advertising and general media communications, as well as certain product characteristics (including the name and the logo or slogan). Information about the brands from the press, opinion leaders and word of mouth also affects the nature of these associations.

Essentially, then, a brand is a collection of perceptions in the mind of the potential buyer. 'It is the psychological, emotional, and (one hopes) motivational link between the customer and the product' (Harrill, 2005: 32).

Long before attempts were made to brand destinations and venues, the concept was applied to consumer goods, where the need for branding arose as a result of increasing global competition and the increasing difficulty for consumers to differentiate what were effectively very similar products in very crowded markets. The impact of branding today can be witnessed in the market for mineral water, for example, where branding is extensively used in order to distinguish near-identical products from others in the range.

But, to what extent can the branding concept be usefully applied to the marketing of venues and destinations?

Since the early 1990s, many hotel chains have branded their conference product, to assist in the differentiation of their meetings facilities and services from their competitors, and to build customer loyalty. Branding was introduced in part to guarantee buyers that they would receive the same quality-assured level of service whichever hotel in the chain was used. From the point of view of the buyer, one of the major advantages of branding was the security of knowing that their meeting would be planned and would take place according to a number of assured, written standards. Such standards may, for example, state how promptly the initial enquiry would be dealt with, exactly how the hotel would assist on the day of the event, how the meetings room would be set up, how the bill would be calculated and how soon after the event it would be sent to the client (Davidson and Cope, 2003).

It may be convincingly argued that hotel chains' use of branding has brought them a considerable measure of *brand equity* in the form of the four major assets described by Aaker's (1991) model of consumer-based brand equity, as explored in Pike (2004):

- **Brand loyalty**: repeat and referral custom, arising from the desire for a reduced risk of an unsatisfactory experience.
- **Brand awareness**: the foundation of all sales activity. Awareness represents the strength of the brand's presence in the mind of the target. There is general agreement that planners' familiarity with hotels' meetings facilities brands has increased through repeated exposure and strong associations.
- **Perceived quality**: there is little point in branding any product that is of poor or variable quality.
- **Brand associations**: a brand association is anything 'linked' in memory to a brand. These associations are a combination of *functional* and *affective* attributes, of which some will represent key buying criteria. 'What is most critical is that brand associations are strong, favorable and unique, in that order' (Keller, 2003, quoted in Pike, 2004).

But while meetings facilities may be close to consumer goods, regarding the way in which branding may be applied to them, there is much more room for debate when considering the role of branding as it applies to destinations. Although the topic of destination branding first appeared in the tourism literature in the late 1990s, research related to the branding of destinations has been sparse, and there has been, in particular, little published research on the long-term effectiveness of destination branding in general or business destination branding in particular.

Advocates of destination branding nevertheless believe that the future of destination marketing will be a battle of the brands, since 'it is likely that most destinations will become increasingly substitutable, if not already so, and therefore commodities rather than brands' (Pike, 2004: 69). They believe that the brand may be the one thing that makes a difference to consumers' thinking about competing destinations all offering features of a similar quality, and that, consequently, branding ought to be at the very heart of marketing strategy, with the purpose of all destination marketing activity being to enhance the value of the brand.

Pike (2004), who has written extensively on this topic, has expressed the belief that since promoting product features is alone not sufficient to differentiate against competitors – branding is required. Consequently, the fundamental challenge for DMOs is to develop a brand identity that encapsulates the essence or spirit of a much-attributed destination, representative of sellers as well as the host community. He is firmly of the opinion that such a brand identity should serve as a guiding focus for all of the marketing activities of the DMO and its stakeholders.

He admits that the processes of brand development, implementation and management would be more complex for destination marketers than for those marketing individual venues, since the former exert no control over the actual delivery of the

Table 4.1 Destination brand hierarchy

Level	Entity
1	Country brand
2	Country business tourism brand
3	State business tourism brands
4	Regional brands
5	Local community brands
6	Individual suppliers' business brands

Source: Adapted from Pike (2004)

brand promise. Part of the reason for this complexity derives from the existence of what Pike calls a destination brand hierarchy, comprising several 'brand' levels, as shown in Table 4.1.

It is clear that, assuming that destinations *can* be branded, one aspect of the complexity of this process would be the need to ensure that the brands of all levels of the hierarchy were compatible – and that a destination's business tourism brand was also compatible with its leisure tourism brand. Harrill (2005) emphasizes the need for destination brands to be supported by different levels in the hierarchy, noting that for a branding programme to prove successful, it must also enjoy the proactive participation of the destination's constituents (at sub-country levels) in their own marketing communications delivery systems.

However, until more destination branding case studies are published, the usefulness of attempting the branding concept to destinations must remain open to debate, and the question must continue to be asked: can an entire country or city really be branded in a meaningful way, or is this necessarily a reductivist and counterproductive approach that may engender unforeseen and undesirable outcomes? The clamour of the destination branders is deafening, however, and dissenting voices are few and far between (one, Holcolm (1999) is quoted by Pike: 'Packaging and promoting the city to tourists can destroy its soul. The city is commodified, its form and spirit remade to conform to market demand, not residents' dreams.').

Nevertheless, there is certainly a degree of truth in Harrill's (2005) statement that branding is today's buzzword for a process that many people wish to employ, but few understand.

Objectives and action plans

After the situation analysis has been completed and used to segment the market and position the product, a venue or destination may proceed to the stage of programme planning, which begins with establishing clear, prioritized objectives. These objectives then help the marketer to devise a set of the most effective marketing strategies based on the marketing mix – a list of action plans designed and implemented for each specific market segment, in order to meet the objectives set.

Objectives

Marketing plans require the venue or destination to establish both short-term and long-term objectives. Typical objectives that might be set could include, for example, achieving a certain level of sales growth within a given period of time or increasing market share by a certain percentage within a certain period. For each established marketing objective, a separate mix of marketing communications activities must be planned.

It is generally agreed that, in order to be effective, objectives should demonstrate certain key characteristics. According to Kotler *et al.* (2003), for example, they should be:

- quantitative (expressed in monetary terms or some other unit of measurement, such as occupancy rate, number of conferences hosted, etc.)
- time-specific (one year, 6 months ...)
- profit/margin specific (such as: an average margin of 22%).

Action plans

The action plan outlines the designated marketing activities required to achieve each specific objective. This usually takes the form of a comprehensive calendar that lists all the major marketing activities month by month for the period of one year. The implementation of these activities is the *action* phase of the marketing plan. For that reason, *timelines* must be clearly stated, to show what must be done by which date in the marketing calendar. The action calendar will take into account fixed dates, such as the dates of major trade shows, the start and finish dates for major promotional campaigns, as well as dates for already arranged familiarization trips and sales trips.

The issue of the resources required to implement the action plan should also be dealt with and recorded in this section of the marketing plan. This involves both staff and money. Those members of staff assigned to lead on various activities in the action plan should also be named, so that there are clear lines of responsibility in the implementation process. And, crucially, the budget required for each activity should be specified in detail.

However, the principal consideration at this stage of the marketing plan is the question of precisely what is to be offered to each market segment – and how – in order to most effectively meet the stated objectives and to yield the maximum return on the destination or venue's investment in its marketing endeavours. The combination of all the tools available to the marketer to plan and implement the marketing strategy and meet the marketing objectives is known as the marketing mix.

The marketing mix

The concept of the marketing mix lies at the heart of all marketing planning. The different variables that constitute the marketing mix are traditionally known as the four Ps: product, place (or process of delivery), price and promotion. For any venue or destination, these are the *controllable* elements of the marketing plan – which clearly distinguishes them from those factors that the organization *cannot* control, such as the PEST elements in the market environments and the actions of competitors.

The marketing mix selected for each particular target segment forms the foundation of the marketing plan's strategy.

- **Product** is what a venue or destination offers for sale in order to satisfy customer needs. This will include all of the tangible elements (the AV equipment, seating, conference food, etc.) as well as the intangibles (such as the manner in which delegates are received, or the atmosphere of the destination).
- **Place** is generally taken to describe those distribution channels the venue or destination uses to make its product available and accessible to prospective customers. These might include trade shows as well as websites through which planners can access information.
- **Price** is the amount charged for services provided – and is therefore a more important consideration for venues than for CVBs, for example, who are less likely to charge clients a direct fee.
- **Promotion** includes all of the marketing communications techniques that may be used in order to reach the selected market segments.

In recent years, attempts have been made to enhance this quartet by the addition of three or four extra Ps. For example, Holloway (2004) suggests adding *People* (the destination's inhabitants) as well as *Physical evidence* (all of the cues present at the destination, based on sight, sound, etc.).

Burke and Resnick (2000) indicate that some travel marketing experts have added four extra Ps – *Physical environment*, *Purchasing process*, *Packaging* and *Participation*. They feel that these additional Ps are necessary to describe the process involved in marketing travel services. A convincing case may be made for applying the same eight Ps to the variables that a venue or destination can control when trying to attain its goal of successfully marketing its facilities and services.

An illustration may be given in the case of a hotel with conference facilities, as in Table 4.2.

Establishing the appropriate marketing mix for each segment may be seen as the culmination of all of the preceding stages in the marketing planning process. A venue or destination, having decided whom it wishes to reach, what it is selling, how much it must charge in order to make a profit, and through which channels it will reach its audience, must then devise a means of communicating its message to its audience. These marketing communications techniques are the focus of the next three chapters of this book.

By recording the marketing mix in an annual marketing action plan, an organization is committing itself in writing to a particular marketing strategy for the 12 months ahead. This does not mean, nevertheless, that no element of the mix can be changed during that period. Changing circumstances in the market environment can produce new opportunities (such as a competitor venue struck by some unforeseen crisis) or threats (a currency devaluation in a country that is a major inbound market, for example). There is therefore a need to avoid absolute rigidity in the marketing plan, without allowing so much flexibility that the plan no longer fulfils its role as a navigational chart.

In any case, while some elements of the marketing mix clearly may be changed at very short notice (promotion, price) others take much longer to alter (product, channels of distribution).

Table 4.2 The marketing mix

The Ps	Definition	Example
Product	What a company is offering for sale	A hotel's conference rooms
Place/process of delivery	Channels of distribution and delivery	A hotel booking agency
Price	The amount of money paid for a product, based by seller on certain factors	A €100 day-delegate rate
Promotion	Activities that stimulate interest in a product	Advertising in a trade magazine
Physical environment	The environment in which the sale takes place	Website, trade workshop
	The environment in which the product is produced and consumed	
Purchasing process	Motivations and information search	Selecting a conference destination
Packaging	Bringing together of complementary products	Providing pre- and post-conference tours and/or partners' programmes
Participation	The transaction or experience	Buyer, intermediary and seller interaction

Source: Adapted from Burke and Resnick (2000)

Monitoring and evaluation

Any plan must be subject to monitoring and evaluation. Constant monitoring of the marketing expenditure is required, to ensure that budgets are not exceeded.

In addition, given the amount of financial resources consumed by a venue or destination's marketing mix, the performance of each element in the mix should be continually monitored to ensure the plan is achieving the results specified in its own objectives.

Constant monitoring of the marketing plan, in order to check that it is accomplishing what it is supposed to, assumes that the results sought in each specific programme area are *quantifiable*. But against what kind of criteria can the plan's results be assessed?

Gartrell (1994) suggests the following, measurable, criteria, most of which may be applied to venues as well as destinations:

- Room-nights booked
- Total delegate attendance
- Distribution of delegate attendance (local, state, regional, national, international)
- Total conventions booked
- Distribution of booked business (local, etc.)
- Types of bookings (convention, exhibitions, trade shows, special events, small meetings)
- Business booked by facilities (convention centre, arenas, hotels)

- Business booked through various marketing techniques (trade shows, direct mail, direct sales, advertising, etc.)
- Number of leads generated
- Conversion rate
- Housing reservations
- Total economic impact of convention business
- Amount of local taxes generated.

Whatever the criteria used, it is only by evaluating the performance of each element in the marketing mix that a venue or destination will be in a position to answer the crucial question of whether it is getting an adequate return on the often costly investment it is making in its marketing activities.

Summary

The tangible manifestation of any destination or venue's marketing planning process is its marketing plan. It is this document that helps managers develop and maintain a clear direction for the set of complex, interrelated marketing activities they undertake on behalf of their destination or venue.

A well-constructed marketing plan based on sound research should culminate in the production of an appropriate marketing mix for each segment to be targeted. In this respect, devising an effective marketing plan is one of the marketing manager's most important tasks.

Case Study 4.1

The branding of the Royal College of Physicians' conference facilities

This case study examines the challenges involved in branding, as a 21st-century conference venue, a 1960s building owned by a 500-year-old professional institution of global repute and distinction.

Background

The Royal College of Physicians' fifth home, overlooking Regent's Park, London, is one of the finest architectural examples of the 1960s. The modern edifice, a grade 1 listed building completed in 1964, embraces the long, rich history of the Royal College, a history that traces its origins back to the reign of King Henry VIII in 1518. In 1992, the architect of the modern building, Sir Denys Lasdun, was awarded a medal by the Royal Institute of British Architects for his design. The RIBA jury described the College, which stands in close proximity to some of Nash's finest Regency terraces, as 'an eloquent demonstration of the marriage between old and new, both in terms of the Classical and Modern traditions of form and the performance of a mixed range of functions'. In 1994 the building won the RIBA Gold Award for British architecture.

One of the College's core roles is that of the oldest and most prestigious medical foundation in England, a professional body that sets the standards and controls the quality of medical

Figure 4.1 Views of the Royal College of Physicians.

practice. It assures the quality of postgraduate medical education and the training of phys-icians, and now has a worldwide membership approaching 20 000 Members and Fellows.

The College offers 11 rooms for the education and training of doctors, of which the Wolfson Theatre (300 capacity) and the Seligman Theatre (140 capacity) are the largest, while the Osler Room, with views of the private garden and adjacent historic buildings, offers the space for 240 people as well as banqueting. The Council Chamber has curved walls and a spectacular vaulted ceiling, and the impressive book-lined Dorchester Library is available for plenary pre-sentations, drinks receptions and other functions. In 2003 a newly built separate facility, the Jerwood Education Centre, was opened adjoining one of the Regency houses offering pur-pose-designed training rooms with state-of-the-art equipment. The Osler Room, with views of the private garden and adjacent historic buildings, offers space for 240 people.

Branding of the Royal College of Physicians' facilities

In 1998 the new President of the College established a change of direction that called for increased levels of activity in the College's medical role. These new initiatives needed funding and, as a result, added focus was placed on increasing revenues from external lettings (the third most important income source for the College after membership and examination fees). Research was undertaken to compare the College's conference and banqueting services against other competitors in London and identify a market positioning for the College. The study revealed that the College could offer a good 4-star standard and had the potential to be a leading London venue. A fundamental decision was taken to accept bookings selectively from the 'non-medical' world.

This change called for the development of a more aggressive marketing strategy and, within this, a specific campaign to develop new business. At that time, it was felt that a major selling point of the College was its superb setting and 480 years of history and heritage 'on display'. In short, the College offered a unique contrast between old and new. It was recognized that the College had the facilities for meetings but lacked a venue brand. There were lengthy discus-sions about whether to brand the facilities as 'The Royal College of Physicians' *or* as 'Regent's Park Conference Centre' or '11 St Andrews Place' or something similar. It was eventually decided to promote the venue as the 'Royal College of Physicians' since this was already an established international brand as a medical college, whose members included some of the most eminent medical practitioners located all around the world.

This crucial decision on a venue name brought with it a number of challenges:

- The term 'college' can be associated with students, cheapness, low quality, and a number of other negative connotations
- As a venue, it was (and still is) required to reflect the values and ethos of a professional med-ical institution in its promotional activity, in its product development, and in the nature of the business it could accept. For example, it might refuse certain conference business (such as a pharmaceutical company wishing to use the venue to gain endorsement for a contro-versial new drug) because that business would be contrary to its ethos as a Royal College of Physicians. Revenue generation is less important than preserving the historic values and image of the institution. Investments in the building and its facilities have to strike the right balance between good quality products and workmanship, on the one hand, without being seen as excessive expenditure creating opulent facilities in the eyes of the College Fellows and Members on the other.

In 2002 brand development experts were employed to establish a brand for the RCP. Their work identified those factors which differentiated the RCP from other London venues as being: landmark location, history, not exclusively a conference and banqueting venue, ethical institution, no accommodation restraints, unique venue, treasure trove, heritage. Subsequently, a more detailed set of Key Selling Propositions (KSPs) and Unique Selling Propositions (USPs) has been devised and these are shown in Table 4.3.

A Value Statement was produced, which states:

> *The quality of our professional service and products depends on each individual's awareness, our commitment and our friendly approach to customers.*

Functional benefits were defined in terms of: state-of-the-art equipment, range of meeting/conference facilities, twin lecture theatres, 5-star banqueting, bespoke exhibitions, and stunning architecture. Emotional benefits were summarized as: success, wonder, discovery, taken seriously, kudos, reassuring.

The quality of staff employed by the RCP is absolutely vital to its success. This means recruiting the right people with the right attitude in the first place, and then investing continuously in their training and ongoing development. Some 54 full-time staff are employed (plus a number of part-time staff) representing 26 different nationalities, and many have previous international hotel experience. The different cultures and perspectives of the RCP team are celebrated and are seen as something that helps to make the team 'special'. Monthly informal get-togethers are held for staff at which examples of high performance by individuals are highlighted and recognized, customer feedback is shared, and ideas for future improvements are put forward.

Detailed training plans are implemented for all staff, while appropriate members of staff participate in at least one teambuilding and values reminder exercise per annum.

As a conference venue, the RCP has achieved international accreditation through ISO 9001:2000 for its provision of quality conference and event management services. It is a member of: Conference Centres of Excellence (www.cceonline.co.uk), the Association Internationale des Palais de Congrès (www.aipc.org), the International Association of Conference Centres (www.iacconline.com) and Unique Venues of London (www.uniquevenuesoflondon.co.uk). These memberships confer a degree of status and endorsement to the RCP, strengthening the promise and assurance contained within its brand.

The College has a truly unique asset in its Dorchester Library, which houses some 50 000 manuscripts, books, maps and other items. These include many original items and form a key part of British history and heritage. The collection has an estimated value of £35 million, and specialist staff are employed to maintain the collection, including a heritage centre manager and an archivist. Some of the treasures can be taken out and displayed for use at dinners and special events, and this feature is an important part of the 'sell' when seeking to attract particularly international medical conferences. The College Bedell (a functionary of the College) can also be employed by event organizers in the role of a toastmaster.

The College's increasing recognition and success as a conference venue can be seen from the following figures summarizing the growth in the number of events held in 2004 compared with 2003. In 2004 1667 internal events (i.e. for members of the Royal College) were staged, a growth of 62% over 2003. There were 621 external events, representing an increase of 28% on 2003. The combined figures give an average increase in business of 30.5% year on year. From a revenue perspective, external events generated more than five times the income obtained from internal events, even though the number of internal events outnumbered external events by almost 3:1.

Source: www.rcplondon.ac.uk/venue

Table 4.3   Royal College of Physicians' Selling Propositions

1	KSP	**Excellent conference and banqueting facilities**
		overall impressive design and layout
	KSP	purpose-built raked lecture theatres
		state-of-the-art audio-visual equipment and technology
	KSP	flexible exhibition space
	KSP	garden area for receptions
	USP	'jewel in the crown' Dorchester Library – in the 16th century it was the most important library outside Oxford and Cambridge
	KSP	has its own generator, preventing interruptions to events in the case of a power failure
	KSP	quality venue with value-for-money prices
	KSP	new purpose-built training centre
	KSP	the College has more resources than other venues linked to a professional body (IT support, photocopiers, scanners, equipment, etc.)
2	KSP	**Central London location**
		good access, road, rail and tube (plus Paddington link for London Heathrow Airport)
		free parking for organizers (outside the congestion-charging zone)
3	KSP	**High quality of food and service**
		eclectic, modern cuisine
		catering managers who are passionate about food
		5-star catering standard
4	KSP	**Professional and friendly multi-lingual/cultural staff**
		excellent back-up team (reception, porters, etc.)
		support services, e.g. hotel bookings
		access to fax, photocopying
5	KSP	**Professional venue experienced in international conferences**
		accreditation to ISO 9001:2000 for the provision of conference and event management services
		member of Conference Centres of Excellence
		member of two international conference centre associations
6	USP	**Award-winning grade 1 listed modern building in a superb setting with 500 years of history 'on display'**
		member of Unique Venues of London consortium
		prestigious medical institution
		overlooking Regent's Park

Continued

Table 4.3 (*Continued*)

		attractive views of Nash houses and medicinal garden
		attractive, light and spacious atrium
7	KSP	**Historical guided tours may be offered to selected groups**
		(particular interest from international medical conferences)
8	USP	**The College collection of books and objects**

Case Study 4.2

Canberra Convention Bureau Business Plan, 2005/2006

All Convention and Visitor Bureaux (CVBs) produce an annual business and/or marketing plan. This case study illustrates the structure and content of one such plan, namely the 'Business Plan 2005/2006' for the Convention Bureau of Australia's capital city, Canberra. The study focuses on the marketing and sales activities and strategies of the Bureau, although the Plan, as can be seen from its Table of Contents (Figure 4.2 below), also covers the wider business and membership development and human resource management of the Bureau.

The stated **vision** of the Canberra Convention Bureau is 'that Canberra be recognized as a leading business events destination shaped by its competitive advantages'. The Bureau's **mission statement** states: 'As the key business events marketing body, the Bureau is committed to increasing meetings, incentives, conventions and exhibition activity for the economic benefit of Canberra and our key stakeholders.'

The following Executive Summary of the Plan gives an overview of the key objectives and activities of the CCB and provides the context and framework for the Bureau's marketing and sales activities.

Executive Summary

Planning for the forward year has been driven by the need to:

- consolidate the new team in the revised organizational structure and build organizational capability
- create positive stakeholder relationships
- build increased ROI confidence for members and government
- promote the bureau services to clients and the wider community.

The overall organizational health of the Bureau will improve as a result of reduced staff turnover and the adoption of a learning culture, leading to increased human resource capability through skills training and professional development.

A knowledge management approach will provide the foundation for increased sales productivity and information systems management. New markets will be targeted in line with

TABLE OF CONTENTS

Figure 4.2 Table of Contents of the CCB Business Plan.

Canberra's knowledge hubs and existing markets expanded in industries in which Canberra has had a successful track record in attracting events. The upgrade of the National Convention Centre (NCC) will be promoted for events from 2007 and beyond.

Marketing activities will include a revised, more targeted familiarization programme, increasing the frequency of national familiarizations from 2 to 4 per year. This will incorporate a greater emphasis on the knowledge advantages of Canberra's institutions, in addition to the traditional reliance on entertainment and destination attributes.

The membership structure and benefits will be reviewed and necessary changes planned for introduction in 2006/07. Growth in membership will come from arresting the previous year's decline and by increasing the current level by 5% in the higher membership categories.

A regional membership programme will also be piloted in response to existing demand and explored as a means of raising income without diluting the Bureau's ACT (Australian Capital Territory) economic impact.

The Bureau will continue to provide market leadership in addressing industry growth constraints. This will include providing advisory services for the scope of work to the upgrade of the NCC, lobbying for a new 'world class' convention centre in 2013, involvement in the city revitalization planning and encouraging investment in new and improved product development in upscale hotels/rooms and associated business event products and services.

Financial management has focused on delivering the greatest number of marketing and sales activities without compromising the medium-term financial position of the Bureau, by retaining a generous proportion of unallocated funds. This allows for flexibility in issues management and the implementation of the board's strategic plans, following a planning session to be conducted later in the year.

A table of contents for the Plan (Figure 4.2) shows it following a logical progression from a SWOT analysis, through marketing and sales objectives and activities, to a consideration of budgetary issues.

CCB's destination marketing and sales strategies are aimed at both the internal market (key stakeholders in the Canberra area) and the external market (the wider industry and clients). Details of the strategies are as follow (section numbers relate to the sections of the Plan as presented in Figure 4.2).

3.1 Brand Image

Establish the Canberra Convention Bureau, in the eyes of industry and stakeholders, as a highly valued resource for increasing meetings and conference business in Canberra.

To create a positive perception of the Bureau in the eyes of all stakeholders by providing consistent and focused messages, in all forms of communications, reinforcing our position and our purpose.

3.2 Destination Marketing

Develop a clear positioning statement for Canberra as a business events destination.

To strengthen Canberra's position for conferences as a serious business destination with a rich variety of cultural and heritage attributes. An incentive product will also be developed to support sales effort in this segment.

Develop positioning in line with:

- Canberra as the national capital of Australia
- Meeting Place of a Nation
- A city rich with culture and heritage attributes – refer to National attractions
- The Business Case for Canberra – a knowledge economy.

3.3 Profile Development

Raise the Bureau's profile and reflect our destination position and brand image through a suite of targeted and co-ordinated collateral.

A suite of collateral that promotes Canberra as a leader in the meetings and events market and promotes the CCB as a convenient conduit to experience will be developed. Collateral design will be in harmony with the 'See yourself in Canberra' message and support our destination positioning and brand image.

Activity	Description
Website re-design	Create a website that is simple to navigate and offers a range of services to both meeting planners and members. This represents the second phase of the upgrade which began in the fourth quarter of 04–05
Meeting Planner Guide	See 'co-operative activities'
Corporate brochure	A brochure that can be used for the promotion of new members and as a sales tool for prospective buyers. The brochure will outline the services the CCB has to offer
Brochure shells	Re-design in keeping with brand position
Corporate gifts	For use as a sales tool
Destination DVD	Create a visual presentation that makes a case for Canberra as a serious meeting destination, while showcasing the services of members and acting as an interactive sales tool
Incentive destination	Create an incentive product as a sales tool for domestic and international incentive business

Figure 4.3 Collateral.

3.4 Communications

Maintain consistent and positive messages regarding the Bureau's activities to the local community, members and other stakeholders.

Build the CCB's perceived value in the eyes of federal and local government, mainstream industry and the general public. This will be achieved through consistent messages delivered via targeted public relations activity, re-designed collateral and destination imagery.

3.5 Co-operative Marketing Activities

Develop and maintain a range of co-operative marketing activities that repeatedly reinforce our brand position, focus on the compelling business case for Canberra and showcase our members' services.

Sales strategies are described in Section 4 of the Plan. They include:

4.1 Sales Overview

The sales targets below reflect historical performance trends and the introduction of the Knowledge Manager resource and increased capability of the new sales team.

The main areas identified for focus and growth are:

- Focus on target market segments that historically have been successful and that have a business case advantage
- Increase international bid conversion from 1 in 04/05 to 3 bid conversions in 05/06

Activity	Description
Newsletter – CCB Update	A monthly update communiqué to members, kindred organizations and local government
Press releases	Develop a minimum of two news stories per month for distribution to media to profile the value of the Business Events industry and the CCB to a mainstream audience
PR consultant exercise	Utilize consultant support to ensure all communications are consistent, targeted and effective across all media
PR events	Attendance at top secret familiarizations by members of the business community, politicians, media and other stakeholders
Launches	Develop a proactive protocol for media launches for confirmed business events. Involve politicians and other stakeholders as a means of engagement
Video and speakers kit (promote role of bureaux in destination marketing)	Utilize Australian Association of Convention Bureaux's 'role of bureaux' video and speakers kit for stakeholder presentations
VIP protocols	Establish protocols for regular contact with local and federal ministers and other VIPs
Co-operative activities with kindred organizations	Reinforce the Bureau's value to the ACT economy and engage the business community through a process of education about the CCB activities
	Provide leadership and work with government and the business community to encourage investment and sound planning for business event-related amenities

Figure 4.4 Public relations.

- Increase national bid conversion from 31% to 40%
- Introduce a more targeted and intelligent national familiarization programme
- Utilization of the Knowledge Manager to assist with bid conversion and target market segment analysis for new lead generation
- Focus on geographic areas that have the ability to grow
- Introduce a 'mature' incentive product including regional attractions.

Activity	Description
Advertising	Promotion of the Meeting Planner Guide through advertising in trade publications including Quorum, CIM, Mice.net. Also through mainstream press Sydney Morning Herald and the Canberra Times and co-operative advertising with other tourism bodies (e.g. Tourism Australia)

Figure 4.5 Advertising.

4.2 Strategies

4.2.1 Market Segment Analysis

Capitalize on our business case and past successes focusing resources on market segments that historically are strong, e.g. Health and Medical, Science and Technology, and Defence/Security.

4.2.2 International Bid Strategy

Increase international bid conversion from 1 bid conversion in 04/05 to 3 bid conversions in 05/06. Based on the international bid selection process, we have the ability to identify and only commit resources to international bids that we have an opportunity to convert.

(a) International Bid Strategy One

Target satellite meetings from other Australian city international bid wins. From Australian bid wins, identify business case opportunities and approach conference organizers with sound business case to either:

    a. Bring satellite meeting to Canberra, or
    b. Create satellite meeting for Canberra.

(b) International Bid Strategy Two

Encourage local organizations that are part of an international body to 'put their hand up for Canberra'.

1 Re-invent 'Bid for Canberra' (this may generate opportunities for national conferences as well)
2 Identify and target opportunities:
    a. Committee member in Canberra
    b. Asia/Pacific area conferences
    c. 5–10-year rotation
    d. Identifiable business case reason to consider Canberra.

As a team we need to identify clear parameters to assist the Knowledge Manager to source the appropriate data for international bid opportunities.

4.2.3 Increase National Bid Conversion

Our aim for 05/06 is to increase bid conversion from 31% to 40%. Based on averages over the last 3 years the average worth of a bid is A\$530 000 and bids are 32% of our annual business. To increase conversion to 40% we need to convert an additional 5 bids per annum, which is an additional A\$2.65 m. Utilization of the Knowledge Manager resource is critical to achieving this target.

Activity	Description
Meeting Planners Guide	The annual directory that is the premier showcase document for CCB members
4 × National familiarization tours	1 × Top Secret destination 2 × National targeted groups that have 'special interests' 1 × National Conference Organizers (PCOs)
3 × Local familiarization tours	For locally based meeting organizers, these familiarizations promote our members' services
2 × CCB CEO market updates	Reinforce the Bureau's value to key members and stakeholders. Highlighting one or two major activities the Bureau is currently undertaking and provide market intelligence to members
2 × Client newsletters	Replacing the Meeting Update and predominantly used as a sales tool, these newsletters will have general promotional information about Canberra, highlight the recent conference bookings and act as a platform for promotions by members
3 × Association executive functions	Held in New South Wales, Victoria and Australian Capital Territory, these events are predominantly sales tools aimed to showcase the CCB services and membership group to association buyers
Networking nights × 10	Continue existing networking night programme
AIME tradeshow	Facilitate and manage the Canberra destination stand in conjunction with member participation
Regional familiarizations	Develop two regional familiarizations subject to regional membership interest and participation

Figure 4.6 Co-operative Marketing Activities.

4.2.4 Review Familiarization Programmes

In 05/06 it was agreed that we would schedule four National Familiarization programmes. The focus for these programmes would be:

1 Target by market segment and by buyer requirements
2 Smaller and more regular familiarizations to assist timely and effective sales follow-up
3 Include business case advantage in the familiarization programmes.

Sales Team Targets 2005/06

Year	Dollar value	Room nights	% Increase on previous year
Budget 05/06	A$28 m	51 538	7.7
Forecast 04/05	A$26 m	45 000	11.5
Actual 03/04	A$25.1 m	52 781	2.5

Geographic Targets 2005/06

Territory	Percentage	Dollar value	Room nights
Australian Capital Territory	38	A$10.64 m	18 754
New South Wales	39	A$10.9 m	20 537
Victoria	18	A$5.04 m	9329
Queensland	3	A$840 k	1871
South Australia	2	A$580 k	1047
	100	A$28 m	51 538

Figure 4.7 Sales targets.

4.2.5 Utilization of Knowledge Manager Resource

To increase business conversion it is essential for the Business Development team and the Knowledge Manager to have a strong working relationship. This is clearly evident when assistance is required to develop a strong business case for Canberra, and when market segment analysis is required to generate new lead opportunities.

4.2.6 Geographic Growth Areas

We are targeting the following geographic areas for growth:

- **Regional New South Wales**: Potential untapped; research in conjunction with Knowledge Manager to identify prospects for Canberra; 2 sales trips per year.
- **Victoria**: Business Development Manager based in the market since October 2004; sales efforts will come to fruition in 05/06; increase of 3% for 05/06.
- **Queensland and South Australia**: Some growth due to increased focus and sales activities; increase of 2% in Queensland and 1% in South Australia due to continuation of serving this market.

The indicators used to test the performance of the above marketing and sales activities are listed in Figure 4.8.

Source: www.canberraconvention.com.au

	04/05 forecast as at May 05	05/06 Budget	% Variance
Sales (measured in delegate expenditure)	A$26m	A$28 m	8%
Room Nights	45 000	51 538	14.5%
Bid Conversion	31%	40%	29%
Membership Income	A$174 800	A$204 410	9%
Membership Numbers	116	122	5%
Staff Turnover	80%	20%	−75%
Total Income	A$1 188 311	A$1 120 478	−6%
Total Expenditure	A$1 144 755	A$1 208 408	5.3%
Surplus/Deficit	A$43 556	(A$87 930)	−149%
Forecast Retained Funds at year end June 05	A$198 930		−44%
Forecast Retained Funds at year end June 06		A$111 000	

Figure 4.8   Performance summary by key areas of business.

Review and Discussion Questions

1 Why should a conference destination or conference venue invest time and other resources in creating a detailed marketing plan for itself each year?
2 What are the principal sources of data available to anyone who is undertaking market research as the first step in preparing a marketing plan for their destination or venue?
3 Discuss market segmentation and positioning with reference to Monaco as a conference destination.

Sources

Burke, J and Resnick, B (2000) *Marketing and Selling the Travel Product*, Delmar Thomson Learning

Davidson, R and Cope, B (2003) *Business Travel: conferences, incentive travel, exhibitions, corporate hospitality and corporate travel*, FT Prentice Hall/Pearson Education

Fifield, P (1998) *Marketing Strategy*, Butterworth-Heinemann

Gartrell, R (1994) *Destination Marketing for Convention and Visitor Bureaus*, Kendall/Hunt

Harrill, R (2005) *Fundamentals of Destination Management and Marketing*, IACVB

Holloway, JC (2004) *Marketing for Tourism*, Prentice Hall

Kotler, P, Bowen, J and Makens, J (2003) *Marketing for Hospitality and Tourism*, Prentice Hall

Middleton, V (2001) *Marketing in Travel and Tourism*, Butterworth-Heinemann

Pike, S (2004) *Destination Marketing Organizations*, Elsevier

Chapter 5

Marketing Communications for Destinations and Venues: Principles and Theories

Summary of Chapter Contents

This chapter examines the principles and theories underlying the various marketing communications techniques that may be employed by conference destinations and venues. It focuses on the principal marketing tools that organizations use in order to communicate with their customers, potential customers and other key stakeholders.

The chapter covers:

- Customer relationship management
- Direct marketing
- Publications
- Public relations
- Trade shows
- Familiarization trips

It includes case studies on:

- The Kursaal, San Sebastian
- Familiarization trip to Cyprus

Learning Outcomes

On completion of this chapter, you should be able to:

- appreciate the uses of customer relationship management
- discuss the main techniques employed in direct marketing
- understand the role played by publications and the various media that can be used

■ appreciate the various techniques used by public relations professionals
■ understand the role played by trade shows and familiarization trips in facilitating communications between suppliers and buyers

Introduction

As was highlighted in Chapter 4, in order to be effective, a destination's or venue's annual marketing plan should include the marketing communications activities that will be undertaken in order to achieve some of the specific objectives of the plan. These objectives will almost certainly involve bringing the destination or the venue to the attention of potential buyers in a cost-effective manner. But comprehensive marketing communications campaigns will include the full range of activities and techniques that focus on developing relationships with buyers and other stakeholders, as opposed to simply concentrating on generating sales.

In this chapter, the various communications activities that may be employed by conference destinations and conference venues are identified and discussed in detail.

Customer relationship management

It may be argued that a company's most important asset is its customer base – nothing happens until a sale is made. But a close second is the valuable information collected about those customers. That information – and how it may be used – is the key to effective customer relationship management (CRM).

CRM is the term used for the 'set of techniques, designed to help build up-close and favourable contacts with an organization's key customers ... over a long time period' (Holloway, 2004: 114). According to Canning (2004), 'CRM is a philosophy that should mobilize an entire organization toward serving the customer better. It is the architecture' behind a successful relationship management programme that puts the customer first. This creates loyal customers who purchase more, cost less to sell to and who will refer other customers to the company.

A key marketing trend since the 1990s, CRM has been widely recognized as a business strategy that enables organizations to identify and manage their relationships with those customers that are most profitable to them. If implemented properly, this strategy can generate a range of benefits including better service provision, higher customer satisfaction, better customer retention and more repeat purchases.

According to Pike, 'The rationale for stimulating relationships with customers is that these will be more profitable over time than one-off sales transactions, since the cost of reaching a continuous stream of new customers will far outweigh the cost of keeping in touch with existing customers' (Pike, 2004: 127).

It is clear that for destinations and venues, loyal customers represent a potential source of considerable profit, because of the opportunity they bring for repeat purchases. Hotels in particular understand that their success in the corporate meetings market depends in part on nurturing quality relationships with key customers in that segment.

The different depths of relationship that a supplier can develop with their customers are illustrated in Kotler's scheme of the five levels of relationships that can be formed with, for example, a hotel's clients who have booked a room for a meetings event (Kotler *et al.*, 2003: 391):

1 **Basic**: The company sells the product but does not follow up in any way.
2 **Reactive**: The company sells the product and encourages the customer to call whenever he has any questions or problems.
3 **Accountable**: The company's representative phones the customer a short time after the booking, to check with the customer and answer questions. During and after the event, the sales person solicits from the customer any product improvement suggestions and any specific disappointments. This information helps the company to improve its offering continuously.
4 **Proactive**: The sales person or others in the company phone the customer from time to time with suggestions about improvements that have been made or creative suggestions for future events.
5 **Partnership**: The company works continuously with the customer and with other customers to discover ways to deliver better value.

CRM, therefore offers the possibility of organizations entering into a relationship with their buyers that is closer to an ongoing partnership than simply a transactional connection. For conference destinations and venues, a CRM approach to marketing is being increasingly used, as a means of strengthening the links between themselves and their actual or potential customers.

A number of specific marketing tools have been widely used for this purpose. Many of these are already familiar, from their use in consumer markets. But their application in destinations' and venues' CRM campaigns is expanding, as the advantages become increasingly evident. Three main benefits may be offered by the users of CRM, to clients.

Financial privileges

Frequency programmes are the most widespread means employed to pass on financial benefits to customers who make repeat purchases from the same supplier. Widely used by airlines and hotels, a number of destinations and venues have experimented with such programmes as a means of rewarding meetings planners who make recurrent use of the destination for their events. Often, it is the planners themselves who are rewarded, as in the case of the scheme operated by the St Paul Convention & Visitors Bureau in Minnesota (www.stpaulcvb.org). That CVB began its St Paul Meeting Miles programme in 1996, awarding those booking events frequent flyer miles on Northwest and KLM airlines. Within the first year of its operation, the programme was credited with generating over 800 room nights, according to a CVB spokesperson (Lenhart, 1998).

Social benefits

Social benefits are those aimed at increasing social bonds with individual customers by recording their specific needs and preferences and anticipating these when repeat purchases are made. For example, one use that hotels make of their CRM programmes is to ensure that staff recognize frequent guests and their preferences (for non-smoking rooms, room-service breakfasts, etc.) and even address them by name. In a conference destination context, one social benefit often used is for buyers to be assigned an individual, named, contact at the CVB, who deals personally and exclusively with those buyers' requests.

Structural ties

These are tangible benefits that take the form of special services to which those buyers whom suppliers wish to nurture are given access. In the airline context, fast-track check-in and lounges for first class customers are obvious examples. For destinations and venues, one way of bonding structurally with particular clients is to invite them to a cocktail event at the destination's stand at a trade show.

Most authors agree that recent advances in technology have facilitated the management of data for operating effective CRM. ICT (information and communications technology) has made it possible for organizations to track the buying patterns of their clients and to purchase and manage databases that highlight potentially profitable clients for future purchases. The use of ICT enables suppliers to manage vast amounts of data quickly and accurately and to use the results to make intelligent decisions about their products, sales strategies and competitive advantage. ICT has also had an immense impact on the next topic for consideration, direct marketing.

Direct marketing

Closely linked with CRM is the marketing tool known as direct marketing. The emphasis in direct marketing, as opposed to traditional sales techniques, is on the interactive or two-way nature of the communication between organizations and their customers or potential customers.

Direct marketing is a term whose meaning has changed over the past few decades. It used simply to refer to any form of marketing where services or products were marketed from the producer to the consumer (or purchase decision-maker) without the use of an intermediate channel of distribution. But Kotler *et al.* note that with the increased use of the telephone and other media to promote offers directly to potential buyers, the meaning of direct marketing was redefined. The authors quote the Direct Marketing Association definition: 'Direct marketing is an interactive system of marketing that uses one or more advertising media to affect a measurable response and/or transaction at any location' (Kotler *et al.*, 2003: 650).

Middleton (2001: 313) also emphasizes the two-way nature of a direct marketing approach: 'the primary objective of direct marketing is to achieve more cost-effective use of marketing budgets based on a deep and evolving knowledge of customers and their behaviour, and direct communication with them. It is this objective that distinguishes direct marketing from traditional forms of direct selling.'

Direct marketing is, therefore, an indispensable tool in CRM. It offers conference destinations and venues opportunities for developing a strong relationship with their customers through dialogue, with the aim of generating responses from them and turning them into loyal clients. The progress made in ICT, in particular the Internet, has radically changed direct marketing. ICT has provided organizations with a fast, effective and convenient means of maintaining regular contact with their customers. It has also facilitated the creation of sophisticated databases to manage customer relations.

The development and use of customer profile databases lies at the heart of effective direct marketing. Rogers (2003: 105) describes the range of data that destinations and venues typically record for each customer or potential customer: 'full contact details (client name, job title, company name and address, telephone and fax numbers and e-mail address, as a minimum) ... then ... a profile of the client's buying requirements (e.g. kinds of conferences organized, types of venues used, sizes of events, locations considered)'.

When these customer profile databases have been established, a number of direct marketing methods may then be employed, to enable organizations to maintain contact with actual or potential clients. The methods most commonly used by destinations and venues are:

- **Direct response media advertising**: the placing of advertisements in, for example, the trade/professional press, inviting readers to respond by post, using coupons, or to call direct-response telephone numbers.
- **Direct mail**: Mail-shots sent to previous customers, or in response to enquiries/returned coupons from advertising. This may take the form of a joint mailing between relevant partners, such as CVBs, and conference centres and airlines serving the destination.
- **E-mail**: An electronic form of direct marketing, this form of communication is frequently used, for example, in the weeks leading up to trade exhibitions, to encourage visitors to come to the destination's or venue's stand at the event. Clearly, one problem of this technique is the issue of buyers already receiving too many e-mails, meaning that many are simply deleted, unread.
- **Telemarketing**: The use of the telephone to reach customers or potential customers. In the consumer market, this method may be used via a call centre. But business-to-business use of call centres is rarer than in the business-to-consumer situation, as is the 'cold call'. In the field of destination and venue marketing, telemarketing campaigns are more often operated using lists of previous enquirers.

Although these four methods have been listed as discrete techniques, they are often used jointly, for maximum impact. Kotler describes the technique known as Integrated Direct Marketing, which comprises a multi-vehicle, multi-stage campaign:

Paid advertisement with a response channel → Direct mail mechanism → Outbound telemarketing → Face-to-face sales call

In the above example, the paid advertisement creates product awareness and stimulates enquiries. The company then sends direct mail to those who enquire. Within 48–72 hours, following mail receipt, the company telephones, seeking an order. Some prospects will place an order; others might request a face-to-face sales call (Kotler *et al.*, 2003: 656). Kotler claims that whereas a direct mail piece on its own may only generate a 2% response rate, it is possible to generate responses of 12% or more using integrated direct marketing.

Publications

Most of the previously described techniques depend on the design and production of publications that are effective in transmitting the destination's or venue's message to potential buyers. Certain publications are also key elements in CVBs' CRM strategies.

Promotional brochures, destination planning manuals, newsletters, and visitor guides are all examples of key marketing and promotional tools used by destinations and venues. According to Gartrell, 'Publications serve as the primary marketing and communications tool for bureaux, and essentially fall into two broad categories: those designed to market services and attract clients and those designed to communicate information and stimulate interest in bureau programmes among its membership' (Gartrell, 1994: 92). Each of these two categories will be examined.

Publications for attracting business

Also known as 'collateral', these publications play a vital role in transmitting the destination's or venue's image to the market. Authors agree that it is essential for publications to be designed, where possible, on a tailor-made basis. McCabe *et al.* (2000), for example, emphasize that collateral material should be developed for the specific market segment targeted. 'The production of a single brochure to satisfy all possible customer needs is not effective … Collateral material should highlight and promote the benefits of the product that are important to the specific customer segment' (McCabe *et al.*, 2000: 180).

The following example demonstrates the rationale behind one such targeted publication:

In 2004, Sydney Convention and Visitors Bureau launched its first incentive meeting planner specifically aimed at the Asian market, to capitalize on strong interest in Sydney amongst Asian corporations and travel agents planning incentivized meetings. The SCVB distributed 2500 copies of the Asian edition of the 28-page 'Imagine Sydney', with another 2500 copies of the booklet issued in the UK, mainland Europe and the United States. The SCVB's Managing Director, Jon Hutchison, explained that the Asian market represented a distinct market segment:

> *Incentive groups from Europe and the US are generally between 50 to 300 people, whilst groups from Asia more commonly range between 500 and 4000. So not only are we seeing more bookings from Asia than other markets, we're also seeing far larger groups. By creating two versions of the brochure we can more easily highlight the most relevant features of our city to different marketplaces and build our business worldwide.*
>
> (Anon, 2004)

Publications for communication with stakeholders

A number of CVB publications have as their key objective the maintaining of communications with stakeholders. These may include actual and potential clients, but their distribution will certainly be much wider than that particular group. The CVB's Annual Report, for example, may serve as an important communications tool, and should therefore reflect the image that the destination wishes to transmit. However, the most commonly used publication for broad communication is the newsletter. Gartrell recognizes the importance of this form of publication: '[Newletters] can serve not only as information tools but as sources for business leads. A newsletter may also carry stories on the bureau's marketing activities, information on what is happening among bureau members, and dates and descriptions of forthcoming meetings and educational forums' (Gartrell, 1994: 92).

Clearly, ICT is also having an immense impact on how publications are created and disseminated to their various audiences. The role played by electronic media in destinations' and venues' promotional and communication strategies has been well documented. Davidson (2004), for example, predicted that as the use of the Internet becomes ever more ingenious and creative, so too will meetings planners' use of that medium continue to expand over the next five years, for the purpose of researching venues:

> More and more event planners will be logging on to the Internet, rather than opening the filing cabinet full of brochures and venue guides. Access to destination and venue information via nearly instantaneous technology has already reduced response times dramatically, as elements of the site-selection process that used to take days or even weeks can now be measured in minutes or hours. Mailing RFPs [requests for proposals] to several properties and waiting for responses to be mailed back will be nothing but a dim and distant memory by the end of the first decade of the 21st century.

> (Davidson, 2004: 9)

One destination's creative use of ICT is illustrated in the following example:

> In February 2004, Meeting News *magazine reported that the Atlanta Convention and Visitors Bureau was using 'video e-mail' to help incoming groups promote their events and the city itself to potential attendees. The service is provided free to the ACVB's largest convention clients, and involves the provision of custom video messages that promote the features of the upcoming meeting and encourage the viewer to register online. One video e-mail features Atlanta Falcons' football star Michael Vick, who invites attendees to visit 'my town, Atlanta'. The streaming-video messages appear in a browser window, playable by Windows Media Player. While the service is free for large convention groups, a sliding-scale fee applies to other groups based on their size, to meet the production costs of their custom clips.*

> *According to the ACVB's director of marketing, the technology places images directly in front of the customer in an accessible and timely manner: 'It's a cost-effective direct outreach, at a time when advertising dollars are stretched and conventions are looking to CVBs for new offerings'.*

> (Ibid: 8)

Public relations

In destinations' arsenal of marketing techniques, public relations is perhaps the most underestimated method of creating and maintaining a positive image. Yet, effectively used, public relations can assist in developing a strong, positive image of a successful conference destination or venue.

Holloway (2004: 339) describes public relations as 'a series of communications techniques designed to create and maintain favourable relations between an organization and its publics'.

According to the Chartered Institute of Public Relations, public relations is about reputation – the result of what you do, what you say and what others say about you. 'Public relations is the discipline which looks after reputation, with the aim of earning understanding and support and influencing opinion and behaviour. It is the planned and sustained effort to establish and maintain goodwill and mutual understanding between an organization and its publics.'

Middleton states that both advertising and PR are 'primary means of manipulating demand and influencing buyer behaviour. Simply stated, they enable businesses to *reach* people ... And to *communicate* to them *messages* intended to influence their *purchasing behaviour*. (Middleton, 2001: 237)

Most authors emphasize the contrasts between PR and advertising. One such contrast is that the range of target audiences for PR is generally much wider than for advertising. It can include local residents, local and central government politicians, existing and potential buyers, employees, the media, shareholders, suppliers, investors, professional/trade associations and pressure groups.

According to Pike (2004: 144), the use of public relations is 'a concerted effort by the destination marketing organization to develop favourable impressions of the destination. This involves both the generation of positive publicity by the DMO as well as the stimulation of positive relations between internal and external stakeholders'. He adds that 'The cost-effectiveness of PR initiatives is usually not lost on DMOs, particularly given the limited resources of most.'

What are the principal techniques that conference destinations and venues can use in their PR campaigns? Holloway (2004) and Kotler *et al.* (2003) agree on the five main activities associated with the role of PR:

1 **Press relations**: Placing newsworthy items of information into the news media, to generate favourable publicity or to diminish the impact of unfavourable publicity.
2 **Product publicity**: Implementing tactics to draw attention to particular products: new or renovated hotels, special events, etc.
3 **Corporate publicity**: Generating a favourable image for the organization itself, both internally and externally.
4 **Lobbying**: Dealing with legislators and government officials to promote a cause or defeat a particular piece of legislation.
5 **Counselling**: Advising management about public issues, particularly with respect to any sensitive issues with which the organization may be associated. In this respect, the PR department has a research and monitoring function.

Two of these techniques will now be examined in further detail.

Using the media

It is clear that, despite the best marketing efforts, much publicity, both positive and negative, about destinations and venues appears in the media without the influence or control of these suppliers. Effective relationships with the media are, therefore, vital to their success.

Positive editorial coverage is essential for the image of destinations in particular – more essential than extensive advertising, according to many commentators. Gartrell (1994), for one, acknowledges the importance of advertising, but maintains that it is *editorial coverage* that can extend and create the image of a destination in a way that advertising cannot. McCabe *et al.* (2000) emphasize the power of PR in correcting negative images of destinations: 'Negative destination images or publicity in the general consumer media … must be addressed. Such negative publicity can rarely be overcome simply by advertising. Responses and "good news stories" must be channelled through the same media that the negative stories appeared in, in order to begin an effective campaign to overcome the bad publicity' (McCabe *et al.*, 2000: 182).

Furthermore, the rapid growth in the volume of advertising 'noise' that decision-makers are exposed to means that many are increasingly immune to the persuasiveness of the claims made in destinations' and venues' advertisements. This has created an opportunity for the role of PR which, when properly used, can generate a greater level of credibility than advertising.

Working in partnership with the media is essential in this context. Organizations' communications staff must liaise with the trade press to stimulate the publication of articles on the destination or the venue; they can host press trips for individual journalists or groups of journalists; and they can produce a media kit that provides basic information about their services and facilities.

It is generally regarded as good practice for organizations to maintain a PR resource library, in order to be able to respond quickly and effectively to the media's requests for material such as photographs, statistics and video footage. A number of destinations and venues have used the power of the Internet to develop their own on-line media centres, where journalists can download press releases, photographs, brochures and newsletters. An example of this facility is the on-line media centre created for Newcastle-Gateshead, two adjoining northern English destinations that are jointly promoting themselves in the leisure and business tourism market (www. 2005alive.com/mediacentre).

Visitors to the site read that:

> 'We [NewcastleGateshead Initiative PR team] work closely with travel and feature writers, local, national and international media and convention trade press to develop and promote stories about NewcastleGateshead – one of Europe's hottest new cultural, leisure and conference destinations.
>
> We can provide you with news stories, feature ideas and copyright-free feature material, facts and figures, quotes and media soundbites, pictures and images, media packs and VHS footage. We also organize, tailor and facilitate media visits, which showcase at first hand the area's world-class attractions and events.
>
> Why not visit our unique media forum – a lively, topical discussion area designed exclusively for NewcastleGateshead media centre users. Post a question, voice your opinion or respond to a comment about NewcastleGateshead ... it's time to join in the latest debate.

Communicating with governments

A key role of PR is the lobbying of governments. Gartrell (1994: 93) emphasizes the importance of effective governmental relations for CVBs:

> This broad arena encompasses more than just monitoring legislative issues and bills. It also means developing rapport and working with those elected officials with whom the bureau comes in contact on almost a daily basis. Those elected officials will have control over the contractual arrangements for public funds. It is imperative that the bureau maintains a positive relationship with such officials, to nurture their understanding of the bureau and its mission.

In this respect, a number of CVBs, particularly in the US, have specific committees whose responsibility it is to oversee the political activities of the bureau.

For example, the Port Arthur CVB, in Texas, has a Political Issues Committee, which has the following roles:

- Monitors and addresses local, county, state and national issues
- Coordinates with appropriate Chamber of Commerce committees to address political issues as needed
- Communicates with officials and agencies concerning legislative issues
- Coordinates candidate forums
- Plans and presents workshops helping to increase the awareness, purpose and operational process of various local, county, state and federal governmental entities
- Works with other entities to address regional issues
- Develops relationships with new officials as they are elected.

The usefulness of PR to destinations and venues is evident. However, as Holloway (2004: 339) points out, PR 'is the most difficult of all marketing techniques to measure results against expenditure. PR generally takes longer to achieve results, and these are by definition dependent upon the attitudes and actions of third parties outside the direct control of the organization.' PR is essentially a marketing tool with a long-term impact, but this should never mean that destinations or venues dispense with its techniques.

Case Study 5.1, presented at the end of the chapter, illustrates a successful PR initiative in transforming an initial negative reaction into genuine enthusiasm for a conference venue in northern Spain.

Trade shows

Trade shows have been defined as: 'presentations of products or services to an invited audience with the object of inducing a sale or informing the visitor' (Davidson, 1994: 194).

Such events represent an additional way in which destinations and venues can develop awareness of their products, generate new leads and nurture relationships with existing customers. They act, therefore, as a useful forum for the two-way exchange of information between exhibitors (CVBs and individual venues) and visitors (buyers of conference facilities and services).

Simply being present and exhibiting at such events is a statement in itself. Gartrell (1994: 194) maintains that: 'The fact that staff are present and visible becomes an important factor in a destination attaining recognition and credibility among meetings planners … There is no question that trade show participation is costly; but it should be looked upon as an investment and a necessary part of any bureau's marketing mix.'

Trade shows for the conference industry exist at different geographical levels, from national to global. A listing of the most relevant trade shows for the conference industry is given in the Appendix to this volume.

In their quest to attract exhibitors and visitors, the organizers of these events offer a number of 'added-value' services. International events such as IMEX and EIBTM, for example, focus on research and education, while more regional fairs such as AIME or EMIF offer a range of seminars and forums for visitors and exhibitors.

Familiarization trips

For many industries, trade shows are not only a forum where exhibitors can meet buyers face-to-face, but also events at which the buyers, or potential buyers, can actually experience the product at first hand. Trade shows for the food and drink industry, for example, offer buyers the opportunity to taste the products for themselves; consumer electronics shows give visitors the chance of having 'hands-on' contact with laptop computers, for instance, that are on display.

Trade shows for the conference industry cannot offer visitors this direct experience of the product. Although some hotels do construct a mock-up bedroom on their stands at some trade shows, building a replica conference venue is a challenge of quite another order entirely.

For that reason, familiarization trips (often abbreviated to 'fam' trips) are used as the only means of giving potential buyers first-hand experience of destinations and the venues within them. A familiarization trip is a visit to a destination or venue offered to potential buyers, designed to acquaint them with specific local facilities and services and to stimulate the booking of an event. Such trips are usually offered to groups of buyers, but sometimes on an individual basis.

Familiarization trips are an important resource for conference planners, venues and for the CVBs responsible for marketing the destination. Planners get a live preview of what their delegates would experience; and sales and marketing representatives of the destination and its venues get the opportunity to share facts and features about a destination to a qualified and captive audience of meetings planners.

In this respect, familiarization trips represent an example of what is increasingly known as 'experiential marketing' – live event marketing experiences where potential buyers interact with products, brands or 'brand ambassadors' face-to-face. Experiential marketing gives customers in-depth experiences with products in order to give them enough information to make the purchase decision. This marketing tool refers to actual consumer experiences or interactions with products for the purpose of driving the sale of that product, and as such it may be contrasted with other techniques which involve the potential buyer seeing, for example, an idealized presentation of a destination or venue in a video, website or brochure. Experiential marketing is the difference between telling buyers about features or benefits within the confines of a promotional brochure or a discussion at a trade show and letting them experience it directly for themselves. This makes familiarization trips one of the most powerful marketing communications techniques available to suppliers and CVBs.

Case Study 5.2, presented at the end of the chapter, offers a detailed example of a venue-led familiarization trip.

Summary

There is no doubt that, in an increasingly competitive environment, destinations and venues the world over are becoming ever more aware of the advantages offered by the marketing techniques discussed in this chapter. Indeed, the 2004 Survey of Destination Management Organizations undertaken by the World Tourism Organization (WTO, 2004) indicated that the two areas of activity projected to be undertaken by significantly more DMOs of all types, including CVBs, in the following three years were:

- E-mail marketing
- Customer relationship management (CRM).

In a buyers' market, it is certain that, in the future, successfully attracting meetings events will increasingly depend on conference destinations' and venues' creative and exhaustive use of all of the marketing communications techniques available to them.

The Kursaal, San Sebastian

In 1999, when the Kursaal Centre opened as a conference and entertainment venue, it was already mired in controversy. The venue, which is named after a 19th century entertainment and casino pavilion which had stood on the same site, is located on the seafront of San Sebastian, a resort of approximately 200 000 inhabitants, situated in the north of Spain, 20 kilometres from the French city of Biarritz. San Sebastian's tourist tradition stretches back to the early 20th century, when it was considered to be the one of the most aristocratic spa centres in Europe.

Integrating a new, state-of-the-art conference centre into such an emblematic setting – facing the sea and right in the centre of the city – was never going to be a straightforward task. But a 1990 competition to design the new venue attracted a number of architects of renown, including Rafael Moneo, whose bold vision for the building – two vast translucent glass cubes portraying 'two rocks washed up on the shore' – was selected as the winning entry. When the Moneo design was chosen by the judges, it was seen as an ambitious project, a spectacular structure of concrete, metal and glass that would endow San Sebastian with a modern, groundbreaking infrastructure, internationally recognized in the world of architecture and design. The 10 000 translucent glass panels of the two cubes cover the venue's 1800-seat auditorium and exhibition centre, two concert halls, various multifunctional meeting rooms, shops, café, and a restaurant.

But from 1995, when construction work started on the building, most local people were firmly against the Kursaal project. Their criticism mainly focused on three issues: the chosen architectural design – extremely avant-garde and 'clashing' with the city's more traditional style; the economic feasibility of the conference centre – given its presumed loss-making activity, which would require public contributions to make it viable; and a potential elitist use of the building. Opposition to the new venue was led by the local press, which ran headlines such as 'El Kursaal de Rafael Moneo monstruoso' (Rafael Moneo's Kursaal 'a monstrosity') (Anon, 1995).

The controversy grew to such an extent that a powerful grassroots anti-Kursaal Citizens' Platform was set up, and the future of the Kursaal as a viable project was called into question.

In response to the negative publicity and widespread public and political opposition, the venue management in association with the Donostia-San Sebastian Convention Bureau created a working party with the declared objective of turning this opposition into positive local support and national recognition for the Kursaal and launching the venue with the full backing of local people. Conference centre staff, representatives of the property's developers, tourist board staff, the city's mayor, shop owners and citizens' representatives were recruited to develop a PR strategy aimed at the project's many detractors.

An external PR communication plan aimed at the citizens and businesses of San Sebastian was channelled through the press, radio, television and the Internet. This included campaigns in different media (on buses, at local fairs, on the web, etc.), advertising a varied cultural programme for the entire public at affordable prices – to challenge the perception that the Kursaal was only for use by out-of-town delegates on generous expense accounts. The campaign emphasized the introduction of the 'plaza concept' – opening the centre to local people for cultural activities of all kinds – to counteract the perception of the building as an exclusive space, closed to the inhabitants of San Sebastian. Another technique for opening up the centre to local people was the promotion of guided tours for members of the public.

To respond to the public's concerns over the economic viability of the venue, the Kursaal's management issued press releases emphasizing that the centre had ended five consecutive years (1999–2003) with its accounts in surplus. An economic impact study was also commissioned from an independent firm of consultants, and this estimated that the economic benefits generated in San Sebastian by the conference market came to 95 million euros in the first 5 years of the Kursaal's operation.

Finally, throughout the PR campaign, the use of the term 'Kursaal', rather than the San Sebastian Conference Centre, was deliberately emphasized to make the venue stand out, with its distinctive name.

By 2003, the campaign to transform the initial overwhelmingly negative reaction into genuine enthusiasm for the Kursaal had been successful. The campaign was given a considerable boost by the widespread, international architectural recognition of the building, which, for example, won the European Union prize for the best contemporary architecture in Europe, in 2001.

The year 2003 saw a number of important tributes made to the venue:

- The 'Kursaal' brand name was selected as 'Business Topbrand' by the Brand Council, together with 42 other key brands such as IBM, Nokia, Mercedes and American Express.
- The Kursaal was voted 5th best conference centre in the world by the AIPC (Association Internationale des Palais de Congrès).
- The Kursaal marketing team won the ICCA Best Marketing Award for their PR campaign.

Most importantly, however, the opinions of the local people and the press had been transformed, and the disparaging headlines of the 1990s had been replaced by newspaper articles celebrating the Kursaal's considerable successes in attracting large, high-profile events to San Sebastian. In October 2002, for example, when a conference on Family and Community Medicine attracted 5000 delegates and a food and drink exhibition drew 55 000 visitors to the city, a local newspaper, *El Diario Vasco*, ran a story vaunting the Kursaal's record-breaking achievements: 'Los records del Kursaal!'

Source: www.kursaal.org

Case Study 5.2

Familiarization trip to Cyprus

This case study shows the programme for a well-balanced familiarization trip to Cyprus for a group of UK-based organizers and an accompanying UK journalist, which took place in November 2004. The trip was organized jointly by Amathus Hotels (see Chapter 9) and the London office of the Cyprus Tourism Organization. A Cyprus-based destination management company, Neon Conferences and Incentives, was used to handle transfers and the activity programme.

A venue-led familiarization trip

Day 1 Thursday 25 November 2004

- Depart London Heathrow Airport at 09.45 hours with Cyprus Airways, flight 327
- Expected arrival at Larnaca Airport at 16.10 hours – meet and greet by Neon
- Transfer to Amathus Limassol Hotel
- Dinner and overnight stay at Hotel

Day 2 Friday 26 November 2004

- Breakfast
- Briefing and departure for jeep safari in Troodos Mountains to include pottery demonstration and lunch in a village tavern
- Return to hotel late afternoon and free time
- Dinner out: Cyprus night at a traditional restaurant in Limassol
- Overnight stay at Amathus Limassol Hotel

Day 3 Saturday 27 November 2004

- Breakfast, followed by showround of hotel
- Departure for Paphos
- En route visit the Kourion Amphitheatre; the birthplace of Aphrodite; a golf club for a lesson in putting and a mini-competition; arrival in Paphos for lunch
- Lunch in a fish tavern by the old port of Paphos, followed by a visit to the World Heritage Site archaeological park with its famous mosaics
- Check in at Paphos Amathus Hotel
- Free time
- Gala dinner with hotel management

Day 4 Sunday 28 November 2004

- Breakfast and showround of hotel
- Treatment session in hotel's spa facilities
- Lunch at hotel
- 14.00 hours depart hotel for Larnaca to catch Cyprus Airways' flight CY326 to London

Review and Discussion Questions

1 How have the principles and practice of customer relationship management changed the way in which conference destinations and venues relate to their clients and potential clients?
2 Discuss the contention that the growing use of information and communications technology will soon mean the end of printed publications.
3 Analyse the differences between the uses of advertising by venues and destinations and their use of public relations.

Sources

Anon (1995) 'El Kursaal de Rafael Moneo monstruoso', *El Diario Vasco*, 29 January
Anon (2004) 'Sydney launches New Asian incentive planner', *Australasian Special Events* (magazine), November

Canning, C (2004) 'Understanding CRM', *The Meetings Professional*, July

Davidson, R (1994) *Business Travel*, Pitman Publishing

Davidson, R (2004) *EIBTM 5-Year Trends Report: Technology and Transport*, EIBTM

Gartrell, RB (1994) *Destination Marketing for Convention and Visitor Bureaux*, Kendall/Hunt Publishing

Holloway, JC (2004) *Marketing for Tourism*, Prentice Hall

Kotler, P, Bowen, J and Makens, J (2003) *Marketing for Hospitality and Tourism*, Prentice Hall

Lenhart, M (1998) 'Can you be bought?', *Meetings and Conventions*, March

McCabe, V, Poole, B, Weeks, P and Leiper, N (2000) *The Business and Management of Conventions*, Wiley

Middleton, V (2001) *Marketing in Travel and Tourism*, Butterworth-Heinemann

Pike, S (2004) *Destination Marketing Organizations*, Elsevier

Rogers, T (2003) *Conferences and Conventions: A Global Industry*, Butterworth-Heinemann

Weber, K and Chon, K (eds) (2002) *Convention Tourism: International Research and Industry Perspectives*, Haworth Hospitality Press

World Tourism Organization (2004) *Survey of Destination Management Organizations Report*, WTO

Chapter 6

Marketing Communications for Destinations and Venues: Practice (I)

Summary of Chapter Contents

This chapter looks at the effective communication and dissemination of promotional messages about destinations and venues through the printed, visual and electronic media. Chapter 7 continues the theme of effective dissemination of promotional messages but focuses on ways in which such communications are carried out primarily on a one-to-one basis with clients.

This chapter covers:

■ Effective use of publications, including websites and electronic brochures
■ Effective PR
■ Effective advertising

It includes case studies on:

■ The Costa del Sol Convention Bureau's Meetings and Incentive Awards Ceremony
■ Harrogate International Centre's appointment of an advertising agency

Learning Outcomes

On completion of this chapter, you should be able to:

■ explain the difference between 'above-the-line' and 'below-the-line' promotional activity
■ assess the relative strengths and weaknesses of printed and electronic communications tools

■ understand the function of public relations in destination and venue marketing
■ describe the role of advertising and the characteristics of effective advertising campaigns

Introduction

Words and pictures or images have a vital and major role to play in the marketing of destinations and venues. They will typically form the first contact or communication between destinations/venues and their target audience, conference and business event organizers. In some cases, of course, it will not be possible to control or manage which words or imagery are being used because these will be conveyed by visitors to the destination or venue after their visit has taken place. Alternatively, words and pictures may be used by radio, television or newspaper journalists reporting on an incident or news 'story' in a particular location, one that is totally unrelated to its use as a conference or convention location – nonetheless, their reports and broadcasts will create an impression of the destination/venue among their listeners or readers.

Having accepted that, in a free world, people are at liberty to write and say (within the confines of libel laws!) what they wish, venue and destination marketers have to focus their energies and creativity on developing and distributing positive messages and communications in order to interest business event organizers in their product offering, one that will provide a platform to enable 'sales' of their product to be achieved. Words need to be used creatively to paint a picture of a destination or venue in the minds of readers, helping them to imagine and visualize what the location is going to be like.

This chapter will explore how marketing communications help to meet this objective, looking primarily at the broadcast media, sometimes referred to as 'above-the-line' promotional activity, which targets a wide audience. Chapter 7 will then look at marketing communications that operate on more of a one-to-one, or 'below-the-line', basis with potential clients.

Effective use of publications

Before examining a number of discrete above-the-line marketing communications tools in some depth, it will be useful to make the general point that, since many venues and destination marketing organizations are small or medium-sized enterprises (SMEs), they may benefit from outsourcing their marketing to a specialist marketing agency or consultancy, rather than trying to maintain this specialist expertise in-house. Such consultancies may operate on a 'full-service' basis (i.e. covering generic marketing planning and marketing mix strategies as outlined in Chapter 4, as well as design, public relations and advertising services) or focus on generic marketing planning and sub-contract design, PR etc. to other specialist companies.

Printed guides

Most destinations and venues produce a printed guide for use by conference and event organizers, updated on an annual basis or sometimes less frequently. The destination guide provides an overview of the destination and its attractions, including details of transport connections and the communications infrastructure, key suppliers (such as audio-visual companies, coach operators, professional conference organizers), together with detailed entries for each of the conference and event venues represented.

Destination guides should:

- use high quality photography
- have two-level maps showing (a) the destination's location within the country and/or region and (b) the location of each of the venues within the destination
- include a comprehensive index
- include a see-at-a-glance summary of the rooms and capacities for all of the venues listed to enable conference organizers to see quickly which venues could potentially accommodate a particular event.

In the authors' experience, possibly the most sophisticated of destination guides is the one produced by Madrid Convention Bureau, which, for 2005, included three separate but integrated wire-bound sections (covering background data on Madrid, the capital city; detailed information on venues; and a section on professional conference organizers and other suppliers) together with pull-out maps (Madrid Convention Bureau, www.munimadrid.es/congresos).

Glasgow City Marketing Bureau (www.seeglasgow.com) produces its own guides, printing them daily using the latest colour printer and web-based technology. Its award-winning conference guide has a 'printed on [today's date]' and a year's life, with a printed 'best before' date. The premise for so doing is that DMOs own nothing but their information: if they provide out-of-date information via their brochures, this compromises their services. As information on the destination changes daily (e.g. new telephone numbers, changes in venue sales managers, new restaurant openings), the brochure or guide is able to keep pace with these changes and remain up-to-date.

While such destination guides are typically produced for local or city destinations, they may also be produced at a national level to promote a whole country. The French Convention Bureau guide, published by the national tourist board, Maison de la France, is one example of a national guide (www.franceguide.com and www. meet-in-france.com), while the British Association of Conference Destinations' national directory adopts a slightly different focus with its descriptions of both discrete destinations and the convention bureaux and conference desks, which promote and service these local destinations (www.bacd.org.uk).

Some destinations opt to complement their largely factual guide with a 'destination sell' publication, designed to convey attractive and positive images of the destination but containing relatively little hard, factual information. In the UK, destinations such as Durham City and South-West Wales have produced destination sell literature.

Venue brochures have an important role in providing detailed information on a specific venue. They also position the venue within the context of a destination. Venue brochures should include:

- detailed maps and location information – again best practice would suggest that at least two maps should be included: one showing the location of the venue within a particular town/city/region, and one showing its detailed position and access within a locality (with names of adjacent roads, details of any one-way traffic systems operating, proximity to railway station, etc.)

- photographs of the venue, showing at least one external shot, plus a number of internal shots to illustrate meeting rooms, bedrooms, restaurant(s), leisure facilities and so forth. Such photographs are always much more effective with people in them, rather than being unpopulated, as is so often the case
- detailed technical information on each of the meeting and conference rooms – capacities for different seating layouts, room dimensions including ceiling height, air-conditioning, whether the room has natural light, and details of any dedicated audio-visual facilities built into the room
- an internal layout plan: this is a particularly useful feature because it illustrates the location of the various meeting rooms within the venue – this assists conference organizers to select the rooms most appropriate to their needs, and gives them the chance to minimize time wasted when delegates have to move between different meeting rooms (for syndicate sessions, for example, or to visit a concurrent exhibition).

Most destination and venue guides are produced in A4 (or quarto) format, and this enables conference organizers to store reference copies easily in standard filing cabinets. Occasionally venues and destinations, driven by the creative flair of design companies, publish guides of a different size and, while this is not a problem if they are smaller than A4, it can cause problems if the guides are larger than A4, because they will not fit into a filing cabinet and, as a result, may be disposed of rather than kept for reference. It is also possible that distribution costs will be higher because special envelopes may be needed and postage/mailing costs are greater. Distribution costs need to be incorporated into the overall marketing budget. Will the guide be distributed principally by post and, if so, will the circulation be national or international? Or will substantial quantities be given to recipients, for example when visiting the destination or venue or from an exhibition stand, incurring minimal or zero distribution costs?

Printed directories (and electronic brochures in the form of CD-Roms/DVDs) pose a dilemma over the quantities to produce, as well as the methods of distribution. Destination and venue marketers have to estimate accurately the print run for a particular brochure. If they under-estimate the quantities required, additional printing can be relatively expensive, making the net cost per brochure higher than it need have been had they printed the correct, larger quantity in the first place. Conversely, printing of too many copies can also waste money if it should prove impossible to put all of the brochures and guides to good use. The solution to this could, of course, be to print on demand or to burn CD-Roms on demand, although the unit costs are likely to be somewhat higher than when printing a bulk supply.

Paper-based or electronic guides?

In this increasingly electronic age, is there still a need for destinations and venues to produce paper-based guides? While it is undeniably the case that more and more resources are being committed to the electronic communications media, there still appears to be a need and a role for printed guides. They have not yet been replaced by CD-Roms and DVDs. The latter have come to be seen as a valuable additional

Benefits of paper-based guides
- Flexibility and portability, e.g. they can be carried around in a briefcase, read on the train or at home
- Speed of access – there is no delay in waiting for the computer to boot up
- Comparability – they facilitate comparisons between venues in the same destination, or between meeting rooms in the same venue

Benefits of electronic guides
- Storage capacity – continuing reductions in costs for electronic communications tools and the rapid development of new electronic devices with huge memory capacities may erode the accessibility advantages that paper-based guides currently enjoy
- Moving images – one of the major advantages that CD-Roms/DVDs have over the static, printed word is their ability to convey moving images and sound in the promotion of a destination or a venue. Video footage of a destination, or a 'virtual' tour of a venue, can bring them to life for the potential client in a way that a printed brochure cannot
- Presentation tool – CD-Roms/DVDs can also play a useful role as a presentation tool, enabling conference organizers to give an audio-visual presentation about a particular destination or venue to their senior management team or to a selection committee
- Lower distribution costs – mailing costs for CD-Roms/DVDs are less than those for printed guides

Figure 6.1 Paper-based *vs.* electronic guides.

promotional tool, complementing the printed word rather than making it obsolete. Figure 6.1 compares the benefits of paper-based guides with electronic information sources.

Websites

Undoubtedly the bigger challenge for printed guides comes from the Internet. Today, practically all destinations and venues active in the conference and conventions sector have their own website, together with links and hyperlinks to other sites. Websites combine the benefits offered by CD-Roms and DVDs with the facility for continuous updating. One of the inherent weaknesses of printed guides is that the data they contain cannot be altered. Many guides and directories are partly out of date even as they are published, and may be very inaccurate indeed once they have been in circulation for a year or more.

Websites can also be accessed 24 hours a day, seven days a week, from anywhere in the world. Distribution costs are minimal, but there are some promotional costs through registration with search engines and the need to inform clients of the website's content and, of course, its address.

Websites can also be used as a valuable promotional tool by conference and convention organizers in helping them to market their event and optimize delegate attendance. The example of Atlanta Convention and Visitors Bureau's 'video e-mail' facility (see Chapter 5) is just one illustration of a destination website being developed in this way. Similarly, many destinations and venues now offer on-line accommodation booking services.

Successful websites for destinations and venues are likely to have features such as:

- be quick loading and have easy navigability
- be visually attractive and make use of the full screen
- contain excellent maps and travel directions
- include virtual tours
- contain factual information on venue layouts and capacities.

Venuemasters, the marketing consortium for academic venues in the United Kingdom (www.venuemasters.co.uk), holds an annual marketing awards competition for the universities, colleges and other academic venues which form its membership. One of the award categories is for best website, which, in 2004, was won by the University of East Anglia (www.ueaconferences.co.uk), whose website epitomized many of the best practice features described above. A screen shot from their website is shown as Figure 6.2. Second and third places were won by City University, London (www.city.ac.uk/ems) and the University of Liverpool (www.livuniconferences. co.uk).

As well as producing their own guides, destinations and venues should also examine the benefits of promoting themselves through other printed directories and websites. Two of the leading Internet-based venue finding and enquiry systems are: www.venuedirectory.com and www.onvantage.com. Sites such as these allow browsers to enter their own venue search criteria on line, and details of venues that match are supplied to them within a matter of seconds. Browsers can then look at detailed information on the venues, including photos, and may also be able to undertake a 'virtual' tour of the venue. There is also the facility to send a specific enquiry ('request for proposal' or 'RFP') to venues shortlisted. Similar information is available in CD-Rom (or DVD) format, with meeting planners receiving updated CD-Roms several times a year.

Newsletters

Newsletters have proved to be a popular marketing medium for destinations and venues for a decade or more. Traditionally produced in printed format, their combination of attractive photos/illustrations and short, snappy news items has proved to be an effective CRM vehicle, strengthening the relationship between destination/ venue and client through the provision of a regular flow of information. Although the production costs can, to some extent, be controlled by limiting the size of the newsletter (6–8 pages would typically be a maximum length), newsletters can prove to be fairly expensive to produce, as budgets need to cover copy-writing, professional photography, design and typesetting, printing, and mailing/distribution costs. Reader surveys also need to be carried out from time to time to obtain feedback on the usefulness and readability of the newsletter, and there should also be an evaluation process to monitor how successful the newsletter has been in meeting the objectives set for it. Such objectives may include: changing perceptions of a venue/ destination, creating a higher profile, or generating specific business leads and enquiries. The newsletter of the Monaco Convention Office (www.monaco-tourisme.com) is one example of an attractively produced, easy-to-read newsletter, often accompanied

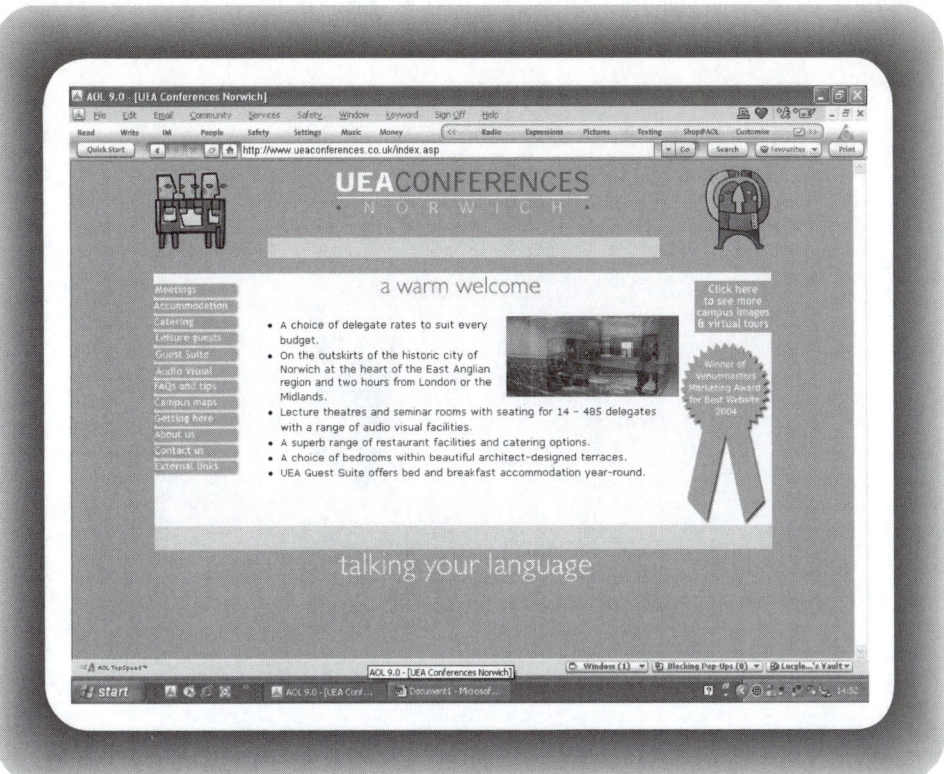

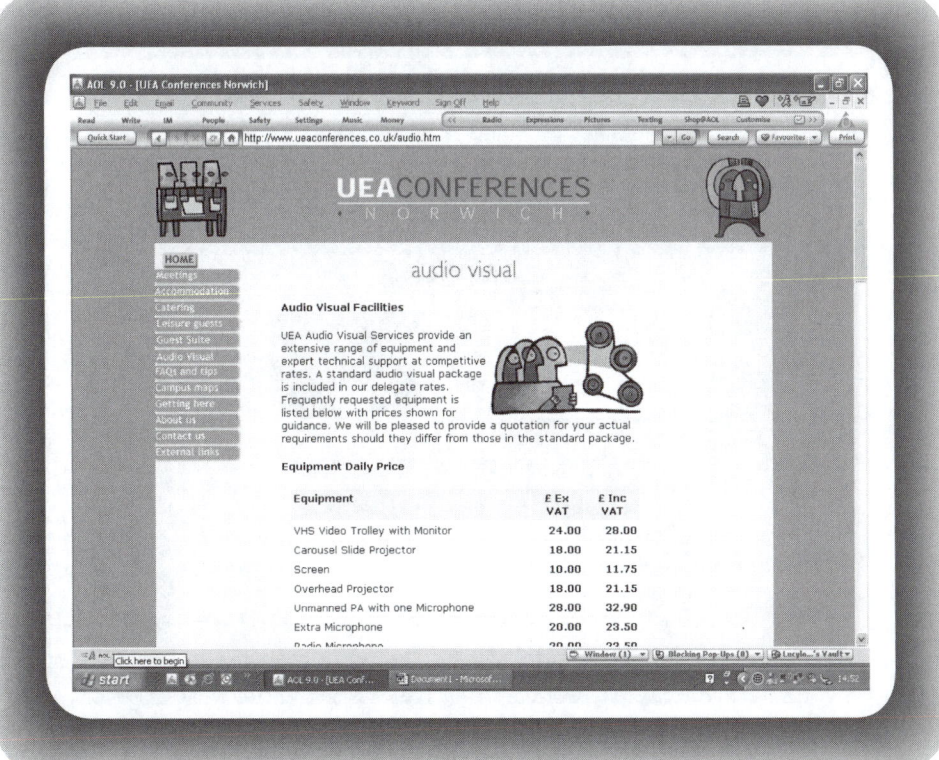

Figure 6.2 Web pages from the University of East Anglia's award-winning website (www.ueaconferences.co.uk).

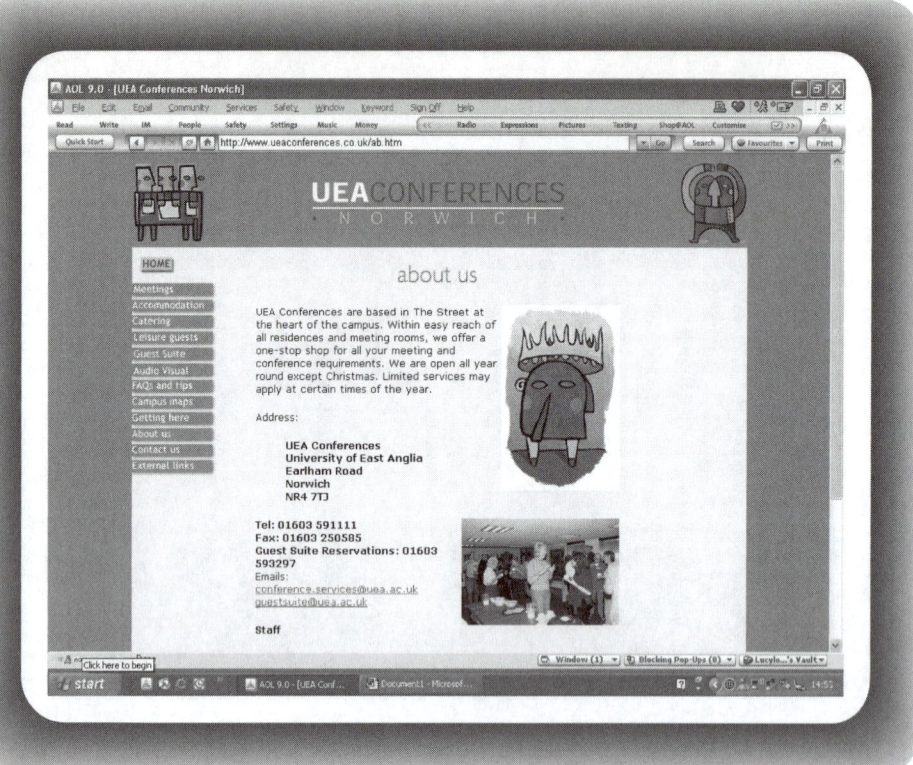

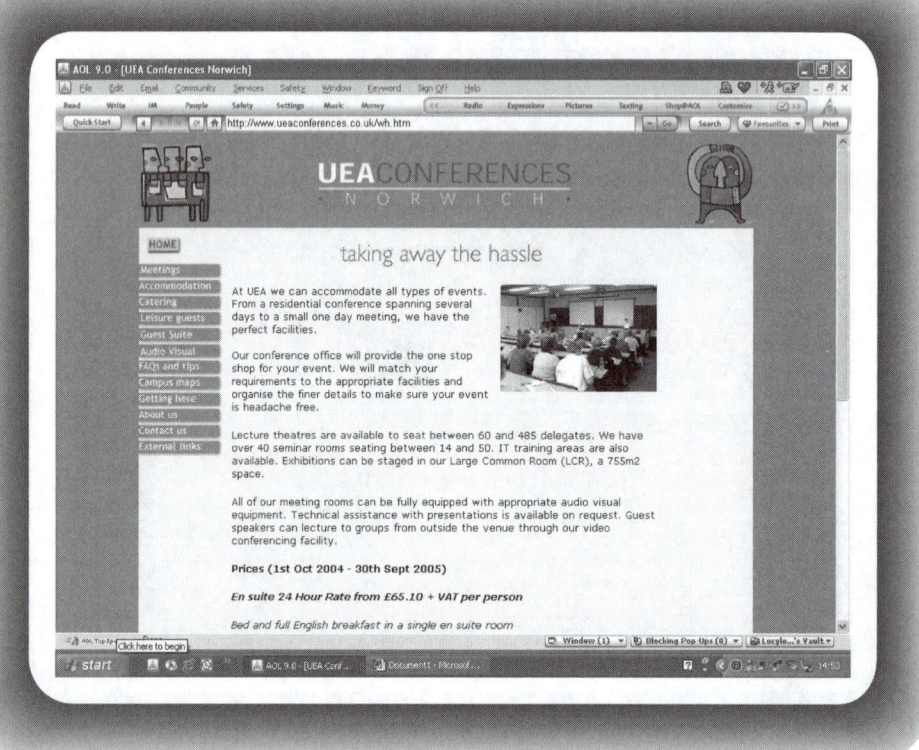

Figure 6.2 (*Continued*)

by an incentive prize draw which requires recipients to read the newsletter in order to be able to answer questions about the destination, for entry in the prize draw.

In recent years the printed newsletter has, to an increasing extent, been replaced by the e-newsletter. This latter is much less expensive to produce and to circulate, and can include significantly more information, if required. E-newsletters are usually distributed as a PDF attachment to an e-mail or as an e-mail with links to the pages of a website, each page containing a different article. The latter option allows the recipient to view an index of the newsletter articles and click on those of particular interest. The newsletters of VisitBritain's Business Tourism Department, (www.visitbritain.com/businesstourism), of the International Congress and Convention Association (www.iccaworld.com), of Best Loved Hotels (www.bestloved.com/data/newsletters/html) and of the trade show EIBTM (www.eibtm.com) are all good examples of this approach.

Effective PR

Another extremely important promotional vehicle is that summarized as 'PR', referring to public (and sometimes 'press') relations. The principles and scope of PR have been explained in Chapter 5 – this chapter gives examples of the practical application of PR, for which many venues and destinations employ the services of a dedicated PR agency, usually one specializing in the conventions and business events sector.

PR has the benefit of giving free media exposure. Its disadvantage is that the destination/venue is not able to control how the message appears, when it appears (if at all) or even where it appears. The coverage given may be negative, or at least inaccurate, and may position the brand incorrectly.

PR is also measurable. Such measures provide key performance indicators (KPIs) for assessing the work of the PR team or dedicated PR agency, enabling targets to be set for individuals against which their performance can be appraised. Tables 6.1 and 6.2 illustrate how PR can be measured, both in terms of the circulation achieved by a piece of news or an article/feature or a photo, and in terms of its value in financial terms.

Table 6.1 Measuring PR by circulation achieved

	Circulation			
	Period under review 2005–6	*Equivalent period 2004–5*	*Year to date 2005–6*	*Year to date 2004–5*
Product PR	2 152 744	4 145 758	6 457 877	8 398 762
Corporate PR	2 840 125	2 474 058	4 954 216	5 065 209
Total	**4 992 869**	**6 619 816**	**11 412 093**	**13 463 971**

Source: Glasgow City Marketing Bureau

Table 6.2 Measuring PR by financial value of coverage achieved

	Advertising equivalence*			
	Period under review 2005–6	*Equivalent period 2004–5*	*Year to date 2005–6*	*Year to date 2004–5*
Product PR (£)	247 503	236 079	2 263 446	1 037 451
Corporate PR (£)	45 954	17 210	76 413	171 299
Total (£)	**293 457**	**253 289**	**2 339 859**	**1 208 750**

*Using the PR industry standard of editorial coverage equating to three times advertising rates.
Source: Glasgow City Marketing Bureau

To be effective, PR activities have to be properly planned, with the PR Plan dovetailing into an overall Venue or Destination Marketing Plan (see Chapter 4), ensuring as well that all appropriate marketing activities are supported by PR. The PR Plan should include sections such as the following.

Setting objectives
These could be:

- To communicate a specific piece of news
- To raise the profile of the destination or venue
- To raise the profile of the destination or venue team.

Identifying the customer
Identifying the customer means identifying the target audience:

- Corporate event organizers
- Association convention organizers
- Agencies or intermediaries
- Local government or public sector bodies.

Identifying possible PR vehicles
These could include:

- Events
  - industry exhibitions
  - specific exhibitions aimed at a certain market (for example personal assistants/ secretaries)
  - association-linked events
  - press events/launches
- Media
  - conference and events industry press
  - vertical press (telecommunications, pharmaceutical, financial services, etc.)
  - job title specific press (e.g. PAs, training managers)
  - general business press
  - local/chamber of commerce press

- ○ national press
- ○ TV and radio
- Awards
  - ○ industry awards
  - ○ job title specific awards (sales team/PAs)
  - ○ national business awards
- Case Study 6.1, which is presented at the end of the chapter, describes an international awards ceremony for the meetings and incentives industry organized by the Costa del Sol Convention Bureau
- Speaker platforms
  - ○ industry conferences or exhibitions
  - ○ destination organized events.

One of the simplest ways of communicating is by press release. Presentation of press material is almost as important as its content: it needs to look professional, and this will significantly enhance the chances of achieving coverage.

Press releases remain one of the most effective ways of promoting a destination or venue, but the reality is that probably more than 70% of press releases end up in the bin! Adherence to the guidelines set out in Figure 6.3, compiled by specialist UK PR agency, Friday's Media Group Ltd, will increase the likelihood of a release being used.

Features

The editorial content of most conference industry magazines can be split into three very different areas: news, comment/opinion columns and issue/destination/venue-led features. While a press release will work to get coverage in the news pages, opportunities to get exposure in the other two sections should not be ignored. Such exposure may be achieved by:

- The provision of appropriate 'comment' from the destination or venue into existing special features and reports
- Venues and, particularly, destinations could also write to magazine editors suggesting ideas for special reports that would include the destination or elements of the destination
- Another approach could be through the promotion of the personalities behind the destination as industry 'gurus'
- Another source of ideas will come from case studies of successful events held in the region. These should be researched and written up and the issues unearthed could form the basis of features and comment columns.

Effective advertising

Advertising, like PR, is a discrete marketing discipline in its own right. Good advertising, as with PR, is likely to require an input from a specialist advertising agency, and again this will probably be from an agency that has developed its understanding and experience of the conventions and business events sector.

Press releases are more likely to be used by media editors if they follow key principles and tips such as:

- Make the story newsworthy – editors are looking for original news (e.g. focusing on 'the first …', 'the best …', 'the biggest …', etc.)
- Aim to create a word picture: rather than simply saying 'the city is 100 per cent occupied, use a description such as a bed can't be found for 30 miles around that hasn't got someone sleeping in it!'
- Use a catchy headline – one that summarizes the story being promoted. Busy editors will ignore a release if the headline does not grab their attention! However, they should not be too tricky. Puns are fun, but should be left to the sub-editors. The content should be clear from the headline
- Summarize the release in the first paragraph as this will help an editor to judge whether he wants further details from which to develop a story – this can come in the body of the release but the opening paragraph must engage their interest
- Remember the 'five W's': Who is involved? What is happening? When is it happening? Why is it happening? Where is it happening?
- Product releases should incorporate information on key features, the benefits to the user, price, availability and a general description, as well as contact details to provide further information
- In stylistic terms, use short sentences and paragraphs. Avoid slang, jargon, opinion and boasts – stick to the facts. Make sure that any statement made can be justified. A press release is not like sales literature. It should be factual and should be written as a news story would appear in a magazine or newspaper
- Include a quote, if possible, preferably from a key person in the organization
- Always print releases in single or double line spacing and avoid elaborate fonts – it is the content that is important

If appropriate, state at the bottom of the release that an image is available upon request. Avoid sending images with the release – if sending by post, this is a costly process. If distributing press releases by e-mail, it is considered bad practice to send unsolicited attachments. At best they will clog up the editor's inbox, at worst they could result in the release being quarantined by anti-spamming software or deleted before it is even opened. The photograph should be professionally taken and can be supplied as a print, transparency or electronically on disk/as a PDF. Ensure that it is supplied with a caption giving all the relevant information, including the names and jobs of anyone featured, listed from left to right. Do not staple prints or transparencies to the press release. When providing the image electronically, ensure that it is scanned at 300 dpi (the standard resolution for most publications) and can be read by PC and Apple Mac computers. Change file names to something relevant to the story and make it clear which caption refers to which file.

Last of all – only issue a press release if there is something newsworthy to say!

Source: Friday's Media Group Ltd

Figure 6.3 Guidelines for effective press releases.

Advertising is typically far more expensive than PR. It is expensive to originate and media costs are high, but the message, media, positioning and timing are totally within the control of the destination/venue.

Traditionally, advertising agencies were either 'above-the-line' or 'below-the-line', i.e. 'above-the-line' refers predominantly to paid advertising talking to a large audience (through television, radio, posters, press advertising), whereas 'below-the-line' focuses on opportunities to reach the audience on a one-to-one basis (e.g. mailing to a database or promoting to customers from an exhibition stand). All agencies are concerned with building brands but for an above-the-line agency it is their main focus. Their advertising (brand marketing) seeks to change minds and create a unique image for the brand. In the words of Chris Arnold, formerly a director with advertising agency Saatchi & Saatchi and now Integrated Creative Director BLAC:

> *Above-the-line advertising seeks to tell you about the brand and change your view of it, direct marketing ...*
> *[below-the-line] seeks to build a relationship between you and the brand, and get you to change your behaviour.*

Some of the traditional distinctions between agencies are breaking down with the same agency now handling both above-the-line and below-the-line activity – the term 'through-the-line' has been coined to embrace such diverse activity.

Advertising has to be planned strategically, carried out over a period of time as a 'campaign', and integrated with the overall sales and marketing plan for a destination or venue. Advertising is an important component in the creation and promotion of a brand for a destination or venue, a process described in more detail in Chapter 4.

The advertising agency assists in setting clear and measurable objectives for the advertising campaign: for example, is the campaign mainly to do with creating an awareness of the destination/venue, changing perceptions, creating a pre-disposition to visit or to 'buy', or to generate actual responses in the form of business enquiries. The agency produces designs for an advertisement or a series of advertisements, advises on where these should be placed (in magazines, business newspapers, or railway stations, for example), and helps in monitoring response. It will normally do this work based on a brief from the destination/venue, finalized in the form of a contract which also includes details of fees and expenses to be paid.

The process employed by the Harrogate International Centre (HIC) (www.harrogateinternationalcentre.co.uk) in England during the early months of 2005, to appoint an advertising agency with responsibility for a new above-the-line advertising campaign to appear in appropriate media (primarily the trade press), illustrates the role and the relationship between venue/destination and agency. The Centre decided against appointing one agency to handle all of its requirements as a full service provision – the purchase of advertising space in the print media, for example, would continue to be handled by a separate agency. The appointment process is presented as Case Study 6.2 at the end of the chapter.

Summary

Above-the-line marketing communications are an essential component in the promotion of a conference destination or venue. While the mix of communications tools will vary (i.e. whether to put the emphasis on an advertising campaign, or PR activity, or web-based promotions, for example), both from venue to venue and from destination to destination, but also from time to time (what may be most appropriate one year may be less so the following year), it is indisputable that the effective use of such communications is fundamental to the future success of other marketing and sales activities. They lay the foundations, namely an awareness of and a positive interest in a destination or venue on the part of clients, upon which further promotional activity can be undertaken, and ensure that such activity has a greater chance of being successful.

Case Study 6.1

The Costa del Sol Convention Bureau's 1st International Meetings and Incentive Awards Ceremony (2004)

The Costa del Sol Convention Bureau (CDSCB) (www.costadelsolconventionbureau.com) is a specialist department of the Costa del Sol Tourist Board, and was formed in 1993 to promote Málaga and the Costa del Sol, located on Spain's south-west Mediterranean coast, to the congress, convention and incentive travel markets. In 2004 it created and organized its '1st International Meetings and Incentive Awards Ceremony', an event which, in the words of the Convention Bureau:

> was the final stage of a long journey, a journey which we undertook with a clear goal in mind – the dream of bringing together top travel industry specialists and members of our Convention Bureau. It was our dream to show the world this fascinating destination and the city of Picasso, to let them experience the magic of the past and the passion of the present.

The CSDCB was assisted in the staging of the awards ceremony by Turespaña, Spain's national tourism authority, and the intention is to stage future ceremonies every two years.

Objectives

While the overt reason for organizing the awards ceremony was to 'honour (and thank) meeting planners, travel managers, congress and incentive organizers and MICE industry media within Europe, the United States and Canada', it also had very clear, underlying marketing objectives. These were:

- to promote the Costa del Sol and all its possibilities as a leading international meetings and incentive destination
- to improve the destination's image and change the market attitudes towards the Costa del Sol
- to strengthen current client loyalty and attract potential clients
- to facilitate face-to-face contact with top decision makers of the MICE industry in a relaxed environment in order to exchange information and ideas.

Target audience

The intention was to invite three key groups to participate in the awards ceremony:

- actual and potential clients
- industry media
- award winners.

Actual and potential clients or buyers were identified from a variety of lists of incentive houses, meetings planners and corporate buyers. It was hoped to attract 100 top buyers (with their partners) from 15 different countries. In the final analysis, 105 buyers with their partners actually attended the event. Table 6.3 shows the numbers participating from individual countries. The timing of the event (2–4 July 2004) was chosen because of its convenience for the greatest number of buyers.

CDSCB recognized, from the outset, that it would be crucial to obtain as much support as possible from key industry trade magazines, and seven specialist titles were selected as partners.

Categories of awards were created to cover:

- Best Product Launch
- Best Creative Programme

Table 6.3 Origin of participants

Country of origin of buyers	No. attending
UK/Ireland	11
Benelux	15
Canada	8
United States	12
Scandinavia	15
France	3
Spain	23
Italy	7
Germany	11
Portugal	1
Poland	2

- Best Costa del Sol Promoter
- Best Scientific Congress
- Best Media Feature

Further details of each category and of the respective award winners are shown on the website: www.costadelsolconventionbureau.com/awards. This site also gives details of the coverage achieved for the event in the industry media.

Marketing campaign

The marketing campaign for the awards ceremony started a year and a half before the event took place, following in-depth interviews with a range of clients and stakeholders to define participants' interests, business concerns, needs, desires, suggestions and preferences. It was decided that the campaign had to meet the objectives for the event (as listed above), capture the interest of the participants, but at the same time reflect the authenticity and character of the destination. Design elements for the event and for the marketing material were examined in detail, and it was eventually decided to base the design theme on 'Picasso', who was born in Málaga and is claimed to be the greatest artist of the twentieth century – the recent opening of the Picasso Museum of Málaga, housing the largest private collection of his works and available for use as a MICE facility, also added weight to this choice of image for the event.

Promotion of the event made use of:

- **Public relations**: through Turespaña and all the networked Spanish Tourist Offices involved in the project. E-mails, telephone, faxes and a website were created for the event.
- **Advertising**: in conjunction with the selected trade magazines. Free advertising was secured in special editions featuring the Costa del Sol.
- **Direct marketing**: through printed material including a specially designed invitation, questionnaires, brochures and newsletters.
- **Internet**: a temporary website was created in order to communicate with the invitees but also to provide a global presence.

CDSCB summarized the most important aspects of their campaign as:

- targeting their audience
- making the appropriate offer
- using the right design.

Throughout the venues and locations used in the programme, different forms of displays were used to create awareness of the event. These included flags, billboards, panels, posters, etc.

Management and financial aspects

The success of the event owed much to good communication. A planning committee was formed by CDSCB from within its membership, comprising representatives of hotels, a coach company, a golf course and an audio-visual company. The committee produced an Action Plan with tight schedules and, as the programme developed, it became a series of mini events, each with their own objectives, administrative requirements, staff considerations, budget and communication needs.

For participants, the only cost was their time in travelling to and attending the event. All of the costs were covered by the organizers and sponsors. A breakdown of the financial and in-kind contributions received is shown in Table 6.4.

Table 6.4 Financial and in-kind support for the event

Organization	Amount contributed (€) and in-kind support
Costa del Sol Convention Bureau	60 000
Turespaña	42 000
Turismo Andaluz	47 000
Málaga Municipality	9000
Iberia	Free air tickets for all international participants
Official hotels	Complimentary accommodation and meals
Coach company	Free transfers
A range of other sponsoring organizations also made specific contributions	

Conclusion

The level and quality of attendance at the 1st International Meeting and Incentive Awards Ceremony, together with the very positive feedback received afterwards from participants, bear testimony to the success of this event. Further assessments of its impact can be made over the next few years when it will be possible to measure the amount of new business being brought to Málaga and the Costa del Sol as a direct result of the event.

The financial and human resources devoted to the promotion and staging of the ceremony were substantial, illustrating the scale of marketing investment that is now necessary in a highly competitive global marketplace in order to differentiate an event and a destination from the competition. But if the destination can get it right, the returns on their investment in the form of new business can also be substantial.

John Keenan, editor of the UK's *Meetings & Incentive Travel Magazine*, described the event in the following words:

> *The 1st International Costa del Sol Awards Ceremony highlighted the variety and quality of the meetings and incentive travel product available in the region. It demonstrated the fine infrastructure, marvellous venues, and value for money offered by a part of Europe too often subject to clichéd opinion. The programme gave organizers a good reason to look more closely at the Costa del Sol.*

Case Study 6.2

Harrogate International Centre's appointment of an advertising agency

A letter was sent by Harrogate International Centre (HIC) in mid-January 2005 to about 12 agencies inviting them to submit proposals for consideration. The letter stated:

> *we are seeking presentations and proposals of visuals and concepts for our new 'above-the-line' advertising campaign to appear in appropriate media (primarily trade press) from Spring 2005, ... together with an indication of anticipated costs of the proposals from concepts to finished artwork and production for supply to various media.*

The letter made reference to the HIC's new Queen's Suite facility, offering additional meeting space, due for completion in February 2005, and further background information was enclosed about HIC and about the Harrogate area as a leisure and business tourism destination. The letter hinted at the possibility of 'extending the remit [in the future] to include holiday/business tourism promotion, print buying, media, PR activities and web-based e-marketing'. On receipt of the letter, interested agencies were invited to contact the HIC Head of Marketing and Sales to 'arrange a further short briefing and agree timescales for subsequent presentation', expected to take place early February, with a view to the new campaign being operative by April. The letter concluded by suggesting that a further, final presentation might be needed in the week commencing 21st February, involving the Director of HIC.

Approximately half of the agencies invited to tender for the HIC contract were asked to present proposals. The criteria used by HIC to assess these agencies included:

Concepts/visuals
These needed to be:

- Engaging
- Relevant
- Dynamic
- Inspiring

and should avoid plagiarism and criticizing competitor venues.

Additional considerations
Other factors influencing the final choice of agency included:

- Costings (concept/artwork/production) and timescales
- Relationships, i.e. the personal chemistry between the agency and the HIC as their client, seen as an essential ingredient in a successful relationship

- The agency's awareness of the market and the HIC product
- The agency's awareness of HIC's competitors and the industry media
- The agency's track record, including endorsements and testimonials from former/existing clients
- Account management aspects
- The opportunities for extending the agency's remit into media buying, PR, web-based activity, etc.

Following submissions and presentations, an agency was appointed and an example of the advertising produced for HIC is shown as Figure 6.4.

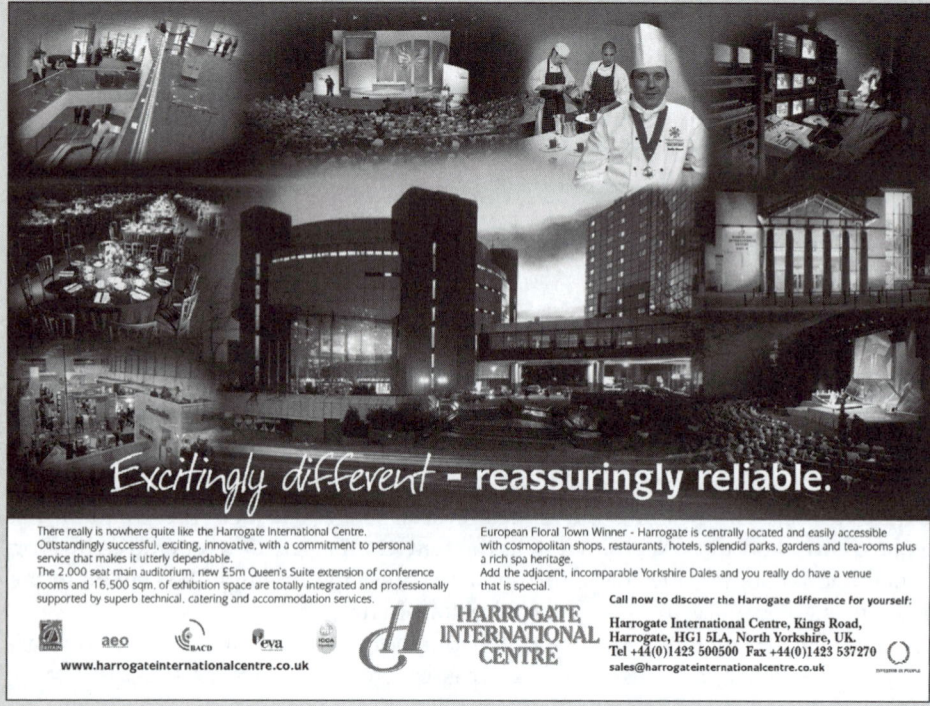

Figure 6.4 Example advertising for Harrogate International Centre.

Review and Discussion Questions

1 Compare and contrast hard copy newsletters and e-newsletters. What are their respective advantages and disadvantages:
  (a) from a venue/destination (i.e. as publisher or producer of the newsletter) perspective?
  (b) from a recipient (i.e. conference organizer/buyer) perspective?

2 Undertake critical evaluations of press releases issued by:
   (a) a venue or venue consortium
   (b) a destination
   (c) an industry association.
   Use the best practice guidelines for press releases in this chapter as the benchmark for your evaluations.
   'The growth in customer relationship management (CRM) and direct marketing will significantly reduce the future use of above-the-line marketing communications in the conference, convention and business events sector.' Discuss the merits of this statement, illustrating your conclusions with examples and/or case studies drawn from the industry.

Source

Arnold, 'What's the Difference between Above, Below and Through the Line', accessed at: www.ad-mad.co.uk/contentstudentforum.htm

Chapter 7

Marketing Communications for Destinations and Venues: Practice (II)

Summary of Chapter Contents

This chapter continues to look at the effective dissemination of promotional messages about destinations and venues begun in Chapter 6, but concentrates on ways in which such communications are carried out primarily on a one-to-one basis with clients.
   This chapter covers:

- Exhibiting at trade shows
- Organizing workshops and roadshows
- Running familiarization trips and educationals
- Organizing effective ambassador programmes

It includes case studies on:

- Venue Italia Workshop in Rome, 2005
- Edinburgh Convention Bureau's Conference Ambassador programme

Learning Outcomes

On completion of this chapter, you should be able to:

- identify the core strategies for successful participation in trade exhibitions
- distinguish between exhibitions, workshops and roadshows, and understand the benefits and opportunities which each provides
- understand the role of familiarization trips in the marketing communications process
- define the detailed planning steps in staging a productive familiarization trip
- explain the purpose, operation and development of ambassador programmes

Introduction

It is perhaps not surprising that, in the business events industry, events themselves can be used as a major tool in marketing communications. The events can range in size from industry exhibitions attracting thousands of visitors and exhibiting companies, workshops and roadshows for tens or perhaps a few hundred people, to quite intimate events such as familiarization trips for just a handful of buyers. In all cases, they are forms of face-to-face marketing, which involve personal interaction with potential customers. Their focus is on below-the-line marketing activity, generating one-to-one encounters with the aim of establishing and building relationships with individual clients.

Ambassador programmes, on the other hand, seek to recruit and work with stakeholders in a particular community to act as the destination's representatives or communicators, in effect to become the medium through whom marketing messages and event bids can be channelled.

This chapter looks in detail at these different forms of below-the-line marketing communications, many of which will be used by both destinations and venues as a key component of their marketing strategies.

Exhibiting at trade shows

Trade exhibitions are a well-established marketing medium, and such exhibitions or shows for the convention and business events sector have existed for several decades. Exhibiting at trade shows is another part of a venue or destination's marketing strategy, part of a planned campaign in the same way that advertising and PR should be. The suggestions for effective exhibiting given below draw heavily on ideas presented by Ray Bloom, Chairman of UK-based Regent Exhibitions Ltd and organizer of IMEX, one of the leading conventions and business tourism exhibitions held annually in Frankfurt, Germany.

Participation in a trade exhibition can often provide the opportunity to launch a new brochure, a new campaign, new products or a new image. The destination or venue's presence and proposed activities at the show can be highlighted nationally or world-wide – in e-mails, letters, news bulletins and advertisements. It is possible to target the world's leading 100 business tourism publications and aim for news coverage that appears just before, during or immediately after the exhibition. One interesting approach is to engineer the sense that a special launch is going to take place during the exhibition … and the deliberate excitement of this beforehand can be added to by using promotional teasers, promised gifts for buyers who come to the stand, and the offer of a fulfilment pack explaining the new product or service in detail.

In addition to ensuring an integrated marketing approach and taking advantage of the exhibition organizer's own promotional activities (such as ensuring a full entry in the exhibition guide and on the show's website, which may well be designed as a year-round 'virtual exhibition'), there are a number of key textbook approaches to exhibition success that should not be by-passed.

Set objectives

The first such requirement is to set more challenging objectives! These, for example, might be to confirm current contracts and thank existing clients, win new business, launch new products, raise profile and awareness, achieve hundreds of good leads, develop new relationships with influential partners, undertake market research, spot industry trends, meet the world's top trade editors, watch what competitors are doing, spark off some creative thinking, or seek involvement in wider initiatives within the industry. In other words, the time-honoured justification for exhibition attendance can be realized – namely, to be commercially successful – but there is further scope to build databases for the future, exploit brand awareness, express market leadership, position or re-position the image of the brand, test reaction to a new product and more.

Stand design

Secondly, the stand design will have an impact on success at the exhibition. In such an environment, where marketing is at its most direct, exhibitors have the freedom to employ all five senses – sight, sound, taste, touch and smell – as weapons in their armoury. Such a sensual approach could be employed to attract and then keep buyers on the stand. Key points of differentiation might be the colours used, open and welcoming stand layout, special eye-catching features and presentation techniques; as well of course as trained professional staff who understand and promote the destination/venue's values and objectives to buyers walking the aisles.

Interacting with visitors

Thirdly, it is important to adopt different approaches to different kinds of visitors to the stand. Mark Saunders, brand experience account director for event management consultancy the George P Johnson company, expressed this as follows in *Exhibiting* magazine:

> *A warm prospect that you know by name and who has interacted with you well in advance of an event needs to be treated very differently from someone coming to your stand cold. For example, a warm prospect who knows and rates your product, but who hasn't yet become a customer, may benefit from having a high-level pre-booked meeting on the stand with your CEO. This will communicate the personal attention they will receive if they become a customer. To underscore this, you might then invite them to a customer reception where they can mix with satisfied customers. In contrast, a browser, someone who hasn't yet proved their value to you as a prospect, and who possibly doesn't know your organization, will need to get a clear 'at a glance' feel for your company and offer. They may need theatre presentations and hands-on demonstrations. All of this will have implications for the layout, architecture and signage on your stand.*

Measuring return on investment (ROI)

Exhibitors are now in a position actually to measure the anticipated revenue outcome of their exhibition investment. For example, this could be done by computing the potential value of the follow-up quotations that are submitted; the actual level of business that has been done; the volume of brochures that were distributed; the degree of response to the stand competitions that were organized; and the total number of centimetres of editorial coverage that was subsequently achieved. More sophisticated approaches could involve the use of market research – by telephone or using focus groups, perhaps – in order to track changing perceptions towards a particular destination. Countries will be keen to monitor the resulting improvement in positive attitudes amongst decision-makers and, therefore, their growing willingness to book and buy. Such measurement may take place over months and years in order to evaluate fully the results from a show's attendance.

Follow-up

This same disciplined and professional approach must, of course, apply also to follow-ups after the event. The exhibition sales team should be de-briefed, their achievements related to the original goals and the subsequent week-by-week progress checked. It is especially important to exploit that immediate exhibition 'afterglow' during which the potential clients can still easily recall their conversation on a particular stand.

Organizing workshops and roadshows

Workshops are a form of mini-exhibition at which destinations and/or venues can interact with a group of invited event organizers or 'buyers'. Typically such workshops last for a few hours rather than for several days (although this is not always the case – see Venue Italia example below), may involve a table-top presence with some literature by the exhibitors instead of a fully fledged exhibition stand, usually offer refreshments to the visitors, and may include a formal audio-visual presentation to those visiting the event as well as the opportunities for one-to-one meetings between exhibitors and visitors. They are on a much smaller scale than an exhibition, and can therefore be held in a hotel or conference centre, or in an unusual or unique venue to provide added appeal to visitors.

Workshops can be held on home territory, with organizers/buyers being invited to visit the destination/venue and experience all that it can offer, perhaps as part of a familiarization trip or educational (see the next section of this chapter). Alternatively, they can be staged in a location identified as an important potential market, in other words taking the destination to the customer and aiming to meet him on home ground. The latter approach has the advantage of convenience for visitors – they can perhaps visit the workshop in late afternoon/early evening, allowing them to do a full day in the office and combine this with participation in the workshop. The disadvantage is that they do not actually experience the destination/venues at first hand, but the provision of such destination visits may well be one of the outcomes from a workshop held in their own area.

Workshops offer considerable flexibility, usually at a much lower cost for exhibitors than participation in a major trade exhibition. They can also take the form of a roadshow, moving from one destination to another during the course of an intensive few days. Such roadshows are often organized by National Tourism Organization, who will invite a limited number of suppliers to join them for a 3-day or 5-day trip to an overseas destination identified as an important potential market, during which workshops will be organized in several leading cities.

To be successful, those planning workshops and roadshows must ensure that:

- Thorough research is done into the target market (i.e. the buyers) to identify those whom it will be appropriate to invite. One of the major causes of dissatisfaction with such events on the part of destinations and venues (i.e. the suppliers) is attendance by inappropriate visitors (some of whom may be 'timewasters' or 'freeloaders' with little or no business to place) – carrying out research on potential attendees can obviate or, at least minimize, this.

- The timing and duration of the workshop/roadshow are suitable and convenient for visitors, and avoid clashes with other industry events.
- The venue to be used is accessible by public transport and is in keeping with the objectives of the workshop. Holding the event in an unusual venue, for example, may increase its appeal to visitors and encourage higher levels of attendance.
- Promotional activity is planned well in advance and is supported by a structured marketing campaign. An important consideration is whether to use above-the-line activity to inform the widest possible audience that the event is happening, or whether to concentrate on below-the-line, direct marketing in order better to control the number and type of visitors.
- A full evaluation takes place after the event in order to gauge both buyer and supplier reactions and to gain ideas for enhancements to any future workshops or roadshows.

The Venue Italia Workshop held in Rome between 30 June and 3 July 2005 (see case study) shows a slightly different approach, with the organizing role being undertaken by a publishing house, presumably on a commercial basis. This particular workshop is held on an annual basis and takes place over four days in total. It offers a carefully balanced programme, mixing formal business sessions (pre-scheduled meetings) with a varied social programme designed to give attendees an experience of Rome and of nearby attractions.

Case Study

An invitation to Rome to attend the Venue Italia Workshop

The Venue Italia Workshop is a high-profile event based on pre-scheduled, one-to-one meetings between European incentive houses, event management companies, congress organizers and corporate meeting planners on the one hand, and a whole range of Italian MICE suppliers, including destinations, hotels, historic hotels and venues, destination management companies, conference centres and convention bureaux on the other.

The Workshop is organized by Convegni, the leading Italian publishing house specializing in MICE publications, including the magazine *Venue Italia*.

You will be accommodated at the Grand Hotel Parco dei Principi, which will also be the venue for the Workshop itself. It is a 5-star deluxe hotel situated right in the centre of Rome, in the Villa Borghese Park and at walking distance from the renowned Via Veneto.

Our provisional programme is as follows:

Thursday 30 June 2005
- Arrival and check-in
- Welcome dinner at the Grand Hotel Parco dei Principi

Friday 1 July 2005
- Pre-scheduled meetings with suppliers – full day
- Buffet lunch at Grand Hotel Parco dei Principi

- Late afternoon: transfer to Villa Adriana archaeological complex at Tivoli (an hour from Rome)
- Visit of facilities and dinner

Saturday 2 July 2005
- Morning: pre-scheduled meetings with suppliers, followed by individually chosen meetings
- Buffet lunch at Grand Hotel Parco dei Principi
- Afternoon: transfer to the Roman Castles region (an hour from Rome)
- Stopover at Hotel Villa Vecchia for a visit of the facilities and a wine-tasting session
- Transfer to historic Grand Hotel Villa Tuscolana; visit of the facilities; open-air concert followed by a typical Roman dinner

Sunday 3 July 2005
- Day at leisure
- Transfer to airport

Complimentary flights, accommodation, meals and activities as per official programme are included. Places are limited.

Running familiarization trips and educationals

Familiarization or 'fam' trips, sometimes also known as 'educationals', are another important part of a destination or venue's marketing mix strategy. They are an activity that combines marketing and sales, but with a greater emphasis on marketing as conference organizers are invited to join the 'fam trip' on a speculative basis. They will have been identified through preliminary research as people whom it would be beneficial to inform and educate about the facilities available in the destination or venue hosting the trip. They will doubtless be organizers of events that the destination/venue would like to attract but will probably not have expressed a definite interest in bringing their event to this destination/venue. Fam trips differ in this important sense from site inspections (see Chapter 9), where the organizer has come to assess a destination and venue(s) with a view to confirming a specific event. Site inspections are very clearly part of the sales process.

Fam trips are organized not only for conference organizers (buyers). They may also be provided for journalists who will subsequently write a feature article on the destination/venue. Fam trips for journalists are offered on an individual basis or for a group. Fam trips for conference organizers are normally planned as a group activity, with the size of the group ranging from 6–8 people upwards.

Figure 7.1 details guidelines for a destination marketing organization when planning a destination fam trip. Mike Lyon of Write Style Communications Ltd (www.write-style.co.uk) has published a useful guide, *Familiarization Trips – How to Maximize Your Return on Investment*, written for convention and visitor bureaux, venues and hotels.

1 **Plan well in advance**
   - Detailed planning should begin at least 3–4 months before the visit is due to take place, with the first batch of invitations being sent out 8–10 weeks prior to the visit. In part this is to ensure that invitees do not already have commitments on the dates in question, in part to give sufficient time for a second mailshot if there has been insufficient take-up from the first mailing.
   - Early planning also gives time to involve suppliers fully in the visit, to clarify how it will be funded or paid for, and to look for assistance from transport providers (airlines and rail companies especially) where appropriate.
   - Agree what role should be played by local professional conference organizers (PCOs) or destination management companies (DMCs).

2 **Clarify your target group**
   - Decide which kinds of buyers to aim for (corporate, association, agency, or a mixture of some or all of these), and tailor the programme to meet their needs as far as possible. Would it be practicable, if you are inviting a mixed group, to split the group up in order to visit different kinds of venues in order to cater more effectively for specific interests? Identify the appropriate participating venues/suppliers relevant to the agreed target group. Consider a possible theme for the trip based on the interests of the participants.
   - What size of group can you accommodate successfully? Bear in mind the need to transport the group around the destination, and also the practicalities of showing them around venues – it's difficult to get more than 5 or 6 people in a hotel bedroom all at the same time, so residential venues may need to run two showrounds simultaneously. For buyers, fam visits provide an excellent opportunity for networking, and so group dynamics is another factor to be considered. A recommended balance of host destination/venue personnel to customers is no more than 8:1, and 6:1 if participants are accompanied by partners/spouses.
   - What is the best time of the week for your suppliers, as well as for the buyers? Corporate and association buyers are usually fairly flexible, but agencies prefer weekends because they cannot afford time away from the office during the week. If the visit is at a weekend, or partly over a weekend, some buyers may expect to bring partners – decide in advance your policy on partner involvement.

3 **Plan a balanced itinerary**
   - The visit should be enjoyable, memorable, creating a positive and favourable impression of your destination, but not a *comprehensive* one. It is better to give a taste and whet appetites rather than try to show too much and create venue fatigue! Consider a separate table-top workshop during the fam trip to give non-participating venues/suppliers a chance to meet the clients.
   - The visit should be mainly business (the buyers expect to work) but with a mixture of pleasure built in, ideally based on the USPs for your destination. Helicopter rides over the Grampian Mountains, a 'ferry ride across the Mersey', clay pigeon shooting, professional tennis tournaments, theatre visits are just a few examples of activities that have been laid on by UK destinations to add enjoyment to a fam visit and ensure that it shows off to maximum effect the unique aspects of their destination. If appropriate, link the fam trip with other events happening in the area which could form part of the social programme or be an additional draw to maximize response.
   - Buyers find it helpful to be given an overview of the destination at the outset, ideally including a short audio-visual presentation as part of a welcome reception. Such a reception would also give them a chance to introduce themselves to each other and outline their buyer credentials by briefly describing the kinds of events they organize. Set a maximum length of time for coach transfers from one venue to another.

4 **Ensure that the venues/suppliers are trained and prepared**
   - The professionalism and preparedness of a destination's venues can make (or break) a fam visit. Venue sales managers should be looking to create a 'memory trail' for the buyers as they show them around their venue, selling benefits and not features.

- Aim to ensure that your venues know as much as possible about the group in advance. It's good for the venue manager to be on hand to welcome the buyers, even if he is not the one to show them around.
- Try to ensure that the venues are ready and waiting for the group, and are fully prepared. And that the venues keep to your timetable, as far as possible.
- Build in the desire for competitiveness between the venues but ensure that details of the whole programme are shared with all venues in order to avoid duplications such as repetitive menus.

5 Sponsorship and/or support in kind
- Look for ways of sharing the costs through the support of your suppliers, whether this is support in kind or some other form of sponsorship. Ultimately, they are the ones who can expect direct benefits from the fam visit.
- Are there other civic budgets that you can tap into to cover a reception or welcome?
- Agree what gifts are to be given to delegates/partners and ensure they are presented at the appropriate time.

6 Plan to follow up and provide feedback
- It is crucial to follow up the buyers after the visit, in part to thank them for their participation and in part to get their feedback on what they have experienced. Such feedback should be circulated to your venues/suppliers, so that any necessary improvements can be put in place for future visits. Agree with your venues/suppliers who will maintain contact with the buyers and with what frequency.
- Follow-up should be an ongoing activity to build on the relationships established with the buyers.
- Consider a face-to-face evaluation meeting with venues and suppliers.
- Track bookings received by venues/suppliers as well as those received via the destination marketing organization.

A fam visit is a significant investment in time and money but, well done, can be a very productive way of promoting your destination and showing your suppliers that you are working with them, in partnership, to generate more business for them.

Figure 7.1 Guidelines for successful destination familiarization visits.

Organizing effective ambassador programmes

Establishing and administering ambassador programmes is another technique employed by CVBs in their efforts to attract meetings to their destinations. Often known in North America as 'Local Hero Programs' or even 'Bring It Home' Campaigns (Spokane Area Convention and Visitors Bureau – www.visitspokane.com), such initiatives involve identifying, recruiting, training and supporting key individuals in the local community who are interested in raising the profile of their own organizations and their cities by bidding for major national or international conferences. A CVB's aim, in establishing an ambassador programme, is to work with those individuals who are willing, and in a position, to influence directly or indirectly the conference destination decisions of the professional institutions to which they belong.

Rogers (2003) lists as likely candidates for inclusion on ambassador programmes: university academics, hospital professional staff, leading industrialists, members of the business community and trade unionists.

The range of assistance that a CVB can offer to its ambassadors is indicated in the following extract from the publicity material distributed by Cardiff Conference Bureau (www.cardiffconferencebureau.co.uk) to its potential ambassadors:

> *By putting Cardiff forward as a future conference destination of your society, association, institution or organization, we can offer the following free and impartial conference support package:*
> - *Venue selection – sourcing potential venues to match your requirements*
> - *Bid document – preparation and presentation in a variety of media formats*
> - *Accommodation booking service – for delegate and HQ requirements*
> - *Inspection visits – accompanied visits to venues in and around Cardiff*
> - *Civic support – advice on applications*
> - *Professional conference organizer (PCO) – we can brief a local PCO to submit costed proposals for your requirements*
> - *Tours/social programmes – suggestions for delegate and partner activities*
> - *Delegate information – a variety of city brochures*
> - *Travel – advice on travelling to Cardiff by road, rail and air*
> - *Local support information – entertainment, audio-visual suppliers etc.*

It is vital that CVBs maintain levels of enthusiasm and motivation among their ambassadors. In order to achieve this, many CVBs publish regular newsletters for their ambassadors, keeping them informed of developments at the destination such as new venues, hotels and forthcoming events of interest. Others host regular Ambassador Dinners, which act as recruiting and networking events, providing opportunities for ambassadors to meet each other, exchange innovative ideas for attracting conferences to the destination and congratulate successful members of the programme.

The Aberdeen Convention Bureau (ACB – www.aberdeenconferences.com) focuses its efforts on the two local universities, the University of Aberdeen and Robert Gordon's University, and research institutes in the north-east of Scotland. At its 2004 Ambassador Dinner, the ACB announced that its ambassadors had attracted conferences from a wide variety of backgrounds, ranging from the Royal Scottish Country Dance Society to the International Association of Energy Economics and that, as a direct result, economic benefits to the area had risen from £1.5m to over £5m in under two years. The ambassadors had already attracted two large conferences for 2005: the World Renewable Energy Conference and the International Council for the Exploration of the Seas. At the same event, the ACB's business tourism manager pointed out that Aberdeen was looking to use its ambassador programme to bridge the gap with its rivals, Edinburgh and Glasgow, where 'over 75% of conferences [were] being booked with the help of a local ambassador' (ACB, 2004).

In 2005 Melbourne launched its 'Club Melbourne' initiative, which involves scientists from the State of Victoria in pitching to secure scientific conventions for the city, working in close partnership with Melbourne Exhibition and Convention Centre (www.mecc.com.au) and the Melbourne Convention and Visitors Bureau (www.mcvb.com.au). Five major events had already been won via Club Melbourne ambassadors at the time of writing (September 2005), including the 13th World Congress on Human Reproduction, to be held in 2011. These events are expected to attract around 7000 delegates who will inject A$32 million into Victoria's economy.

Case Study 7.1 below describes the operation and development of Edinburgh Convention Bureau's Ambassador Programme.

Summary

Destinations and venues experiment with a variety of marketing communications activities and constantly assess their effectiveness and the return being provided. Over the past ten years, the number of conference industry exhibitions has increased dramatically but the budgets and staff resources available to destination and venue marketers have not necessarily increased, and indeed may have decreased, and so the importance of selecting the right exhibitions to attend becomes ever more crucial. Some destinations and venues are showing a preference for smaller-scale, niche events such as workshops and roadshows, but the growth in these over recent years has, in some cases, led to lower-than-expected attendances by buyers because buyers simply do not have the time to participate.

From the buyers' perspective, below-the-line marketing communications demand a greater response from them. They are asked to respond by participating in some form of activity which requires time, some expenditure, possibly inconvenience and maybe a commitment of their personal time (for example, to attend a fam trip taking place over a weekend). While the benefits may be greater in the medium to long term, because of the relationships established with suppliers and the direct experience gained of venues and destinations, buyers have to weigh up these benefits against many competing demands on their time and their increasingly busy work schedules.

Destinations and venues must constantly assess the returns generated by their above-the-line and below-the-line marketing communications, and adjust the balance of their investments in such activities on a regular basis.

Case Study 7.1

Edinburgh Convention Bureau's Edinburgh Ambassador Programme

This case study is based on a presentation given by Ellen Collingsworth of Edinburgh Convention Bureau to the 2004 convention of the British Association of Conference Destinations held in Birmingham, England, updated to take account of developments subsequently in Edinburgh.

Edinburgh is a city of half a million people and is an international destination for leisure visitors, primarily because of the Edinburgh Festival. The city's focus on business tourism began in the early 1990s.

The Edinburgh Ambassador Programme was founded in 1991, with re-funding and resurgence in 1996, immediately following the opening of Edinburgh's International Conference Centre (EICC). The Programme was created to influence and secure the association conventions market for Edinburgh, giving all the support that very busy professionals need in order to take on the role of a destination ambassador. Each destination has its own strengths and a local Ambassador Programme should focus on these strengths. Edinburgh's strengths are: its impressive universities and associated research parks, together with its medical science institutes; biotechnology, finance, arts and the law are its key market sectors, and the city has major institutions related to all of these.

The Edinburgh Convention Bureau (ECB) database has details of 1400 Edinburgh Ambassadors, 600 of whom are active in some way. Many of the others are used to refer other people to the ECB and are part of the network. An individual may be inactive for several years until finally deciding to bring a bid to the city. In the meantime, such individuals are visiting other destinations and informally promoting Edinburgh. So even as inactive ambassadors, they serve a vital function for the city.

ECB does not have any entrance requirements or qualifications for someone to become an Edinburgh Ambassador. Based on ECB research, staff will invite an individual to become an Edinburgh Ambassador. Or ECB will be approached by a potential ambassador who wants information about how to bid for a conference. It is a very flexible and open programme of membership.

The Edinburgh Ambassador Programme is linked to the economic development of the destination's key market sectors. For this reason, it receives funding support from the regional development agency, Scottish Enterprise Edinburgh & Lothians. By hosting national and international conferences, Edinburgh's profile as a centre of excellence in the key market sectors of finance, law, life sciences and biotechnology, and creative industries is enhanced. Conferences provide rich opportunities for networking on the home base; deals are made, contracts are signed, students get jobs. Edinburgh benefits and so indeed does the rest of Scotland by hosting such major events.

Edinburgh Convention Bureau is committed to developing this long-term market. For example, in 1999 Edinburgh Convention Bureau identified an Edinburgh Ambassador to lead the bid for the International Primatological Society Conference for 2004. Losing this bid was followed by several quiet years until, in 2002, another Edinburgh Ambassador volunteered to bid in 2004, winning the conference for 2008. Parallel to this development, a consortium of Scottish Universities and the Edinburgh Zoo won a funding proposal for a new primate research centre to reside in Edinburgh.

ECB also provides the focus for all of the bureau suppliers who do not have the time to work on the long-term market. For example, hotels are not keen to give bedroom allocations 5, 6, 10 years in advance because they themselves are evaluated on annual targets.

What are the ingredients to a successful ambassador programme? It requires patience and passion, an appreciation of the various professional commitments Edinburgh Ambassadors must meet and a recognition of the importance of their work. Somebody in the destination has to have the focus and the time and energy to work on the long-term market, and this role is fulfilled by ECB.

The development of Edinburgh's Ambassador Programme has been based on three core elements:

1 A commitment to research of events, key market sectors and potential ambassadors
2 A strong brand image
3 Building a strong network that works for the ambassadors.

Commitment to Research

ECB's research sources are varied. The source of information, the initial inspiration to go for a bid, can come from any one of these sources: web-based research, a lead from VisitScotland's consultant in another country, or a request for proposal from an association headquarters with supplementary information from ICCA data. ECB researches to see if the city has a key player on the decision-making committee of the association, and seeks to recruit him as an Edinburgh Ambassador. Equally, the first spark may come directly from the Edinburgh Ambassador who already knows the importance of ECB's bid support. A further source of leads is the marketing consortium, BestCities Global Alliance, of which Edinburgh is a founder member (see Case Study 10.2 for further details of the Alliance).

Create a strong brand image

Establishment of a strong brand image, based around the letter 'A', was a vital step in the development of the Ambassador Programme. The brand is used, for example, on the covers of ECB's twice-yearly ambassadors' newsletter. The newsletters help to give ECB's ambassadors recognition among their colleagues, and assist in developing their own support network.

The newsletters communicate what ECB can do for its ambassadors. But they also give exposure to the venues and suppliers who are the members of ECB, especially when they contribute to hosting ambassador events.

The conference industry is awash with suppliers eager to get to the key decision-makers. Edinburgh Convention Bureau uses strong branding to ensure it is clear that ECB manages the Edinburgh Ambassador Programme on behalf of the ambassadors and the City of Edinburgh.

Building a strong ambassador network

ECB organizes ambassador events approximately six times a year. One purpose of the events is to inform ambassadors about new developments in the city. For example, The Hub hosted an Edinburgh Ambassador event to illustrate that it was not only the headquarters of Edinburgh International Festival, but a stunning venue for meetings and conference dinners. At the same time, the organizers of the Festival talked about what was new in the upcoming Edinburgh International Festival programme. Ambassadors are busy sharing their expertise about what worked or what to avoid as a conference planner, so plenty of informal time needs to be built into these events for socializing. ECB has identified critical concerns that make potential ambassadors hesitate to undertake conference organizing. To address these concerns, more formal educational presentations provide information on topics such as how to develop a draft budget.

Challenges

The ECB Ambassador Programme is now a mature one, which brings its own challenges. Such challenges include:

1 The cost of hosting events for local ambassadors: the costs were found to be soaring while ECB budgets remained finite. The annual ambassadors' dinner, for example, was costing over £10 000, and ECB decided that this could not continue. The rationale for the events was to show appreciation from the city for all the work the ambassadors had put into working on bids, and to reassure ambassadors that, even if their bid failed, they were still part of the Programme. It was also an effective and quite classy way to recruit ambassadors. Nevertheless, it was too expensive.

2 Profile amongst suppliers and ECB members: it became evident that the Ambassador Programme's profile was very low among ECB suppliers and members. Members found it difficult to comprehend that a conference that took place in 2004 was actually won as far back as 1999 or 1998. Suppliers and members were found to move around too much in their own jobs to be able to take a long-term perspective. They were often unaware that ECB had

submitted a bid and perhaps even promoted the conference before it came to Edinburgh. Much of ECB's Ambassador Programme work went unseen and was frequently unrecognized by the time the event was actually staged. It was also clear to ECB that their suppliers did not understand what the association convention market required. ECB needed high allocations but lowest prices. The challenge was to educate members and suppliers about ECB's ambassadors: they were not the same as corporate clients, and needed to be treated differently.

3 Funding partner requires new direction: ECB's funding partner, Scottish Enterprise Edinburgh and Lothians, was interested in providing further funding but required the Ambassador Programme to have a new angle. They could not justify funding the same programme for a third time – it was beyond their remit.

Innovations

Member venues now host the ambassador events, at a considerable saving to ECB while at the same time raising ECB's profile amongst suppliers. The venues have access to an important local market through the Edinburgh Ambassadors who attend their events.

Ambassador-exclusive events, such a private viewing of an exhibition at the Royal Museum of Scotland, gave ambassadors the feel-good factor that a supplier was treating them very specially. ECB also realized that these events give Edinburgh Ambassadors a certain kudos among

Figure 7.2 A workshop event for Edinburgh Ambassadors.

their peers. Ambassadors could go back to their office after one of the hosted events and tell a colleague that they had been, for example, to 'Underground Edinburgh' and that it was a great place to have a dance and a dinner.

Recently, ECB invitations were extended to include their ambassadors' partner/spouse/colleague leading to an advantageous discovery. The first event was a chefs' display. ECB found that a lot of the wives knew each other, and realized how much influence partners had in making conference decisions, and in making decisions about how delegates spend their free time. The presence of ambassadors' partners became a real benefit and the events themselves acquired much more of a 'buzz'. The hosting venue also became more interested in an event because it was reaching a larger audience.

ECB's funding partner's demand for a new angle to the Programme meant that ECB had to demonstrate that there would be direct links to Edinburgh businesses from conferences that were being brought to the city. This was achieved, for example, by giving the small biotech companies access to the meeting planners and to ECB's calendar so that they could exhibit at the conferences, and had opportunities to host or to be a sponsor – the local business community is now much more involved with conferences taking place in the city.

Edinburgh Convention Bureau Limited* manages the Edinburgh Ambassador Programme and provides the same free services as ECB. Now an independent company, Edinburgh Convention Bureau Limited also operates as a commercial body for consulting purposes. Edinburgh's expertise is now available to ambitious suppliers.

*ECB is now Edinburgh Convention Bureau Limited, no longer part of Edinburgh & Lothians Tourist Board, which was dissolved in 2005. Edinburgh Convention Bureau is responsible for promoting the city to the business tourism market.

Review and Discussion Questions

1 'Attendance at conference industry trade exhibitions will decline in direct proportion to the growing use of the Internet by conference organizers.' Is the accuracy of this statement supported by the facts? Substantiate your answers with evidence taken from attendance figures for at least three trade exhibitions, as well as from research among conference organizers on how they source conference destinations and venues.

2 Plan a 2-day familiarization visit to a city destination of your choice. This should include details of the marketing of the event and of the preparations made within the destination in advance of the visit to ensure its success. Provide details of the familiarization visit itinerary, and also of the kinds of buyers invited to participate, demonstrating how these buyers would be appropriate for your chosen destination.

3 Analyse two discrete destination ambassador programmes, comparing their structures, activities, and administrative resources. How successful have they been in meeting the objectives set for them? What recommendations could be made to other destinations looking to establish an ambassador programme?

Sources

ACB (2004) Press Release, Aberdeen Convention Bureau, September

Lyon, M (2004) *Familiarization Trips – How to Maximise Your Return on Investment (A Guide for Conference Bureaux, Venues and Hotels)*, Write Style Communications Ltd

Rogers, T (2003) *Conferences and Conventions: A Global Industry*, Elsevier, Butterworth-Heinemann

Saunders, M (2005) 'Down to experience', *Exhibiting* (magazine published by Mash Media), April

Chapter 8

Sales Strategies for Destinations and Venues: Principles and Theories

Summary of Chapter Contents

This chapter examines the principles and theories underlying the strategies employed by venues and destinations to sell their facilities and services.
  The chapter covers:

- The role of personal selling
- The uses of sales promotion
- The management of a sales force

It includes case studies on:

- The De Vere Golden Ticket booking incentive competition
- The 'Make It Singapore PLUS' campaign
- Leipzig and the ICCA Database

Learning Outcomes

On completion of this chapter, you should be able to:

- understand the role of personal selling in generating sales and maintaining long-term relationships with customers
- understand the different approaches to personal selling
- discuss the range of personal sales activities undertaken by professional sales representatives
- analyse the different techniques and roles of sales promotion
- understand the issues involved in the management of a sales force

Introduction

Advertising and promotion alone are not enough, in themselves, to guarantee a destination's or a venue's success. Sales is an essential part of the marketing process, and success in the conference and convention industry ultimately depends on the ability to sell effectively.

Many people use the terms 'marketing' and 'selling' interchangeably. However, they are not, in fact, the same activity. It has already been established in earlier chapters of this book that marketing is a broad process involving a number of stages:

1 Discovering what product, service or idea customers want.
2 Producing a product with the appropriate features and quality, to meet customers' needs.
3 Pricing the product correctly.
4 Promoting the product; spreading the word about why customers should buy it.

These stages may be considered to have as their primary aim the setting up of the sale itself, which is the next, crucial, stage in the marketing process. Selling the product or service to the customer should be the culmination of this entire process, if an effective marketing process has already created a high degree of customer awareness and a propensity to buy. If conference facilities and services are not actually purchased, then all of the preceding marketing efforts will have been in vain.

Advertising, public relations and direct marketing are the elements of the marketing communications mix that were considered in Chapters 5, 6 and 7.

As shown in Figure 8.1, personal selling and sales promotion are also key marketing communication activities. They will be the primary focus of this chapter. Chapter 9

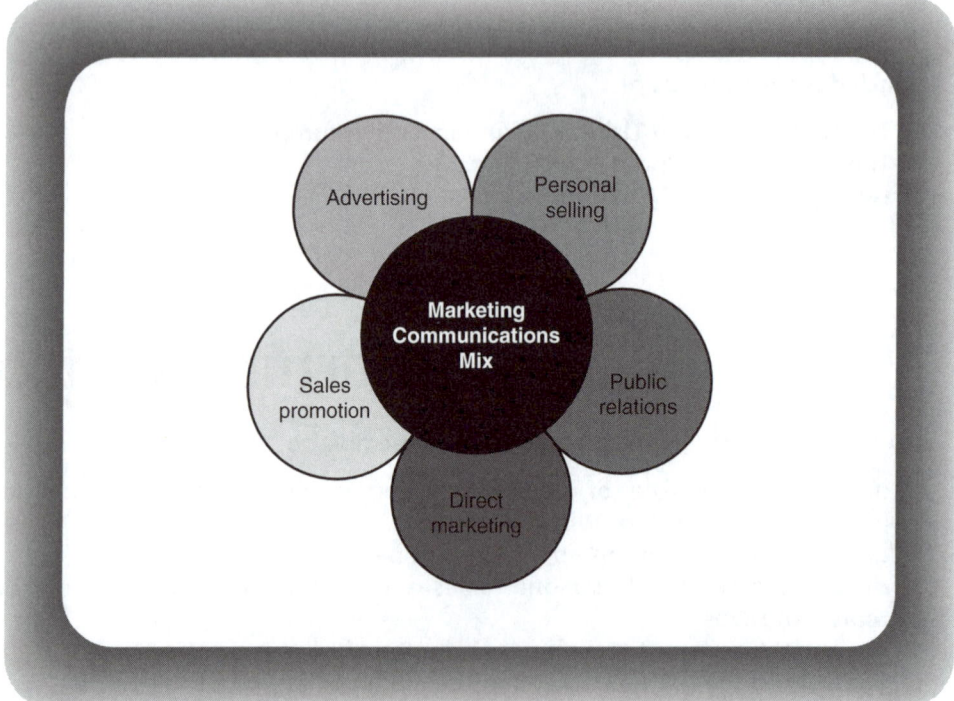

Figure 8.1 The marketing communications mix.

will examine how conference venues and destinations put their sales strategies and techniques into practice.

Personal selling

Personal selling, or direct selling as it is also known, is a vitally important form of interpersonal communication between sales staff and potential buyers. It is a two-way process with great potential for, on the one hand, influencing buyers' preferences and purchasing behaviour, and, on the other hand, for generating useful feedback that can lead to important adjustments to what is being sold.

Personal selling may be defined, then, as the element of the communications mix that consists of direct, personal interaction, either face-to-face or by telephone, between sales people and potential customers.

It has two main, and linked, objectives:

- to generate sales, and
- to build and maintain long-term relationships with clients.

Generating sales

The immense power of personal selling to generate sales for an organization is a common theme in the marketing literature:

> Personal selling is a powerful element of the promotional mix. Despite the millions of dollars spent on advertising and sales promotion, personal selling is usually superior in converting demand for ... products and services into actual purchases, because its message can be tailored to individual customers and it allows for immediate feedback and reaction. Person-to-person communication is a potent and persuasive sales technique.
>
> (Burke and Resnick, 2000: 226)

Unlike other elements of the marketing mix, such as advertising and public relations, personal selling is an interactive relationship between buyer and seller, involving direct communication and the opportunity for immediate response. Much of the effective nature of personal selling arises from the fact that it allows sales people to adapt their presentation to the individual customer or potential customer with whom they are in discussion, either across the table or on the telephone. Effective sales people use this feature of personal selling to their advantage, by using their communications skills to tailor their sales presentation according to the customer's responses.

Personal selling also offers sales people the opportunity of increasing existing customers' levels of spending by suggesting that they purchase additional products or higher-value products. The marketing literature contains a rich vocabulary to describe these techniques, but those with most relevance for the conference and convention industry are:

- **Upselling**: the technique of suggesting that the buyer purchase higher priced products, rather than those already selected. For example, replacing a conference coffee break consisting of simple coffee and biscuits with one offering coffee, fruit smoothies and Danish pastries.

* **Cross-selling**: the technique of introducing existing customers to additional products that are not necessarily linked with their usual purchases. For example, a hotel might try to sell leisure weekend break packages to guests staying in the hotel for the purpose of attending a conference. Destinations endeavouring to persuade conference delegates to extend their business trips in order to spend more time enjoying the leisure attractions of the city or resort are engaging in cross-selling. 'Business extenders' will be discussed in Chapter 9.

It is, however, important to note that although one objective of upselling and cross-selling is to increase profitability for the seller's organization, such techniques can only be said to be truly successful if they add real value to the buyer's purchases in such a way that the buyer remains loyal to the organization and its products. The buyer-seller relationship is the subject of the next section.

Building and maintaining long-term relationships

It was argued in Chapter 1 that organizations that focus on their customers' needs are better positioned to achieve long-term success than are companies that do not.

Since personal selling provides organizations with the opportunity to listen directly to their customers' needs, its significance goes beyond the achievement of a single sales transaction. Properly used, this element of the marketing mix can be effective in converting purchasers into regular customers. In this respect, it may be considered to be a component of customer relationship management (CRM) – which aims at building and maintaining long-term relationships with clients. City-centre venues seeking regular bookings from local businesses for their management meetings, for example, depend on this form of long-term relationship with their clients.

It is important to distinguish, however, between the two basic approaches to personal selling: a sales-oriented approach and a customer-oriented approach. Kotler *et al.* (2003) are among the numerous authors who highlight the contrasting behaviour and tactics used in these two approaches to personal selling:

A **sales-oriented** approach (using high-pressure sales techniques; exaggerating the product's merits; criticising competitors' products) assumes that customers are only likely to buy under pressure, are influenced by a slick presentation, etc.

A **customer-oriented** approach (using customer needs analysis; listening and questioning in order to identify customers' needs; proposing appropriate product solutions) assumes that customers have latent needs that present company opportunities, and that they will be loyal to sales representatives who have their long-term interests at heart.

These two approaches to selling are almost universally recognized in the literature on selling and sales techniques. Indeed, over 20 years ago, Robert Saxe and Barton Weitz devised a questionnaire to find out which of the two approaches was taken by practising sales people. The statements listed in Figure 8.2 make clear the marked contrasts between the two orientations.

It is clear that sales people who use a customer-oriented approach tailor their sales strategies to help customers make purchase decisions that will meet their (the customers') needs. They demonstrate behaviour that is aimed at increasing long-term customer satisfaction and they avoid behaviour that might result in customer dissatisfaction. In this way, they are contributing directly to their company's CRM efforts.

Selling orientation	Customer orientation
• If I am not sure a product is right for a customer, I will still apply pressure to get him to buy • I imply to a customer that something is beyond my control when it is not • I try to sell as much as I can, rather than to satisfy a customer • I spend more time trying to persuade a customer to buy than I do trying to discover his needs • I pretend to agree with a customer to please him • I treat a customer as a rival • It is necessary to stretch the truth in describing a product to a customer • I begin the sales talk for a product before exploring a customer's needs with him • I try to sell a customer all I can convince him to buy, even if I think it is more than a wise customer would buy • I paint too rosy a picture of my products, to make them sound as good as possible • I decide what products to offer on the basis of what I can convince customers to buy, not on the basis of what will satisfy them in the long run • I keep alert for weaknesses in a customer's personality so I can use them to put pressure on him to buy	• I try to give customers an accurate expectation of what the product will do for them • I try to get customers to discuss their needs with me • I try to influence a customer by information rather than by pressure • I try to help customers achieve their goals • I answer a customer's questions about products as correctly as I can • I try to figure out what a customer's needs are • A good salesperson has to have the customer's best interest in mind • I try to bring a customer with a problem together with a product that helps him solve that problem • I am willing to disagree with a customer in order to help him make a better decision • I offer the product of mine that is best suited to the customer's problem • I try to achieve my goals by satisfying customers • I try to find out what kind of product would be most helpful to a customer

Figure 8.2 The SOCO (Selling Orientation–Customer Orientation) scale (adapted from Saxe and Weitz, 1982).

With its emphasis on mutual trust and shared responsibility for the success of any meetings event, the conference and convention industry provides little, if any, scope for the use of selling-oriented techniques. For that reason, it is increasingly important in this sector that sales people understand marketing as well as selling, if they are to be fully effective.

Who sells?

The characteristics distinguishing conference and convention products that were analysed in Chapter 1 have important consequences for the role of staff selling those products.

(1)   The intangible nature of conference and convention products means that the customers of this industry are highly dependent on the advice and guidance they

receive from the professionals who are responsible for selling venues and destinations. The overall experience of holding a convention in a particular conference centre or in a particular city cannot be tried in advance of the event itself. Consequently, the onus is on sales people to represent their venues and destinations accurately and to fulfil all of the promises they have made, implicitly or explicitly, during the sales process.

(2) Being created and supplied by a service industry, the conference product is indivisible from the staff who deliver it. Salesmanship therefore forms a part of the consumption of the product itself, and is not limited to the transaction stage before consumption.

It is clear that the word 'selling' may relate to the activities undertaken by a wide range of staff employed by venues and destinations. In a sense, every staff member of a CVB or a conference hotel, for example, plays a sales role at one or more stages of the purchasing and consumption process. And although this chapter focuses on the activities of professional sales people, it is important to bear in mind that selling is something that continues long after the sales contract has been signed by the client.

It is useful to think in terms of different levels of sales creativity. Burke and Resnick (2000) are among the many commentators who contend that personal selling ranges from simple order-taking (routine requests from customers) to truly creative selling.

At one end of the sales creativity scale are the order-takers who deal with routine requests from existing customers, and who may include front-line staff such as hotel receptionists and waiters. At the other end of the scale are the sales professionals employed primarily for the purpose of selling the venue or destination. The activities of these professional sales staff will now be examined. However, before focusing on the more creative sales activities, it is worth emphasizing that many order-takers also have the potential to sell and to increase their organization's profitability while at the same time enhancing the customer's experience. The receptionist who suggests that delegates use the hotel's spa facilities and the waiter who proposes a finer bottle of wine are both engaging in genuine sales activities.

Professional sales activities

The main characteristic that distinguishes the activities of professional sales staff from order-takers is that the former are engaged not only in servicing existing clients but also in demand creation: identifying potential new customers – known, in marketing terminology, as 'prospects' – and motivating them to buy.

In this sense, it can be seen that professional sales staff may do much more than simply sell.

Kotler *et al.* (2003: 667) list the possible tasks of sales representatives as follows:

- Prospecting: finding and cultivating new customers
- Targeting: deciding how to allocate their scarce time among prospects and customers
- Communicating: communicating information about the company's products and services
- Selling: Approaching, presenting, answering objections, and closing sales
- Servicing: Consulting on customers' problems, rendering technical assistance …
- Information gathering: Conducting market research and intelligence work
- Allocating: Deciding which customers to allocate scarce products to, during product shortages (for example, allocating hotel accommodation during a major convention).

Two of these tasks, however, are almost always undertaken by professional sales staff: prospecting and selling.

Prospecting

Burke and Resnick (2000) note that selling to groups and businesses is more complicated and time-consuming than selling to individuals, sometimes requiring additional steps in the personal selling process. This is certainly the case in the conference and convention industry, where the selling usually takes place between businesses or between businesses and organizations, and what is being sold is a product designed for consumption by a group, as opposed to an individual or a family.

One of the additional steps required in the conference and convention sector is the preparation of bids, and this will be examined in detail in Chapter 9. Another is the process of prospecting – conducting research to identify new customers. A common theme in the marketing literature is that one of the main reasons enterprises fail is that people do not spend enough time and resources prospecting for new business.

For many organizations, this is necessarily an ongoing process: a hotel may find that some of the local businesses that hold their meetings there have moved away or have gone out of business or have decided to change to videoconferencing; a destination may find that the political party that held its annual conference there every year has switched to a competitor destination. Associations, as stated in Chapter 1, rotate their annual conferences between destinations. For that reason, CVBs are obliged to spend considerable resources prospecting for future association events – since their competitors are doing exactly that.

There are two main steps involved in prospecting:

- identifying 'suspects' or leads – potential customers who may eventually be persuaded to purchase
- qualifying these – determining which suspects are the most promising (most likely to become 'prospects' of high potential).

Prospecting for conference and convention business can involve professional sales staff researching a range of sources, including responses to advertising and promotions, computerized databases, business directories and other listings, and even Internet searches using key words to identify companies, organizations and associations that fit their customer profile.

For the conference and convention industry, Harrill (2005) lists other potential sources of suspects as:

- leads generated at trade shows
- MINT – Meeting Information Network, for members of DMAI
- telephone directories
- Chamber of Commerce member lists
- networking – meeting with people in their environment.

He also emphasizes the importance of using existing clients as potential sources of new business:

> Customers currently doing business with you are the most important group to research. Not only might they buy from you again, they can be excellent sources for referrals. A careful analysis of current customers can yield a profile of the ideal prospect. Customers will respect your enquiry once they understand that you are trying to expand a market and could use their advice on potential customers.
>
> (Harrill, 2005: 18)

Qualifying suspects involves using professional judgement to decide which of them are most likely to become customers. This judgement may be partly based on the past buying patterns of the suspect. For example, an association that has recently held its annual conference in a particular city is unlikely to return for several years, at least. Consequently, for that city's CVB, the association will have low potential as a customer for the immediate future.

For the more promising suspects, the next task for the sales professional is likely to be arranging an appointment to meet. If that appointment is granted and the suspect and the sales person meet face-to-face, then begins the actual selling.

Selling

It is generally agreed that in presenting their products and services, professional sales staff follow a structure designed to encourage the successful achievement of a sale. A customer-oriented approach to personal selling will include a series of steps that apply in almost any situation where sales staff and potential clients come face to face. There is general agreement that those steps are as follows:

- Establishing rapport with clients
- Investigating client needs
- Presenting the product to clients, selling strengths and benefits
- Handling objections
- Closing the sale: getting the clients to commit themselves
- Follow-up/maintenance.

The exact skills required for the effective implementation of this sales sequence in the context of the conference and convention sector will be explored in Chapter 9. However, at this stage, Harrill's (2005) distinction between two types of objection that may be raised by prospects is of interest here. These are:

- **liabilities**: something which the venue or destination simply cannot provide (for example, a conference requiring a venue for 10 000 delegates, when the destination's largest venue is half that size)
- **misunderstandings**: perceptions that can be corrected (the objection that the venue's room rates are too high may be overcome by suggesting that it is possible to negotiate at certain times of the year).

Sales promotion and yield management

Sales promotion

Closely linked to personal selling is the technique of sales promotion. Commonly referred to as 'below the line' promotion, sales promotion, according to the Institute of Sales Promotion, is, 'any scheme designed to sell more product'. Burke and Resnick (2000) define sales promotion as specialized activities designed to stimulate demand for a particular product. They emphasize that sales promotion is distinct from the general term 'promotion', and that it has as its specific purpose the encouraging of sales, often in a very direct manner. Used effectively, sales promotion can be an extremely powerful device in organizations' efforts to boost sales volume.

In the market for consumer goods, sales promotion has generally been defined as a tactical example of marketing used to generate additional sales at the point-of-sale in retail outlets, through the use of inducements such as money-off vouchers, two-for-the-price of one offers, and 'free' gifts. However, in recent years, sales promotion has seen increasing respectability as a discipline and has come to be regarded as more of a strategic tool used across the marketing mix. Sales promotion is now believed by many to be a core part of any integrated marketing programme, and it is a technique that is widely used by conference venues, in particular.

Middleton describes the use of sales promotion in the context of travel and tourism, but his comments apply equally to the conference industry: 'the 'perishability' of tourism products means that marketing managers are constantly preoccupied with the necessity to manipulate demand in response to unforeseen events, as well as the normal daily, weekly or seasonal fluctuations (Middleton, 2001: 255). Those responsible for marketing destinations and venues are also faced with the challenge of dealing with unforeseen events (SARS, 9/11, the 2004 tsunami, currency devaluations, etc.) and fluctuating levels of demand, such as the lower levels of business in the summer months and at weekends.

Sales promotion techniques are particularly suitable for dealing with such demand adjustments, and as such, may be regarded as vital weapons in the marketing armoury of many conference and convention organizations.

How may sales promotion techniques be applied in the conference and convention industry? It was stated that these techniques are usually used at the point-of-sale. But it is clear that, unlike the case of the distribution of consumer goods, the conference and convention industry has no retail outlets or showrooms. However if a point-of-sale may be said to be any place at which a purchase transaction takes place, then it is clear that this will include, for the booking of venue services:

- Customers' own places of work: when they make bookings in response to direct mail and telephone calls from venues
- A venue's own website – the primary target for sales promotion
- Trade shows/workshops where venues take bookings.

Middleton (2001) highlights three main targets to which sales promotion techniques may be applied in order to stimulate the sale of specific products at particular times:

- Individual buyers
- Distribution networks – in the case of any organization that achieves a large proportion of its sales through intermediaries, such as hotel booking agencies, Venue Finding Services
- Sales force – in the case of larger organizations, such as international conference centres. Any additional effort required on top of routine sales efforts requires some additional form of incentive/reward.

The actual sales promotion techniques that may be used are listed in Table 8.1. Although these apply primarily to the use of sales promotion in the travel and tourism sector, many of them are commonly used as direct inducements to boost bookings for conference venues also.

Table 8.1 Sales promotion techniques

Individual buyers	Distribution networks	Sales force
Price cuts/sale offers	Extra commission and overrides	Bonuses and other money/incentives
Discount vouchers/coupons	Prize draws	Gift incentives
Disguised price cuts	Competitions	Travel incentives
Extra product	Free gifts	Prize draws
Additional services	Parties/receptions	
Free gifts		
Competitions		
Passport schemes for regular customers		
Prize draws		

Source: Adapted from Middleton, 2001

Of all the techniques listed, price cuts are generally acknowledged to be the most effective of incentives to purchase (or, in the case of intermediaries and sales forces, to sell). However, most commentators also emphasize the perils associated with price-cutting, a technique that is easily matched by other venues, and raises the possibility of 'price wars', if over-used. In addition: 'there is a danger … that if sales boosts are achieved through money-off or bargain offers, this can have the effect of demeaning the brand' (Holloway, 2004: 304).

For these reasons, organizations often prefer to use special offers and packages (which, in reality, are disguised price cuts) such as three delegate nights for the price of two, or 'free' food and drink during coffee breaks. In this way, the venue is able to maintain its regular price structure while still offering added value to customers and an incentive to buy.

Also widely used by venues, such as hotel chains, are the 'passport' schemes – designed to promote loyalty and frequency of purchase by customers, by rewarding them for their loyalty to an individual venue or to a chain of venues. Competitions can also be used as a sales promotion technique, as the De Vere case study shows.

Case Study

The De Vere Golden Ticket booking incentive competition

De Vere is a chain of 19 4-star and 5-star hotels in the UK. On Thursday, 19 June 2003, De Vere Hotels arranged for the De Vere Belfry in North Warwickshire to be decorated in Scottish tartan and for a lone Scottish piper to welcome 75 winners to the grand final of their 'Golden Ticket' booking incentive competition. The incentive, which ran from 15 December 2002 to 15 May 2003 was open to all business travel agents and conference agents who booked and confirmed a residential conference for ten or more delegates at any De Vere or Village Hotels & Leisure Clubs property.

Over 40 agencies had qualified for the evening and there was much excitement and anticipation amongst the guests at the climax of the evening as the draw was made.

The first prize went to BTI (Business Travel International) in Leicester, who won ownership of a luxury lodge at De Vere Cameron House, Loch Lomond, for one week every year for life.

The prizes awarded to the runners-up were:

- a two-night break for two at the Algonquin in New York plus flights
- a two-night break for two at the De Vere Grand Jersey plus flights
- a two-night break for two at De Vere Cameron House, Loch Lomond.

All other winners of the Golden Ticket incentive received a bottle of wine.

Commenting on the evening Paul Dermody, Chief Executive of De Vere Hotels, said: 'We have always valued the contribution that business travel and conference agents provide to our business. It was a tremendously exciting evening and I was thrilled to present the awards and was delighted to see their enthusiasm for De Vere Hotels.'

It is clear that sales promotion can be an effective device for boosting sagging sales volumes. However, the short-lived, temporary nature of the results they can have means that they must be used with caution. In particular, it is generally agreed that sales promotion techniques are not effective at building long-term brand preferences.

There is, therefore, need for a genuine balance to be struck between short-term sales increases and the longer term need for organizations to develop a sound reputation and solid brand image. The two are not incompatible, however:

Sales promotion techniques should be seen first and foremost as aids in building a relationship between organizations and their customers. They should not be viewed merely as a 'quick fix' to unload surplus stock, even where this may be one of the objectives within a promotional campaign. Behind any such campaign, there should always be the overall aim of building loyalty and adding value to the product, rather than undermining it.

(Holloway, 2004: 303)

Holloway emphasizes that sales promotion techniques are complementary to advertising (the main tool used to achieve longer-term strategic objectives, such as building the corporate image of the organization and its products). Sales promotion and advertising work together most effectively when they are mutually reinforcing.

Yield management

Yield management programmes also generally reflect fluctuating levels of demand, and for that reason they are closely linked with sales promotion campaigns in venues' efforts to maximize revenue by adjusting prices to suit market demand. Yield management is essentially derived from the basic economic theory of supply and demand, which dictates that in times of high demand, high prices can be charged, but when demand is low, prices will drop. Similarly, when supply is limited, prices rise (a sellers' market), and when there is an over-supply, prices fall (a buyers' market).

Widely used by the airlines since the 1980s and by hotels since the 1990s, yield management has now been recognized by conference venues as an essential element in the marketing and selling process. Basically, yield management is an inventory management system that allows venue managers and their sales staff to forecast supply and demand and adjust their pricing strategies accordingly – in order to maximize revenue. It is, therefore, a systematic approach to simultaneously optimizing both average rate and occupancy for a venue, the ultimate aim being 100% yield – i.e. 100% occupancy at the published rack (non-discounted) rate.

Clearly, a venue's forecasting must be based on what the patterns of purchasing behaviour the venue's management have observed in the past, as well as what they think will happen in the future.

Peckinpaugh (2000) gives this example of yield management at work at a 700-room conference hotel with a maximum group block of 500:

Rack rate: $175 (peak season)
Peak seasons: March–May, September–November
Meeting space: 25 000 square feet
Desired catering revenue per room, per night: $74–$65 peak season, $64–$50 shoulder season, $50 or below off season
Peak demand days: Midweek (Monday–Thursday)
Slow days: Weekends (Friday–Sunday)
Desired patterns: Thursday–Sunday, Wednesday–Sunday, Sunday–Wednesday
Peak season transient (individual traveller) demand: 200 rooms

If your meeting profile matches most of the hotel's guidelines based on the above considerations, your ability to negotiate will be excellent. But if you want to book 200 rooms in April, arrive on Tuesday and depart on Friday, use all of the meeting space, and hold only continental breakfasts on site, the property will most likely turn down your business. The decision hotels must make is: Do they book your meeting today or do they wait to book a higher revenue group and risk having empty rooms and meeting space if they're unable to do so?

Rogers (2003: 178) outlines the 'conference capacity strategy' devised by Hartley and Rand for use by venues' sales teams in order to maximize yield from conference bookings. The strategy looks at business mix, market strength and competitive edge, profitability, lead times and refused business. The authors expound the factors and techniques involved in allocating capacity to particular enquiries, and give practical tips on how to secure the business.

Sales management

Any organization investing in employing a sales force is making a long-term commitment to sales and selling. The sales peoples' salaries and commission make personal selling one of the most expensive of the promotional tools available. But, used effectively, the sales force can hold the key to any organization's sustained growth and profitability. It is vital, therefore, that an organization's sales force is managed in such a way that it achieves the desired sales objectives. This is one of the principal aims of sales management.

Sales force objectives

A key initial step is to establish clear objectives for the sales force. This is a vitally-important task for the sales manager, as everything else that follows rests on effective decisions being made at this stage. According to Kotler *et al.* (2003), objectives are typically established for sales staff for two reasons:

- to ensure that corporate goals are met (these may include revenue, market share, improving corporate image …)
- to assist sales staff to plan and execute their personal sales programmes effectively.

Berkowitz *et al.* (2003) also place emphasis on the importance of setting objectives, noting that these are used to give direction and purpose, and to act as a standard for evaluation of the sales force's performance. For the members of the sales force, the main objective will always be the converting of customer interest into actual sales. However, other possible features of sales force objectives include:

- A time-frame: sales objectives are generally expected to be accomplished within a certain period of time
- Objectives may be set for the total sales force as a whole and/or for each individual sales person
- They may be measured in terms of revenue earned, units sold, or market share achieved, for individual sales persons. They may also include results measured in terms of average order size, average number of sales/time period, and ratio orders/calls.

Sales objectives must be reviewed regularly, and may be changed in the case of circumstances changing considerably, such as natural or man-made disasters.

Recruiting and training the sales force

Given the importance of direct interpersonal communication to the sales process, it is generally agreed that recruiting and training the sales force are vitally important sales management tasks. Berkowitz *et al.* (2003) recommend that a set of required qualifications be established before beginning to recruit, and suggest that preparing a job description that lists specific tasks the sales person should perform and analysing traits of the successful sales people within the organization are additional tasks for the sales manager. They also advise that whether using formal training programmes, or informal on-the-job training, training should focus on:

- the company
- its products
- selling techniques.

Furthermore, Berkowitz *et al.* contend that training should not be limited to new staff, but should also be made available to experienced personnel. Holloway (2004: 239) makes the additional point that training in sales should not only be reserved for members of the sales force: 'In any company's marketing strategy, adequate training must be built into the marketing plan to ensure that personal selling, with all its associated social skills, is effectively communicated to all staff who are likely at any time to come into contact with customers' (Holloway, 2004: 239).

Structuring the sales force

A useful distinction is often made between the 'inside sales staff' (or 'in-house staff') and the 'outside sales staff' (or 'field staff') who may work for a sales manager.

McCabe *et al.* (2000) define the respective tasks of the two groups as follows:

- Inside sales staff support outside sales activities and co-ordinate sales direction in relation to the overall marketing plan. They also:
  - (a) provide timely follow-up on all sales leads and enquiries
  - (b) maintain customer databases
  - (c) assist in the planning of sales calls/industry promotional events
  - (d) develop collateral material
  - (e) conduct site inspections/familiarization trips
- Outside sales staff operate in the external environment. They:
  - (a) obtain market feedback on sales and marketing opportunities, competitive activities and client needs
  - (b) conduct direct sales calls in order to educate, develop customer relationships and create sales.

The inside sales staff category may also include telemarketers who use the phone to find new leads, qualify them and either sell to them or pass their details to outside sales staff. Venue reservations staff and CVB conference desk staff dealing with enquiries are further examples of in-house sales staff with an important selling role.

Outside sales staff may be directly and exclusively employed by the organization or they may be independent sales representatives normally representing a number of different venues or destinations. Hotel representatives who sell hotel rooms and meetings facilities in a given market area often work independently, for several chains or properties. Kotler *et al.* (2003) maintain that it is often more effective for a hotel to hire a hotel representative than to use its own sales person. This is true when the market is a distant one where the market potential does not justify employing a salaried sales person, and when cultural differences may make it hard for an outsider to penetrate the market.

Whether inside or outside, and regardless of whether or not they work on an independent basis, when there are several sales staff, they must be organized according to particular criteria. The three most commonly-used criteria are shown in Table 8.2. Most sales forces are organized using one or more of these.

Organizing the sales staff by territory is certainly the most straightforward of methods. However, it is considered by many to be unsuitable in cases where the products are varied, complex or where deep technical knowledge is required.

Compensating and motivating the sales force

In order to attract, motivate and retain the most effective sales people, it is important to determine the best level of compensation required, and the best method of calculating it. The sales manager must decide between a number of possible remuneration packages:

- a straight salary
- a salary plus benefits (commission, bonus, profit-sharing …)
- straight commission – a simple percentage of the value of the sale, or a sliding scale of commission
- a combination.

Table 8.2 Structures commonly used in organizing sales staff

Structure	Definition	Advantages
Territorial-structured	Each sales representative or sales team is assigned an exclusive territory in which to represent the company's entire offer: for example, Scotland or Western Europe	Results in a clear definition of the sales person's responsibilities Increases the sales representative's incentive to cultivate local business and personal ties Travel expenses are relatively small, as each sales representative travels within a small geographic area
Market-segment structured	Each sales representative or sales team specializes in selling to a different market segment: for example: the association meetings market or the corporate meetings market	Each member of the sales force can become knowledgeable about their specific market segment
Customer-structured	Each sales representative or sales team serves one or more of the major (or 'key') accounts of specific customers whose business is critical to the success of the organization: for example, large companies with many divisions operating in many parts of the country, such as General Motors in the United States	Follows the trend towards increasing buyer concentration resulting from mergers and acquisitions, meaning that fewer buyers account for a larger share of some companies' sales Follows the trend towards more buyers centralizing their purchases instead of leaving them to local units Sales staff can become familiar with major customers, understand trends that affect them, and plan appropriate sales strategies and tactics

Source: Adapted from Kotler *et al.*, 2003

Finally, the sales force must be motivated to sell and to keep selling effectively. Berkowitz *et al.* (2003) note that a systematic approach to motivating all sales staff is required, since due to burn out, even the best need motivating. They advise that any motivational scheme must also satisfy the important non-financial needs of the sales force:

• job security
• good working conditions
• opportunities to succeed.

A commonly-used method of increasing sales is through the use of a competition as a motivational programme, with the reward being either cash, or travel, or symbolic awards, such as a plaque for Sales Agent of the Year, as recognition of the extra effort made.

Summary

This chapter has examined the key elements that must be taken into account when a sales strategy is being devised. Designing an effective sales strategy demands an understanding of the complex set of variables that constitutes any organization's approach to selling its products. If undertaken successfully, the sales strategy can be the blueprint for the organization's sustainability and growth.

As stated at the beginning of this chapter, sales should be the culmination of the entire marketing process. To be successful, it must be fully integrated within the overall marketing communications mix, in such a way that it is supported by advertising and public relations which create awareness of the product and the desire to buy it; and it must be fully co-ordinated with sales promotions that motivate customers to purchase.

Above all, the selling function must be undertaken by men and women who are motivated by a genuine desire to serve the customer and provide them with real value for the money they are spending. The conference and convention marketplace is crowded and competitive, and sales people who can deliver high levels of service and value-for-money to customers have the potential to bring a distinct advantage to the venues and destinations that employ them.

Case Study 8.1

Make It Singapore PLUS! sales promotion campaign

The 'Make It Singapore PLUS' sales promotion campaign run by Singapore Tourist Board (STB) was an extension of an earlier campaign, 'Make It Singapore', a S$15 million initiative launched by STB in November 2003 which ran until December 2004. The objective of 'Make It Singapore' was to reinforce Singapore's reputation as a business hub and to attract more MICE events to Singapore. The campaign was successful in winning 40 business events for Singapore, generating an estimated 60 000 visitor nights* and S$50 million in direct tourism receipts. Examples of events won included: The Amway India incentive group with 1400 incentive award winners in November 2004; and the International Conference on Materials for Advanced Technologies (ICMAT) with the International Conference on Advanced Materials (ICAM), attracting 1500 overseas delegates in July 2005.

*Visitor nights is calculated by multiplying the number of visitors by the number of nights of their stay, e.g. 1000 delegates attending a 3-day conference (but just staying over for 2 nights) would equate to 2000 visitor nights. Visitor nights differs from 'room nights', which are calculated by multiplying the number of rooms booked by the corresponding nights' stay, e.g. 1000 delegates for 3-day conference, assuming that all are staying on a twin-sharing basis, would total up to 500 (twin rooms) for 2 nights, making 1000 'room nights'.

In order to build on the positive response to the 'Make It Singapore' (MIS) campaign, STB decided to extend the campaign until December 2005, but cleverly refreshed the image of the campaign by re-naming it 'Make It Singapore PLUS'. The re-launched campaign was supported by more than 40 hotels, MICE venues and Singapore Airlines. It offered revised criteria and enhanced incentives for event planners who confirmed an event for Singapore by 31 December 2005 and held the event before December 2007.

To qualify for support under the campaign, events had to involve a minimum of two consecutive nights' stay in Singapore. Other eligibility criteria varied according to the type of MICE event under consideration. For example, an international corporate board meeting for CEO or director level attendees had to involve a minimum of 150 visitor nights (this compares with a minimum of 400 room nights* under the MIS campaign), while a convention required a minimum of 400 visitor nights. An exhibition, on the other hand, had to meet the following criteria:

- be held in Singapore for the first time
- have a minimum of 1000 overseas visitors
- occupy a minimum of 1000 square metres of net exhibition space
- have a minimum of 50% of exhibitors from overseas.

The financial support offered for qualifying events was not a standard package but was customized by STB to the specific and individual needs of clients, within the parameters set in Figures 8.3 and 8.4.

In addition to the financial support available to event planners (decision-makers), there were also various forms of non-financial or in-kind support on offer. These included:

- assistance to secure a Guest of Honour
- welcome messages for delegates at the airport

Eligibility criteria	Support*	Qualifying costs
Event must bring at least 150 visitor nights	Financial support for qualifying activities	• Local DMC/event management fees • Programme enhancements • Entertainment for function • Speaker fees • Teambuilding • Welcome performance • Welcome gift pack • Welcome banner • Photography and • Videography
International corporate board meetings	50% financial support for qualifying activities	

Figure 8.3 STB financial support for corporate meetings and incentives. (*Financial support subject to a maximum limit based on the number of visitor nights achieved)

Eligibility criteria	Support*	Qualifying costs
Event must bring at least 400 visitor nights	30% financial support for qualifying activities	• PCO management fees • Speakers fees • Overseas marketing costs

Figure 8.4 STB financial support for conventions. (*Financial support subject to a maximum limit based on the number of visitor nights achieved)

Hotels	For site inspections: • 2 complimentary rooms for up to 3 nights each for MICE decision-makers For confirmed events: • 1 complimentary room for every 25 rooms confirmed, up to a maximum of 5 rooms for the duration of the event room upgrades for VIPs (up to 3 rooms) late check-out (based on availability)
Venues (hotel and non-hotel based)	• Discount off food bill for welcome or opening reception at the official venue where the main event is being held *and/or* special rates for set-up and break-down days
Airlines	Offer mutually beneficial commercial arrangements based on net flown revenue generated by organizers. The incentive to be in the form of tickets which organizers can draw upon for the marketing of their future event

Figure 8.5 STB industry support.

- assistance to secure exclusive venues
- assistance with immigration clearances
- publicity.

Singapore's industry partners were required to provide support, as outlined in Figure 8.5.

A new feature of the MIS PLUS campaign was what was entitled a Channel Support Scheme, the purpose of which was to encourage intermediaries locally and overseas to develop packages and/or outreach programmes in order to push out the campaign with the objective of business conversion. The scheme provided matching funds for agreed activities that generated new business.

The MIS PLUS campaign was promoted through:

- PR and media activities, including the dissemination of factsheets
- Roadshows, MICE seminars, functions and direct mail activity – STB regional offices helped to push the campaign direct to (i) end users and (ii) intermediaries, using these platforms to allow influencers and decision-makers to disseminate information to their own delegates/clients before the deadline of 31 December 2005
- Collateral, including MIS PLUS brochures, a revamped MIS PLUS website, and e-mail blasts.

At the time of writing (July 2005), the results of the MIS PLUS campaign were not available, although the targets set were known: to generate 100 000 visitor nights and an estimated S$100 million in tourism receipts.

In 2004 Singapore welcomed an estimated 2 million business visitors, accounting for 26% of the total visitor arrivals of 8.3 million. Business-related visitor arrivals in 2004 represented an increase of approximately 60% over 2003, and of 30% over 2002.

Case Study 8.2

Leipzig and the ICCA database

Prospecting for new conference business is a key role played by sales staff in venues and in CVBs. Many of these employ staff as full-time researchers, with the task of identifying associations likely to consider the venue, the city or the country as a location for a future conference. But while finding information on international meetings is relatively straightforward, with so many online resources at hand, the difficulty lies in finding those international meetings that have not already been to a particular venue or destination but may have the interest and the potential to come.

ICCA

Many researchers are therefore grateful for the ICCA (International Congress and Convention Association) database. ICCA was founded in 1963 by a group of travel agents. The association's aim was to evaluate practical ways to get the travel industry involved in the rapidly expanding market of international meetings and to exchange actual information related to their operations in this market. This initiative soon proved to have been taken at the right moment: the meeting industry expanded even more rapidly than the founders had foreseen, as a result of which candidates from all over the world applied for ICCA membership – not only congress travel agents but representatives from all the various sectors of the meetings industry.

ICCA now is one of the most prominent organizations in the world of international meetings. It is the only association that comprises a membership representing the main specialists in handling, transporting and accommodating international events. With over 700 members in almost 80 countries worldwide, it is certainly the most global organization within the meetings industry. ICCA has offices in the Netherlands, Malaysia, the United States and Uruguay.

ICCA's mission is to enable its members to generate and maintain significant competitive advantage. One of the ways it achieves this is by compiling its association database.

The ICCA Database

In 1972, ICCA's research department started compiling details of international association meetings. The present sophisticated system enables ICCA data researchers to produce data in various formats, tailored to users' needs. The information comes from ICCA members, international organizations and from continuous project research. A group of seven researchers works full-time to process all data.

This computerized online Association Database provides historical overviews of thousands of association meetings, plus details on the contracted suppliers and attendance figures. In June 2005, the database contained: 87 000 individual events, 6000 international organizations (all addresses checked in the past 2 years) and almost 11 000 meeting series. Regarding their size, these 11 000 series break down as follows:

- 64% attract more than 250 delegates
- 14% attract between 150 and 250
- and 22% attract between 50 and 150 delegates.

Thirty per cent of all meeting series are on the subject of medical sciences; science constitutes 12% of the total; technology 9%; industry 8%.

It is estimated that some 14 000 different association meetings are organized on a regular basis. The ICCA Database holds information on 80% of them.

The Association Database has easy search capabilities, is updated weekly and is free to all members, password protected.

With this user-friendly tool, ICCA assists members in identifying business leads and opening up direct lines of communication with potential clients.

Information in the database includes current contact addresses (including hyperlinks with website and/or e-mail addresses), meeting room requirements, decision procedures and destinations that may be eligible for the future – all that it is essential to know for destinations that intend making a bid to host the meeting.

ICCA members can only profit from this valuable tool if they know how to use it properly. To this end, ICCA runs a number of Data Workshops at its Head Office in Amsterdam and at members' request anywhere else in the world. Workshops are also a regular feature at events such as IMEX and EIBTM and at ICCA's own annual International Congress and Convention Researchers Meeting ICCRM, which is in itself a major international event, attracting several hundred delegates and celebrated speakers.

A typical ICCA workshop is divided into different sessions such as: Case Studies, Bid Strategies and Targeting Leads.

Leipzig's use of the database

Ronald Kotteritzsch, Director of Marketing & Sales, at the Congress Centre in Leipzig, has made effective use of the ICCA database:

We have been working with the ICCA Association Database for several years, and in several ways.

When you exhibit at a trade show (such as the EIBTM or IMEX), you come home with a large number of new contacts and follow them up. The difficult thing is to find out which of these contacts represent any realistic potential for you at all, and on which of them you should focus your energy and resources. The ICCA Database has always been of invaluable help in making these decisions.

For example, in the late 1990s, two women contacted me at the EIBTM trade show and asked me if I could send them some information on our city. I would have asked them a number of questions to make sure that they got the information they actually wanted, but they had many appointments at the show and hence little time.

Back in my office, I found their organization, the European Society for Therapeutic Radiology & Oncology (ESTRO) in the ICCA Database. The information contained there (capacities required, case history, previous venues, etc.) told me that they were indeed potential customers for us. Also, the database gave me important indications about which information is or is not relevant to them. For example: 'Should I mention in detail that we co-operate with a number of excellent and experienced PCOs, or will they bring their own PCO anyway?'

When I started to communicate with them, I did so in the full knowledge that I was really telling them those things about our city and our venue that they actually wanted to know. When you communicate with your potential client in this way, they will:

- *see that you are genuinely interested in them*
- *appreciate that you are willing and able to understand their specific needs*
- *be convinced that they are talking with professionals who do their homework*
- *know that they can expect the same attention and commitment if they actually decide to come to your city.*

Consistency and patience was needed. We communicated for several years, and it was in November 2003 that they accepted our invitation to visit Leipzig for a site inspection. In summer 2004 we were officially informed that we will have the honour of hosting the Meeting of the European Society for Therapeutic Radiology & Oncology in October 2006. I stress again that the ICCA data information was extremely helpful to us, in achieving this success.

Whenever we have won a bid for a major international conference – Eurelectric in June 2002, the EACTS Annual Conference with 2000 delegates in September 2004, ESTRO, the World Filtration Congress in 2008 – ICCA Data has also always tremendously helped us to identify our local 'ambassadors', and to address the right people at the right time in the right way.

Another important aspect of our work with the database should be mentioned. Leipzig has been a university town since 1409. The city has a great wealth of scientific and academic institutions, foundations, renowned hospitals etc. Many local professionals, doctors etc. would have the potential and the influence in their organizations to be involved in a conference bid. When they find the time for an appointment with us, we make sure that we are well equipped with ICCA data information about what conferences in their field could come to Leipzig. This gives them confidence in our professional approach, and we are actually working with some of them on future bids.

Review and Discussion Questions

1 Discuss the roles of personal selling in the conference industry.
2 What are the principal sales promotion techniques that are employed by conference venues?
3 What are the main tasks that must be undertaken by a sales manager with respect to organizing the work of his or her sales force?

Sources

Berkowitz, E, Crane, F, Kerin, R, Hartley, S and Rudelius, W (2003) *Marketing*, McGraw-Hill

Burke, J and Resnick, B (2000) *Marketing and Selling the Travel Product*, Delmar Thomson Learning

Gartrell, R (1994) *Destination Marketing for Convention and Visitor Bureaus*, Kendall/Hunt

Harrill, R (2005) *Fundamentals of Destination Management and Marketing*, IACVB

Holloway, JC (2004) *Marketing for Tourism*, Prentice Hall

Kotler, P, Bowen, J and Makens, J (2003) *Marketing for Hospitality and Tourism*, Prentice Hall

McCabe, V, Poole, B, Weeks, P and Leiper, N (2000) *The Business and Management of Conventions*, Wiley

Middleton, V (2001) *Marketing in Travel and Tourism*, Butterworth-Heinemann

Peckinpaugh, D (2000) 'The Conferon Guide to Meeting Management', *Convene*, September

Rogers, T (2003) *Conferences and Conventions: A Global Industry*, Elsevier Butterworth-Heinemann

Saxe, R and Weitz, BA (1982) 'The SOCO Scale: a measure of the customer orientation of sales people', *Journal of Marketing Research* 19 (August): 343–51

Chapter 9
Sales Strategies for Destinations and Venues: Practice

Summary of Chapter Contents

This chapter explores the practical implementation of sales strategies and identifies the skills, knowledge and activities required by destination and venue sales teams. It also suggests ways through which the economic impact of successful bids can be maximized by encouraging leisure extensions to business trips.

The chapter covers:

■ Destination and venue selling strategies
■ Handling enquiries effectively
■ Submitting professional bids and sales proposals
■ Managing site inspections and showrounds
■ Negotiation skills
■ Maximizing impact through cross-selling (business extenders)

It includes case studies on:

■ Amathus Hotels' sales strategy
■ The International Confederation of Midwives' Conference, 2008
■ The International Textile Machinery Exhibition – best practice in maximizing business extenders

Learning Outcomes

On completion of this chapter, you should be able to:

■ understand the key factors influencing the selection of destinations and venues
■ appreciate the importance of destination knowledge and expertise in the sales process

■ **define the skills needed in professional enquiry handling, bidding for events and negotiating with clients**
■ **identify appropriate strategies for successful site inspections**
■ **understand the added economic value accruing through maximizing extended visits by convention attendees**

Introduction

There are many books that describe the sales skills and techniques generic to the selling of any product or service. Price and Ilvento (1999), for example, suggest that the approaches to be adopted by the 21st-century sales person will include:

- An ability to customize the sales presentation in order to answer the question in the customer's mind 'What's in it for me?' The sales person 'must present a value-laden presentation customized to the exact needs of their prospect' (p. 35).
- A consultative approach which asks questions (what they describe as 'strategic probing') of the customer, and is based on doing one's homework about the customer before any interaction takes place.
- Building trust between the sales person and the customer (p. 47): 'decisions will still be made based on facts – price, services, features, benefits, warranties and guarantees – but more than ever, the decision [to buy] will be based upon perceptions of trust, comfort and credibility of you and your company'.

Such generic sales skills are important no matter what product or service is being sold. But, when selling a destination or a venue in the conference and business events sector, additional and specific skills, knowledge, tools, resources and activities are used by sales professionals. These will be explored further in this chapter.

Destination and venue selling strategies

Destination and venue selection criteria

An understanding of the factors and criteria influencing buyers when they are selecting destinations and venues is essential. Such an understanding will need to be complemented by knowledge of the specific requirements and selection factors deemed critical by the individual buyer, which might be as quirky as ensuring that the destination has the right kind of shopping to satisfy the tastes and needs of the Chairman's wife! This understanding will enable the destination sales person to focus on selling the benefits of the destination, rather than its features. In other words, not simply informing the client of the total number of bedspaces in the destination but demonstrating that the destination has ample 4-star hotel bedrooms in the right locations to meet the specific requirements of the client's event. Similarly, at a venue level, an understanding of the key venue selection criteria for conference organizers will assist the sales staff in demonstrating how their venue's meeting rooms and other facilities and services can be used and configured to ensure the successful staging of a particular event.

Destination and venue selection criteria may show some variation from year to year, and also from country to country, dependent upon economic, social, political and technological factors. Such factors are examined in more detail in Chapter 12 of this book. Table 9.1 illustrates the key determinants of UK buyers' purchasing of destinations and venues in 2004, and is taken from annual research published as the 'UK Conference Market Survey'.

Commenting for this book on destination and venue selection criteria, Scott Taylor, chief executive of Glasgow City Marketing Bureau, said (October 2005):

> *Glasgow understands that 80% of the decision-making process by a conference organizer is influenced by the image of the destination, and that price is secondary. Organizers will only ever select a destination if it has a positive image. The destination has to attract delegates to it. If it fails to do this, convention registrations will fall and convention income will be compromised. Destination imaging is now recognized as the primary driver for demand. Put it another way: a poor destination image leads to poor attendance which results in a poor profit. Conferences are not in business to make a loss. Some research has suggested that price is the overriding influence, implying that the cheapest destination will always win. There are many examples of destinations that are not selected by organizers because they know that there will be little demand from delegates to attend, irrespective of how cheap it is.*

Destination and venue selling 'Hierarchy'

The importance of location in the selection process is paramount, always featuring among the top three criteria. In selling location, account should always be taken of what might be termed a hierarchy of location. In other words, if selling within the international arena to attract an international event, the first priority is to get one's

Table 9.1 Factors influencing destination and venue selection (listed in priority order)

Ranking	Selection criteria for associations	Selection criteria for companies/corporations
1	Location	Location
2	Price/value for money	Previous experience of venue
3	Access: road, rail, air links	Price/value for money
4	Capacity of conference facilities	Availability
5	Availability	Quality of service
6	Quality of service	Access: road, rail, air links
7	Staff awareness of needs	Quality of conference facilities
8	Quality of food	Capacity of conference facilities
9	Quality of conference facilities	Provision of leisure facilities
10	Cleanliness of venue	Staff awareness of needs

Source: UK Conference Market Survey 2004

own country on to the shortlist before putting forward a specific city or destination, and then a venue and other suppliers. For example, Cardiff, the capital city of Wales, might wish to put forward the Cardiff International Arena as the ideal setting for a major corporate or association conference. A key element of the sales process would be to persuade the client to consider firstly bringing the event to Wales (rather than to France or Thailand or Canada), and then to focus on the city (i.e. Cardiff) and, finally, on the venue itself. Even when, as with international association conferences, it would normally be the city rather than the country that would be bidding to host the event, the destination and venue sales teams must also promote the benefits and attractions of the country. Clients or buyers have to be convinced that the national context for their event is appropriate (taking account of such things as language, culture, environment, access, political stability, etc.) before they can be persuaded to look in detail at the discrete destination or destinations, and then venues, within that country.

Destination expertise

To be effective in selling any product or service, the sales person must have expert and in-depth knowledge of that product or service. This principle applies equally to selling a convention or business event destination, whether operating in a destination or venue sales role. This will mean having good first-hand knowledge of the destination through visits to, and experience of, the facilities and infrastructure that make up the destination. It means becoming an expert on the destination to be sold, combining that first-hand knowledge with a database or library of information and intelligence on the destination. Such a database resource should hold information on the following:

Venues
- Number, types and location of conference and business events venues
- Their capacities in terms of number and size of meeting rooms and number of bedrooms
- The special features and facilities or unique selling propositions (USPs) of the venues (e.g. swimming pool, golf course, Michelin-star restaurant, videoconferencing suite)
- Quality assessments, including an assessment of the quality, experience and professionalism of the venue staff
- Prices
- Accessibility of venues and their ability to handle delegates with disabilities
- The venues' client portfolios – this will give an indication of the kind of conference and convention business currently being attracted to individual venues. It does not necessarily mean knowing the names of client companies but it should include details of the kinds of business by industry sector, by organization type, by size and duration of events, etc.

Local suppliers
Another important aspect of a destination's overall 'product' are the local companies supplying specialist services to incoming conferences and events, such as:

- Audio-visual and production companies: some organizations prefer to work with the same audio-visual companies no matter where the event takes place because they have worked with them over a period of time and have confidence in their ability to provide an efficient and cost-effective service. They may not, therefore, have a need to appoint locally based audio-visual companies. Even so, it strengthens the overall image and profile of the destination if it can demonstrate that it has good quality, local audio-visual companies.

- Exhibition contractors: similarly to audio-visual companies, exhibition contractors often work on a national rather than local basis, but the destination can gain added credibility if it can point to locally-based exhibition contractors and suppliers. It demonstrates that the sector's importance is recognized within the local economy.
- Marquee and furniture hire companies.
- Speciality caterers, who can be hired for a convention banquet or for a special function that forms part of the convention programme, and which will often be held in one of the destination's unique venues.
- Interpreters.
- Activity providers, e.g. companies offering flights in hot air balloons, teambuilding activities, off-road driving.
- Transport providers (e.g. coach companies, taxi services, car rental companies, helicopter hire, train chartering), to emphasize the facilities that exist for transporting delegates within the destination.

Transport, communications and accessibility

Here the focus is on showing the range and ease of access to the destination from other areas or from other countries. Intelligence needs to be gathered, stored and regularly updated on:

- Rail services, showing direct services with other major cities/destinations, and holding information on the length of journey (in miles/kilometres) and duration (in hours/minutes), frequency of service, price
- Air connections, with similar information to that collected on rail services above. If the destination does not have its own airport, there should be information on the nearest airports and their services, plus details of transfer times between the airport and the destination
- Road links/communications with details of average journey times from other major hubs
- Good quality maps that position the destination on at least two levels: showing the destination (a) within the national context, and (b) within its local/regional context. The latter should ideally show where the major venues and hotels are located within the destination.

Attractions and events

Visitor attractions and major events taking place within the destination can both be important as components of social programmes, partner programmes, pre- and post-convention tours. The database should, therefore, feature details of:

- Visitor attractions – information on local attractions (e.g. country parks, castles or stately homes, museums, zoos, theme parks) which can be visited during any free time or as part of the convention social programme and/or pre- and post-convention tours

- Restaurants
- Shopping
- Activities (outdoor and indoor) – theatres and cinemas, sports facilities and leisure centres, golf courses, etc.
- Major events – conference organizers may want their conference to coincide with a major event taking place in the area because it will be of interest to their delegates, perhaps linking in with the theme of the conference in some way. Conversely, they may prefer to avoid a clash with a major event because of possible transport problems, congested accommodation, price rises, or other factors
- Tourist/Visitor Information Centres – the destination sales person must know about the range of information and services available through the local tourist and visitor information centres, with full contact/address details and information on their hours of opening.

Local economy and infrastructure

- Business sectors and major companies – it is vital to know about the key businesses and companies operating in the destination. At one level, such businesses will doubtless generate many local conference and meeting bookings in the destination's venues, making them very important clients. On another level, these businesses and the business sectors they represent should give some strong clues about the types of future conference business to be sought. If a destination has a strong financial services sector, or engineering industry, it is likely to have more success in winning conferences and business events from the financial services or engineering industries because of the natural synergies and links that will exist.
- Inward investment successes – the term 'inward investment' is used to describe the relocation of a company or organization to a particular destination, or a decision by such companies to establish a subsidiary operation in another destination. Inward investments are beneficial because they also give indicators about the inherent strengths and potential growth sectors of the local economy. Inward investment success stories provide valuable promotional material ('we have a vibrant local economy which has attracted the following new businesses in the past year ...') but they are also, in their own right, an important source of future events business.
- New infrastructure developments: the database should hold information on proposed and actual development to the destination's physical infrastructure e.g. new roads or bridges, an extension to the airport, developments to the railway station, new retail parks, new leisure facilities, etc.
- New transport services: information on new or planned air or rail services, for example.
- Road traffic volumes – road congestion and traffic jams are an increasingly common phenomenon in our twenty-first century cities and on our motorways. Local government and central government agencies capture statistics on road traffic volumes – a destination that can demonstrate that, for example, driving is a pleasure because the roads are uncluttered could promote this as one of the benefits and pleasures of holding an event there.

The intelligence held within this database can be used in sales proposals and bids to clients, but also as an invaluable resource in communicating with the trade media, with consultants and potential investment companies.

Case Study 9.1, presented at the end of this chapter, gives details of the sales and marketing strategy of Amathus Hotels and the group's approach to developing its conference and incentive travel business.

Handling enquiries effectively

Destination and venue marketing and sales activity has, as its objective, the generation of leads and enquiries from clients which can be converted into actual business. For a venue, winning business is essential for its survival while, for the destination, success in securing conventions and business events creates increased economic benefits in terms of visitor expenditure and job creation, thus providing a key measure for the destination marketing organization's effectiveness.

Destination level

The destination marketing and sales team will, for the most part, act as a conduit or intermediary organization between the client/customer and the venue with which the business or event will finally be contracted. The sales team's role is to stimulate and then direct enquiries to those venues within the destination that most closely match the client's requirements. They may also make referrals to professional conference organizers (PCOs) or destination management companies (DMCs) to assist them in securing the business. They act as an honest broker or match-maker, seeking to bring together two parties (buyer and supplier) in the hope and expectation that they will reach agreement, strike up a relationship and work together in partnership to ensure a successful event, with further potential events to follow through repeat business.

The destination sales team may also fulfil a role in reassuring buyers and providing consistency of support, especially in countries where high turnover among venue staff can threaten to undermine buyers' confidence that their event will be delivered successfully. Gartrell (1994: 178) writes: 'Convention and visitor bureaus have become the stabilizing influence in an industry that has a reputation for high turnover. This continuity of sales and marketing personnel provides a positive image for a city.'

The stimulation of sales enquiries is achieved both proactively and reactively. The proactive approach is based on researching or 'prospecting' for sales leads by identifying potential clients whose event requirements match what the destination can offer. Contact is made with such clients by telephone or e-mail (or through a personal visit) with the aim of building a rapport and clarifying whether there might be forthcoming events for which the destination could tender. These initial contacts or 'cold calls' seek to generate leads for onward referral to appropriate venues within the destination. Gartrell (1994: 181) sets out the proactive approach diagrammatically. The reactive approach entails responding to enquiries received as a result of the types of marketing communications activity outlined in earlier chapters.

Once the introduction between buyer and supplier (venue and/or PCO/DMC) has been effected, the destination team generally pulls back to allow the venue and possibly other service suppliers to deliver the event for and with the client. The client signs a contract with the venue, not with the destination. The destination team are available to offer support and additional services (such as assistance with pre- and post-tours, social programme planning, the provision of a civic reception), if required, and to follow up after the event to check that the client has been satisfied with the facilities and service experienced from the destination – and clearly also to check on the likelihood of repeat business at some future point.

The process outlined above will certainly apply to the smaller meetings and conferences and to the majority of corporate events. Where, however, the event is of a larger scale, perhaps justifying the description of a 'destination event' involving hundreds or even thousands of delegates, the destination team may also be involved in the whole bidding process, adopting a team approach with the major conference venue, and possibly a PCO, to bid for the event.

Venue level

At a venue level, the sales team seek to maximize appropriate business for their venue. As with the destination sales team, the venue sales team should also adopt both a proactive and reactive approach to sales leads and enquiries. It may well be that, especially for hotel venues that are part of a large chain, sales activity will be co-ordinated through a regional sales team, with national call centres established to handle initial enquiries and bookings. Chapter 10 gives examples of venue marketing consortia and hotel brands, many of which offer a centralized enquiry or booking service.

The venue sales team seeks to win business that gives the best occupancy but which also provides the highest possible yield or revenue (see the section on yield management in Chapter 8). There may well be other factors influencing how they handle an enquiry and respond to a client: for example, if they are new clients who have not used the venue before, how flexible does the venue wish to be in meeting the clients' requirements and making an 'offer they can't refuse', sometimes known as 'buying the business'? If the event is from an existing client, a similar weighing of commercial benefits may be needed, balancing the benefits of retaining the client and getting further repeat business against opportunities to win higher-yield business but from just a one-off event, with no further events forthcoming. Do they take the short-term view and fill their rooms now or do they take a medium- to longer-term view in order to achieve a sustainable business balance, bearing in mind that client retention is normally less expensive than having constantly to find new clients, and generally makes good business sense anyway.

Venues are sometimes criticized for taking the short-term perspective rather than investing in longer-term business relationships. This may not be surprising when general managers of hotels (especially), but other venues as well, have to justify and defend their sales figures for the next few months, but not normally for two or three years in the future. Gary England, Head of Corporate Sales for the Barbican (www.barbicanconferences.co.uk), a large non-residential conference venue in central London, argued against this short-term approach using the following rationale (*Conference & Exhibition Fact Finder* magazine, December 2004):

> One of the many buzz words for the moment is relationship management. Let us not forget that this is a volatile market, reactive to international events, so investing in relationships is one sure-fire way of managing against disaster. It is sometimes the case that, during the better times, good relationships are forgotten. I have recently experienced a frustrating example of this: a large hotel chain, with which I have a 5-year relationship, put a 45 per cent price increase onto its rooms! For me this is five years of good relationship building down the drain. A reactive decision taken at head office against an upturn in business. Of course, I understand the economies of supply and demand, but for me this does not take into account the economies of the local marketplace. If, God forbid, another 9/11 or SARS scare should hit the industry, not only has the relationship

been lost, but you could bet the subsequent price drop would be equally both dramatic and unhealthy. It is these short-term, reactive strategies that we need to move away from as an industry. Not just milking every upturn and struggling against damage limitation when things go bad. A long-term strategy is where business growth leads to business investment. The benefits are that, during the good times, you will gather a budgetary surplus that will help pay for your plans during the not-so-good times.

Another issue with which some venues have to wrestle, particularly those belonging to a chain or consortium, concerns the onward referral of business. If they are unable to handle an enquiry because, perhaps, of lack of availability, do they offer to refer the enquiry to another venue in the locality (i.e. keep the business in the destination) or do they pass it on to other venues in their chain (but which may well be in a different part of the country) in order to try to win the business for the chain? Practice varies enormously but the overriding consideration should be: what is best for the client?

How, then, do destinations and venues gain a clear understanding of clients' requirements for their events. What enquiry handling skills and procedures are needed, how is event intelligence to be gathered, how should sales teams seek to empathize with clients to appreciate their priorities in achieving a successful event?

Enquiry handling skills

Destination and venue sales staff must understand, from the outset, that the clients and customers who contact them with an enquiry are, in many cases (possibly as high as 80%), not full-time conference and event organizers. They may be secretaries or PAs, trainers or human resource managers, marketing or public relations staff, with only limited experience and knowledge of convention and event management. They may well not be the decision-makers: their role is to collect information on destination and venue options for an event, perhaps make recommendations and attempt to sell a destination, but then leave senior managers or directors, or a selection committee, to make the final choice. It is, therefore, important, when handling an enquiry, to establish at an early stage the status of the enquirer and to clarify the scope they have to influence the final choice of event location.

The limited professional expertise of enquirers, or perhaps their limited ability to influence the choice of destination or venue, can prove frustrating. It can frequently mean that enquirers do not have complete information on the event for which they have been asked to locate a suitable destination and venue. Their 'brief' may lack some of the essential detail required by the destination and venue sales teams to enable them to put forward a full and properly tailored sales proposal. It may also be unclear when a decision will be taken on the choice of destination and venue, complicating the processes for follow-up sales calls once a bid or proposal has been submitted to the enquirer.

Customer frustrations, on the other hand, often centre upon the destination or venue's perceived inability to supply appropriate information within a specified time frame. Comments such as 'they didn't listen to us' or 'they didn't interpret our needs correctly' are sometimes heard. The destination sales team may respond that customers only wanted to know about venue availability and price, and that they gave the customers what they wanted. In doing so, the sales team has failed to gain a proper understanding of the customers' real needs, and has missed the opportunity to give a response different from that being submitted by other destinations. Where they do adopt a more customer-focused approach, they enjoy a higher success rate with more enquiries being converted. All customers have different needs and experiences. They organize different types of events with quite different requirements. The destination sales team must understand these differences and then assess and present the destination's unique 'product' or offering in order most closely to match the customers' unique requirements.

In practical terms, it means not only obtaining the factual information necessary to process an enquiry (such as size, dates, type of event) but also seeking other information to enable the sales team really to understand the objectives for an event and what will be its critical success factors. This means asking the client open questions. Rudyard Kipling's apposite verse is one that should be known to all sales professionals:

> I kept six honest serving men.
> They taught me all I knew.
> Their names are What and Why and When
> And How and Where and Who

Table 9.2 illustrates how such open questioning can be used to gather the crucial and distinctive support information, in addition to the basic factual event information,

Table 9.2 Enquiry support information (Who? What? Where? Why? When? How?)

1 DATE	How flexible can you be with your chosen date? If we were able to offer you a better deal on an alternative date, would you be interested?
2 THE EVENT	What is its purpose? How confidential is it? How frequently is it held? Who are the delegates? How much free time will they have?
3 DESTINATION KNOWLEDGE	When did the client last visit the destination? How many times have they been previously? What is their source of knowledge about the destination?
4 LOCATION	How will the delegates be travelling to the destination? Where will they be travelling from? How important is location in the overall decision?
5 OTHER VENUES AND DESTINATIONS	Which other venues/destinations have you used previously? What was your experience like? Which other venues/destinations are you considering for this event? Why have you decided not to return to last year's venue/destination?
6 DECISION	When will the decision be taken on the choice of destination? (This question will often also elicit information on who will be making the decision) Who is the main organizer? When do you expect delegates to book?
7 BUDGET	What is the budget for the event? How will payment be made? To what extent is the price important to you in your choice of venue/destination?
8 SITE VISIT	When can you visit us? How long can you stay? What are you looking to achieve from your visit? Who will be visiting?
9 CLIENT'S PRIORITIES	What is important to you about the destination/venue you select? How will the success of the event be judged?
10 EXTRA SERVICES	To what extent do your delegates appreciate a welcome pack or a gift from the area? Do any of your delegates have special needs? What other services can we offer you to support the success of your event?

Source: BACD Summer School, 1999 (presentation by Peter Rand)

which will enable the destination and venue sales teams to get under the customers' skin, understand their priorities, and hence tailor the destination bid and venue sales proposal in such a way that they will have a much higher chance of success.

As well as asking open questions, it is vital to listen actively and carefully to the answers being given. People speak on average at 125 words per minute but the mind is capable of hearing and receiving up to 500 words a minute. It is very easy to get bored or distracted, and to miss some key words unless listening very closely to what the customer is actually saying.

The advent of the Internet and e-mail has meant that customers increasingly supply their enquiry details in electronic form and do not necessarily have any direct interaction with another human being. There may not be the telephone conversation between the destination/venue sales team and the customer, which often signals the first steps in building a relationship between both parties. It is, therefore, crucial to design the electronic enquiry questionnaire (which, when completed by the customer, is then submitted to the destination/venue as a document known as an 'RFP' or 'request for proposal') in a way that adheres to the principles outlined above, and elicits the maximum amount of information from the customer.

In order to increase their own efficiency and to respond to customer demands for information in an electronic format, many destination sales teams have invested in dedicated enquiry handling software that, to a large extent, automates enquiry handling systems while still enabling them to provide a personalized and tailored response to the client. One example of such software in the UK is known as 'Chaser BUREAU', developed by Velvet Software Ltd (www.velvetsoftware.co.uk). 'Chaser BUREAU' was designed and developed specifically for UK convention bureaux and it has the following features:

- It is designed for destinations as the complete solution for conference enquiry management, automating time-consuming processes associated with enquiry handling, report generation and financial administration.
- It integrates information on a destination's venues, attractions and suppliers into the enquiry response process.
- It maintains entire client profiles including venue preferences and history of past events.
- It is central to the national venue-finding service operated by the British Association of Conference Destinations. The web-based 'Chaser HUB' distributes BACD enquiries to destinations, collates destination responses and aggregates information on the economic impact of enquiries for inclusion in national business tourism statistics.

Submitting professional bids and sales proposals

Submitting a professional bid for a high-profile national or international convention can be a lengthy and costly undertaking, and may involve the bid team travelling to another country in order to present its bid to a selection panel or committee. It also requires considerable sensitivity to the situation of the bid's recipients, appreciating that it is possible to oversell or 'over-egg' a destination and provoke a negative response from those whom it was intended to impress. For example, it might not be appropriate to stress the luxuriousness of the facilities to be found in a bidding city from a developed country if many of the expected delegate attendees will be travelling from under-developed or third world countries. A sensitivity to different cultural, political and economic situations when bidding for international conventions, in particular, is a vital requirement.

Destination level bids

Once the enquiry or RFP has been received, the destination sales team has to decide whether it can match the event requirements and, if so, what scale and type of response will be suitable. Some events are, of course, very large and have complex requirements but also detailed stipulations about the format and content of the bids to be submitted by those destinations interested in securing them. If the event is simply a small meeting with relatively straightforward needs, the destination may establish systems that direct the enquiry to appropriate venues in the destination for them to respond to the client, with minimal involvement by the destination sales team. Edinburgh Convention Bureau in Scotland, for example, has implemented such a system following considerable research and a decision to benchmark their system against Boston's (USA) successful www.meetingpath.com. The Edinburgh sales team only gets involved in an enquiry when the event is over a certain minimum size (i.e. more than 150 delegates). The web-based system (www.meetingedinburgh. com) assists meeting planners and conference organizers to access information on all the members of Edinburgh Convention Bureau; to develop a shopping list of members selected; to e-mail RFPs directly to suppliers; and to maintain a record of RFPs sent to suppliers. The system cost some £47 000 to develop and it came into operation in March 2004. By February 2005 it had already generated more than £800 000 of business for Edinburgh venues.

Once it has been established that the enquiry is an appropriate one for the destination, the sales team begins the process of assembling its response or bid document. Computerized and web-based systems do allow bids to be compiled very speedily (i.e. within hours). Vienna Convention Bureau (www.vienna.convention.at) in Austria has the proud boast that it will respond to any enquiry, from any part of the world, within 24 hours, and the city's success in the international congress and conventions market in recent years is testimony to the Bureau's ability to respond quickly, effectively and professionally.

Glasgow (www.seeglasgow.com), Stockholm (www.congressstockholm.se) and Madrid (www.madridconventionbureau.com) are among cities to have developed on-line bid documents. Glasgow was the first city to win a congress (the International Crustaceans Congress) using an on-line bid. Stockholm's bid-on-line system was launched in 2001 and has been found to be very useful when there is a large group of people, spread all over the world, who are involved in the voting process. So far, the bid-on-line format has been built as a traditional website with the same headings, sub-headings and contents as the paper bid. Since the web bid has been used as a complement to Stockholm's paper bid, it has been important for the layout to be the same in both. Stockholm's experience has been that there is still a need for the traditional paper bid alongside its web bid, presumably because it is easier to compare bids from different destinations in hard copy format. Another significant factor has been the big differences in web knowledge and web access over the world. Until now Stockholm has been operating two different systems: one for hard copy documents and one for its bid-on-line. It plans, in the future, to integrate the two systems in order to reduce the work required from the Convention Bureau staff in submitting major bids.

Yukon Convention Bureau in Canada (www.ycb.ca) has developed a 'bid kit' which has proved highly successful in its bids to host meetings in the province. The kit includes a box filled with a customized written bid, a CD-Rom including a Powerpoint presentation of the proposal, redeemable coupons for Yukon products and services, and speciality Yukon products such as teas, smoked salmon, CDs and cosmetics, all donated by members of Yukon Convention Bureau. The kit also contains personalized letters of invitation from the Premier and the Minister of Tourism, as well as photos and stories that reflect the nature of the recipient group.

Ljubljana (www.ljubljana-tourism.si), capital of Slovenia in central Europe, when bidding for international conventions and similar events, uses a bid document which combines pre-printed, static information with individual sheets personalized to the client and his event. The document is assembled in spiral, wire-bound format inside a folder replete with full-colour photographs of Ljubljana. Visible on the outside front cover is the wording: *Ljubljana invites ...[name of congress]*.

The document has separate sections on:

- Letters of invitation (e.g. from the Mayor or other civic or government dignitary inviting and welcoming the convention)
- Letter/information from the host organization (involved in co-ordinating the bid and in organizing the event)
- Host city (i.e. Ljubljana): pages on location/climate/geography/culture/economy; its expertise and reputation as a conference destination; impressions of Ljubljana quoting travel writers' comments about the city; history of Ljubljana; architecture; entertainment/cuisine/arts and culture/recreation and shopping; useful information sources
- Access and transportation: how to reach Ljubljana by air, road and rail
- Venues and accommodation: photos and data on the main congress centre; details of major hotels; a map showing the location of main venue(s) and hotels
- PCO and references: details of professional conference organizer services
- Preliminary programme
- Budget: quotations for the costs of different elements of the convention
- Tours and excursions: city tours and excursions; ideas for excursions outside Ljubljana.

Spain's second city, Barcelona (www.barcelonaturisme.com), when bidding in December 2001 to persuade the organizers of EIBTM (the annual European Incentive, Business Travel and Meetings Exhibition – www.eibtm.com) to move this trade show from Geneva, Switzerland to Barcelona, assembled a 100-page bid document, supplemented by a 'Powerpoint' presentation. EIBTM is one of the leading international trade exhibitions for the business tourism sector, organized by Reed Travel Exhibitions. It was held in Barcelona for the first time in November 2004 where it attracted 6100 visitors (including 2500 hosted buyers) and 700 exhibiting companies from 95 countries. Barcelona's contract to stage EIBTM runs for an initial 5-year period (2004–2008). Figure 9.1 gives further details of Barcelona's bid document for EIBTM.

Section No.	Title	Page No.
1	BARCELONA LOVES EIBTM	2
	• Introduction and letters of support	3
2	THE HOST CITY: BARCELONA	21
	• Introducing Barcelona	23
	• Cost of living overview	25
3	ACCOMMODATION	26
4	VENUE	40
5	TRANSPORTATION	50
	• **Transportation/airline:**	51
	• Barcelona Airport	51
	• Official carrier	65
	• **Ground transportation into the city:**	67
	• By road	67
	• By train	69
	• High speed train	69
	• By sea	73
	• **Ground transportation within the city:**	74
	• Public transportation and new projects	74
	• Taxi	78
	• **Ground handling**	80
6	SOCIAL FUNCTIONS	82
	• Event venues in Barcelona	83
	• EIBTM social events	92
7	ADDITIONAL CONSIDERATIONS	94
	• City support	95
	• Hosted buyer programme	95
	• Civic local personality support	95
	• Banner and poster sites	97
	• Tecnomeeting	97
	• Universal Forum of Cultures 2004	98

Figure 9.1 The index of contents for Barcelona's 2001 bid document.

An insight into the steps and processes involved in bidding for a conference is given in the summary of Glasgow's approach when bidding to attract a major international conference – the International Confederation of Midwives' (www.internationalmidwives.org) conference – to the city (see case study).

Case Study

The International Confederation of Midwives' Conference, 2008

This case study illustrates the importance of adopting a cohesive, partnership approach when seeking to win major international conventions and congresses for a destination. It demonstrates how a city convention bureau worked with a local ambassador and a trade association, two national tourist boards (Scotland and Britain) and other government agencies to secure a high profile event that will bring an estimated 3000 delegates to Glasgow in 2008. The event is likely to generate economic benefits for the city in excess of £5 million.

It began with desk research by the International Association Sales Executive of Greater Glasgow & Clyde Valley Tourist Board's Convention Bureau (GG&CVTBCB – since April 2005 known as the Glasgow City Marketing Bureau), researching through databases such as that of the International Congress and Convention Association (ICCA), to identify those large medical conferences that had not been held in the UK for a number of years. These were matched with conference subject matters where the UK had expertise and a strong UK association in place. This research brought up the International Confederation of Midwives, among others.

The GG&CVTBCB's Ambassador Executive then set about identifying through local research a potential Ambassador. The ideal candidate was found at Glasgow University: Professor of Midwifery, Edith Hillan. Professor Hillan was a member of the Royal College of Midwives' Executive Board and a leading academic in this field. The Manager of the Convention Bureau and the Ambassador Executive then met Professor Hillan and outlined the support that the Bureau and city would give to the Royal College should they be persuaded to put forward a bid.

The Manager and International Association Executive next travelled to The Hague where the head office of the International Confederation of Midwives is based and met the Secretary General. They went to assess the likelihood of a UK bid being successful and to find out as much as possible about both the international association and the bid procedure so that they could report back to their local Ambassador with valuable market intelligence. Professor Hillan duly presented to the Executive Council and it was agreed that the Royal College would bid with Glasgow as the chosen UK destination.

The Bureau worked with the Royal College and the proposed venue – the Scottish Exhibition and Conference Centre – to produce the bid presentation, which was to be given by Dame Karlene Davis: the General Secretary of the Royal College. The bid was to take place in Vienna in 2002 and the competing destinations were Montreal and Buenos Aires.

In preparation for the bid and despite the six years' lead time, GG&CVTBCB had to work closely with their local accommodation and transportation suppliers to put together a bid package that would satisfy the needs of the midwives and their professional conference organizer, Congrex Holdings.

The year 2002 was the centenary of the Royal College. Working with support from their colleagues at VisitBritain (the pan-British government agency tasked with promoting Britain internationally) and VisitScotland (the national tourist board for Scotland – www.conventionscotland.com), GG&CVTBCB were able to arrange a reception in Vienna prior to the bid, attended by 150 voting members of the International College of Midwives. The reception was hosted by the British Ambassador to Austria at his official residence.

For the bid presentation itself, a short video was produced in which the British Prime Minister (Tony Blair) spoke, encouraging delegates to vote for Glasgow. The presentation was preceded by a piper piping delegates into the auditorium, giving an immediate flavour of Scotland. Glasgow was successful, attracting 90 votes compared with 25 votes for Buenos Aires and 12 for Montreal.

Venue sales proposals or bids

A sales proposal or bid from a venue must 'sell' the reason why clients should choose this venue for their event. It is *not* purely an acknowledgement that the venue is available, giving details of costs.

The document has, historically, been sent through the post but is increasingly likely to be submitted by e-mail with a link to the venue's website for additional information including a 'virtual' tour of the venue. Whether sent in hard copy format or electronically, the bid proposal should include (*inter alia*):

- A short covering letter (accuracy of the client's contact details is crucial) to include: thanks and personal comment (if appropriate); summary of initial event requirements; clarification of status of booking; invitation to visit; reassurance of venue's experience/flexibility/enthusiasm for the booking; name of contact for further information/assistance.
- The sales proposal (set out in an attractive, easy-to-read format):
  - full client contact details
  - event dates (arrival and departure)
  - numbers of delegates (minimum and maximum numbers, with agreed timescales for notification)
  - general introduction personalized to the client and emphasizing 'you'
  - benefits of the venue's location (with details of travel and communications, parking, special deals); situation (i.e. rural/city centre) selling the style of the venue, with map
  - event requirements in chronological order with an outline programme
  - meeting rooms/exhibition space, selling the benefits of individual facilities, and giving an internal location plan and photo(s)
  - accommodation, with details of the venue's strengths and any special access requirements
  - catering requirements, with specific benefits and names of room(s)/restaurant(s) to be used
  - terms and conditions, including deposit requirements
  - draft contract/booking form
  - prices, tailored specifically to the event and giving rates 'up to' a specified maximum; listing items including before stating the price, clarifying whether inclusive of any applicable taxes
  - testimonials from previous clients
  - timetable for handling the event
  - experience of similar events over a period of 'x' years

○ any accreditations, such as ISO 9000
○ a copy of the venue's promotional brochure
○ key reason why the client should choose this particular venue.

Managing site inspections and showrounds

Once the destination and/or venue sales team has submitted its bid or proposal, this is normally followed up after a few days to check that the client has received the information safely and to clarify that it provides all the information needed. There may also be questions that arise from the contents of the bid and this follow-up sales call gives the client the chance to raise such questions.

The sales team will be hoping that their bid has convinced the client to shortlist their destination/venue for further consideration, which will often take the form of a site visit by the client to view the destination/venue at first hand and to assess how well it matches the requirements for their event.

Site visits are different from the familiarization visits and 'educationals' described in Chapter 7. Familiarization visits and 'educationals' take place at an earlier stage in the promotional process. They are designed to stimulate an interest in the destination or venue, to develop an understanding and experience of what it can offer, and to create a predisposition on the part of the client to consider the destination or venue seriously when placing future business. The site visit, on the other hand, takes place with a specific event in mind, the requirements and success criteria for which will be known, so that the destination and venue sales teams can focus their efforts on converting the enquiry by giving the client the confidence and assurance that his event will be even more successful with them than with any of the other destinations/venues the client has on the shortlist.

One of the keys to a successful destination site visit (as opposed to venue site visit – see below) is cross-destination communications. All of the destination's suppliers (venues, hotels, attractions, transport providers, civic or municipality representatives, etc.) to whom the client will be introduced during the inspection visit must be properly briefed on the characteristics of the client's event and on its critical success factors. This will enable them to prepare their information accordingly and to sell their product or service in a way that is customized to the client's needs. It will also demonstrate to the client a cohesive and united approach by the destination, giving confidence that the destination will indeed deliver on the day. For major events the briefing should take the form of a get-together of all the main supplier contacts in order to run through the detailed arrangements of the site inspection, to ensure that the appropriate co-ordination takes place and to minimize unnecessary duplication.

Other important aspects in the staging of good site inspections include the following:

• Good timekeeping. Adhering to the schedule of the visit programme is essential, as this conveys a sense of professionalism.
• A welcome to the client from the general manager or senior representative of the facilities being visited, underlining the prestige of the event and the importance

attached to winning the client's event for the destination. This senior representative will not necessarily be the one to undertake the showround for the client (this should be left to the sales staff who are more likely to have at their finger tips the answers to questions raised by the client), but their involvement at the outset of the visit is crucial in setting the right tone.

- A programme schedule that allows some flexibility. It may become apparent during the visit that the client has concerns or questions that need to be addressed by showing him some aspect of the destination that was not originally planned. Such flexibility will also show that the destination is listening actively to the client and is not making false assumptions about what his requirements are.

For the venue, a site inspection and showround is the best opportunity to win new business, but it needs to be planned and prepared for with great attention to detail. Such attention to detail must assess:

- The length of the visit and the appropriate level of hospitality to be offered, and whether this should include an overnight stay
- Which of the venue's staff should be introduced to the client, and how will they be briefed for this
- How the meeting rooms should be laid out and best brought to life, and how the client can be introduced to any rooms that may be in use for another event during the client's visit
- What is the most logical order for the showround, showing those parts of the venue relevant to the client's needs, with an appropriate layout plan
- Where a quiet area can be found in which to sit down with the client, check and overcome any concerns, clarify the next steps and ask for the business!

Once the site inspection is over, a follow-up sales call should be made to deal with any further queries, unless the client has made clear that the onus is now on him to make contact with the destination/venue sales team. Even if no sales call is to be made, a letter should be sent to the client thanking him for his time in visiting the destination/venue, expressing the hope that he has been impressed by what he has seen, and reminding him that the destination/venue is available to answer any further questions he might have. By this time, a rapport and relationship should have been established with the client, one that has given the client a sense of trust and comfort in the destination's ability to deliver a successful event.

Negotiation skills

The principles of yield management (see Chapter 8) provide the context for a venue's sales activity and, especially, for its approach to negotiating with clients. A successful site visit will have persuaded the client that the destination and venue are suitable for his event but the client may still wish to negotiate further to secure the best possible deal before signing a contract with the chosen venue. From a venue perspective, there are a number of factors to be considered as part of this negotiation process, all of which link with the objectives of maximizing occupancy and yield, and help in determining whether the venue wants the piece of business and, if so, at what rate. Rogers (2003: 181–2) suggests that such factors include:

- Decisions on the correct business mix for the venue (identifying the most appropriate conference market segments (see Chapter 1) as well as other types of business if, for example, the venue is a hotel also seeking individual business travellers, leisure tourists, coach groups, etc.)
- Dates – accepting business that allows the venue to maximize bookings on 365 days a year, including factors such as whether the event is weekday or weekend or a combination of the two
- Timings of a meeting or conference – if, for example, the event does not start until the afternoon or evening, is there an opportunity to sell the meeting room(s) to another client for the first part of this day?
- Duration and seasonality
- Numbers of delegates, bedroom occupancy and overall value of the piece of business
- Numbers of meeting rooms required, and implications this may have for other potential business that might have to be refused
- Future opportunities for business from this client.

The venue sales team should not begin negotiating with a client without a detailed knowledge of the market. This market knowledge should include:

- Knowing the main sources of business for the venue
- Understanding market segmentation and the different types of conference clients with different types of events, objectives, budgets. What is the market position of the client?
- Keeping abreast of the current state of the conference market (strengths and weaknesses, trends) and of the general economy (local/national and increasingly international)
- Being aware of the venue's principal competitors
- Being fully informed of major events in the locality (sporting, cultural, business), which will have an impact on demand for bedrooms and possibly function rooms.

The venue needs to decide, prior to negotiation, what the ideal outcome would be, but also what a realistic outcome would be and, finally, what its fallback position should be.

Once negotiations start, it is important to establish at an early stage what are the important criteria (i.e. critical factors in determining how successful an event has been) for the client; what alternatives are available (both other venues being considered but also alternative dates and formats for the event to allow maximum flexibility); whether the buyer/organizer has any concessions to offer and, if so, what he might be expecting in return; and what concessions the venue can bring to the negotiating table which will cost little but be perceived as valuable by the client.

Successful negotiation is about achieving a 'win/win' situation for both the client and the venue. This requires both parties to be willing to give in order to get. A win/win situation is achieved by joint decision-making and discussion, and therefore:

- Meets the needs of both parties
- Leads to a decision which is not unacceptable to anyone
- Requires two-way communication

- Has an emphasis on flexibility
- Concentrates on objectives
- Maintains a long-term relationship.

Peter Rand, one of the leading UK convention industry trainers, contends that critical mistakes leading to unsuccessful negotiations include:

- Inadequate preparation
- Ignoring the give/get principle
- Use of intimidating behaviour
- Impatience and loss of temper
- Talking too much and listening too little
- Arguing instead of influencing
- Ignoring conflict.

Maximizing impact through business extenders

While launching successful bids for events is, of course, the principal *raison d'être* of the destination and venue sales team, it is not the only one. It is now recognized that it is also of paramount importance to maximize the economic benefits of the event for the destination, and revenue for the venue, by ensuring the highest possible number of delegates (and, where appropriate, accompanying persons) and by encouraging the delegates to extend their stay through pre- or post-convention tours.

It can be very difficult for business visitors to change their return travel dates or organize extra time off work at the last minute, so leisure extensions to business trips need to be planned far in advance. This means that information on available options needs to be available well before the event is due to take place, information that is actively circulated to the delegates.

Understandably, the priority for conference organizers and hosts is for the event to be successful, so their main concern is with the logistics of the conference itself. But most organizers also realize that selling the attractions of the destination can be an effective way of boosting attendance figures, particularly in the association conference market. Making conference organizers fully aware of the destination's attractions and leisure opportunities is, therefore, essential.

Davidson (2003) suggests that actions to be taken by destination sales teams to encourage business extenders and to maximize delegate attendance can include:

- The incorporation of information on local tours, attractions and events in familiarization trips, bid documents and presentations to organizing committees.
- Attendance at an association conference in the year prior to its being held in their destination to showcase the leisure opportunities on offer by the destination and the surrounding area. This usually entails having a stand with tourist literature in the reception area of the conference, and/or being given the opportunity to sponsor a reception at the conference and say a few words of welcome on behalf of the destination for the following year's event.

- Offering conference and trade show organizers photographic material and tourism information to be included in their printed publicity material and on their websites.
- Providing bulk supplies of tourist literature to be sent out to delegates by the event organizer. Philadelphia Convention and Visitors Bureau (www.pcvb.org) – motto: 'Come early, Stay late' – arranges for a brochure promoting the leisure, cultural and gastronomic attractions of its city to be sent to every convention delegate with the initial invitation to attend the event. The information in the brochure is tailored to the specific leisure interests of the delegates and carries the name and logo of the association. A reply-paid card in the brochure, which asks if delegates are bringing guests and/or extending their trips, is used to request further tourist information.
- Encouraging destination management companies to tailor tours, guest programmes and excursions to the interests of the particular delegate group.
- Suggesting to the conference organizers and meeting planners that they time their event to begin just after, or end just before, key cultural/sports events in the destination.
- Setting up discount schemes for business visitors by involving local suppliers such as restaurants, shops, car hire companies and attractions. For example, New York City Convention and Visitors Bureau (www.nycvisit.com) operates a 'Convention Delegates Pass Program' in association with American Express, offering discounts and promotional offers at local restaurants, attractions, theatres and shops to delegates who present their conference name badge and redeemable coupon and pay with an American Express card. Details of the scheme and participating businesses can be sent to delegates in advance, posted on the conference website, or included in registration packs. The Detroit Convention and Visitors Bureau (www.visitdetroit.com) has a similar discount scheme to that run in New York, based on the use of coupons, but available only at weekends. By tracking the number of coupons used, Detroit is able to estimate the volume of business visitors extending their trips over the weekend.

Davidson (2003) recommends that residential conference venues can drive leisure business through their corporate base and increase occupancy rates at weekends by:

- Offering to business visitors, at the time of booking, weekend extensions at a special discount, lower than the conference rate, if attending an event as a delegate
- Offering business extenders complimentary 'add-ons' such as dinner
- Offering special discounts on leisure breaks for the employees of key corporate customers booking meetings in the venue, as an incentive
- Teaming up with local attractions to offer business guests special themed packages.

Maximizing the impact of a major event can also involve collaboration with adjacent destinations in order to provide the necessary bedstock and also to give visitors knowledge of, and access to, attractions and experiences within the wider region, thus further increasing the enjoyment of their visit and encouraging them to extend their stay. Case Study 9.2, presented at the end of the chapter, on the International Textile Machinery Exhibition (ITMA) illustrates how cross-destination partnerships can be used to excellent effect in order to ensure the successful staging of a large event and to lever the maximum economic benefits for a region.

It is vital, therefore, that all stakeholders are made aware of the full value of this type of incremental spending by business visitors. That means taking care to measure the benefits of business visitors who extend their trip, return or bring guests, or any combination of these. Only when these indirect benefits are demonstrated will the full contribution of conventions and business events to national and local economies be recognized.

Summary

Destination selling is a challenging but exciting and stimulating occupation. It demands skills that are generic to the selling of any product or service, but it requires additional skills, expertise and information resources, commensurate with the task of selling and promoting a living, changing and constantly evolving entity: a place. Destination selling is a crucial component in place marketing activity, essential for the conversion of a convention organizer's interest in a destination into confirmed business for the destination. Similarly, venue sales activity calls for a high level of skill and a broad knowledge base. Destination and venue selling both require a planned, strategic approach, one that will be implemented by marketing and sales teams whose professionalism should infuse their enquiry handling, event bidding and overall customer relationship management in order to be successful in an extremely competitive marketplace. It will follow through into their strategies for maximizing the economic benefits and revenue generation of conventions, meetings and other business events.

Case Study 9.1

Amathus Hotels' sales and marketing strategy

This case study traces the development and implementation of a sales and marketing strategy by Amathus Hotels in respect of the conference and incentive markets.

Amathus Hotels is a division of Amathus Navigation Ltd, a Cypriot company with a base in Limassol. The company is part of a much larger group of companies, the Lanitis Group, which has interests in construction, tourism, banking, farming, leisure, retail and entertainment.

Amathus Hotels is the largest of all the divisions in terms of turnover and operates three 5-star hotels with a total of 837 rooms in Cyprus and Rhodes. The Amathus Beach Hotel in Limassol is the flagship of the division and the first hotel of the group to become a member of the prestigious 'Leading Hotels of the World' consortium. The Paphos Amathus Beach, in Cyprus's west coast town of Paphos, is also a member of the same consortium while the Rodian Amathus Beach Hotel, at Ixia on the north-west coast of the Greek island of Rhodes, has recently been acquired by the division. All three properties enjoy beach-front locations and are renowned as luxury hotels in the leisure tourism and MICE segments.

Creation of a Sales and Marketing Department

Originally each hotel employed its own specialist sales and marketing manager but the acquisition of the Rodian Amathus Beach Hotel led the company to question the efficiencies of such a way of operating, both in terms of the costs and in respect of the levels of occupancy being achieved. Serious consideration was given to the establishment of a group sales and marketing department to provide a more consistent level of performance across the different target markets and to address the issue of marketing two hotels in Cyprus and one in Rhodes. In June 2001 a sales and marketing director was appointed to lead a new, centralized department and to work closely with the existing sales and marketing staff at the individual hotels. The objective of cross-selling all three properties became a core focus of all marketing plans.

Marketing plans

Each hotel is required to prepare a draft plan of costed activity for the whole year towards the end of the previous year. Once each hotel has prepared its proposed plan, this is presented to the Central Sales and Marketing Committee, consisting of the three hotel general managers, the central sales and marketing director, and the divisional chief executive officer. This committee meets bi-monthly and, among other responsibilities, gives final approval to the central marketing plan. The individual plans of each hotel are presented, and the committee ensures that unnecessary duplication (such as two executives attending the same exhibition or two hotels advertising in the same publication) and poor communications are avoided. Such bad practice occurred regularly until the creation of the central marketing office, also contributing to increased marketing costs.

The Sales and Marketing Committee agrees a final, central marketing plan which involves activities for the benefit of all three hotels in all segments and in all markets. The plan also determines training needs to ensure that all marketing staff are able to promote all three properties. The new structure has produced higher occupancy levels as well as economies in marketing expenditure. Savings included reductions in travelling and entertaining costs and a 50% saving in advertising costs. At the same time, the department looked to develop common brochures and gifts, as well as branded display and advertising material.

The next issue to be tackled was that of an international presence. It was evident that, while 99% of total arrivals to all three hotels came from Europe, there were no marketing staff based in any of these markets. The first such overseas office for Amathus Hotels was created in the UK in 2003, the UK being the largest market for all of the hotels. An office in Germany followed and soon after, one in France. These three offices divide the whole marketplace between them, dependent upon the language skills and capabilities of each office manager: Germany is responsible for all German-speaking countries while France looks after the French-speaking countries, and the UK office in London (the largest office to date, with three staff) is responsible for the UK and Italy. The overseas office staff are responsible both for leisure tourism and conference/incentive markets.

The target market segments

All hotel guests are found through different 'distribution channels'. Historically, guests would have engaged in private correspondence with the establishment where they wished to stay. Then the travel agent was born and today there is the Internet travel agent. Others who may be involved in the booking process can include tour operators, airlines, incentive and conference organizers, business travel agents, company implant agents (i.e. staff of a travel agency or business travel house being physically based in the offices of a major corporate client), hotel consortia and consumers booking direct. All of the above are known as the distribution channels or the travel industry segments.

Amathus Hotels views all of the above as its target segments and it is here that the whole divisional marketing team searches for its business. Each and every segment will have its importance and contribute towards the properties' profitability and, depending on exactly this level of contribution, the Sales and Marketing Committee will decide on the degree of investment and effort towards a particular segment. Each segment requires a different approach, a separate plan and an individual campaign of activities. The unique selling propositions (USPs) of a hotel are known but the beach, for example, might be a primary reason for choice by the leisure traveller as opposed to the conference delegate, while the meeting room of the same hotel will be of no interest to the leisure traveller but of utmost importance to the delegate. The spa, however, of the same property could surely be of interest to both types of client. The promotion of various elements of a hotel, therefore, differs from segment to segment.

Amathus Hotels has an objective to increase business deriving from the MICE segment because of its higher profitability or yield. Each hotel is currently active in this segment but with different occupancy levels being achieved. A variety of sales strategies and activities is now being employed to meet the set targets.

Sales and marketing activities

Sales and marketing activities employed by Amathus Hotels include advertising, use of PR agencies, publication of dedicated hotel brochures for the MICE segment, and familiarization and venue inspection visits for conference/incentive organizers. Amathus Hotels has adopted an open invitation policy towards the MICE segment by which it attempts to host as many organizers as possible in its hotels. This hospitality is not only extended to the organizer with a specific brief for a specific event but also to any serious organizer at any time, to enable them to sample the hotels' facilities and services.

Amathus Hotels also attends many of the specialist MICE exhibitions provided that they are included in its central marketing plan. Amathus exhibits from its own stand or as part of the Cyprus or Greece stands. Prior to attending such events, the hotels will write or call all their existing conference/incentive organizer contacts to invite them to visit the Amathus stand. The main objective of this presence is to create new contacts within the MICE segment and to strengthen relationships with existing clients. There is not usually an expectation that such organizers will bring lots of specific enquiries with them to the exhibition. After the exhibition, Amathus Hotels follows up each contact with a 'thank you' letter for the opportunity to meet and with a telephone call in which the person calling will try to set up an appointment to visit the organizer at his workplace. It is at this stage that Amathus is trying to establish an ongoing relationship with the client. Amathus ensures that these contacts continue to receive updated information on each hotel, newsletters of the division and eventually an invitation to see the properties at first hand. Visits to the client's workplace also help to assess the overall quality of the contact and the likelihood of his providing any future business.

Case Study 9.2

The International Textile Machinery Exhibition – best practice in maximizing business extenders

The International Textile Machinery Exhibition (ITMA) is one of the largest international trade exhibitions in the world. In October 2003 it was staged at the National Exhibition Centre (NEC), Birmingham (England), the first time that it had been held in the UK. The exhibition is held every four years and had previously only been staged in continental Europe (Hanover,

Paris and Milan). The challenge for Birmingham and the NEC was, therefore, to introduce exhibitors and potential visitors not only to a new venue but also to a new host city and region. To meet this challenge, a big confidence-building task had to be undertaken in order to reassure both sets of visitors that this new location could, and would, provide an appropriate environment for a successful business event, and could also offer opportunities for enjoyable leisure and recreational experiences.

The exhibition itself occupied 18 of the NEC's 20 halls (a total of 200 000 square metres of display space plus a mass of associated storage space) for a total of 38 days (22 days for stand building, 8 open days, 8 breakdown days). It featured more than 1300 stands and welcomed more than 125 000 visits. Around 90% of visitors and exhibitors travelled from overseas, representing more than 140 countries.

A dedicated website (www.itma.com/what2do) was developed by the NEC Group through funding provided by Advantage West Midlands (AWM), the regional (economic) development agency – this website was linked to the main exhibition website. The website became operational in May 2003 and, following its launch, was actively promoted by e-mail to ITMA exhibitors and visitors as a source of information on entertainment, eating out, attractions, arts and sporting events. The information was supplied and updated by a range of sub-regional and regional agencies, to encourage visitors to extend their stay and to expand the range of activities they undertook in the region.

The website provided up-to-date information based on the diverse spread of regional destinations where visitors and exhibitors were going to be staying and spending money. The e-mail marketing campaign peaked in September 2003, promoting the site to 1300 exhibiting companies (with 20 000 exhibiting staff) and more than 8000 pre-registered exhibition visitors.

Statistics on usage of the site reveal the following:

- Hits to the entire site   277 025
- Average per day   945
- Page views   63 976
- Document views   35 372
- Average visit length   7.14 minutes

In addition to the website development, briefing meetings were held with tourism and leisure staff from the local authorities and municipalities across the West and East Midlands regions, to alert them to the nature of the ITMA event and its potential economic benefits through staying visitors, and to urge them to do all that they could to promote their own areas to these visitors and encourage extended visits. The first such briefing was held in January 2003, and this was followed by two further briefings in different parts of the English Midlands. A national-level briefing meeting also took place, at the Houses of Parliament, to inform government, airline, travel trade and embassy contacts about ITMA and to enlist their aid in educating exhibitors and visitors, unfamiliar with locations outside continental Europe, about this new UK destination.

The purpose of the ITMA 'Welcome Programme' was to reinforce the importance of ITMA as a landmark event which, if successful, would provide credible evidence to attract future peripatetic events of a similar scale to the NEC. The funding from AWM complemented the investment and event welcome infrastructure developed over the previous decade by the City of Birmingham and the NEC Group to welcome major events. Marketing Birmingham allocated £75 000 towards ITMA welcome activity, embracing city dressing, posters, welcome desks, media reception and briefings for the hospitality industry.

A consistent design approach was agreed with Marketing Birmingham to produce a set of welcome materials for use in both Birmingham and the other main locations in the region where ITMA visitors would be staying. The programme included:

- A major presentation to 150 hospitality, entertainment and transport suppliers from Birmingham, Solihull, Coventry, Worcestershire and South Warwickshire
- Dedicated promotions in conjunction with Black Country Tourism and Leicester Promotions to hoteliers
- Distribution of around 1000 information packs to hotels and attractions across the West and East Midlands
- Welcome posters displayed in Birmingham City Council information sites and at Birmingham International Airport
- Welcome badges worn by information, catering, cleaning and parking staff at the NEC.

Underpinning all of this activity, and key to its success in maximizing business extenders, was the partnership approach involving a myriad of influential regional players, including: NEC Group, Advantage West Midlands, Birmingham City Council, Birmingham Convention Bureau and Marketing Birmingham, MARCH (Midlands Association of Restaurants, Caterers and Hotelkeepers), regional destinations/attractions/hotels, and regional transport operators.

ITMA was assessed by consultants KPMG as delivering:

- Additional visitor spending in the West Midlands of £85 million
- Total UK additional spending estimated at £110 million
- Support for the equivalent of 1550 jobs in the region
- 47% of its visitors through Birmingham International Airport
- 45% of visitors reporting that they were 'likely' to return and bring friends/family to Birmingham in the future
- 25% of visitors reporting that they would spend time visiting other regions of the UK
- £25 million expenditure on accommodation (mainly hotels)
- £24 million expenditure on food and drink.

Review and Discussion Questions

1 You have been asked to develop a destination database of the kind outlined in the section on 'Destination Expertise'. Describe the steps you would take, the information sources you would use (i.e. how and where you will find the information needed), and the data access and retrieval systems required in order to store the requisite information and data on:
   (a) venues
   (b) transport, communications and accessibility
   (c) local economy and infrastructure.
2 'Destination selling is very different from selling a car or a washing machine.' Discuss the merits and accuracy of this statement, giving full reasons for the conclusions you draw.

3 Your destination has been shortlisted for consideration as the host destination of the 2010 congress of the International Association of Chiropodists and Podiatrists (fictitious as far as is known). The congress is held every two years and typically attracts around 1000 delegates from around the world, half of whom bring with them partners/accompanying persons. How would you approach the compilation, content and presentation of your bid? One of the underlying objectives of the bid is to maximize the economic impact of the event for your destination – outline separately how your bid, if successful, will meet this objective.

4 Compare and contrast the sales team structures for:
(a) a major purpose-built convention centre, and
(b) a hotel venue which is part of a national or international chain.
What are the key target markets for each, and what kinds of performance measures and incentives are in place? How effective are they?

Sources

Davidson, R (2003) *Making the Most of our Business Visitors*. Business Tourism Partnership (www.businesstourismpartnership.com)

Gartrell, RB (1994) *Destination Marketing for Convention and Visitor Bureaus*. Kendall Hunt Publishing Company

Meetings Industry Association (2005) *UK Conference Market Survey 2005*

Price, D and Ilvento, J (1999) *License to Sell*. Applied Business Communications, Inc.

Rogers, T (2003) *Conferences and Conventions: A Global Industry*. Butterworth-Heinemann

Chapter 10

Building Effective Marketing Partnerships

Summary of Chapter Contents

The marketing of conference destinations and venues requires substantial financial and human resources and expertise. Greater success can often be achieved by destinations and venues through working, not in isolation, but in partnership with others that may be similar in type or geographically close together.

This chapter, therefore, explores:

- The role of CVBs in forging partnerships at the destination level
- Membership recruitment and retention for DMOs
- Working with marketing consortia
- Maximizing the benefits of membership of trade associations
- Harnessing political support through effective lobbying

It includes Case Studies on:

- England's North-West Conference Bidding Unit
- BestCities Global Alliance
- 'National Meetings Week'

Learning Outcomes

On completion of this chapter, you should be able to:

- describe the ways in which a CVB or DMO provides leadership to a destination
- understand how a CVB or DMO stimulates collaboration, team working and partnerships across a destination
- understand the different types of membership structures for CVBs and DMOs
- identify strategies used by CVBs and DMOs to recruit and retain members
- describe the different kinds of marketing consortia available to venues, and the potential benefits from joining such consortia
- understand the role played by industry trade associations, and the membership benefits they offer
- appreciate the value of industry lobbying and representational activity, and give examples of how such activity is carried out

Introduction

Speaking at the 2004 convention of the British Association of Conference Destinations, Rick Taylor, Chief Executive of Cape Town Convention Bureau, said:

> *I've talked about the importance of working together. You cannot do it on your own. We came up with a single-minded proposition, going back 4–5 years, with a campaign under the strapline that 'Tourism is Everyone's Business'. We went into the communities, we went into business, we met the national government and just started talking about the economic impact of tourism, the job creation, all those great things.*

Rick Taylor was very keen to stress that Cape Town's rapidly growing success as a convention destination was being achieved through collaboration and partnership with the whole community. And this has been the experience of most other successful destinations and venues. Positioning and profiling a brand, creating recognition and trust, generating a predisposition to buy on the part of conference clients, are the result of developing appropriate strategies and campaigns as outlined in earlier chapters. They demand huge investments of time and resources in a world that, today, is often described as a 'global village'. Competition is intense and increases by the day.

At the same time marketing budgets, especially those deriving from public sector bodies, may be reducing rather than expanding. Yet there is still the challenge and requirement to produce ever-greater returns on the investments in marketing that are being made.

It is in this context that the benefits of working with key strategic partners become a major consideration for destination and venue marketers. This chapter will look at how such collaboration works in practical terms and will illustrate the kinds of advantages to be gained.

The role of CVBs in forging partnerships at the destination level

A fundamental requirement for the successful implementation of a destination marketing strategy is the ongoing collaboration of skilled, flexible and committed people who develop a strong team culture. A strong team culture is built upon mutual trust and respect, complementary strengths and abilities, an understanding of and commitment to goals that are larger than individual goals, with everyone pulling together to achieve extraordinary results. Success can be achieved when all partners are motivated, inspired and encouraged, working together with a commitment to clear and focused goals and shared values.

In destination terms, this means identifying where there is a need to co-operate but understanding where there is still a need to compete – and the balance required between the two. When managed effectively, working together and developing a real team culture can also become a learning experience, enabling partners to discover what they are already doing well but also, importantly, what they could do better.

Elizabeth Jeffries, Head of Jersey Tourism, speaking at the 1997 convention of the British Association of Conference Destinations, suggested that the development of a high-performing team is said to go through the following evolutionary process:

- **Forming**: as the team comes together, tasks, rules and methods are established
- **Storming**: conflict starts to emerge as people test the task, each other and the leader
- **Norming**: co-operation begins to develop with some cohesion and unity of purpose; agreed canons of behaviour emerge
- **Performing**: constructive work surges ahead; energy is focused.

Successful teambuilding could be summarized as follows:

- **Caring**: of each other; being respectful of different views; and being mutually encouraging
- **Daring**: being innovative and adventurous
- **Sharing**: of objectives, responsibility and one another's roles.

However, it is vital that the team is supported by appropriate training, development and education. This needs formal education, a commitment to ongoing training and development and, finally, organizational learning, i.e. organizations that will truly excel in the future will be those that discover how to tap people's commitment and capacity to learn at all levels within an organization, and do not simply rely on a grand strategy being handed down from the top. Teams must learn also how to harness and nurture leadership at all levels, both bottom-up and top-down, empowering individuals and the whole team to take responsibility for the achievement of the team's goals, both in principle and in practice.

A convention and visitor bureau (CVB) or destination marketing organization (DMO) needs to offer leadership to the destination and create a sense of cohesion within that destination. In doing so, clients will feel that they are dealing with a single, united entity where the various suppliers are seen to be co-operating fully with one another to ensure the success of the clients' events. In practical terms, this could mean, for example, that the CVB will discuss accommodation rates being offered by a number of hotels and seek their commitment to a set of rates that can then be guaranteed to the client as part of the event bidding process, even though the event itself may be several years ahead. It might be, as in the case of Vancouver's taxi drivers described in Chapter 2, that the CVB or DMO will put in place a destination training programme to drive up standards and enhance the overall quality of the destination product.

The essence of CVBs and DMOs is that they bring together, under a common umbrella, a variety of venues and other suppliers for collaborative marketing activity – venues and suppliers that, at another level, might see themselves in direct competition with one another. They can unite the public and private sectors in partnerships across a city or local community, often to a degree that is rarely replicated in other business sectors. The most successful partnerships are those that develop a real team ethos but also continue to recognize and respect the strengths and needs of the individual team members, reflecting the unique features of each while, at the same time, portraying them as components of a greater whole: the destination itself.

The CVB can fulfil an important communications role in ensuring that venues, visitor attractions, restaurants, retail outlets, transport operators, the local municipality and the wider business community are all aware that a major convention is coming to town. Each of these can then prepare their products and services accordingly, maximizing the economic opportunities afforded by the event but also tailoring these in a way that is personalized to the client and to the event participants. These latter will, in turn, be given the feeling that the whole destination is aware of their event and is working together to make them feel welcome and at home. For convention delegates and attendees, anticipation of an enjoyable and worthwhile event will be increased if they arrive in a city and see welcome banners profiling the event, experience taxi rides with drivers who are informed and able to initiate friendly conversations and make specific reference to the convention, and meet hotel reception staff who have been briefed on the importance of the convention and, as a consequence, treat the delegates as VIPs.

The CVB is probably the only destination body able to fulfil this vital co-ordinating role, combining its strengths as a neutral, impartial body with its detailed knowledge of the network of destination suppliers to create a true destination partnership and an image of a properly co-ordinated destination. Where the CVB fails to achieve such collaboration, client perceptions are of a weakened or non-existent destination brand, on the one hand, while their task of organizing a successful event is made so much harder, on the other, because there is no one pulling everything together on behalf of the destination, for the benefit of the client.

Scott Taylor, chief executive of Glasgow City Marketing Bureau (www.seeglasgow. com), describes destination partnership opportunities in terms of 'linkages'. Commenting specifically for this book (October 2005), he expressed his views in the following terms:

> *Conventions across almost every sector provide opportunities that are rarely fully exploited. From conventions and conferences come study visits, research profile opportunities, engagement with local economic development teams for inward investment, and business expansion through networking. To win a congress or convention for a city isn't good enough on its own. It is not good use of a city's resources if there is a collective failure to maximize the significant business opportunities afforded. It requires team-working, a 'can-do' attitude, and a hunger on the part of city or destination agencies to explore avenues outside the norm. Conventions are a form of inward investment by any other name. If a city were to secure a new manufacturing plant, the economic agencies would be all over it like a rash. It's critical to wake up to the linkages that discretionary business tourism provides.*

A truly innovative example of destination partnership marketing is to be found in the north-west region of England, where a regional bidding unit has been established to research and secure national, European and international conventions and meetings for the various regional players. This is described in detail as Case Study 10.1, which is presented at the end of the chapter.

Membership recruitment and retention for DMOs

The majority of convention and visitor bureaux and destination marketing or management organizations operate as membership bodies, although in some cases the term 'industry partners' instead of 'members' is coming into vogue, usually describing an even closer relationship between the CVB and the partner organization. With some destinations, membership is defined in relatively narrow terms and will just encompass a destination's conference/convention venues, hotels and perhaps audio-visual suppliers. In other instances, membership is extended to a much broader section of the business community, including: transport companies, retailers, visitor attractions, restaurants, professional conference organizers, even banks and utility companies.

Whichever type of membership structure is adopted, the challenge is always to recruit and retain the members because they provide a key income stream for the DMO, sometimes the largest single income stream. Managing and satisfying a potentially diverse membership is never easy, as each member will come with different needs and expectations. It is increasingly the case that membership of a DMO must demonstrate 'bottom line' business or commercial benefits (i.e. generate new business and revenue for members), rather than simply offer networking, education or accreditation benefits to members. However, as Walters (2005: 163) writes: 'Most CVBs don't want members unless they can help the member to secure business. No one wants to damage the CVB's reputation in the community by signing on companies that will not be helped by bureau membership and that might disparage the bureau at renewal time if they thought they did not receive the services promised.'

Effective recruitment strategies demand good quality promotional materials or 'collateral' (both printed literature and electronic information) that sets out clearly the services to be provided by the DMO/CVB, and quantify the costs and benefits of membership. Such materials should not over-state the benefits because a member who has joined with unrealistic expectations will almost certainly be disappointed and will not renew membership – nonetheless, promotional materials need to be positive and upbeat. It is always worth including quotations from existing members or peers on what they have gained from being a member. There may be opportunities to invite potential members as guests to DMO events and activities, using these as appetizers to give these likely recruits an insight into, and experience of, membership. Special receptions or presentations can be organized where potential recruits meet the DMO's Board members and executive team. Most DMOs have a dedicated 'membership services team' with both a sales role (to sell membership to new members) and a servicing role (ensuring effective communications with, and care for, all members).

Retention of members is, in part, about delivering good commercial benefits to members. But it is also about making them feel valued and important, and this in turn links back to the development and maintenance of accurate member databases. It is vital that members receive regular and appropriate communications from the DMO, and it is crucial that the data held on members is comprehensive and up-to-date – mis-spelling a member's name, holding a wrong e-mail address, omitting them from distribution lists, may all be relatively small mistakes in themselves but they invariably give a member the impression that he is not valued and that the DMO is not a professional organization.

Retention is a 12-months-of-the-year task. It is hard work. It requires attention to detail. It needs a listening ear. Walters (2005: 165) suggests that:

a membership services person should make six to ten calls a day, especially to members who do not seem to be participating. This person should ask questions such as whether they are getting the CVB's mail and leads, whether their brochures are at the local visitor centre, and whether they plan to attend an upcoming mixer or other event. At renewal time, CVBs should send a letter with the invoice, stress that renewal is optional, and offer to meet with the contact person if they have any doubts about renewing. This is especially important if the contact person has changed and the new person receiving the mail is not sure what the bureau is or why the firm is even a member.

Working with marketing consortia

It is difficult, and certainly very expensive, for an individual conference venue to market itself effectively by operating on its own. Venues seeking to establish a market presence must contend with factors such as the scale of the competition, the substantial costs of marketing, and the predisposition of buyers to buy 'location' first.

It is for these reasons that most venues work in partnership with the destination in which they are located to create awareness and to stimulate enquiries from potential clients. The venues build links with the appropriate destination marketing organization, be this a convention and visitor bureau or conference office, an area or regional tourist board, or a national tourism organization. Many venues are also members of marketing consortia (groupings of similar properties interested in the same types of clients), which give them a higher market profile and through which they engage in collaborative marketing activities. Consortia can also provide tangible business benefits such as bulk purchasing discounts, networking, benchmarking and training. Belonging to a consortium can also give a venue credibility in the eyes of the buyer. Examples of major consortia operating in the conference industry include:

- **Hotel groups** such as Hilton, Accor, Six Continents, Marriott, Starwood Hotels & Resorts, Sol Melia, Intercontinental and Holiday Inn. These are not strictly consortia as they are groups of hotels under common ownership and management systems. Most, if not all, have central reservation and marketing departments that undertake national and international marketing campaigns and which control the promotional activities of the individual properties to a greater or lesser degree. Even so, the majority of hotels within these chains are also allowed some discretion and budget to engage in their own marketing campaigns, for which the broad strategy and promotional materials are determined by head office. Over recent years, all of the large chains have developed their own branded conference products.
- **Best Western** claims to be the world's largest global hotel brand, established for more than 50 years, with over 4100 independently owned and operated hotels in membership worldwide (covering 80 countries). It is a non-profit-making organization whose sole purpose is to enhance the success and profitability of its member hotels. It has reservations centres in four countries with fully automated links to global distribution systems. Its recruitment brochure claims that 'Best Western brand markets to, and attracts, a bigger universe of customers than any single property on its own could ever hope to reach'. For the conference and meetings market, 'Best Western First Place' is the consortium's venue sourcing service. Best Western also offers joint marketing opportunities for its members, such as a presence at trade shows like 'International Confex'. For more information see: www.bestwestern.com.
- **Unique Venues** is a grouping of more than 7000 non-traditional meeting facilities and function rooms in the United States, Canada and the United Kingdom: colleges, universities, museums, mansions, cinemas or movie theatres, conference centres, entertainment venues, cruise ships, restaurants, business centres and others. In this case, the common theme is the individuality or uniqueness of the venues involved, with a particular focus on their ambience, memorability, flexibility, technology and affordability. Unique Venues has administrative offices in Colorado, Pennsylvania and South Carolina (USA). Further details can be accessed via: www.uniquevenues.org.

- **Conference Centres of Excellence (CCE)** is Britain's largest consortium of dedicated, specialist conference and training venues, with some 41 such venues in membership (as at March 2006). It was formed in 1992, with objectives to:
  - undertake joint marketing through pooling marketing resources
  - share PR activity designed to enhance the image of management centres in membership
  - investigate opportunities to market the centres in mainland Europe
  - share information and expertise.
- One of the main aims of CCE has been to promote and market the unique benefits of conference venues that offer first-class facilities and professional standards (making comparison with other venues that do not dedicate staff or facilities to the business conference, meeting or training sector). Members are required to meet certain minimum criteria, which include 'actively seeking to attract conference, meeting or training events as their main Monday–Friday source of business' and to 'embrace and maintain the *Hospitality Assured Meetings* accreditation'. Criteria are also laid down to cover the standard of conference rooms, bedrooms and other facilities provided. They are also expected to participate in the consortium's booking referral system and to promote its hotline 'One Call'. Would-be member venues are required to submit to inspection by the CCE's membership committee before being accepted into membership.
- Whilst users of the CCE venues are guaranteed to receive excellent service in quality surroundings, the individual nature of the member properties offers contrasting atmospheres ranging from country houses in beautiful settings to purpose-built centres often attached to academia. Further information: www.cceonline.co.uk (tel: +44 (0)1306 886900).
- **Historic Conference Centres of Europe** is a network of conference centres located in historic buildings, spanning the length and breadth of Europe. As at September 2005, 22 centres were members of the network, which has administrative offices in Amsterdam. HCCE's promotional material claims that 'there is nothing standardized about these conference centres. Each facility has a unique architectural heritage, an attractive location and a management approach based on personal service.' Further details from: www.hcce.com (tel: +31 (0)20 618 95 40).

The BestCities Global Alliance is, on the other hand, a marketing consortium for DMOs rather than venues. The role and activities of BestCities are set out fully in Case Study 10.2, which is presented at the end of the chapter.

Maximizing the benefits of membership of trade associations

There are a number of trade associations in the conference industry, some operating at a national level, others at a continental or truly international level. Many cater for a particular niche in the market (the Destination Marketing Association International, the European Federation of Conference Towns, the Association Internationale des Palais de Congrès, for example) while a few aim to attract a wide variety of members (such as the International Congress and Convention Association, or the UK's Meetings Industry Association).

Boléat (2003: 1) defines trade associations in the following terms: 'Trade associations provide representative and other collective services to businesses, generally in a specific sector, with common interests. There are a number of different types of association. At the margin, trade associations overlap with other industry bodies.' He describes their role as a representative body in 'putting forward the collective position of members, generally to government departments and agencies and regulators, but also to the media and to other opinion formers'. He adds that 'many associations also provide other services such as industry statistics, general market information, training, conferences and exhibitions'.

It can be seen from this description that trade associations are not primarily marketing entities, although it is often the case that members join specifically in the expectation of gaining new business through their membership. However, some associations do provide direct sales and marketing opportunities to their members through the organization of stands at exhibitions (and may even organize the exhibitions themselves), by forwarding on business leads, by maintaining databases of clients or buyers that can be accessed by their members as a unique membership benefit. Many associations produce newsletters and issue press releases to highlight the activities and services of their members, thus giving good PR exposure.

Trade associations can also provide indirect marketing benefits to their members, as membership can confer a sense of accreditation on members, particularly if a rigorous new member recruitment policy is in force requiring potential members to meet certain quality or commercial criteria before being granted membership. Members are then entitled to display the association's logo on their stationery and promotional material, and it is anticipated that this will give buyers confidence that they are dealing with a reputable organization that will perform to certain minimum standards.

Individuals who get fully involved with the running of a trade association may progress to becoming one of its officers, serving as chair or president or treasurer, for example. While this can give invaluable experience to the individual and enhance their own career prospects, the venue or destination that they represent can also benefit through 'association' – one of their employees becomes a recognized figure in the trade association and in the wider conference industry and the exposure that they receive can also reflect positively on their employing organization.

A survey into associations' 'Membership Recruitment and Retention in Europe in 2005', undertaken as a joint initiative between IMEX (www.imex-frankfurt.com), The Association Gateway and Resources for Associations (www.associationgateway.org), found that successful associations 'focus clearly on delivering good business networking opportunities, a relevant education programme and up-to-date industry news and best practice guidance. Other factors cited as important for member satisfaction were sound strategic planning, well-delivered services and professional management.'

Hendrie (2005) suggests that people join trade associations for 'leadership, innovation, representation and "bang for our buck"'. He goes on to outline some of the challenges facing trade associations, as well as the recipe for success:

We recognize what trade associations face: competition for member dues, sensitive community, regional and national issues, a tight economy, internal and external politics, restrictive practices, unenlightened management and directors, and perhaps the worst enemy … ennui. But it all comes back to worth! The successful organizations are not static. They continually assess their resources, realign the process, people, products and services to maximize value. Regularly, they survey their constituency, evaluating satisfaction and seeking input. This also includes their allied members and the organization's staff. Communication is constant, reliable and germane. They are always connected, imaginative and decisive, recognizing that flexibility and adaptability make for progress. But it all starts with knowing their stakeholders ... their needs, their aspirations and their expectations. Then they deliver like crazy.

While it would be a mistake for a venue or a DMO to join a trade association solely for the purpose of business generation, it is undoubtedly the case that many trade associations can and do offer a range of direct and indirect commercial development benefits. To take full advantage of these, trade association members need to participate actively in the opportunities on offer, and work hard to maximize the benefits of their membership. Members who sit passively at their own workstations expecting business to fall into their laps simply because they have joined a trade association are likely to be severely disappointed.

Harnessing political support through effective lobbying

The kinds of local, national and international partnerships and consortia outlined in this chapter offer a range of examples and models for emulation or adaptation. However, none of these replaces the complementary need for activity that will raise overall understanding of, and support for, the conference and business events sector. Ours is still, as we have seen in Chapter 1, a young industry, one that is all too frequently misunderstood and under-recognized by the political and business communities. It is vital that this situation is addressed urgently in order to ensure that support structures, educational and career frameworks, product investment, funding for marketing, political support in bidding for major international events, for example, are provided at levels commensurate with those given to other industry sectors. Changes and improvements will only be achieved through professional lobbying and representational activity by the industry itself, and these need to be undertaken at both international and national levels.

Some worthwhile initiatives are already under way. At an international level, for example, the Joint Meetings Industry Council (JMIC – www.themeetingsindustry.org) has launched its 'Power and Profile' campaign as a way of raising the profile of the meetings industry and of those who work in it. The JMIC membership includes leading associations from the meetings, incentives, conventions and exhibitions (MICE) segments: Meeting Professionals International (MPI), Association Internationale des Palais de Congrès (AIPC), the Society of Incentive & Travel Executives (SITE), the European Federation of Conference Towns (EFCT), the International Association of Professional Congress Organizers (IAPCO), the International Congress & Convention Association (ICCA), Association Internationale des Villes Francophones de Congrès (AIVFC) and the Confederation of Congress and Events Organizing Bodies (COCAL).

JMIC's 'Power and Profile' campaign was still being finalized at the time of writing (July 2005), but their own documentation stated:

> *The idea of this program is that by improving community and governmental awareness of the importance of what we do, and the benefits it creates for our communities, we'll all be in a much better position to influence decisions that affect our future.*

> *The basis of the program is that awareness begins in our own individual communities, and that is where a program of activities such as these must be carried out. It is here that each of us has the connections, the impacts and the specific information required to make a difference in how both governments and the public see us, and to create better awareness of the benefits we generate.*
>
> *With this approach, we believe the best role for an organization like JMIC is to support your individual efforts by providing some of the resources necessary to make it easier to participate and creating a thematic framework to link all these individual efforts together and make them even more effective.*

JMIC envisaged three elements to the programme:

- Publication of a guidebook on community and government relations. This included a number of templates for articles, advertisements and presentations designed for easy adaptation
- Development of an 'International Meetings Industry Week' as a way of creating a focus for activities world-wide that feature the meetings industry and the benefits it creates
- Collection and dissemination of best practice ideas and activities through a dedicated website
- Linked to this will be the launch of special 'Power and Profile' awards to recognize the accomplishments of individuals from across the international meetings and business events industry.

'At the same time, JMIC would be seeking new ways to interact with international media, business organizations and government in promoting the overall meetings industry message, for example creating forums where local politicians can explore issues and concerns about the industry.' Although the 'Power and Profile' campaign is still in the early stages, its successful development and fulfilment will do much to spread the word about our great industry and lever additional resources and recognition for it.

An example of an initiative that has been under way for several years and has established a track record of significant achievement can be found in the UK. The Business Tourism Partnership (BTP – www.businesstourismpartnership.com) was formed in 1999 by the leading industry trade associations and national tourist boards (18 bodies in total as at July 2005), supported by key government departments. The mission of the BTP is:

> *To lead the way in supporting a competitive, high quality and more profitable business tourism sector in Britain.*

One of its important roles is to bring together most of the key industry players in order to discuss contemporary issues and to seek a common and united position on these, so as to speak on them with one voice. Other important activities include: presentations to politicians and to leading civil servants; meetings with other related industry organizations; identification of industry research needs; compilation and dissemination of briefing documents and more substantial reports; circulation of regular media releases; and maintenance of a BTP website.

There is no doubt that the BTP has succeeded in creating a much higher level of awareness of the business tourism and business events sector among national politicians in the UK. Translating such awareness into appropriate and effective support structures is an ongoing task, but at least the communications networks are now in place to facilitate progress to such an objective.

The UK also has an annual 'National Meetings Week', a specific campaign of the kind envisaged by JMIC, and this is detailed as Case Study 10.3, presented below.

Summary

This chapter has stressed the importance, for both destinations and venues, of exploring the myriad opportunities for building marketing partnerships with like-minded organizations and with destinations and venues having similar product characteristics. It is undeniably the case that, in a world where more than 200 countries are now competing aggressively for their share of the conference and business events 'cake', competition is tough and will only get tougher. To be successful by working in isolation, 'doing your own thing', is extremely difficult and certainly very expensive. Collaborative marketing ventures should be investigated, not only because they can offer better returns and prove a more cost effective way of spending finite budgets, but also because they frequently bring with them other benefits, such as the creation of information networks and the sharing of best practice, as experienced by the members of the BestCities Global Alliance.

As an industry there is also a need, at local, regional, national and international levels, to establish a higher profile for, and better understanding of, the many benefits to the world community brought about through meetings, conventions and business events. A cohesive representative voice for the sector is a 'must' if it is to grow and flourish, and gain its deserved share of political, economic and social support.

Case Study 10.1

England's North-West Conference Bidding Unit

This case study provides an example of a different form of marketing partnership, offering an approach that is original and may be unique. It demonstrates the benefits of collaborative marketing for a number of destinations that, at one level, could be seen as competitors but which have recognized that there is more to be gained from working in partnership with their geographical neighbours.

England's North-West Region

This region stretches from the Scottish border down to the Cheshire plain, and includes such renowned tourism attractions as the Lake District, Blackpool, Southport and Chester, plus the cosmopolitan cities of Manchester and Liverpool. In terms of their conference and convention product, the key features are:

- **Cumbria and the Lake District**: Country-house hotels, independently owned hotels, training centres and tourist attractions with meetings facilities typify the range of venues. Many are in stunning rural and lakeside locations and can frequently offer outdoor pursuits activities to occupy delegates in their free time, or perhaps as part of a teambuilding programme. Many of the events are relatively small in terms of delegate numbers (typically fewer than 100 delegates), but will often be residential providing an opportunity for participants to focus on the business in hand free from the usual distractions and pressures.
- **Blackpool and Lancashire**: Blackpool and, to a lesser degree, Morecambe are much more interested in the bigger 'town' conferences staged by trade unions, political parties, associations and voluntary organizations. They have an established track record in staging many

high profile conferences, and the impending investment in Blackpool to transform it into the 'Las Vegas' of the North-West can only contribute further to its success in winning more convention business. Lancashire has a mix of unique venues, including historic houses, castles, football stadia, chain hotels and even high-capacity venues such as Preston Guildhall.

- **Manchester**: Manchester is especially strong in its hotel product, with many of the leading hotel chains now represented in the city, all with substantial meetings facilities. It is also well-known for its academic venues, and larger purpose-built venues based around its 'convention quarter'. Venues such as the Manchester International Conference Centre, Bridgewater Hall and G-Mex are enabling Manchester to compete aggressively for international association conventions, national association conferences, and corporate meetings. The proximity of Manchester International Airport, providing access to over 200 destinations world-wide, is also key to attracting more of the lucrative international meetings business to the city.
- **Liverpool**: Like Manchester, Liverpool too is witnessing huge investments in its hotels and in the overall infrastructure necessary to host business tourism events. The investment programme will continue to gather pace as the city gears up to 2008, when it becomes the 'European Capital of Culture', and this same year will see the completion of the Liverpool Arena and Convention Centre, the city's first purpose-built conference centre. The burgeoning provision of low cost airline routes from Liverpool John Lennon Airport is also giving greater access into mainland Europe. **Southport**, a few miles up the coast from cosmopolitan Liverpool, was born as an elegant Victorian seaside resort. It too has invested heavily in its attractions, hotels and facilities, making it a regular choice for association and trade union conferences, which take over the Southport Theatre and Floral Hall complex. It also lays claim to being 'England's Golfing Capital', with a number of superb links courses having hosted major championships, including The Open Championship.
- **Cheshire and Warrington**: Cheshire and Warrington boast a variety of quality hotels, conference and training centres, and a myriad of unusual venues (Chester Racecourse, Blue Planet Aquarium, Jodrell Bank, Chester Zoo, for example), in the main catering for the corporate meetings and smaller association conference market. Easy accessibility to Manchester and Liverpool airports and to the national motorway network are significant advantages in enabling the area to attract business from around Britain and from further afield.

Formation of a Regional Conference Bidding Unit

The five sub-regions described above receive some tourism funding from the North-West Development Agency (NWDA), one of nine such bodies established by central government to oversee the economic development and regeneration of the English regions. The sub-regions contribute to a regional tourism development strategy for 'England's North-West', and a key objective of the strategy is to maximize equal partnership between the public, private and voluntary sectors.

In 2004 the decision was taken to establish a Regional Conference Bidding Unit with the aim of generating £20 million of economic benefit by attracting more association convention business to England's North-West. The initiative was spearheaded by Marketing Manchester, the body responsible for tourism development and marketing for the Manchester sub-region, in association with the Mersey Partnership, the body fulfilling a similar role for the Liverpool and Merseyside sub-region, together with active support from the other sub-regions detailed above. In addition, funding was also provided by NWDA, giving a total operational budget of £600 000 for an initial 3-year period. This enabled a Bidding Unit team of seven to be recruited: a Unit manager, a UK sales manager, a European sales manager (based in France), a bid co-ordinator and three researchers. Two of the researchers are full-time and are based at the offices of Marketing Manchester – the other works two days per week and is 'in kind' support from the Mersey Partnership. In July 2005 the Bidding Unit established a presence in the United States, with Manchester's Gateway marketing manager working one day a week in order to develop contacts with US-based associations.

The specific aims of the Bidding Unit are to:

- Generate additional revenue for the region by increasing the number of international meetings held
- Further enhance Manchester and Liverpool's profile as international conference destinations in the North-West
- Maximize opportunities for international conferences in the other North-West sub-regions
- Maximize the potential of the North-West for conference extenders and partner programmes.

The Bidding Unit is not intended to replace the work already being done by the sub-regions in bidding for events, but rather to complement and extend this, especially in respect of European and international events. The sub-regions are still expected to provide their own subvention funding, and can opt to retain their own ambassador programmes, where these exist, although Marketing Manchester's ambassador programme has been subsumed into the work of the Bidding Unit. The Bidding Unit seeks to enhance the existing work of the sub-regions by providing:

- Bid preparation
- Civic letters of support
- Hosting inspection visits
- Guidance on civic funding and subvention
- Unbiased venue sourcing
- Support materials
- Ideas for social events and partner programmes
- Introductions to professional conference organizers (PCOs)
- An accommodation booking service.

The bidding process

The initial phase of work focuses on proactive research to identify potential association conferences and conventions. The Unit seeks particularly to identify events that meet the ICCA criteria for inclusion in the ICCA cities' rankings, i.e.

- have a minimum of 50 delegates
- be held on a regular basis and rotate around the world.

If the event requires subvention (financial or in-kind support), the Unit needs to be able to demonstrate that there will be a return on investment of at least 15%. Events should ideally have an economic impact of at least £600 000, and there would need to be a venue in the North-West region able to accommodate the event successfully.

'Hot' leads are passed to either the UK or the European sales manager, who will then meet the client to determine their conference specification in more detail. Following this meeting, the sales manager forwards a detailed event specification to the bid co-ordinator, who in turn passes this on to the appropriate sub-region(s) as an RFP (request for proposal) – the selection of sub-region(s) being determined by the client's requirements. The proposal submitted by the sub-region is discussed with the client by the sales manager before a detailed bid document is assembled by the Unit's bid co-ordinator. This bid document is passed on to the client by the sales manager. The content of the document is similar to other bid documents described in Chapter 9. There is always a paper version of the bid, and on occasions a PDF version is also supplied. The Bidding Unit prepares bid documents on behalf of all the sub-regions, but each has a different appearance and imagery in order to maintain the individuality of the sub-regions (although the actual content is essentially the same). Documents are prepared in Quark, colour-printed and wire-bound, costing around £6.50 per document. The Unit can produce a full bid within a 48-hour turnround time.

Impact of the Bidding Unit

In the first six months of activity, the Unit produced 22 bid documents and won seven bids with an estimated economic impact of £1.6 million. Forty-one enquiries were generated with a total economic benefit of over £39 million. The Unit established a database with more than 3000 contacts. A website for the Unit went live in March 2005 (www.nwcbu.org.uk), and purpose-designed enquiry handling software came into full effect in Summer 2005. Interestingly, two of the successful seven bids in the first six months of operation were for Chester, even though, when the Unit was being established, it was anticipated that there would be no 'wins' for destinations other than Manchester and Liverpool until year three.

Other English regions are now considering the creation of their own regional bidding unit.

Case Study 10.2

BestCities Global Alliance

The BestCities Global Alliance (known as BestCities.net until August 2005 – www.bestcities.net) was formed in 2000 and comprises the convention bureaux of eight cities: Cape Town, Copenhagen, Dubai, Edinburgh, Melbourne, San Juan, Singapore and Vancouver. The Alliance was launched with the notion that convention bureaux could learn from strategies successfully practised in other industries: the airline industry, financial institutions and automotive manufacturing all provide examples of the formation of global alliances which have become an essential business strategy for the long term.

The Vision for BestCities is 'to be recognized globally for being innovative and setting and delivering the world's best convention bureau practices for the meetings industry'. The BestCities Mission Statement says that it 'will deliver the world's best service experience for meetings planners and will help its partners earn more business as a result'.

The primary objectives of BestCities are:

- to access and lever resources through an exclusive, partner-based network of convention bureaux with a common purpose; these resources include financial, new markets and organizational expertise
- to facilitate the exchange of best practices, ideas and knowledge, market intelligence and the development of new convention bureau programmes among the partners
- to share costs for joint activities of collective benefit, particularly in the areas of sales, research and marketing

- to gain a competitive advantage by developing an alliance brand that raises the profile and increases the exposure for all partners as key players in the international congress market.

Organizationally, the Alliance is based on goodwill among its partners and works to by-laws, operational policies, client service standards and a code of practice. It has a Board of Directors (comprising chief executives of the member bureaux), which provides overall strategic direction and approves major policies; an Operations Group to manage the running of the Alliance; Sales, Marketing and Servicing Groups; and a general manager based in Copenhagen.

The Alliance promises clients 'quality, expertise and professionalism', with guaranteed service levels built around reliability, assurance, innovation, empathy and responsiveness, all underpinned by a Service Charter. All members of the Alliance are required to adhere to some 35 service standards agreed between the members. The lack of standards within the convention bureau environment (see also Chapter 11) can cause frustration for both buyers and suppliers. The essence of BestCities, according to Paul Vallee, Executive Vice-President of Tourism Vancouver (the Greater Vancouver Convention and Visitors Bureau), is 'the Service Charter and the 35 client service standards that outline the commitment made by the partners to deliver exceptional service'. Client satisfaction levels had reached 92% by 2005.

The service standards are organized into five main categories:

1 Destination expertise
   (a) Dedicated meeting planner website
   (b) Dedicated meeting planners' guide
   (c) Request for proposals (RFPs) that serve as a brief for site selection
   (d) Expertise on local products and services
   (e) Facilitation of educational visits (on application)
   (f) Access to local industry and government contacts
   (g) Itinerary planning and suggestions
2 Bid assistance
   (a) Detailed event research using the BestCities global network to ensure a thorough knowledge of the bid requirements
   (b) Customized bid strategies
   (c) Customized bid document
   (d) Bid presentation support, e.g. promotional stands, bid presentations, promotional literature (on application)
   (e) Provision of audio-visual aids, e.g. multimedia, video, slides
   (f) Venue and accommodation selection and recommendations
   (g) Secure provisional room and venue allocations
   (h) Access to event budgeting and financial planning services
   (i) Site inspection support
   (j) Local government and industry liaison
   (k) Co-ordination of letters of support
   (l) Bid promotion, e.g. mailings, PR assistance (on application)
3 Convention planning
   (a) Site inspections of local venues, accommodation and infrastructure (on application)
   (b) The appointment of a professional conference organizer (PCO) if required
   (c) Introductions to local industry and government
   (d) Development of social programmes
   (e) Development of pre-convention and post-convention tour programmes
   (f) The selection of other products and services relevant to the event

4 Building attendance (i.e. maximizing the number of delegates/attendees at an event)
   (a) Access to promotional collateral (some items at cost), i.e. videos, slides, brochures
   (b) Assistance in developing recruitment strategies
   (c) Global network through BestCities partner locations
   (d) Destination weblinks to a conference registration website
5 On-site event servicing and post-event support
   (a) Complimentary visitor guides for delegates
   (b) Visitor Information booths for events over 1000 delegates
   (c) Information listings on local services, e.g. restaurants, entertainment and shopping
   (d) Post-event debrief to gain client feedback on how effectively the city facilitated the conference.

A Client Advisory Board reviews the standards on an annual basis. Each year the partners (members) conduct a self-assessment on where they stand with their service practices. The evaluation is shared with other members and areas of improvement are identified and discussed.

The Alliance is planning to establish joint service development programmes and joint certification of its members. Each partner will align its own corporate objectives with those of the Alliance and establish the necessary processes so that all partners will serve clients in the same way.

The BestCities Global Alliance works to the following premises:

- Alliances are *not*:
   ○ A single policy applied to all members
   ○ A signed document without implementation plans
   ○ A plan to create monopolies
   ○ An end to competition
- But they *are* built for the customer:
   ○ They provide convenient global access
   ○ They offer world-wide status and privileges
   ○ They are designed to generate more customers for the members
   ○ They are useful as a means of exploring synergies in offering consistent service.

Members of BestCities have identified a number of other benefits and opportunities arising from the Alliance:

- It maximizes their return on investment in the international markets: by working together members achieve greater market penetration.
- It provides cost efficiencies: each $1 invested gives a return equivalent to $8.
- It addresses marketplace needs by setting standards of service.
- It gives positive brand association, bringing together top cities and bureaux.
- It offers opportunities to learn from other members and share best practice.

The primary business focus is on conventions and congresses of international associations with a minimum of 300 delegates. The secondary focus is on international corporate meetings of 100-plus delegates. Additionally there is a focus on meetings that have already been held in one or more Alliance member destinations.

Members engage in cross-promotions which include the placing of BestCities advertisements in each of their destination guides, as well as advertisements from the partner destinations. The BestCities logo is used on all partners' websites, and the business cards used by employees of the respective bureaux all contain the BestCities logo, tailored to match the colour scheme of each bureau. Cross-promotions are estimated to be worth US$20 million a year. In the three years 2002–2005, more than 400 business leads were exchanged between members. Vancouver, in 2004, attributed three out of 11 successful international bids to BestCities, namely:

- International Harm Reduction Association – 1500 delegates generating 3700 room nights
- International Society of Ultrasound in Obstetrics & Gynaecology – 1500 delegates and 3000 room nights
- World Confederation for Physical Therapy – 3000 delegates and 10 900 room nights.

One of the unique features of the Alliance is in bringing together destinations from five continents. As each member is active in targeting international convention business, the Alliance recognizes and seeks to exploit the rotational nature of many international events, which move from continent to continent according to a pre-determined cycle. But this does not mean that Alliance members do not participate in marketing initiatives undertaken by their own countries. In fact, at industry trade exhibitions, for example, Alliance members normally share stands with their national marketing organizations (e.g. Edinburgh exhibiting as part of the VisitScotland stand, Melbourne on the Australia stand, etc.), but there will sometimes be a discrete booth for BestCities providing them with additional exposure to visitors.

While each of the destinations represented in the Alliance is geographically diverse, their adherence to a common set of service standards makes it easy for clients to compare information and to know what they may expect from the destination. The BestCities promotional literature states that all of the members offer:

- Easy access from all major airports
- Natural beauty
- Cleanliness and comfort
- Good friendly service
- Safety and security
- Pedestrian-friendly city centres
- Historical and cultural depth
- Strong scientific and research environments
- High standard of living.

BestCities is dependent upon the commitment made by each of its members, and it strives hard to engender a sense of ownership. This means that members are not simply required to pay an annual fee but must also participate in one to two meetings a year, as well as in monthly conference calls among peer groups, e.g. calls between chief executives of the bureaux to discuss strategic issues, calls between sales staff to discuss the referral of leads and enquiries.

The goal of BestCities is to become a preferred source for clients seeking potential meeting destinations, so that the BestCities brand will be widely recognized as a standard for trustworthy convention bureaux and desirable destinations.

Commenting on his time as Chair of the Alliance for three years, Paul Vallee says (*DMO World*, Issue 2, January 2005): 'A key learning for me has been to understand what it takes to make a strategic alliance successful. In this industry, we are constantly working together but the complexities of working with varying cultures, attitudes, conditions and needs is beyond other partnerships that I have been involved with. I find it fascinating that such a diverse group can come together with a common purpose and do so without politics. Perhaps it is the distance from one another that keeps us close?'

The current BestCities Chair (Steen Jakobsen, Director, Business Development and Industry Relations, Wonderful Copenhagen) predicts: 'In the future we will be looking to add new partners in North America, South America, South/East Europe and Central/North Asia to increase the impact of the Alliance in the marketplace and to offer an even broader geographic and cultural appeal to our clients.'

Case Study 10.3

'National Meetings Week'

'National Meetings Week' (NMW – www.nationalmeetingsweek.co.uk) has been staged in the UK since 2001 and is organized by CAT Publications Ltd, with support from major conference sector trade associations. In 2005 such support was enhanced by inclusion of a number of industry partners (major venues, convention bureaux and intermediary companies).

The objectives of NMW are:

- To promote understanding of the financial value of the conference and events industry to the exchequer
- To promote the effectiveness of meetings and events to the business community as a business tool, staff motivator and communications medium
- To promote awareness of the meetings and events industry outside of it.

In 2004, NMW achieved 43 radio interviews, coverage in the regional press across the UK, coverage in the national press and in the business press. Linked with NMW is a charity ('Meeting Needs') designed to raise money for worthy causes – in 2004 over £15 000 was raised.

The specific objectives for the 2005 NMW campaign (held 3–7 October 2005) were to:

- Create a central voice for the meetings industry
- Raise awareness of NMW to a national and international audience
- Be seen as leading the campaign in Europe
- Raise awareness in both trade and business press of the UK meetings industry
- Encourage the industry to participate in events/initiatives
- Engage the industry in further debate and discussion
- Raise funds for 'Meeting Needs'.

Key audiences were identified as: the conference and meetings industry, stakeholders, the business community, students and graduates, local and national government. The key messages to be disseminated through NMW were seen as:

Messages for the business community	Messages for consumers
There is a UK meetings industry	The value of face-to-face communications
The value of meetings	Making the most out of a meeting
Economic benefit	Meetings versus new technologies
Employment opportunities	Meetings are good for you
Pride and the 'feel good' factor	What is a meeting?
The productivity of meetings	'Meeting Needs'
'Meeting Needs'	

As well as support and 'buy-in' from the industry, the organizers of NMW seek support from celebrities from the entertainment and sporting world. In 2004, over 100 Members of Parliament also pledged their allegiance to the campaign.

Activities planned for NMW 2005 at a national level included:

- A 'kick-off' event at Chelsea Football Club
- A Careers Fair and a Careers Week
- A MORI poll
- The 'Meetings & Incentive Travel Show'
- The Meetings Industry Marketing Awards
- A Grand Finale event.

Initiatives such as 'National Meetings Week' complement the ongoing work of the industry's representative bodies and lobbying agencies. They offer an important peg on which positive messages about the industry can be hung, and through which topical issues and concerns can be raised.

A number of other countries are now initiating their own National Meetings Week or its equivalent. Such countries include: Australia, Belgium, Canada, Finland, Holland and Norway.

Review and Discussion Questions

1 'Convention and visitor bureaux (CVBs) play a unique role in facilitating partnerships across a destination.' Discuss this statement and compare the functions and achievements of CVBs with those of partnership bodies in other industry sectors, e.g. an inward investment agency, a public transport authority, a health care trust or board.
2 Are the benefits of participating in a marketing consortium outweighed by the potential loss of brand identity? Illustrate your answer with examples of either conference venues or conference destinations which have (a) joined a marketing consortium (b) opted to act independently.
3 Recognition of the economic benefits of the conference, convention and business events sector has increased significantly over the past five years. Discuss the accuracy of this statement with reference to a specific country. How effective has industry lobbying been in this country, and what forms has it taken?

Sources

Boléat, M (2003) *Managing Trade Associations*, Trade Association Forum

Hendrie, JR (2005) 'The value of membership: what makes a good trade association?', *DMO World* e-newsletter, Issue 6 (September), accessible at: (www.frontlinecommunication.co.uk/dmoworld/feature9.html)

Walters, J (2005) Chapter in *Fundamentals of Destination Management and Marketing*, Educational Institute of the American Hotel and Lodging Association and the International Association of Convention & Visitor Bureaus

Chapter 11
Current Initiatives in the Conferences, Conventions and Business Events Sector

Summary of Chapter Contents

As an industry grows and matures, it faces challenges and issues that need to be overcome if it is to progress. The conference, convention and business events industry is no exception. This chapter focuses on some of the current initiatives designed to take the industry forward in a number of fundamental areas.

It covers:

■ Research and market intelligence
■ Terminology
■ Education and training
■ Quality standards

It includes case studies on:

■ Australia's National Business Events Research Project
■ The Performance Measurement Handbook of the Destination Marketing Association International

Learning Outcomes

On completion of this chapter, you should be able to:

■ appreciate the need for, and importance of, industry research
■ give examples of best practice research programmes

■ understand the rationale for a clearer and more consistent use of terminology and jargon
■ understand the crucial role of education and training in enhancing the overall professionalism of the conference industry
■ identify different types of quality assurance schemes now in operation

Introduction

Many might argue that statistics, terminology, quality standards, even education programmes, are all rather dry and somewhat esoteric industry features, of interest only to academics and bearing little relation to the exciting and 'real' world of marketing. The reality is that these form the foundations on which a young industry can be built and nurtured into maturity.

Research provides parameters against which an industry's performance and growth can be measured, and through which new trends can be identified. The adoption of a standard terminology and consistent interpretation of both words and statistics are both essential if, at an international level, the industry is to develop data and intelligence that are robust and reliable. Such data are essential to support benchmarking and to enable countries to compare their performance with other countries. The industry's workforce is expanding rapidly, as are education and training programmes to go with this, but is there sufficient coherence and standardization in the provision of such programmes, or are they being developed with only passing reference to market demands? How should quality benchmarks for both venues and destinations be brought on stream in ways that will have meaning also for clients, the purchasers of the venues and destinations?

This chapter will examine each of these topics in more detail and also highlight a number of best practice initiatives from around the world.

Research and market intelligence

It has been seen that, in comparison with many other industries, the conference industry is still very young, less than one hundred years of age in Europe and North America and still in its infancy in much of the rest of the world. Although it is maturing at a very rapid rate, it is indisputable that one of the consequences of its relative immaturity is a lack of reliable statistics and regular research to provide a base of intelligence and information on trends and on the size and value of the industry. Statistics produced annually on international conventions and congresses by the International Congress and Convention Association (ICCA) and the Union of International Associations (UIA) are something of an oasis in what has, until recent times, been a rather barren statistical landscape. This, in turn, has meant that governments have not taken the industry seriously as a major benefactor to national economies because it has been impossible to demonstrate clearly the positive economic impacts that conferences can generate.

It is pleasing to report that, while many gaps still remain, some genuine progress is being made in gathering better market intelligence and there are increasing numbers of best practice examples from around the world, which themselves deserve recognition and emulation. Some of these are summarized on the following pages, but first it will be useful to take note of developments in the system of tourism satellite accounts and the Standard Industrial Classification, which, in the medium to longer term, could lead to significantly enhanced industry statistics and research at both national and international levels.

Tourism satellite accounts and the Standard Industrial Classification

A tourism satellite account (TSA) provides a means of separating and examining both tourism supply and tourism demand within the general framework of the System of National Accounts approved by the United Nations. The term 'Satellite Account' was developed by the United Nations to measure the size of economic activities that are not defined either as industries in national accounts or as a cluster of them. Tourism, for example, impacts heavily on industries such as transportation, accommodation, food and beverage services, recreation and entertainment and travel agencies. Calvin Jones and David James (2005) state that:

> *Tourism is a unique phenomenon as it is defined by the consumer or the visitor. Visitors buy goods and services both tourism and non-tourism alike. The key from a measurement standpoint is associating their purchases to the total supply of these goods and services within a country. The TSA:*

- Provides credible data on the impact of tourism and the associated employment
- Is a standard framework for organizing statistical data on tourism
- Is a new international standard endorsed by the UN Statistical Commission
- Is a powerful instrument for designing economic policies related to tourism development
- Provides data on tourism's impact on a nation's balance of payments
- Provides information on tourism human resource characteristics.

Agreement was reached in 2004 between the World Tourism Organization (a specialized agency of the United Nations), the International Congress & Convention Association, Meeting Professionals International, and EIBTM (the international trade exhibition for the conventions and incentives sector) for the TSA to incorporate meeting industry data for the first time, allowing studies to be made into the relationship between expenditure on meetings and other economic measures such as Gross Domestic Product and job creation.

A project team led by Sustainable Tourism CRC has begun (as of November 2005) to develop a standard methodology for measuring the value of the meetings industry based on a TSA. It seeks to:

- Identify the basic data units for collection of statistics
- Explore how these fit into existing TSA statistics
- Develop survey instruments to capture meetings-related expenditure and costs

- Identify the indicators/variables to be used for quarterly measurement of the performance of the meetings industry
- Create guidelines for the collection of statistics adapted to the functioning of the TSA
- Describe the roles of the stakeholders in the process to ensure credibility.

The industry has rightly interpreted these developments as a major step forward in gaining recognition for the meetings industry and in enabling industry data and intelligence to be gathered in a more comprehensive and structured way.

Current examples of industry research activity

This section will highlight a number of best practice examples of industry research, at international, national and local/city levels.

International research programmes

Some of the longest-running industry research programmes are those undertaken by the **Union of International Associations** (UIA: www.uia.org/statistics) and the **International Congress and Convention Association** (ICCA: www.iccaworld.com). Both of these organizations monitor the staging of international congresses and meetings, identifying trends and producing annual rankings of the most successful cities and countries as per the example shown in Tables 11.1 and 11.2. It is not possible to make direct comparisons between the UIA and ICCA data because they use different criteria when defining which events to include in their surveys (see Rogers, 2003: 8–13) for details of the criteria used), but they nonetheless provide valuable information on which destinations are maintaining or increasing their market share, and which may be losing their position in the international meetings market. Destinations themselves take the results very seriously, and those achieving a high ranking can use such positive and objective data as a key part of their own promotional and PR campaigns. The data held by the UIA and ICCA on international associations and organizations can also be purchased for direct marketing and CRM activities, and such data is well used by those destinations active in the international conference and conventions sector. Both the UIA and ICCA will conduct specific research for destinations on market share, competitive performance and trends.

ICCA identified approximately 4800 international association meetings occurring in 2004 which take place on a regular basis and circulate between at least three countries.

UIA and ICCA DATA can also be used as part of the sales research process (see Chapter 8) to identify potential leads, which then become the focus of marketing and sales activity. Figure 11.1 shows a request submitted to ICCA DATA by a congress centre in Vietnam for details of events matching specific criteria, i.e. rotating around their part of the world, covering a particular subject area (science), attracting a certain number of people (750), not having being held in Vietnam for at least 15 years, and the international organization staging the event must be represented in Vietnam (key contact). Figure 11.2 shows the series and address details, including information on frequency, preferred venue and first open year (the next future year for which a destination/venue is not yet confirmed). It also provides an historical overview of the event, which helps destination and venue marketers to forecast whether a congress is likely to come to a certain destination in the (near) future. Figure 11.3 shows key contact information for the member organizations of the international body – these are very important individuals who need to be motivated to put in a bid to host a future

Table 11.1 UIA rankings – top international meeting cities in 2004

Ranking	City	No. of meetings	% of all meetings	Ranking	City	No. of meetings	% of all meetings
1	Paris	221	2.41	26	Amsterdam	59	0.64
2	Vienna	219	2.39	27=	Hong Kong	58	0.63
3	Brussels	190	2.07	27=	Istanbul	58	0.63
4	Geneva	188	2.05	29	Strasbourg	57	0.62
5	Singapore	156	1.70	30	Dublin	53	0.58
6	Copenhagen	137	1.50	31	Buenos Aires	50	0.55
7	Barcelona	133	1.45	32	Oslo	49	0.53
8	London	131	1.43	33	Tokyo	47	0.51
9	Berlin	110	1.20	34	Moscow	46	0.50
10	Seoul	109	1.19	35	Cairo	44	0.48
11	Budapest	104	1.14	36	Cape Town	43	0.47
12	Washington DC	102	1.11	37	Reykjavik	42	0.46
13	New York	94	1.03	38	St Petersburg	41	0.45
14	Beijing	88	0.96	39=	Melbourne	40	0.44
15	Prague	83	0.91	39=	Munich	40	0.44
16	Stockholm	82	0.90	41	Warsaw	39	0.43
17	Helsinki	76	0.83	42=	Orlando	38	0.41
18	Rome	71	0.78	42=	San Francisco	38	0.41
19	Madrid	70	0.76	44	New Orleans	37	0.40
20	Bangkok	69	0.75	45	Shanghai	36	0.39
21	Sydney	68	0.74	46=	Vancouver	34	0.37
22=	Athens	65	0.71	46=	Mexico City	34	0.37
22=	Lisbon	65	0.71	46=	Brisbane	34	0.37
24	Kuala Lumpur	64	0.70	49=	Frankfurt	33	0.36
25	Montreal	59	0.64	49=	Venice	33	0.36

Source: Union of International Associations (website: www.uia.org/statistics)

Table 11.2 ICCA rankings – number of international association meetings per city in 2004

Ranking	City	No. of meetings	Ranking	City	No. of meetings
1	Barcelona	105	26	Istanbul	35
2	Vienna	101	27=	Rio de Janeiro	34
3	Singapore	99	27=	Taipei	34
4	Berlin	90	29	Melbourne, VIC	33
5	Hong Kong	86	30	Vancouver, BC	31
6	Copenhagen	76	30=	Glasgow	31
7	Paris	75	30=	Cape Town	31
8	Lisbon	67	30=	Sydney, NSW	31
9	Stockholm	64	34	Brisbane, QLD	29
10	Budapest	64	35	Montreal, QC	28
11	Beijing	58	36	Shanghai	26
12	Amsterdam	58	37	Tokyo	25
13	Seoul	53	37=	Brussels	25
14	Kuala Lumpur	51	37=	Munich	25
15	Madrid	49	37=	Sevilla	25
16	Prague	47	41=	Chicago, IL	24
17	Bangkok	46	41=	Valencia	24
18	Helsinki	45	41=	Santiago de Chile	24
19	London	44	44	Uppsala	22
20	Athens	39	45	Buenos Aires	21
21=	Rome	38	46=	Kyoto	20
21=	Oslo	38	46=	Göteborg	20
21=	Dublin	38	46=	The Hague	20
24	Edinburgh	37	49	Ljubljana	19
25	Geneva	36	49=	Havana	19
			49=	Venice	19

Source: ICCA DATA (website: www.iccaworld.com)

congress. Figure 11.4 provides vital information about the requirements of the international organ-ization and its expectations of how the event will be planned and managed.

At a European level, the European Commission and its statistics agency, Eurostat, published in 2000 a 'Methodological Manual for Statistics on Congresses and Conferences', which sets out 'agreed guidelines for the production of statistics on congresses and conferences'. The Manual was developed in co-operation with the National Statistical Institutes in Member States and with the Joint Meetings Industry Council (JMIC), representing a number of the industry's leading international associations. The Manual is in four parts:

1 Introduction, defining objectives, presenting information needs, identifying current problems in congress and conference statistics, and proposing a common methodology
2 Outlines demand for congresses and conferences

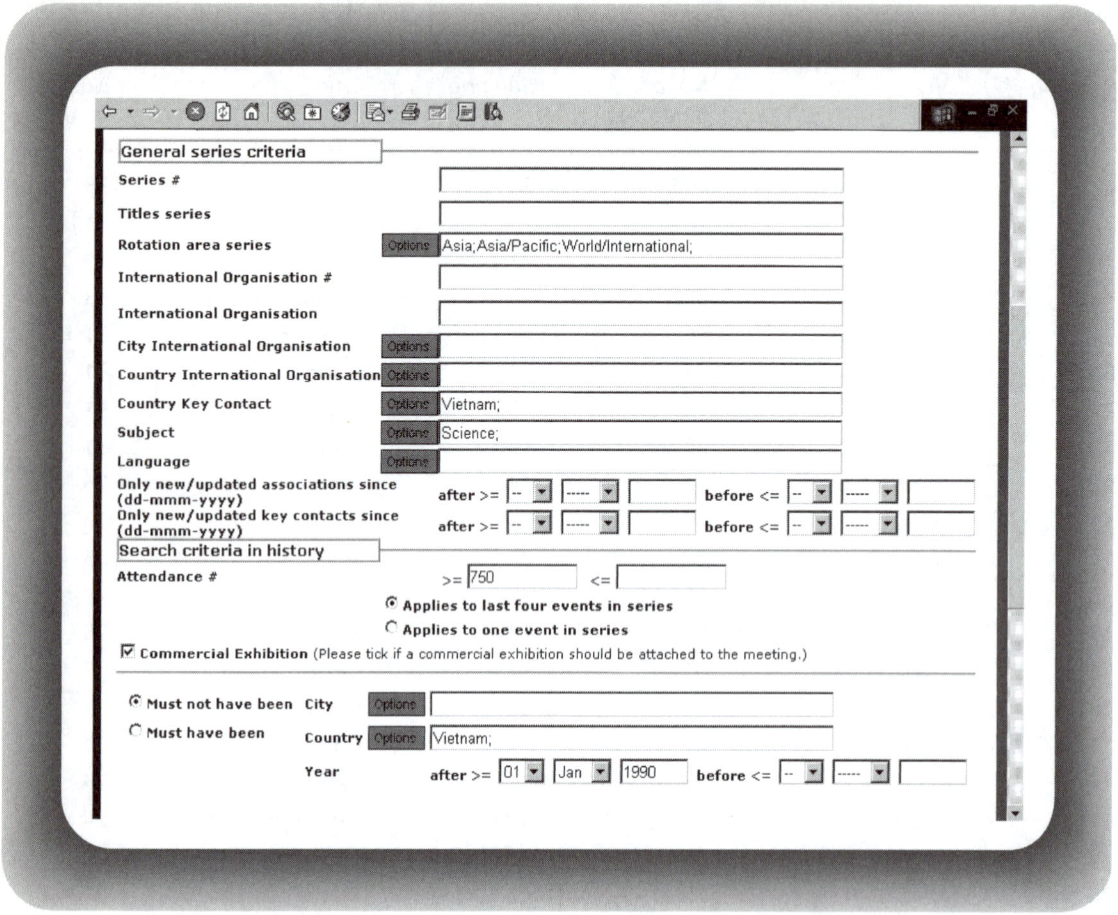

Figure 11.1 Specimen research request criteria. (*Source*: ICCA DATA – website: www.iccaworld.com).

3 Outlines supply aspects of congresses and conferences
4 Provides guidelines to measure the impact of congresses and conferences on the economy.

The Manual can be downloaded free of charge from: http://forum.europa.eu.int/irc/dsis/bmethods/info/data/new/embs/tourism/congresses.pdf

From a purely DMO or CVB perspective, a valuable insight into the funding, structure, operation and marketing activities of DMOs and CVBs is provided by surveys including:

- 'ICCA Category D Survey' carried out by Christian Mutschlechner of Vienna Convention Bureau. Category D members of ICCA are CVBs and tourist boards, and this survey has been carried out every three years since 1994. Further details: mutschlechner@vienna.info
- 'Benchmark Survey of Convention and Visitors Bureaux', published in 2004 by Dr Dimitris Koutoulas. Further details: d.koutoulas@ba.aegean.gr
- The Destination Marketing Association International (formerly the International Association of Convention and Visitors Bureaus) also undertakes surveys of its members from time to time. Further details: www.iacvb.org.

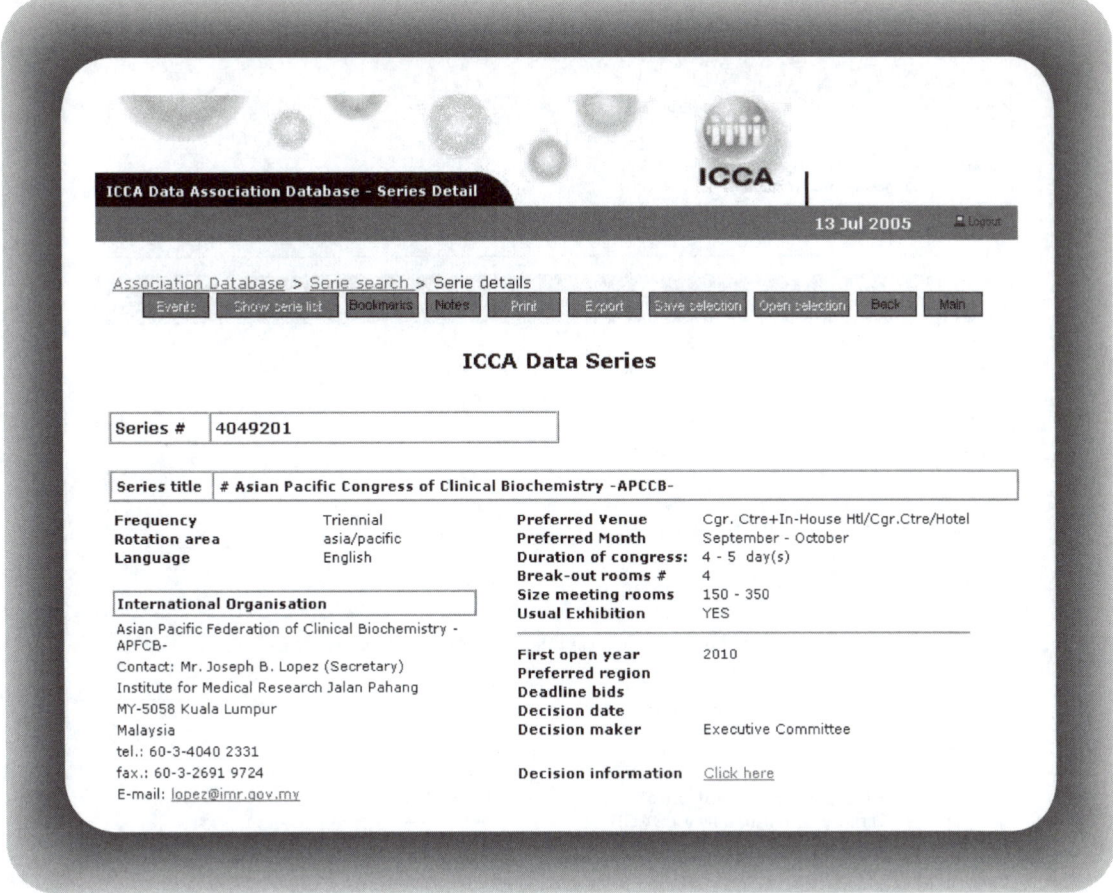

Figure 11.2 International Congress 'Series' – ICCA DATA website screen shot.

DOME (an acronym for 'Data on Meetings and Events') is a programme originally launched in 1997 with the aim of improving 'the quality and accessibility of global research and data on the world's convention and meetings industry'. In recent years the core focus of DOME has been in measuring the economic impacts of conventions by asking delegates to provide information on types of accommodation used and the duration of their stay, as well as details of air seats used by airlines, flight segments and class of service (for examples of data see Rogers (2003: 77–8). The data enable hotels and airlines to know what share of business they achieved for a specific convention, where the convention has been certified by DOME. Further details: www.domeresearch.com.

The organizers of industry exhibitions such as IMEX and EIBTM also commission research on different aspects of the international conventions industry. An example of IMEX-sponsored research is given in Chapter 10 on the topic of trade association membership. The annual 'Industry Trends & Market Share Report', compiled by the co-author of this book, Rob Davidson, is sponsored by EIBTM. Such research activity typically has two objectives: first, to supply useful, up-to-date intelligence on hot topics affecting the industry and, second, to position the exhibition itself as being at the cutting edge of all that is happening in the industry, one that will be an important,

Homepage: http://www.apfcb.org
Keycontact link: Click here

#: 40492 Keycontact list Remarks

International organisation address check: 23-Feb-2005

Subjects science/biology/biochemistry
science/chemistry/clinical
science/biology/immunology

Series profile last updated: 23-Mar-2005

Overview of events

Event #	Dates	City	Country	Attendance
200700473	14 - 19 Oct 2007	Beijing	China-P.R.	
200400135	20 - 25 Sep 2004	Perth, WA	Australia	1000
200100165	11 - 16 Nov 2001	New Delhi	India	2000
199800644	11 - 16 Oct 1998	Kuala Lumpur	Malaysia	1650
199500418	17 - 22 Sep 1995	Bangkok	Thailand	753
199300099	14 - 19 Nov 1993	Melbourne, VIC	Australia	3000
199100438	29 - 04 Oct 1991	Kobe	Japan	990
198800444	28 - 02 Sep 1988	Hong Kong	Hong Kong, China	915
198500273	15 - 20 Sep 1985	Denpasar, Bali	Indonesia	900
198200388	19 - 24 Sep 1982	Singapore	Singapore	1000
197900276	14 - 19 Oct 1979	Singapore	Singapore	800

Home | Site Index | Privacy Policy | Terms of Use | Inquiries | Copyright Policy | Log Out

© 2005 ICCA - all rights reserved.
ICCA - International Congress & Convention Association
Entrada 121 NL-1096 EB Amsterdam

Singapore Association of Clinical Biochemistry (SACB)

Assoc Prof Sunil Kumar Sethi,
Dept of Laboratory Medicine,
National University Hospital,
5 Lower Kent Ridge Road,
SINGAPORE 119074.
patsks@nus.edu.sg
Fax: 65-775-1757

Association for Clinical Biochemistry, Taipei, China (CACB)

Prof Ching-Shan Huang
c/o Dept. of Laboratory Medicine,
Cathay General Hospital,
No. 280, Jen-Ai Road Sec. 4, Taipei,
TAIWAN 106.
REP of CHINA.
Fax: 886-2-27025104

Thailand Association of Clinical Biochemists (TACB)

A/Prof Busaba Matrakool,
Faculty of Medical Technology,
Huachiew Chalermprakiet Univ,
18/18 Bangna-Trad Road, Km 18,
Bangplee,
Samutprakarn 10540,
THAILAND.
Busaba@hcu.ac.th
Fax: 662-3126237

Vietnamese Association of Clinical Biochemistry (VACB)

Assoc Professor Dai Duy Ban, MD, PhD
Institue of Biotechnology,
1 Hoang Quoc Viet, Cau Giay -Ha Noi,
VIET NAM
Ban@im-ibt.ac.vn
Fax number: (84 8) 7 564 483

Figure 11.3 International Congress 'Series' – ICCA DATA website screen shot.

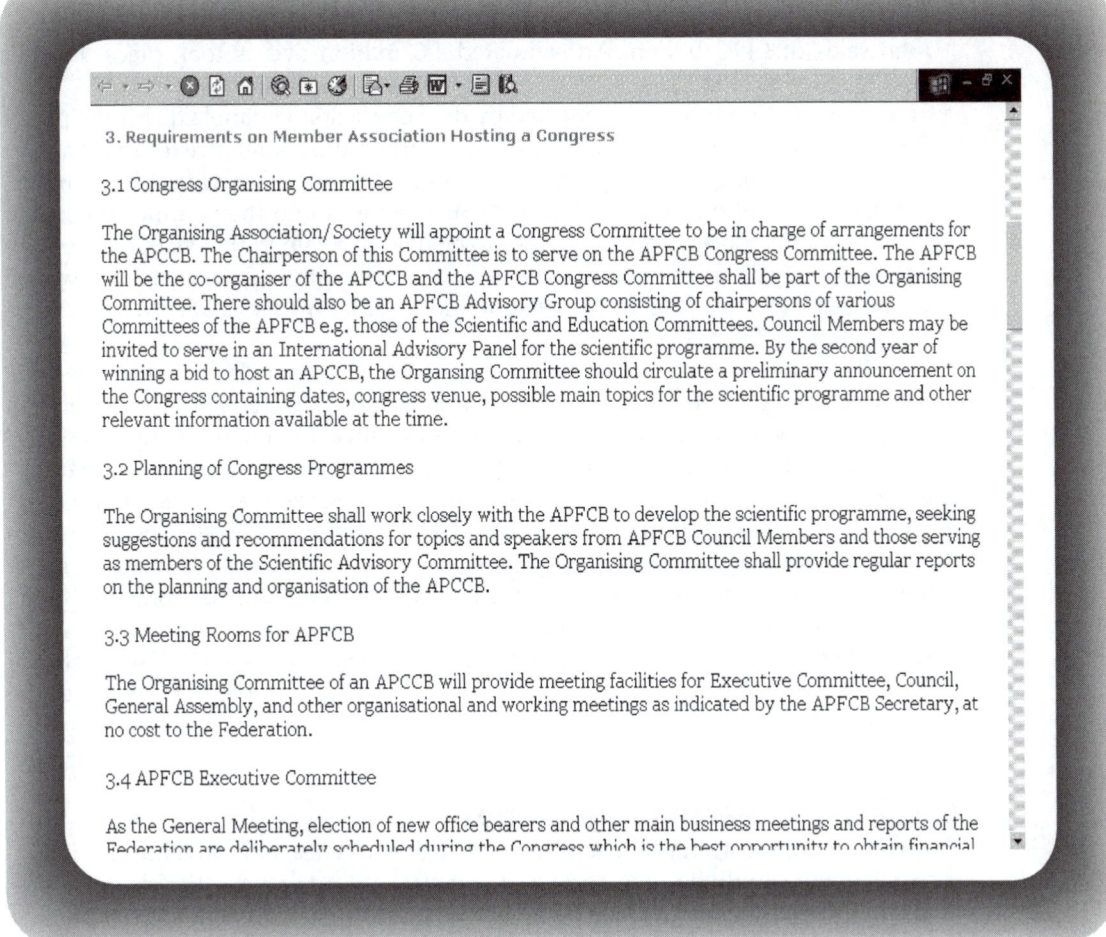

Figure 11.4 International Congress 'Series' – ICCA DATA website screen shot.

not-to-be-missed communications event for the industry as a whole. Further details: www.imex-frankfurt.com and www.eibtm.com.

National research programmes

Growing numbers of countries are now carrying out regular or one-off studies into their conference and convention sectors. A few examples of such studies are shown below. An important step in the maturation of the industry will be taken once some standard and consistent methodologies for these types of research are established, ensuring that countries are using the same approaches and definitions in their research activity. This will then enable comparative studies to be undertaken between countries, as well as the aggregation of data by groups of countries and perhaps even continents.

• The German meetings market is measured by the German Convention Bureau, typ-ically every three years through the medium of an in-depth study. The last study was in 2002 and this showed, for example, that there were 69 million participants in conferences, meetings and seminars throughout Germany in that year, generating total sales of £49.3 billion. An estimated 1.3 million events took place. Further details: www.gcb.de.

- Spain Convention Bureau, supported by the Federación Española de Municipios y Provincias, provides an annual statistical report on the conference tourism market in Spain, compiling and analysing data supplied by individual cities (the members of Spain Convention Bureau). The 2003 Survey measured the volume and size of meetings, conventions and congresses to be held in Spain in that year, plus a more detailed analysis of the characteristics of these events (e.g. seasonality, type of venue used, expenditure, industry sector, location). Further details: www.scb.es/ (see section on 'Statistics').

- The UK conference market is monitored through two separate annual surveys: the 'UK Conference Market Survey' assesses trends and characteristics from a demand perspective by undertaking in-depth interviews with 600 conference organizers (300 corporate, 300 association) (further details from the Meetings Industry Association – www.mia-uk.org); the 'British Conference Venues Survey' examines trends and volume and value features from a supply-side perspective, collecting data from conference venues. The 2005 Survey, for example, estimated that the value of meetings business to venues was some £11.7 billion (further details from the British Association of Conference Destinations – www.bacd.org.uk).

- A detailed look at Australia's major industry research project ('The National Business Events Study') is shown as Case Study 11.1, presented at the end of the chapter.

Local/city research programmes

For many, if not most, cities that are active in the conference and conventions market, research is and should be an integral part of their day-to-day work. For example, systems should be in place to record the volume and type of business enquiries being handled by the DMO, and it will be possible to analyse these enquiries in a variety of ways. The DMO may undertake client feedback research, or 'mystery shopper' surveys (where a research consultant poses as a genuine client in order to test the quality of service provision by the DMO), in order to ascertain how the destination has performed, to identify areas for improvement, and to inform future marketing activity. Statistics on website usage offer valuable insights into the source of business leads for the destination, and contribute to assessments of e-marketing campaigns. Similar kinds of research information should also be collected by conference venues – much of this will be available to them through their day-to-day work but systems do need to be put in place to make sure that data are captured fully and accurately, and interpreted consistently.

There will also be a need, from time to time, for destinations and venues to commission discrete research programmes, perhaps to assist them in drafting a new business strategy, to assess client demand for new facilities and infrastructure, or to undertake economic impact studies for use in lobbying. Examples of two such research programmes are:

- **Vienna Congress Survey 2004:** the Austrian capital city of Vienna's Convention Bureau, in conjunction with its University of Economics and Business Administration, carried out interviews with 2500 Vienna congress participants over an 18-month period. The survey was designed to elicit information on the following topics:

○ Duration of stay including details of congress 'extenders'
○ Gastronomy and hotel accommodation
○ Leisure and cultural behaviour
○ Expenditure and economic impact
○ Travel patterns
○ Social demographic data
○ Perceptions of Vienna's conference venues
○ Perceptions and image of Vienna as a conference destination

- **Further information**: www.vienna.convention.at
- **Sydney Convention Delegate Study**: the CVB of Sydney, Australia, undertakes every 2–3 years a study into the characteristics of the delegates attending conventions in the city. It covers similar ground to Vienna's survey. The study findings are used for advocacy purposes, demonstrating the economic benefits of convention business and the role of Sydney Convention and Visitors' Bureau (SCVB) in attracting this business. They are also used by the members of the Bureau as a marketing tool. Further information: www.scvb.com.au.

In the UK, research into delegate expenditure undertaken in the late 1990s by the UK National Tourist Boards produced average expenditure figures per day and per trip for different types of conference and convention, disaggregated into expenditure on conference registration fees, accommodation, restaurants, entertainment, shopping, etc. These figures have been adjusted twice subsequently to take account of inflationary increases over the past few years. They are used by many UK destinations as 'multipliers' to measure the economic impacts of different kinds of conference. Further details under the heading 'Estimating the Direct Expenditure Benefits of Conferences to a Local Area', can be accessed on the website of the UK's Business Tourism Partnership: www.businesstourismpartnership.com/publications.html.

Terminology

Non-standardized terminology

One of the reasons for the limited statistics on the size and value of the industry is the lack of an accepted and properly defined terminology. At a macro level, arguments still rage over whether the term 'business tourism' is an accurate or appropriate one to describe the sector encompassing conferences, conventions, exhibitions and incentive travel. The link with 'tourism' is thought by many to be confusing and overlaid with a number of negative perceptions ('candy floss' jobs of a seasonal and poorly paid nature, for example, and dominant associations with holidays and leisure tourism). While the phrase 'business tourism' may be considered an oxymoron in some quarters, it is now widely in use in Europe as the accepted generic term. In Australia, the industry has adopted the term 'business events' to describe the sector's essential focus.

The acronym MICE (for meetings, incentives, conferences and exhibitions or events) is also still in widespread use around the world, despite its somewhat unfortunate connotations! In Canada this is adjusted to MC&IT: meetings, conventions and incentive travel.

At the micro level, words such as 'conference', 'congress', 'convention', 'meeting' even, are often used synonymously or indiscriminately. Other words are also used with similar but more specialized connotations, such as 'symposium', 'colloquium', 'assembly', 'conclave', 'summit', though it is probably only the last of these for which it might be easy to reach a consensus on its precise meaning (namely, a conference of high level officials, such as heads of government).

There are a number of current initiatives designed to bring some coherence and standardization to the terminology in use across the global meetings industry. One such initiative is the 'Dictionary of Meeting Industry Terminology', a dictionary with definitions in English for 900 terms in use in the industry, including translations of these terms into 11 other languages. Further details of the dictionary are available from the website of the International Association of Professional Congress Organizers (www.iapco.org/dictionary).

A second initiative comes under the aegis of the Convention Industry Council and has the acronym APEX (Accepted Practices Exchange). The overarching aim of APEX is to bring increased standardization and consistency to the systems and procedures in operation throughout the industry, in order to create greater efficiencies and better services for customers. Among several 'accepted practices' now completed is the APEX Industry Glossary, which is an interactive, on-line tool, intended to be a comprehensive reference for the terminology, jargon and acronyms used industry-wide. It is available free at: www.glossary.conventionindustry.org.

In June 2005 it was announced, following two specialist United Nations meetings, that the profession of meeting and exhibition organizing had been recognized by the UN in their 'International Standard Industrial Classification of All Economic Activities' (ISIC, Rev 4 provisional draft) as follows:

8230 Convention and trade show organizers
This class includes the organization, promotion and management of events such as business and trade shows, conventions, conferences and meetings, whether or not including the management and provision of the staff to operate the facilities in which these events take place.

7920 Other reservation service activities
This class includes the activities of marketing, promotion and arrangement of accommodation and other services including tours for conventions and visitors, tourist guide services, condominium time-share exchange services and other travel-related reservation services (including for transportation, hotels, restaurants, car rentals, entertainment and sport). Activities of ticket sales, theatrical sports and all other amusement and entertainment are also included.

This United Nations initiative has huge potential benefits for the industry in encouraging greater professional recognition, stimulating much better employment data, and in supporting the provision of appropriate education and training programmes.

Education and training

Elizabeth Jeffries – Chief Executive of Jersey Tourism – speaking at the 1997 convention of the British Association of Conference Destinations, said:

Destination marketing is facing increasing competitive pressures with the speed of change, technological advances, shorter product cycles and rising customer expectations. Destination marketing involves three sets of stakeholders whose needs and wants must be satisfied in balance: visitors, suppliers and the host community. The critical success factor in destination marketing will be the ability to create a high-performing team culture – in learning organizations committed to the ongoing education and training of their employees. This will enable the delivery of consistent quality in the successful development and implementation of a conference destination strategy, including turning complex destination information into targeted and integrated communications to potential conference organizers and delegates. The ability to learn faster than one's competitors may be the only sustainable competitive advantage.

The conference and conventions sector is all about high quality and high yield. But high quality demands high levels of professionalism and productivity on the part of the industry's practitioners, and the delivery of customer service that not only meets but regularly exceeds expectations. If clients do not enjoy such experiences, they will certainly not return.

Research has consistently shown that where conference organizers and meetings planners have problems with venues it is not, for the most part, with the facilities and equipment but with staff service, specifically a lack of professionalism and friendliness. As the physical attributes of conference venues become more standardized and of a generally acceptable level, it is likely to be the quality of the staff which will differentiate one from another. This point was expressed very lucidly in a report published in the UK by the Department of National Heritage (DNH – now known as the Department for Culture, Media and Sport) in 1996. Entitled 'Tourism: Competing with the Best – People Working in Tourism and Hospitality', the report said that:

> *The quality of personal service is perhaps more important to tourism and hospitality than to any other industry. Consumers who buy one of this industry's products will often have made a significant financial investment, but also an emotional investment and an investment of time. Of course the physical product – the facilities of the holiday village, the distinctiveness of the tourist attraction, the appointments of the hotel, the quality of the restaurant's food – is very important to them. But during the period customers are in the establishment, they will have many interactions with people: some indirect, with the management and chefs and cleaners; and many direct, with the front-line staff. The quality of those interactions is an integral part of the experience and has the potential to delight or disappoint the consumer. We do not believe that this potential is there to the same extent in any other employing sector.*

The DNH report rightly claims that:

> *Excellent service at a competitive price can only be provided by competent, well-managed and well-motivated people. This means recruiting the right people in the first place, equipping them with the skills they need, managing staff well to create motivation, job satisfaction, and high productivity.*

The type of quality standards described above can only be met through the establishment of effective education, training and lifelong learning programmes. Such programmes are necessary at post-school vocational and higher education levels, and on a continuous basis through short course provision and flexible distance learning that allow 'students' to combine learning with employment. In order to be fully effective, the programmes must be backed up by an integrated qualifications infrastructure, ideally one that is international in its scope and validity, enabling employees to move between countries and continents, possessing qualifications that are truly portable and that are accepted in many countries around the world.

Some examples of best practice education and training provision are given below.

International courses and qualifications

'Certification in Meetings Management' programme

The Certification in Meetings Management (CMM) has been developed by Meeting Professionals International (MPI) and is the first university co-developed global professional qualification for meeting professionals. It represents a major step towards encouraging and recognizing professionalism in meeting and conference management. The CMM focuses on strategic issues and executive decision-making. Once accepted onto the CMM programme and registered for a course, participants are required to complete four components:

1 Pre-residency (or pre-residential): preparatory reading and assignments, including a 'virtual' assignment requiring a number of participants to 'meet' through technology
2 Residency (residential): a 4½ day full immersion course, with sessions covering strategic thinking and acting, strategic negotiation, strategic marketing, strategic management, strategic leadership, organizational culture, and technology
3 Examination: composed of essay questions requiring participants to apply what has been learned to their own organization/situation
4 Post-residency (post-residential) business project: requires participants to produce a business plan based on what they have learned during the programme.

While the core curriculum taught in the CMM varies only slightly from programme to programme, the curriculum is adjusted to take account of different cultures and industry realities in the country or continent in which the programme is being offered. MPI strives to ensure an appropriate balance of faculty members (teaching staff) from the geographic culture, while still offering global input from tutors from outside that culture. Some attendees have found it beneficial to attend a course outside their own region in order to broaden their perspectives, and build their skills in global meeting planning.

The CMM is open to anyone working in the conference industry, such as:

Planners (Buyers)	Suppliers
Corporate planners (full- or part-time)	Hotels and conference centres
Association planners	Staff of convention bureaux
Professional conference organizers	Audio-visual/production companies
	Airlines
	Destination management companies, etc.

Further details on the CMM are available from: MPI International Headquarters, 4455 LBJ Freeway, Suite 1200, Dallas, Texas 75244, USA. Tel: +1-972-702-3000; fax: +1-972-702-3070; e-mail: education@mpiweb.org; website: www.mpiweb.org

MPI European Office, 22 Route de Grundhof, L-6315 Beaufort, Grand Duchy of Luxembourg. Tel: 352-2687-6141; fax: 352-2687-6343; e-mail: dscaillet@mpiweb.org

'Certified Destination Management Executive' programme

The Certified Destination Management Executive (CDME) programme has been developed by the Destination Marketing Association International (DMAI) and is relevant to those working in the convention and visitor bureau (CVB) and destination management/marketing side of the conference industry.

The CDME programme is delivered under the auspices of the World Tourism Management Centre at the University of Calgary, Canada, in collaboration with Purdue University (Indiana) and DMAI. It is an advanced educational programme designed for experienced CVB executives who are looking for senior-level professional development courses as well as an industry designation.

The main goal of the CDME programme is to prepare senior executives and managers of destination management organizations for increasing change and competition. The focus of the CDME is on vision, leadership, productivity and implementing business strategies. Demonstrating the value of a destination team and improving personal performance through effective organizational and industry leadership are the expected outcomes. Those completing the programme successfully are entitled to use the CDME designation.

The course has three core modules:

- Strategic issues in destination management
- Destination marketing planning
- Destination leadership.

Participants also choose from a variety of elective modules, including:

- Destination information and research
- International tourism and convention marketing
- Destination financial management
- Rural and small community destination management
- Destination community relations planning
- Sustainable destination development and marketing
- Human resources in destination management
- Festivals and events tourism
- Communications and technology in destination management
- Resort destination management
- Destination promotion planning
- Wine destination marketing and management
- Gaming and destination management
- Visitor servicing in destination management
- Convention/tradeshow marketing and sales management
- Destination partnership development
- Destination product development.

Further details on the CDME programme are available from: Professional Development Co-ordinator, DMAI, 2025 M Street, NW, Suite 500, Washington, DC 20036, USA. Tel: +1-202-296-7888; fax: +1-202-296-7889; website: www.iacvb.org

University education programmes

A significant number of universities and higher education institutions offer tourism and hospitality courses that include modules in conference and event management. The University of Nevada, Las Vegas is one of the leaders in the field both nationally and internationally. Other key players in North America (according to Weber and

Chon, 2002) include the Appalachian State University, George Washington University, Georgia State University, Northeastern State University, the University of Houston, the University of New Orleans and the University of Central Florida, all offering specific conference sector-related courses which have close links with, and are supported by, the industry.

Universities in Europe are also rapidly developing programmes at undergraduate and postgraduate levels. In the UK, for example, the University of Westminster launched, in October 2003, a Masters degree in 'Conference Management', while Leeds Metropolitan University offers a number of programmes in 'Events Management'. Several European universities (Sheffield Hallam in the UK, Università degli Studi di Bologna in Italy, the Universidad de Deusto, Bilbao (Spain) and the Berufsakademie in Ravensburg, Germany) have been collaborating since 2000 to run the European Masters in Congress Management – this is a two-year full-time course, incorporating both general management subjects and industry-specific subjects in addition to an industry-related research project in the form of a dissertation.

In the Asia–Pacific region, Hong Kong Polytechnic University offers specific programmes at both undergraduate and postgraduate levels. In Australia, Southern Cross University has been at the forefront of course development, with provision that includes a Masters in 'Convention and Event Management'.

Educational provision is improving but there is a need to put in place effective education, training and lifelong learning programmes, ideally on a flexible basis that will allow 'students' (employees) to combine short courses with employment or follow distance learning programmes while being employed. Such programmes must be backed up by occupational standards and an integrated qualifications infrastructure, ideally one that is international in its scope and validity, enabling employees to move between countries and continents, possessing qualifications that are truly portable and which are accepted in many countries around the world.

Quality standards

Reference was made earlier in this chapter to the work of the Convention Industry Council, through its Accepted Practices Exchange (APEX), in enhancing industry standards and developing 'accepted practices', including the publication of an Industry Glossary covering the terminology, jargon and acronyms used industry-wide. APEX has also developed a range of other accepted practices:

- Post-Event Report: this provides a format for collecting, storing and sharing accurate and thorough post-event report data on all types of events. It includes best practices as well as a Microsoft Word template for a Post-Event Report.
- Event Specifications Guide: this is a tool for preparing and sharing complete instructions and details for events and also provides a Microsoft Word template.
- Housing and Registration: this covers accepted practices for collecting, reporting, and retrieving complete housing (accommodation) and registration data for meetings, conventions and other events.

Other accepted practices are being produced and will cover: requests for proposals (RFPs), meeting and site profiles, and contracts. Further details on all the APEX topic areas are available from: Convention Industry Council, 8201 Greensboro Drive, Suite 300, McLean, VA 22102, USA (tel: +1 (703) 610 9000; website: www. conventionindustry.org, offering free on-line access to the published practices).

APEX is just one of a number of programmes designed to improve the quality and professionalism of the conference and convention industry world wide. The rapid growth of the global meetings industry over the past few decades has, perhaps inevitably, meant that quality issues have not always received the attention they deserve. It is an indication of the maturation of our industry that quality standards, consistency of delivery and performance measurement are all beginning to feature strongly in the operations of venue and destination marketers. Certain quality initiatives are particularly appropriate to event venues while others have been developed for application at a destination level. Some examples of quality initiatives are given below.

Wales Tourist Board's Business Class scheme

In 2003 the Wales Tourist Board (WTB) re-launched its Business Class accreditation scheme under which venues are inspected and can be awarded a Platinum, Gold or Silver grading for either their meeting rooms or/and business class bedrooms. Meeting venues in Wales are as diverse as the country itself. Be it a large conference venue or a more intimate meeting room in a country-house hotel, the scheme aims to inform the potential business traveller or conference organizer of the standards of business meeting facility or bedroom accommodation a venue can provide. By September 2005 some 75 venues had been awarded Business Class accreditation, with a further 11 having failed to meet the criteria. Venues must be a minimum of 3-star standard to participate in the scheme. It is WTB's policy that all meeting venues/hotels that have received capital funding/grants for new developments or upgrading of their establishment must take part in the Business Class scheme.

Table 11.3 provides a checklist of the requirements to be met for accreditation. Further details can be accessed at: www.wtbonline.gov.uk.

At the time of writing (September 2005), discussions were under way in the UK about the feasibility and desirability of developing a pan-UK system for assessing and grading meeting and conference venues.

ISO 9001:2000

ISO is the International Organization for Standardization. It is located in Switzerland and was established in 1947 to facilitate international trade through the provision of a single set of international standards that people everywhere would recognize and respect. Such standards are applicable to all kinds of organizations in all industry sectors. The members of ISO represent over 120 national standards bodies.

ISO 9001:2000 is an international quality management system designed to help both product and service-oriented organizations. The Royal College of Physicians, described in Case Study 4.1, is one example of a conference venue that has achieved ISO 9001:2000 certification.

For ISO 9001:2000 certification or accreditation to be achieved, a number of requirements have to be met. These are summarized in Table 11.4. Further information on ISO 9001:2000 is accessible at: http://praxiom.com/iso-9001.htm.

Standard CVB performance reporting

The Destination Marketing Association International has developed a handbook for CVBs which sets out a series of standards for measuring, evaluating and reporting on performance. The handbook is summarized in Case Study 11.2.

Table 11.3 Wales Tourist Board's Business Class award scheme: checklist of meeting room requirements

Requirement	Platinum	Gold	Silver
Adequate space	✓	✓	✓
Catering service tailored to customer needs: refreshments provided	✓	✓	✓
Appropriate lighting	✓	✓	✓
Appropriate ventilation	✓	✓	✓
Comfortable chairs	✓	✓	✓
Even height tables	✓	✓	✓
Appropriately sited power points	✓	✓	✓
Drapes or modesty panels	✓	✓	✓
Blackout curtains	✓	✓	✓
Efficient portable fans	✓	✓	✓
Dedicated meeting personnel	✓	✓	✓
At least one breakout room	✓	✓	
Sound proofing	✓	✓	
Flip chart	✓	✓(H)	
OHP available	✓	✓(H)	
Projection equipment with stand	✓	✓(H)	
TV and video	✓	✓(H)	
Lecterns	✓	✓(H)	
PA system	✓	✓(H)	
Controllable lighting level	✓	✓	
Availability of phone	✓	✓	
Space for back projection	✓		
High speed Internet access	✓		
Simultaneous translation facilities	✓(H*)		
Air conditioning	✓		
Video conferencing	✓(H*)		
Range of breakout rooms	✓		
Temporary staging	✓(H*)		
Dedicated conference team	✓		

Notes: Although not stipulated above, it is expected that there will be an adequate number of WCs and hand-washing facilities available, commensurate with the total number of delegates attending at any one time

The room must be a dedicated meeting room, i.e. a restaurant or public area would not be acceptable

(H) = For Gold award, 50% of the items marked H may be hired in, the other 50% must always be on site. The venue chooses which

(H*) = For Platinum award, items so marked may be hired in

Additional explanatory notes are provided to assist with interpreting the requirements

Table 11.4 Requirements for meeting the ISO 9001:2000 Standard

A: Systemic Requirements

I. Establish your quality system
- Develop your quality management system
  - Identify the processes that make up your quality system
  - Describe your quality management processes
- Implement your quality management system
  - Use quality system processes
  - Manage process performance
- Improve your quality management system
  - Monitor and improve process performance

II. Document your quality system
- Develop quality system documents
  - Develop documents to implement your quality system
  - Develop documents that reflect what your organization does
- Prepare quality system manual
  - Document your procedures
  - Describe how your processes interact
  - Define the scope of your quality system
- Control quality system documents
  - Approve documents before you distribute them
  - Provide the correct version of documents at points of use
  - Review and re-approve documents whenever you update them
  - Specify the current revision status of your documents
  - Monitor documents that come from external sources
  - Prevent the accidental use of obsolete documents
  - Preserve the usability of your quality documents
- Maintain quality system records
  - Use your records to prove that requirements have been met
  - Develop a procedure to control your records
  - Ensure that your records are usable

B: Management Requirements

I. Support quality
- Promote the importance of quality
  - Promote the need to meet customer requirements
  - Promote the need to meet regulatory requirements
  - Promote the need to meet statutory requirements
- Develop a quality management system
  - Support the development of a quality system
  - Formulate your organization's quality policy
  - Set up your organization's quality objectives
  - Provide quality resources
- Implement your quality management system
  - Provide resources to implement your quality system
  - Encourage personnel to meet quality system requirements

Continued

Table 11.4 (*Continued*)

- Improve your quality management system
  - Perform quality management reviews
  - Provide resources to improve the quality system
II. Satisfy your customers
- Identify customer requirements
  - Expect your organization to identify customer requirements
- Meet your customer's requirements
  - Expect your organization to meet customer requirements
- Enhance customer satisfaction
  - Expect your organization to enhance customer satisfaction
III. Establish a quality policy
- Define your organization's quality policy
  - Ensure that it serves your organization's purpose
  - Ensure that it emphasizes the need to meet requirements
  - Ensure that it facilitates the development of quality objectives
  - Ensure that it makes a commitment to continuous improvement
- Manage your organization's quality policy
  - Communicate your policy to your organization
  - Review your policy to ensure that it is still suitable
IV. Carry out quality planning
- Formulate your quality objectives
  - Ensure that objectives are set for functional areas
  - Ensure that objectives are set at organizational levels
  - Ensure that objectives facilitate product realization
  - Ensure that objectives support the quality policy
  - Ensure that objectives are measurable
- Plan your quality management system
  - Plan the development of your quality management system
  - Plan the implementation of your quality management system
  - Plan the improvement of your quality management system
  - Plan the modification of your quality management system
V. Control your quality system
- Define responsibilities and authorities
  - Clarify responsibilities and authorities
  - Communicate responsibilities and authorities
- Appoint management representative
  - Oversee your quality management system
  - Report on the status of your quality management system
  - Support the improvement of your quality management system
- Support internal communications
  - Ensure that internal communication processes are established
  - Ensure that communication occurs throughout the organization

Continued

Table 11.4 (*Continued*)

VI. Perform management reviews
- Review quality management system
  - Evaluate the performance of your quality management system
  - Evaluate whether your quality system should be improved
- Examine management review inputs
  - Examine audit results
  - Examine product conformity data
  - Examine opportunities to improve
  - Examine process performance information
  - Examine corrective and preventive actions
  - Examine changes that might affect your system
  - Examine previous quality management reviews
- Generate management review outputs
  - Generate actions to improve your quality system
  - Generate actions to improve your products
  - Generate actions to address resource needs

C: **Resource Requirements**
  I. Provide quality resources
- Identify and provide quality resource requirements
  - Identify and provide resources needed to support the quality system
  - Identify and provide resources needed to improve customer satisfaction

  II. Provide quality personnel
- Use competent personnel
  - Ensure that your personnel have the right experience, education, training and skills
- Support competence
  - Define acceptable levels of competence
  - Identify training and awareness needs
  - Deliver training and awareness programmes
  - Evaluate effectiveness of training and awareness
  - Maintain a record of competence

  III. Provide quality infrastructure
- Identify and provide infrastructure needs
  - Identify and provide building needs
  - Identify and provide workspace needs
  - Identify and provide hardware needs
  - Identify and provide software needs
  - Identify and provide utility needs
  - Identify and provide equipment needs
  - Identify and provide support service needs
- Maintain your infrastructure

  IV. Provide quality environment
- Identify and manage needed work environment
  - Identify and manage factors needed to ensure products meet requirements

Summary

We live in a world of constant and, it seems, ever-faster change. It is encouraging to witness some very positive changes affecting the conference, conventions and business events industry which will enhance the quality, professionalism and stature of the industry. Robust research, consistent use and interpretation of terminology, education and continuing professional development programmes attuned to market needs, and the establishment of quality standards and performance measures, are all vital building blocks in the creation of a strong and appropriate infrastructure for the sector. Much good work is being done but there is also an important need to ensure that all these developments and innovations are managed in a coherent way, in a way that will minimize duplication of effort and maximize their benefits for venues, destinations and the industry as a whole.

Case Study 11.1

Australia's National Business Events Research Project

In Australia the business events sector is recognized as a high-yield component of the tourism industry with direct connections to other key areas such as trade, foreign affairs, education, science, training and communications. It has great potential for further expansion. An important study into Australia's meetings and exhibitions sector was undertaken by the Bureau of Tourism Research and was published in 1999 under the title of 'Meetings Make their Mark'. This study estimated that business events contributed A$7 billion to the Australian economy. In the light of substantial developments to the sector in the early years of the new millennium, it was felt to be timely to undertake a comprehensive evaluation of the sector and to include other components such as incentive travel. The findings of this major research project were published in 2005 as the 'National Business Events Study', a report that runs to almost 150 pages. This Case Study will focus on the methodology and scope of the research as an example of national best practice, which could be emulated by other countries. Certain key findings from the study will also be highlighted.

The National Business Events Study (NBES) data were based on business activity in the 2002–3 financial year. The key objectives for NBES were identified as:

- To provide an estimate of the sector in relation to its:
  ○ size, and economic contribution
- To provide increased knowledge on the decision-making processes of delegates/attendees in the Business Events sector
- To provide key indicators for monitoring performance of the Business Events Sector in subsequent years.

For the purposes of the study, a business event was defined as:

> *Any public or private activity consisting of a minimum of 15 persons with a common interest or vocation, held in a specific venue or venues, and hosted by an organization (or organizations). This may include (but not be limited to): conferences, conventions, symposia, congresses, incentive meetings, marketing events, special celebrations, seminars, courses, public or trade shows, exhibitions, company general meetings, corporate retreats, training programmes.*

The method used in the study was a quantitative survey approach based on a number of questionnaires designed to capture an understanding of business event activity within Australia. Each of the questionnaires was devised by the NBES Steering Committee, a committee comprising industry experts and researchers with relevant expertise. The method of questionnaire distribution varied with each component of the study with the delegate, trade visitor, exhibitor and venue questionnaires being administered on-line. This method of distribution was used because of its ability to reach large groups of potential respondents and its cost-effectiveness. Other questionnaires, such as the incentive travel and the organizer surveys, were faxed, e-mailed or mailed.

The following components were identified by the steering committee as the key areas for research:

- Venues
- Meetings and conference delegates
- Meetings, conference and exhibition organizers
- Exhibitors
- Trade visitors
- Incentives.

All data collected in the study were confidential and were aggregated to avoid identification of any person, entity or event.

Sampling frame

Each component of the study required a sampling frame that included a range of event types and every attempt was made to ensure the representativeness of the sample.

The sampling frame for the meetings and conferences delegate survey considered the following:

- **Location:** different states and territories; metropolitan; regional
- **Size of meeting or conference:** small; medium; large
- **Category:** corporate; association; government; private
- **Participants:** international; interstate; local.

The exhibition sector sampling frame included:

- **Location:** different states and territories
- **Size of exhibition:** floor space
- **Industry type:** across a range of industries
- **Participants:** international; interstate; local
- **Exhibitors:** international; interstate; local
- **Trade visitors:** international; interstate; local.

The sampling frame for exhibition and event organizers included:

- **Location:** metropolitan; regional
- **Type of event/exhibition:** international; interstate; local
- **Size:** small; medium; large.

The sampling frame for the incentive travel sector included inbound tour operators (identified by Tourism Australia as being involved in this sector), accommodation properties with incentive travel business and destination management companies.

Key findings

An immense range of detailed information was collected through the study and is included in the published report. Key findings include the following:

- The overall estimated expenditure associated with business events in 2003 was in excess of A$17 billion
- The direct contribution to employment was estimated to be 116 000 jobs
- 316 000 business events were held in the financial year 2002–3 (284 000 of which were meetings and conferences)
- 28.4 million delegates attended these events. By event type the breakdown was:
  - association: 8.3 million delegates
  - corporate: 4.8 million delegates
  - government: 5.3 million delegates
- The busiest quarter for business events activity was October–December, which accounted for 29% of all events
- The greatest influence on all respondents to attend a conference was the business or educational content of the conference programme; the opportunity to network was the second most important motive
- Meeting and conference delegates spent an estimated total of A$11.5 billion in Australia in 2003, with A$949 million being expenditure by international visitors and the remainder being associated with domestic delegates
- On average, each delegate spent A$558 within Australia, although this varied substantially according to the type of delegate:
  - local: A$430
  - intrastate: A$892
  - interstate: A$2019
  - international: A$3526
- Average large exhibition organizer expenditure was A$459 000 per event, and average revenue per event was A$678 000
- An estimated total of 2.4 million trade visitors attended exhibitions in 2003, generating an estimated expenditure of A$540 million
- Expenditure on incentive travel was estimated to be in excess of A$585 million, with A$46 million being domestic business and approximately A$539 being international business representing new expenditure in Australia
- The average expenditure per incentive delegate, including some non-domestic airfares and personal expenditure, was:
  - Long haul delegates: A$2560
  - Short haul delegates: A$2180
  - Australian delegates: A$1224.

The NBES sets out several recommendations for future action, as follows:

1 Future studies of the business events sector should be conducted periodically to track changes in the sector and these studies should adopt the definition of business event venues used in the NBES, which will facilitate longitudinal comparison.
2 Business event venue data should be collected in collaboration with the Australian Bureau of Statistics under the Census Act in order to maximize the accuracy of the data which underpins any assessment of the business events sector. Many of the venues involved in the NBES did not have systems that facilitated the gathering of the required data. In order for

consistent and timely data to be collected for future research studies, a systematic method of data collection should be provided for venues to collect automatically the required data. This may be in the form of an electronic 'kit' that facilitates the data collection.

3 A template should be devised and distributed to venues that would facilitate their ongoing collection and recording of data relevant to assessing the overall size of the sector. This would overcome the problem of having to trawl back through records in order to complete the questionnaire, and the potential for error this creates. Ideally this template should be in the form of a software package and it is suggested that the industry should invest in the development of this.

Source: The published study was written by Margaret Deery, Leo Jago, Liz Fredline and Larry Dwyer. Further details may be accessed at: http://sustainabletourism.cgpublisher.com/. The study is published by Common Ground Publishing Pty Ltd, with ISBN 1 86335 576 6.

Case Study 11.2

The Performance Measurement Handbook of the Destination Marketing Association International

Accountability has become an integral part of any company's activity and reporting in the 21st century. This is certainly the case among CVBs, where stakeholders – whether they are a Board of Directors, government entities, members, or corporate partners – are increasingly asking their CVBs to show that they are effectively using their resources to generate the greatest possible return on investment (ROI) to the local community – the ultimate stakeholder.

In a perfect world, a CVB would know exactly how many of its destination's visitors were motivated to come solely by the CVB's efforts. And further, the CVB would be able to pinpoint exactly which of its sales and marketing effort(s) was responsible for that visitor. However, the CVB and its local tourism industry do not function in a perfect world. And potential visitors are constantly bombarded by such a myriad of stimuli (the CVB, its industry partners, national sales offices, the news, and so on) that it becomes impossible to say that a visitor was motivated 100% by the CVB and *only* by the CVB. In practice, when addressing the issue of visitors generated, CVBs can, at the very least, set into place monitoring and research programmes that identify visitors who were *clearly and significantly* generated by their efforts.

This Case Study looks at a tool developed by the Destination Marketing Association International (DMAI) (formerly the International Association of Convention & Visitor Bureaux) to assist CVBs to evaluate, calculate and report on their performance. The tool is in the form of a handbook entitled *Recommended Standard CVB Performance Reporting*, updated in February 2005. The handbook seeks to provide CVBs with a resource that will enable them to measure and report on their performance in a credible and auditable fashion that is consistent with other CVBs. Performance reporting also gives CVBs benchmarks and a platform by which they can clearly articulate their contribution to their stakeholders and the local community.

The handbook has been created as a result of the efforts of the DMAI Performance Measurement Team which, in 2003, began the process of standardizing CVB sales and marketing definitions, activity and performance measures, and productivity metrics including an ROI model. Initially, three CVB functional areas were examined individually: convention sales, travel trade sales, and marketing and communication (direct-to-consumer). In order to develop a performance reporting programme for each function, the purpose, or *mission*, for each function was defined first. From this mission flowed operational definitions and measures needed to illustrate, in an accountable and auditable way, the function's (and eventually the CVB's) performance as measured against the mission. These definitions and measures include:

1 Activity: a physical action taken by the CVB functional area that ultimately supports its mission, e.g. attending a trade show, conducting a familiarization visit, writing and distributing a press release.
2 Performance measure: a measure that helps to define and quantify the results of the CVB activity. Implementation of this system of measures should yield actionable tools that the CVB staff can use for short- and long-term enhancements of its efforts.
3 Productivity metric: a metric that illustrates the relationship between the CVB performance and its resources. Typically expressed as a ratio (cost per lead, number of bookings per sales manager), productivity metrics assist the CVB in managing its resources in the most cost-efficient and cost-effective manner possible. Many of the recommended productivity metrics are designed with the intent that the CVB establishes a benchmark year and recalculate these metrics regularly (e.g. every quarter, once a year). By examining these metrics over time, the CVB will be able to monitor its progress towards achieving desired resource efficiencies.

The handbook provides detailed activity measures, performance measures and productivity metrics for the three functional areas listed above (convention sales, travel trade sales, marketing and communications). It also gives ROI formulae for each of these areas together with practical examples illustrating the application of these formulae.

Source: The handbook can be viewed and downloaded free of charge at: www.iacvb.org under 'Performance Measurements'.

Review and Discussion Questions

1 Analyse critically the methodology of one of the industry's research programmes (international, national or local) to identify its strengths and weaknesses. Suggest ways in which the weaknesses might be addressed and the strengths further enhanced to produce a more robust and more valuable piece of research.
2 'To be successful, it is no longer sufficient to have an excellent congress centre, plenty of four- and five-star hotel rooms, good air and ground access, excellent IT and telecommunications, and a team of multilingual, experienced individuals in your local DMCs, PCOs, CVBs and venues. Everyone already has or is swiftly developing these attributes, so the competitive playing field is flatter – and the world smaller – than ever before.' (Martin Sirk, CEO of the International Congress & Convention Association, September 2005). Discuss this statement, with particular reference to the education, training and skills of the industry's workforce. If, in general terms, you agree with the statement, suggest what will be the key factors in the future by which a destination will seek to differentiate itself from the competition and so gain the crucial competitive edge.
3 How feasible would it be to develop a quality grading scheme for conference venues applicable to all types of venues? Which features and aspects of venues should any such scheme seek to measure and assess? Support your conclusions with feedback from conference organizers.

Sources

Jones, C and James, D (2005) 'The tourism satellite account (TSA): a vision, challenge and reality', *Tourism*, Issue 123, Quarter 2 (The Tourism Society)

Rogers, T (2003) *Conferences and Conventions: A Global Industry.* Elsevier/Butterworth-Heinemann

Union of International Associations, Brussels (2005) International Meeting Statistics for the Year 2004: International Meeting Statistics: Comparative tables on their development, geographical distribution, organization, participation and other matters

Weber, K and Chon, KS (2002) *Convention Tourism: International Research & Industry Perspectives*, The Haworth Hospitality Press

Chapter 12

Future Trends and Challenges for the Conferences, Conventions and Business Events Sectors

Summary of Chapter Contents

This chapter looks at some of the most important trends that will present opportunities and challenges to the global conference industry in the years ahead. Many of those trends are already emerging, and others may be anticipated because of changes in the wider market environment.

The chapter covers:

- The principal economic and social trends that will shape the future of the conference sector
- The future challenges and opportunities presented by ICT
- Emerging markets: new destinations and new types of venue
- Anticipated changes in demand for conference facilities and services

Learning Outcomes

On completion of this chapter, you should be able to:

- appreciate the role that will played by emerging markets, in particular India and China
- discuss how companies will try to obtain better value-for-money for the conferences they hold
- understand how developments in ICT will be adopted by the conference industry

- understand how changing social and demographic trends will have an impact on the profile of the conference delegate
- appreciate how trends in corporate accountability will lead to a more responsible conference industry.

Introduction

Those responsible for the marketing of conference destinations and venues understand that the market for their services and facilities is an extremely dynamic one, and one that is highly sensitive to even subtle changes in the political, economic and social environment. The conference sector is also affected by the accelerating rate of innovation in information and communications technology, which on the one hand offers significant opportunities for more effective marketing and more attractive products, but on the other hand may also create certain threats to the long-term prosperity of this sector.

This chapter focuses on some of the general trends and changes in the broad market environment that will affect the marketing of conference destinations and venues in the short- and medium-term.

Economic trends

Emerging markets

In the middle of the 20th century, practically all of the supply of, and demand for, conference services and facilities was located in two world regions: North America and Western Europe. These were the earliest industrialized regions, and therefore the first to construct the infrastructure necessary for a fully functioning conference industry.

But, as the world economy has developed over the past 50 years, many other nations have emerged as conference destinations in their own right, after investing in the building of new venues and marketing them both nationally and internationally. The supply of these 'emerging markets' appears inexhaustible as more and more countries attempt to reap the benefits of hosting *international* conferences in particular. The first major wave of new conference destinations began in the 1990s, when South-East Asian countries such as Thailand, Malaysia, Korea and Indonesia joined Hong Kong in investing heavily in conference facilities, relishing the prospect of welcoming overseas delegates and their dollars, and receiving a new stimulus to local economies.

A second wave of emerging conference destinations was seen in the early years of this century, when Central and Eastern European countries, newly admitted into the European Union, successfully marketed their rich supply of venues in cities of history and culture such as Warsaw, Krakow, Prague and Budapest, as well as the capitals of the Baltic States.

But each of these newly developed conference destinations has challenged the positions of the established ones, and added to the development, identified in Chapters 2 and 3, of an over-supply of venues and destinations in many parts of the world. At the same time, however, developing economies also create additional demand for conferences, as their new businesses fuel the need for corporate meetings and members of the expanding professional classes increasingly have the means to travel to association meetings in other countries.

Nowhere is this phenomenon more in evidence than in China and India, two of the world's fastest-growing economies, and countries widely believed to be major sources of international conference business in the years to come – as well as attractive destinations for international events. These two countries represent the two economies that are set to generate the greatest expansion in outbound business tourism for the short and medium term. Citizens of these countries are already travelling to other destinations in their regions, on business, but they will extend their scope to Europe and other long-haul destinations in rapidly increasing numbers in the years ahead.

At the World Travel & Tourism Council's 3rd Global Travel & Tourism Summit in May 2003, Peter de Jong, CEO of the Pacific Asia Travel Association, said that the opportunities, for tourism in general, presented by the emerging economies of China and India were unparalleled, adding:

> In Asia, we have a great deal of intra-regional travellers who are set to venture further afield in the very near future. Because the populations of India and China are so huge, a modest percentage growth in international travel could have a significant impact on the rest of the world – and if managed correctly, will become our bread and butter business for the next decade or two.

(Davidson, 2004: 6)

The same conditions that will stimulate mass long-haul travel from China and India – the combination of rising consumer incomes, growing freedom to travel and travel itself becoming increasingly affordable – will also create a massive market for outbound conference travel to corporate and association meetings in destinations around the world. In the October 2004 issue of *TravelSmart Asia Watch*, India was described as a market undergoing an incredible transformation, one that has given rise to what is potentially the most powerful consumer bloc in the world – the great Indian middle class: 'Numbering more than 300 million – larger than the entire population of the United States – India's middle class is leading the country's change from a subsistence economy to an economic powerhouse' (Anon, 2004). There is no doubt that members of India's middle-class will be as motivated as professionals in Europe and the United States to travel internationally to professional association meetings and corporate events.

But if any country can surpass India as an outbound travel market and as an emerging conference destination, it is the People's Republic of China. Predicted by the United Nations World Tourism Organization to be the world's leading tourism destination by 2020, China is also preparing itself to receive a very substantial share of the world's international conferences.

The Chinese government has already declared its intention to have 120 world-class convention centres by 2020. Preparations for the 2008 Olympics in Beijing have accelerated the expansion of that city's infrastructure and facilities, adding considerably to China's existing stock of conference venues. In April 2005, construction of the National Convention Centre began, as part of the Beijing Olympic infrastructure. After the Games, the 270 000 square metres will be used for conferences and exhibitions. But

Beijing is already home to 25 major conference centers, such as the Great Hall of the People with its plenary space for 10 000 and 30 meeting rooms, or the Beijing International Convention Centre for up to 2500 delegates in 60 meeting rooms. Meetings facilities are also offered by hotels such as The Great Wall Sheraton with plenary facilities for 1200 participants and 1007 rooms, and it is estimated that by 2008 Beijing's hotel facilities will grow to 800 properties with 130 000 rooms (Davidson, 2005).

Shanghai is also preparing its infrastructure for the 2010 Expo that will be held there. But that city has already successfully hosted a number of high-profile events, such as Fortune 500 (the annual meeting of the largest companies in the United States) in 1999 and the Asia Pacific Economic Co-operation conference in 2001. These events were held at the 3000-seat Shanghai International Conference Centre, which doubles as the Oriental Riverside Hotel, with 260 bedrooms (Antrobus, 2005).

However, it is China's status as an emerging economic superpower that will ensure that it becomes a major source of demand for outbound conferences as well as a successful destination. By October 2005, China's manufacturing sector had sustained growth for 19 months, and the most important current trend in the Chinese economy was the growth of the private sector, which had already supplanted state industries as the most important driver of economic growth. Growing levels of personal disposable income, Chinese companies' investment overseas, and a fast-increasing number of international air connections with cities in major destinations, are all factors that will ensure the rapid growth of Chinese outbound corporate meetings and of Chinese delegates at international association meetings in the near future.

A clear indication of the potential of this outbound market was given in 2005, when Reed Travel Exhibitions launched a new travel trade show in Beijing. The first China International Business & Incentive Travel Mart (CIBTM) was held at the China World Trade Center. Spread across 4300 square metres, it showcased 172 participating companies from 25 countries around the world, including National Tourism Authorities from Belgium, France, Hungary, Malaysia, Philippines and Qatar. The three-day event attracted 2460 professional visitors including 102 hosted buyers and 195 VIPs.

Growing corporate cost-consciousness

As competition between venues and between destinations intensifies with the arrival in the market of every new supplier and every new country, buyers have become aware that they are buying in what is, in most regions of the world, a buyers' market. Much of the corporate market in particular has lost no time in reaping the benefits of this situation, and meetings buyers have quickly learned how to negotiate to their best advantage. With no sign of imminent change in the relationship between supply and demand, corporate buyers are set to become even more cost-conscious in the years ahead.

Although almost every survey of demand for conferences suggests that corporate buyers expect the number of events they organize to increase in the immediate and short-term future, there is no corresponding indication that their budgets are going to increase at a proportional rate. For example, in a speech delivered at the OPC Spain annual congress near Cadiz in February 2005, Ray Bloom, chairman of IMEX, a European exhibition for the conference and incentive travel industry, said:

> *Our surveys reveal a general tightening of per-delegate expenses, as the central issue for many companies becomes that of ensuring better overall value and a higher (and more demonstrable) return on their investment.*

This reminds all destinations, and the venues within them, that they must constantly look for ways to manage their tariffs and demonstrate the cost-effectiveness of these. Quality, but at a keen price, will be a dominant requirement for the foreseeable future. It is the inevitable outcome of the 'want more – pay less' mentality of the many global businesses that have now come to recognize the strengths of their volume-driven purchasing power.

In a buyers' market characterized by an over-supply of venues and destinations, companies' concern with getting more value for the money they invest in off-site meetings has emerged as a central theme. One indication of this is the fast-growing number of companies who are making determined efforts to take control of how much they spend on their off-site meetings. Such companies are increasingly using their position of power, as high-volume purchasers of meetings-related facilities and services, to negotiate with suppliers, in order to achieve their meetings' objectives at the most competitive prices.

It has been a long-established practice for most medium-sized and large companies to control and streamline the ways in which individual members of staff travelling on business on the company's behalf book their travel and accommodation. It has become a standard procedure for companies, often through their dedicated corporate travel departments, to negotiate competitive rates with a restricted number of 'preferred suppliers' such as hotels and airlines, on the basis that they tend to purchase travel and accommodation in considerable volume year after year. By rationalizing and consolidating their business travel-related purchasing in this way, and imposing adherence to use of the preferred suppliers through a company travel policy, many companies have been able to achieve cost savings and efficiencies across all of their business travel spending.

In the past few years, however, the effort to streamline travel costs has extended into the field of companies' spending on off-site meetings. This new trend is certain to gain momentum in the years ahead, as a growing number of corporate buyers come to understand the, at times considerable, cost savings that can be generated by consolidating and centralizing the purchase of all meetings-related services and facilities.

A convincing argument in favour of this approach is made by those who have identified significant inefficiencies in the ways in which companies book meetings facilities. West (2005: 4), for example, quotes these anecdotes told by corporate meetings planners at a round-table discussion on the subject of consolidation:

For example, one participant who is now implementing a consolidation programme discovered that two different groups from the company were using the same hotel during the same week for two unrelated programmes. Both programmes had been planned by administrative assistants, but one had negotiated a room rate that was significantly lower than the other. Another participant found out when trying to book a certain property for a meeting that another planner [from the same company] had a large attrition penalty that the company had to cover.

However, in the United States, where this trend finds its roots, a powerful legal measure has also played a part in accelerating moves towards the strict monitoring and controlling of corporate spending on meetings.

For many publicly traded companies, one of the catalysts to track meetings spend was the Sarbanes–Oxley Act that passed through Congress in 2002 and went into effect last year for large companies. These new laws govern corporate fiscal reporting, and are demanding strict compliance in the wake of corporate accounting scandals. The relatively untagged spending that was taking place in the meetings sector is now seen by some companies as a legal liability should the firm undergo an audit. In these situations, the entity within the

company driving regulation and compliance is often the finance or purchasing department. Realizing synergies
and cost savings in the process has been an added benefit of capturing this spend and has cemented its value.

(West, 2005: 4)

The initial step in the meetings consolidation process is for the company to identify which members of staff actually book meetings facilities and which destinations and suppliers are the most commonly used – in order to detect where their purchasing volume might be leveraged to create cost-saving opportunities; the next step is to establish a limited number of preferred suppliers, or preferred 'vendors', that should be used by all company staff members involved in booking meetings; finally rates are negotiated for items such as room-hire, the use of audio-visual equipment and food and beverage. Such pre-negotiated contracts not only save money by preventing mistakes by inexperienced meetings planners but can also save time in the individual negotiating process and therefore increase planner productivity.

The meetings consolidation process is often initiated and monitored by the company's *procurement* department. Within companies, such departments are traditionally responsible for guiding and shaping purchasing decisions and contracting procedures, covering anything from buying a new photocopier to sourcing a firm of window cleaners for the company's offices. In today's increasingly cost-conscious companies, these departments guide purchasing decisions and contracting procedures, reducing costs through negotiating volume discounts from preferred suppliers and by tracking payments more effectively. And they now increasingly undertake this role across the company as a whole – including the company's spending on meetings.

How does this trend affect suppliers, in particular conference venues? It is clear that when faced with the challenge of marketing and selling their facilities and services to corporate customers who now purchase these through their procurement departments, traditional methods of cultivating and keeping meeting planners' business will no longer suffice. A position paper published by MPI makes the following observation:

With the increased involvement of procurement departments in meetings management, suppliers are under-
standably concerned that established relationships with planners will no longer matter even though meetings
are an inherently relationship-driven business. Deals aren't made on handshakes any more; suppliers must
continually show their value to planners and their stakeholders.

(MPI, 2005: 5)

The MPI position paper goes on to offer specific guidelines to suppliers, which those responsible for marketing venues will increasingly need to consider. These include:

- Evolve strategically along with the planners you serve rather than relying on previously established relationships to secure future business. The more contemporary your relationship with a planner whose job is evolving to involve larger business issues, including procurement, the more likely you will serve that planner better.
- Continually articulate or demonstrate how you are inherently different and valuable to a planner and/or organization beyond just the cost of your service. Focus on how you can help an organization fulfil its strategic meeting objectives through your services.
- Understand the fundamental changes in how organizations are doing business in more stringent regulatory environments. Many planners have strict rules regarding how often they can accept gifts (and of what value), travel on familiarization trips, or receive other amenities. In the US, with Sarbanes–Oxley and other legal changes, these limitations are becoming more widely enforced.

- If you have achieved an established preferred-vendor relationship with an organization, don't rest on your laurels. You must continue to indicate increasing value because companies are going out to bid more frequently in search of better performance, service and pricing.
- Be more flexible in your negotiations. Parameters are built into standardized contracts, and planners often can work only within those parameters.
- Suppliers should be flexible in the alignment of their sales forces to meet this shifting paradigm. With the convergence of travel, meetings and procurement, it becomes challenging to assign resources geographically. Also, as organizations attempt to better leverage the company-wide meetings-related spend, it is likely that one person/office will need to be held accountable for the corporate level account – instead of many representatives calling on many planners within one company.

The increasing involvement of corporate procurement professionals in the meetings purchasing process will mean that a growing number of suppliers will need to take steps to understand how procurement managers think and work, as well as the dynamics of the relationship between themselves and their corporate clients.

Technology trends

Information and communications technology has already transformed many aspects of the conference sector and there is no doubt that further advances in ICT will continue to have a profound impact on how conferences are planned, promoted and experienced in years to come. Young people now entering this sector will never understand the extent to which the Internet alone has revolutionized many practices in destination and venue marketing. Yet, as recently as at the end of the 20th century, e-mail had not yet achieved the almost universal presence it now enjoys as a means of professional and personal communication; mobile telephones were still relative curiosities, owned essentially by early adopters; most small and medium-sized enterprises were still using dial-up connections to the Internet; and flip charts were still equally likely to be used for conference presentations as Powerpoint.

Chapters 2 and 3 discussed some of the key technological developments that are currently being used by conference destinations and venues. There is little doubt that, by the end of the first decade of the 21st century, such applications of information and communications technology will have been refined and even superseded by new developments in this field, as in every field of human endeavour.

Corbin Ball, a renowned specialist in conference-related technology, has made a number of predictions as to how ICT will be used by the conference sector in the years ahead:

> *Technology will continue to evolve at a remarkable pace. Computers will get smaller and cheaper; processors will get faster; batteries will hold a charge longer; displays will have better resolution and be more flexible; data projectors will get smaller, cheaper and brighter; and broadband Internet will get faster and ubiquitous. Experts predict a doubling of performance tied to price every 18 months into the next decade. The phrase 'faster, better and cheaper' will continue to apply to most of the technology products we buy.*

Technology is revolutionizing business in general, and, specifically, the meetings industry. We will see many developments in the next few years, including:

1 *Wi-Fi and broadband Internet will be in nearly all public meeting space: The rate of Wi-Fi deployment in convention centers and large meeting hotels is skyrocketing. Even McDonalds is starting to provide 'free' Wi-Fi access.*

2 *More mobile products: With access to wireless broadband, today's cell phones will evolve to long-lasting mini-PDA phones that can access high-speed Internet access through multiple channels including Wi-Fi, Bluetooth and even faster wireless formats. We are seeing a number of products that are being developed on these mobile platforms for the meetings industry, including mobile registration, networking, surveys, audience response, interactive programs, electronic attendee lists, product directories, lead retrieval and more.*

3 *We will see tablet PCs develop as a platform to manage meetings specifications and site inspections.*

4 *RFID (radio frequency identification), the barcode of the future, will work its way into a number of lead retrieval, access verification, and attendance tracking systems in the next few years, despite concerns regarding privacy.*

5 *Web services (.NET) are emerging as the new platform for meetings technology products. The benefit is that it becomes much easier for different programs (for example online registration and housing) to work together even if not made by the same company. As there is a huge range of web-based technology products for meetings planners (more than 1100 categorized links at www.corbinball.com/bookmarks), this interoperability between programs will be of significant benefit as it will allow the planner to more easily mix-and-match different applications.*

6 *Voluntary standards will continue to make slow but steady progress. APEX (Accepted Practices Exchange), led by the Convention Industry Council (www.conventionindustry.org) in North America, will provide technology standards in this next year for: résumés/work orders, request for proposals (RFPs), housing and meeting/site profiles. It will only be by adopting standards that the meetings industry can truly digitize its business process. This will reduce laborious clerical inputting and proofreading that both meeting planners and hoteliers/convention service managers are now required to do for nearly every meeting.*

7 *Procurement will increasingly drive more meeting purchasing decisions, especially for large corporations. Combined meetings consolidation/attendee management software will save large companies millions of dollars annually due to increased efficiency, reduced liability exposure (centralizing meetings contracts), and better buying leverage by more accurately knowing actual meeting spend by vendor from previous years. Meetings consolidation products include: Arcaneo, PlanSoft MMS, StarCite, SeeUThere, Plan2Attend and Carlson.*

8 *Technology will assist in strategic meetings management to track and communicate return on investment (ROI) metrics to all meeting stakeholders – many of the products listed in Prediction 7 will lead the way.*

9 *Matchmaking programs, popular in the singles scene, will work their way into the meetings arena to bring people of like interests together at meetings. Matchmaking programs include: Columbia Resource Group's Rio, and Smart Event from ExpoExchange.*

10 *VoIP (Voice over Internet Protocol): people will use broadband Internet (wireless and wired) to make phone calls around the world at little or no cost. Calls can then be more easily linked in with data management and customer relationship management systems to better serve client needs. This change will happen for both wired and mobile phones and will impact the way that the meetings professionals communicate.*

(Source: www.corbinball.com)

Social trends

More female delegates

Changes in the profile of the working population have had a very significant effect on the profile of conference delegates, and the most prominent of these is the ongoing increase of the proportion of women in professional employment. Women's overall share of professional jobs increased in the first two years of the 21st century, in the vast majority of countries, and this trend shows every sign of continuing.

A survey conducted by the International Labour Office (ILO, 2003) showed that in most Western European countries between 2000 and 2002, women's share of professional employment rose to between 40% and 60% of the total workforce, reaching, for example, 58% in Portugal and 55% in Italy. However, the same source indicates that the percentage of women in the professional working population was highest in Central and Eastern Europe and in the Confederation of Independent States.

In 2003, most developed countries also saw modest rises in the percentage of women in senior management jobs, according to the ILO (2003). Women are already well represented in a number of professions, such as healthcare and finance, that are considered to be expanding rapidly in most countries. Women are also making inroads into traditionally male-dominated professions. For example, in some countries, women's share in the ICT sector is already significant.

This continuing trend means that there are more women travelling on business, for all work-related purposes, including participation in conferences. The Visa EU Business Travel Survey 2004, which included responses from 901 executive travellers from the UK, France, Germany, Italy and Spain, showed that female executives were spending almost as many nights away from home on business (average 15.1) as men do (average 15.9).

However, a survey of 600 female business travellers, by New York University on behalf of Wyndham Hotels (NYU, 2003: 57), revealed that, in the United States, although 40% of all business travellers are women, they are not necessarily made to feel like valued customers. The report notes that:

> *Although most respondents feel valued by hotels, less than one third feel valued by the airlines. Overall, there is an opportunity for both hotels and airlines to improve their standing among women business travellers. Even constant business travellers, who are the industry's most valuable customers, don't feel valued often enough.*

Nevertheless, the growing presence of female delegates at conferences has had a number of impacts on the conference industry, from how venues are designed (more toilet facilities for women), to the food served during conference breaks (lighter and generally healthier). Another indication of the femininization of the market is the increase in popularity of spas as conference products – and not only for women. Wakelin (2004: 75) has noted the vast expansion in spa developments around the world and their popularity with corporate incentive or 'concentive' groups in particular:

> *Seek the opinion of any potential female incentive prize winner and the spa is top of her list. ... It would certainly appear that luxurious treatments and hedonistic pampering are perfect incentive options in our time-poor, stressed-out culture.*

Partly through the influence of female participants, the spa has become an amenity that a growing number of delegates expect at conference hotels and resorts. In a 2005 survey by *Convene* magazine (*Convene*, 2005), almost 90% of responding meeting planners said that they believed that a spa is an important amenity at a headquarters hotel. Half rated it very important to attendees and 40% that it was somewhat important; only 10% not think it was important. Many companies are realizing that a spa-based incentive is a wise investment in the well-being of their employees, both male and female. By combining healthy food, exercise, beauty treatments, and seminars on topics such as stress relief, relaxation, and aromatherapy, time spent at a spa can rejuvenate the mind and body – meaning that participants are more productive when they get back to the office.

More older delegates

The European and North American working population is ageing significantly, and will continue to do so for the foreseeable future, adding to the proportion of those in employment who are in the older age categories.

Since 1980, the number of US workers over the age of 40 has increased significantly. By 2010, more than 51% the workforce is expected to be 40 or older, a 33% increase since 1980, while the portion of the workforce aged 25–39 will decline 5.7% (BLS, 2001). The number of workers aged 55 and older will grow from 13% of the labour force in 2000 to 20% in 2020 (BLS, 2002). And in Europe, 24% of those in what is considered to be the working age population (15–64 years old) were over 50 years old in 2003. This is likely to grow to 27% by 2010 (EC, 2003).

Increasingly, people in these age groups and older are remaining in employment, either through choice or through necessity. The older profile of the EU workforce is due to various factors:

1 Sectoral restructuring has resulted in the deferral of planned retirement.
2 Pre-retirement schemes are not as prevalent as they used to be, and the postponement of pension age is currently being considered in several member states.
3 Information and communications technology is also facilitating the tendency for people to remain longer in employment – for example, providing opportunities for employees to work from home ('teleworking') rather than face the daily commute to work.

With a significant proportion of workers in the older age-groups working in managerial and professional positions, it is highly likely that they will continue to attend conferences, for a number of reasons:

• Because they can! As members of the 'baby-boomer' generation start to enter their 60s, it is clear that they are considerably healthier, fitter and more socially involved than the previous generation was at that age. Travelling to events and fully taking part in them presents them with none of the physical challenges that their parents would have faced in their 60s.
• Older workers understand that networking is particularly important for them, since the type of upper-level positions they are often seeking are not as likely to be advertised. Attendance at conferences of their professional associations provides them with a valuable opportunity for networking.
• It is widely recognized that there is a positive relationship between older workers staying in the workforce and the provision of on-going training opportunities. Particularly with so many older workers continuing to work in the fast-evolving 'knowledge industries', constant in-service training events are vital to them, for keeping their skills up-to-date.
• A growing number of retired people are choosing to continue being members of their professional associations – in many cases, for the mental stimulation that profession-based meetings provide, as well as for the opportunity to maintain contact with colleagues.

The challenge of attracting 'Generations X and Y'

It is generally agreed that over the next few years associations will face growing difficulties in attracting attendees to their events. This is partly due to the prevalent phenomenon of 'time poverty', experienced by the growing number of association members with extensive demands on their limited time. But it appears that the new and upcoming generation of association members – 'Generation X' (reputedly those born between 1964 and 1977) and Generation Y (born between 1978 and 1994) – may also take some convincing as to the value of attending conferences. McGee (2005) quotes a spokesman representing Conferon, the US's largest independent meeting planning company, who claims that Generation-Xers, unlike their parents, do not so readily see the value of face-to-face events. As they have grown up with electronic media as a primary communication tool, face-to-face events are less attractive to them (and this is even more the case with Generation Yers). If this contention proves to be accurate, it presents serious meeting-attendance issues for associations, since these two generations between them account for a combined demographic of 120 million people in the United States alone, although the Ys outnumber the Xs by approximately 2 to 1.

What can be done to reach this vast and growing section of the workforce? Understanding their profile, developing strategies and targeting each group with the appropriate messages could be the key to motivating Generations X and Y to join associations and attend their conferences.

Although there are important differences between them, the Generations X and Y do share common ground. Both groups have a sophisticated understanding of technology and expect it to be well utilized; the web wins over traditional media as a primary source of information; they often select personal fulfilment over monetary rewards, seeking a casual work environment, telecommuting options, and time off to enjoy life; they also desire personal attention on the job. These groups are interactive and appreciate immediate feedback. Generations X and Y also want opportunities to lead.

The magazine *Recruiters World* has provided its readers with advice on how to attract these groups into employment in their organizations. Some of that advice may be adapted in order to attract them into association membership and conference attendance:

Emphasize the Internet in your recruitment strategy. Create media that are modern and upbeat, focusing on unique ways to deliver information. Also, provide online tools to help candidates learn about the association/conference and interact with other members.

Create a high-impact recruiting message. Generations X and Y are used to being marketed to and need a very distinctive message to get their attention. Be careful not to go overboard though: a genuine, straightforward approach usually works best.

Deliver an event with plenty of options. Work–life balance is very important to Generations X and Y. These groups want flexibility, learning opportunities, relationships with decision-makers, challenging projects, responsibility and personalized career development.

Members of Generations X and Y are clearly high-maintenance individuals. But the future of association conferences as a market segment depends on their regular presence at such events. As time moves on, their behaviour and preferences will come to shape corporate and associative life. Therefore time spent now in convincing them of the rewards of attending face-to-face events will reap rewards in the future.

Corporate social responsibility

In the face of the current globalization of economies and financial markets, and in an industrial climate characterized by restructuring, relocation and subcontracting, the social, environmental and ethical roles of businesses of all kinds have come under increasing scrutiny, and will continue to be monitored closely in the future. Pressure groups have turned the spotlight on a range of dubious business practices, from the food industry's role in promoting obesity, through oil and mining groups' payments to corrupt leaders in some developing countries, to conditions in Chinese sweat-shops producing expensive branded sportswear.

As a result, the field of corporate social responsibility (CSR) has grown exponentially in the past decade, as companies increasingly seek to engage with their stakeholders and deal with potentially contentious issues proactively, instead of waiting until campaigners' accusations lead to disastrous press coverage. Now, more companies than ever are engaged in integrating CSR into all aspects of their business, encouraged by a growing body of evidence that CSR has a positive impact on businesses' economic performance.

A variety of terms are used to discuss CSR, including business ethics, corporate citizenship, corporate accountability and sustainability. The US-based organization Business for Social Responsibility (BSR) defines corporate social responsibility as 'achieving commercial success in ways that honour ethical values and respect people, communities, and the natural environment'. This organization also says that CSR means addressing the legal, ethical, commercial and other expectations that society has for business, and making decisions that fairly balance the claims of all key stakeholders.

In Europe, CSR has moved to a prominent place in both the business and policy agenda. The European Commission has placed CSR at the core of Europe's competition strategy, and has issued a Green Paper on CSR and a subsequent communication outlining the Commission's definition of CSR and steps that companies, governments and civil society can undertake to refine their commitments to it.

The conference industry itself is beginning to show increasing awareness of the need to demonstrate its CSR, and this will intensify in future years. As the drive for greater transparency grows, all industries and organizations, public as well as private, will be increasingly obliged to demonstrate their ethical, environmental and social credentials. All stakeholders in the conference industry, from airlines, hotels and venues to intermediaries and the delegates themselves, will need to examine their own commitment to CSR.

Concern for the environment

With growing awareness of the potential detrimental impacts of conferences, as discussed in Chapter 1, this sector will be required to take more practical steps to limit the damage that meetings can inflict on the natural environment. Venues, for example, will be under increasing public pressure to emulate the type of 'green' credentials typified by the example of the Tampere Conference Centre, described in Chapter 3. The Environmental Protection Agency in the United States has a Green Meetings website (www.epa.gov/oppt/greenmeetings/) that lists a number of current initiatives, which demonstrate that awareness of environmental issues is growing in the conference sector.

A number of agencies and industry associations are already active in promoting environmentally friendly conferences. These include:

- The Green Meetings Initiative, developed by the US Environmental Protection Agency's Pollution Prevention Division to provide conference planners and suppliers of conference services easy access to information on the planning of environmentally friendly conferences.
- Oceans Blue Foundation/La Fondation Oceans Bleus, which is a Canadian environmental charitable organization established in 1996 to help conserve coastal environments through environmentally responsible tourism. They are the first organization in North America to focus on developing and promoting best practices and standards for all sectors of the tourism industry – including the development of guidelines for 'green' meetings.
- Meeting Professionals International's (MPI) Green Meeting Task Force, which has authored a White Paper guide giving general recommendations for the greening of all areas of meetings operations (accommodation, meetings facilities, exhibitions, food and beverage, transportation and communication), with specific recommendations to planners as to how they can effect an environmentally responsible meeting.
- Fairmont Hotels EcoMeet Program. Fairmont Hotels & Resorts have developed an environmental programme, a product option specifically for conference planners which allows them to order a 'ready made' green conference when organizing through the Fairmont Hotel chain. All of the greening initiatives available at the Fairmont Hotels are automatically incorporated into the conference events when this 'EcoMeet Program' is chosen. Greening initiatives include transportation alternatives, environmentally friendly meals and conference facilities, and incorporation of environmental educational opportunities for conference delegates.
- The Convention Industry Council's Green Meetings Report, which lists comprehensive examples of environmentally friendly best practice for stakeholders such as CVBs, venues and meetings planners.

These are promising signs, but such initiatives must take steps to clearly demonstrate their effectiveness if they are to be considered as anything more than just sticking-plaster gestures.

Concern for the host community

A growing number of stakeholders in the conference sector are also acknowledging the need for a CSR-oriented approach to forging relations with the community that lives in the host destination. This is particularly the case when the standard of living of the host community is markedly below that of the conference delegates or the incentive trip participants. The apparent luxury and extravagance that characterize certain events can stand out in very stark contrast to the abjectly poor and chronically disadvantaged conditions in which some of the local inhabitants live. For that reason, it is encouraging that a number of conference organizers have begun taking steps to invest time and money in the communities that reside in the destinations where their events are held. Such initiatives are often taken in partnership with charities or non-profit organizations operating at the destination.

Enlightened conference planners are increasingly willing to include elements in their programmes that are designed to make a real difference to the disadvantaged members of the local community. For some, this has become a matter of routine. Linda Pereira, the executive director of CPL Events, based in Lisbon, is one example of a new generation of progressively thinking event organizers. At conferences held in destinations such as Mozambique, Romania, Cape Verde, the Azores and Brazil, her company has invited delegates to make a contribution to the local communities through fundraising campaigns and voluntary work. For example, during the 'free' day of the event, delegates are invited to devote their time to helping build a local school, to planting a garden or to raising money to equip a school gymnasium. And the good deeds are not necessarily confined to the country where the conference takes place. In 2005, at a meeting organized in Australia by CPL, the delegates raised money to buy books for a school library in the neighbouring country of East Timor.

Some conference associations themselves are also setting an example to the industry, in terms of their own approach to corporate social responsibility. In 2004, the annual ICCA Congress & Exhibition was held in the Cape Town International Convention Centre, in South Africa. Through an initiative taken in association with Dirk Elzinga, Managing Director of the CTICC, the ICCA event left its mark on some disadvantaged local townships located close to that city. Delegates were requested to hand in their conference bags at the end of the congress. These were then donated to local township schools to be used by their students as school bags. In addition, the bright orange tee-shirts worn by ICCA conference staff and the local PCO staff during the event were also donated to the local townships, providing the children with uniforms for their rugby, soccer and netball teams.

The charitable nature of the conference also manifested itself after the closing speech, which was delivered by Archbishop Desmond Tutu. As the archbishop refused to accept a fee for his speech, he was presented with a cheque for 40 000 rand (€5200) to be donated to a local charity, the Trauma Centre for Survivors of Violence and Torture, a non-governmental human rights organization that promotes and inspires the healing of survivors of violence and torture.

The traditional argument in favour of this form of CSR is that businesses rely on the communities in which they operate, and this is certainly the case for conference destinations that depend, for part of their appeal, upon harmonious relations between visiting delegates and the host community.

But it is undeniable that positive displays of CSR are also directly beneficial for the conference buyer's, organizer's or destination's reputation. Since well-publicized acts of generosity can be regarded as generators of favourable public relations, these can be regarded as a highly effective element of the stakeholder's marketing mix. This point is underlined by Plimmer (2005) in an article on corporate philanthropy:

> *At a time when traditional means of advertising are less effective than in the past, a charitable donation can be a means of attracting favourable attention. Likewise, with corporate behaviour under increasing scrutiny …a public show of goodwill can do much to engender faith in a brand.*

In the years ahead, more conference sector stakeholders will become aware of the benefits to themselves, and to host communities, of investing time and money in giving something back to underprivileged people living in some of the destinations where their events take place.

Summary

This chapter has reviewed some of the key trends and challenges that the conference sector is already dealing with now and will continue to face in the future. There can be no doubt that the market environment will continue to evolve and mutate in ways perhaps impossible to predict at the present time. But it is in this very unpredictability that lie the challenge and the excitement of marketing destinations and venues in the conference sector.

However, in the complex, volatile flux of market trends and market forces, one element that will remain reassuringly constant is human nature itself. Delegates will continue to attend conferences, not only for the opportunity to obtain personal and professional development for themselves and business growth for their organizations, but also for the simple pleasure of meeting those with whom they share a common interest or goal. Buyers and participants will be drawn to attractive destinations and venues that deliver efficiently-run and memorable events, using state-of-the-art technology, as well as distinctive cultural experiences in a healthy and unique environment.

Those responsible for marketing venues and destinations have a crucial role to play in satisfying this timeless demand.

Review and Discussion Questions

1 What are the principal emerging trends that will make the role of marketing staff in the conference industry more demanding in the future?
2 How is the profile of conference delegates in the 21st century different from the profile of those who attended conferences towards the end of the 20th century?
3 What evidence is there to support the prediction that businesses operating in the conference industry will become more responsible and more accountable in the future?

Sources

Anon (2004) 'Asia's new travel giant', *TravelSmart Asia Watch*, October
Anon (2005) 'Help wanted: Generation X and Generation Y', *Recruiters World*, January
Antrobus, A (2005) 'Is Asia getting it right?', *Association Meetings International*, November
BLS (2001) Bureau of Labor Statistics, *Monthly Labor Review*, November
BLS (2002) Bureau of Labor Statistics, *Monthly Labor Review*, May
Convene (2005) 14th Annual Meetings Market Survey
Davidson, R (2003) *EIBTM Social and Political Trends Report*, Reed Travel Exhibitions
Davidson, R (2004) *EIBTM Economic Trends Report*, Reed Travel Exhibitions
Davidson, R (2005) 'My encounter with Chinese MICE', *Conference News*, December
EC (2003) *The Social Situation in the European Union 2003*, Office for Official Publications of the European Communities, European Commission
ILO (2003) *Yearbook of Labour Statistics*, International Labour Office
McGee, R (2005) 'Emerging trends: marketing is king for convention groups', *Association Meetings*, October

MPI (2005) *The Power of Partnership: Capitalizing on the Collaborative Efforts of Strategic Meeting Professionals and Procurement Departments*, Meeting Professionals International

NYU (2003) *Coming of Age: The Continuing Evolution of Female Business Travellers*, The Tisch Center for Hospitality, Tourism and Sports Management, New York University

Plimmer, G (2005) 'Giving is good for business', *Financial Times*, 'Philanthropy' supplement, 16 December

Wakelin, J (2004) 'Spas in your eyes', *Meetings & Incentive Travel*, September

West, E (2005) *Gathering Planning Today: The Move to Consolidate*, VNU Travel Network

Appendix

Major Trade Shows for the Conference Industry

Trade show	Description	Held in	Website	Logo
AIME	AsiaPacific Incentives & Meetings Expo	Melbourne	www.aime.com.au/	
CBITM	China International Business and Incentive Travel Mart	Beijing	www.cbitm.com/	
EIBTM	The global meetings and incentive exhibition	Barcelona	www.eibtm.com	
EMIF	European Meeting Industry Fair	Brussels	www.aboutemif.com	
IMEX	The worldwide exhibition for incentive travel, meetings and events	Frankfurt	www.imex-frankfurt.com/	

Name	Description	Location	Website	Logo
IT&CMA	Incentive Travel & Conventions Meetings Asia	Pattaya	www.itcma.com.sg	
International Confex	The UK's biggest event for people organizing events	London	www.international-confex.com/	
LACIME	Latin America and Caribbean Incentive and Meetings Exhibition	São Paulo	www.lacimexpo.com/	
The Motivation Show	Business solutions that move people	Chicago	www.motivationshow.com/	

Index